Advance Praise for *Navigating Cultural Memory*

"David Mwambari offers a powerful revisionary account of the memory of the 1994 Genocide in Rwanda. His book works simultaneously on two levels: it illuminates and challenges what he calls the hegemonic master narrative of the genocide memory while offering an account of the plurality of memories of multiple violence in Rwanda's history; and it models how the study of collective remembrance can take inspiration from decolonial methodologies and move beyond its Eurocentric origins. This is an important contribution to a variety of fields, including genocide studies, African studies, and memory studies. Highly recommended!"

—**Michael Rothberg**, author of *The Implicated Subject: Beyond Victims and Perpetrators.*

"David Mwambari's nuanced study explores the lived experiences of the 1994 genocide and its commemoration, over twenty years, recentring a wide range of Rwandan voices, and examining the powerful dominant narrative of the 1994 Rwandan Genocide Against the Tutsi. Mwambari has a unique positionality as one of the few Rwandan international scholars to carry out such complex scholarly work. This is a scholarly journey which is both restorative and productive, and one in which the humanity of the author is fully engaged."

—**Molly Andrews**, Honorary Professor of Political Psychology, University College London

"This innovative study explores how Rwanda's master narrative about the 1994 genocide became hegemonic through a process spanning several years and involving multiple actors. Particularly noteworthy are profiles of how three Rwandan artists contributed to commemoration events—yet the celebrated musician Kizito Mihigo was punished when he dared diverge from the dominant narrative; several years later he died in police custody. Despite its extensive research, the cautious tone of Mwambari's book will likely stimulate spirited debates on a central political issue today—that of creating a hegemonic ideology in the wake of massive social violence."

—**Catharine Newbury**, Professor of Government, Smith College

"This book has evolved both as a biographical excavation and intellectual inquiry into what memory and memorialization can do for societies disrupted by genocide. In focusing on memory and how remembering is the subject of ever-changing dynamics, this study advances our understanding of knowledge, of how we know and what we know. This is the reason the intellectual contribution of this book is urgent and valuable. The book reminds us that lived experiences, coded in memory, give intellectual work authenticity. In daring to write this book, and in doing it so well, David Mwambari has taken memory studies a notch higher and invited us to accept the fluidity of memory without denying its very value in society. The book is an indispensable contribution to a growing interdisciplinary field of memory studies."

—**Godwin R. Murunga**, CODESRIA Executive Secretary

EXPLORATIONS IN NARRATIVE PSYCHOLOGY

MARK FREEMAN
Series Editor

BOOKS IN THE SERIES

Narrative Imagination and Everyday Life
Molly Andrews

Decolonizing Psychology: Globalization, Social Justice, and Indian Youth Identities
Sunil Bhatia

Beyond the Archive: Memory, Narrative, and the Autobiographical Process
Jens Brockmeier

Speaking of Violence
Sara Cobb

Not in My Family: German Memory and Responsibility After the Holocaust
Roger Frie

Entangled Narratives: Collaborative Storytelling and the Re-Imagining of Dementia
Lars-Christer Hydén

Narratives of Positive Aging: Seaside Stories
Amia Lieblich

The Ethics of Storytelling: Narrative Hermeneutics, History, and the Possible
Hanna Meretoja

Rethinking Thought: Inside the Minds of Creative Scientists and Artists
Laura Otis

The Narrative Complexity of Ordinary Life: Tales from the Coffee Shop
William L. Randall

A New Narrative for Psychology
Brian Schiff

Life and Narrative: The Risks and Responsibilities of Storying Experience
Brian Schiff, A. Elizabeth McKim, and Sylvie Patron

Words and Wounds: Narratives of Exile
Sean Akerman

The Transformative Self: Personal Growth, Narrative Identity, and the Good Life
Jack Bauer

Navigating Cultural Memory: Commemoration and Narrative in Postgenocide Rwanda
David Mwambari

Navigating Cultural Memory

Commemoration and Narrative in Postgenocide Rwanda

DAVID MWAMBARI

OXFORD
UNIVERSITY PRESS

Oxford University Press is a department of the University of Oxford. It furthers the University's objective of excellence in research, scholarship, and education by publishing worldwide. Oxford is a registered trade mark of Oxford University Press in the UK and certain other countries.

Published in the United States of America by Oxford University Press
198 Madison Avenue, New York, NY 10016, United States of America.

© Oxford University Press 2023

All rights reserved. No part of this publication may be reproduced, stored in a retrieval system, or transmitted, in any form or by any means, without the prior permission in writing of Oxford University Press, or as expressly permitted by law, by license, or under terms agreed with the appropriate reproduction rights organization. Inquiries concerning reproduction outside the scope of the above should be sent to the Rights Department, Oxford University Press, at the address above.

You must not circulate this work in any other form and you must impose this same condition on any acquirer.

Library of Congress Cataloging-in-Publication Data
Names: Mwambari, David, author.
Title: Navigating cultural memory : commemoration and narrative in postgenocide Rwanda / David Mwambari.
Description: New York, NY : Oxford University Press, [2023] | Includes bibliographical references and index. |
Identifiers: LCCN 2023004666 (print) | LCCN 2023004667 (ebook) | ISBN 9780190942304 (hardback) | ISBN 9780190942328 (epub) | ISBN 9780190942335
Subjects: LCSH: Genocide—Rwanda—History—20th century. | Genocide—Rwanda—Psychological aspects. | Collective memory—Rwanda.
Classification: LCC DT450.435 .M883 2023 (print) | LCC DT450.435 (ebook) | DDC 967.57104/31—dc23/eng/20230210
LC record available at https://lccn.loc.gov/2023004666
LC ebook record available at https://lccn.loc.gov/2023004667

DOI: 10.1093/oso/9780190942304.001.0001

Printed by Integrated Books International, United States of America

To the Rwandan Youth

Contents

Foreword   ix
Acknowledgments   xvii

Introduction: The Complexities of Living after Mass Violence   1

1. Decolonial Approaches to Memory   26
2. Rwandan Narratives and Rwandan Pasts   45
3. Shaping the Emergence and Evolution of the Genocide Master Narrative   74
4. Imprinting the Land with the Materials of Memory   112
5. Localizing Commemoration and Individual Responses to the Master Narrative   145
6. Expressing Memory after Genocide: The Art of Commemoration   178
7. The Media, Commemoration, and the Enforcement of the Master Narrative   217

Conclusion: The Malleability of Memory and Reflections on the Future of Knowledge Production on Rwanda, Dignity, and in Memory Studies   252

Bibliography   273
Index   301

Foreword

Self-Reflexivity: The Challenges and Opportunities of Researching One's Own Society

Paul Zeleza reminds researchers that "our individual scholarship is enmeshed in specific historical geographies, current political economies, and generational aspirations and anxieties."[1] I am part of a generation that lived through and witnessed Rwanda's complex history of the 1990s and the genocide in 1994 and have inherited anxieties from these events. In postgenocide Rwanda, where one's choice of vocabulary speaks to one's past, present, and future politics and aspirations, one's identity is sometimes sensitive. I have spent a considerable amount of time researching my family history from various sources to understand myself and my past. So far, I can articulate that I am of "mixed" heritage with family backgrounds from both Hutu and Tutsi affiliations. Identifying and acknowledging one's mixed heritage is a complex process in a context where violence happened because of the politicization of these affiliations. Having a Tutsi background in Rwanda's current context is associated with royalty, victory, and power. The history of violence and power exercised by the royal family against each other and the rural and poor Rwandans over which they ruled is a distant memory, as I show in chapter 2.[2] I have grown up in an environment in which Hutu identity has become associated with recent genocidal violence, leading to guilt, shame, and stigma in postgenocide Rwanda and among the diaspora. The victimization of Hutus and the Twa in Rwanda's history, meanwhile, merits only meager mention in the country's official memory. The postgenocide master narrative does not recognize nuances in this history.

My generational (meaning those who were young during the genocide) anxiety is that "when there is trouble" the youth with mixed heritage "are the first to be rejected by both sides because they are considered accomplices of one or the other ethnic group."[3] My healing journey is incomplete. I am also not a "genocide survivor" because the term is officially defined in Rwanda to apply exclusively to those who are deemed fully Tutsi. I do live with traumas of the genocide and, like many Rwandans, have faced political, economic, and social consequences of the genocide and the civil war in the two decades since 1994. I am yet to reconcile internal contradictions of my mixed heritage and the contradictions of victory, violence and victimhood that accompany it. I have not mustered enough courage and self-acceptance to choose either of the two ethnicities that make me. I am not sure that it is even important or desirable. I am a son of my mother and father. I reject both patriarchal and matriarchal systems that force one to select to which parents we culturally belong. My deliberate omission is a form of personal protest against these politicized categories, which have led to bloodshed, including the 1994 Genocide Against the Tutsi and 1990s civil war. I am not alone in this. Some of my respondents and contemporaries share similar anxieties, albeit at different levels.

My identity is further complicated by the fact that I have lived outside Rwanda—in different African and European countries and in North America and Australia. My earlier education was Eurocentric, and later in graduate school I was exposed to different pedagogies. As a result I remain embattled within myself to decolonize my mind and to unlearn and rethink certain approaches to studying and writing about the past. It is for this reason that in the first two decades of this century I embarked on multiple journeys and visited different regions of Rwanda frequently, including while conducting this research. My interlocutors and many others trained me to listen to multiple voices and exposed me to diverse perspectives that depart significantly from the previous curricula of my training. Thus, my insider/outsider perspectives on these issues are inherently influenced by my own career and life trajectories. Significantly, in learning to listen to the multiple voices of those around me, I have begun to learn how to listen to the multiple voices within me.

As a Rwandan who has lived much of his adult life in the "sixth province"—as Rwandans refer to its diaspora—over a decade has shaped the research process and writing of this book.[4] My insider/outsider positionality has at times been both a restriction and an essential precondition to the sort of research I sought to conduct in Rwanda.[5] Some researchers view all knowledge as positioned; thus, in discussing these stories I did not simply play "a mechanistic role in the collection and analysis of data but rather an active, critical role that embraces the complexity of the social and psychological."[6] My positionality in this research is explained by three aspects.

First, on the level of language, my deep knowledge of Kinyarwanda and Rwandan culture helped me understand the verbal and nonverbal forms of communication commonly used by my respondents when doing field research. It was also helpful to be aware of cultural nuances around particular language choices that were used in the research and analysis of data.[7] As a native speaker of Kinyarwanda, I was able to interact with Rwandans who do not speak any other languages. My fluency in Congolese Swahili, meanwhile, allowed me to conduct interviews with Rwandans who returned from Congo with the Rwanda Patriotic Front (RPF) or those who had fled in 1994. My English gave me access to elites and those who returned from Uganda and the anglophone diaspora. My familiarity with Kirundi allowed me to interact with respondents who had previously lived in Burundi.

Beyond ethnicity, one's family history of migration matters for how one understands the official discourse of the past, present, and future.[8] Thus, my familiarity with these languages and the cultures and histories around them allowed me to not only access a wide range of views but also translate and analyze them within the larger context that has shaped postgenocide Rwandan society. I know to what extent studies on Rwanda or any other context that are based on translations of interviews have the potential to lose nuance.

Second, on the level of generational anxiety and aspirations: I was 11 when the civil war started in 1990, 13 when the genocide happened, and in my late 20s and early 30s when I traveled around Rwanda and around the world doing this research. As a Rwandan who lived in diaspora contexts for most of my adult life, there are many events that I researched and discussed in this book that I did not experience directly, the way my compatriots did. Thus, I might have a different perspective on and arguments about these events from someone who lived through them in Rwanda. This is why I interviewed individuals whose lived experience brought them into closer contact with these events, including some who were my age-mates. We shared similar anxieties when discussing the genocide or commemorations. For instance, we had to use the correct vocabulary, which has been in a state of flux in the two decades following the genocide. In this case, I kept in touch with a colleague who was familiar with official changes so that I could continue to use the appropriate and sensitive language, especially when interviewing political elites and writing this book.

For respondents who were educated and well read on Rwanda, we shared another frustration—that of constantly reading new books that reconstructed Rwanda's history with exaggerations, reproduced colonial tropes about Rwanda, and provided frustration on learning Rwanda's history analyzed through a Western lens, in scholarship produced often for Western publics. Rwanda became a topic of interest to many young and seasoned scholars, journalists, and commentators, who were able to publish in high-ranking presses after a few days or weeks of being in Kigali or one or two rural towns. The result is that available research on Rwanda's past is laden with colonial and agenda-setting scholarship that in some instances alienates the complexity of Rwandans' lived experiences and how Rwanda as a society has emerged, evolved, and negotiated various aspects of life after the genocide and civil wars in Rwanda and the region. It is for this reason that this book also uses proverbs and analyzes popular songs and other carriers of memory that capture this complexity throughout the analysis of the emergence, evolution, and responses to the master narrative with multiple readers in mind, including Rwandans.

I also shared aspirations with some of my young respondents regardless of their family background or if they resided in rural or urban areas. The language of peace was part of everyone's vocabulary, and we agreed, mostly, that seeking to understand what happened to our society in the 1990s as well as the memorialization of those events was a crucial exercise. We might have disagreed on interpretations of the history of our country and on what our parents did or did not do in the genocide or civil wars in Rwanda and in the Great Lakes Region, but we all showed empathy and sympathy to each other's mourning experiences. Some of my respondents also spoke of the importance of understanding this past as a useful avenue through which to contribute to present and future peace in Rwanda and the wider region. Older interviewees often spoke to me frankly and were more critical of the master narrative. They hoped their words would contribute to a future they will not live to see. However, these elders also insisted younger Rwandans should not be like them and live through wars and violence every time one government and its hegemonic master narrative gave way to another. In that sense we also shared aspirations of a peaceful Rwanda. These shared aspirations are part of what motivated me to research, analyze, and reflect in writing about this complex and sensitive topic even as I am aware many will disagree or question my arguments. The book therefore relies on these respondents and secondary sources to encourage debate and engagement with the sensitive tone the topic requires. It is a book born of struggle to understand personal, family, and Rwandan society's pasts remembered in the present. I hope some of my respondents who read this book, and that other Rwandans, and readers in general, will appreciate the sensitivities of this debate, especially given some of the analyses on contemporary debates that remain highly emotional and still evolving. This is important. Politics of master narratives around the world are increasingly turning into polarization. There is a need for constructive, nuanced debates and care especially when dealing with examining recent mass atrocities. With this book, I therefore hope to inspire a broader call to action among researchers attempting to navigate the murky waters of memory studies and the fragile shores of qualitative research in conflict-affected contexts: to acknowledge, integrate, and centralize sensitivity, personal dignity, and individual complexity.

Third, on the level of personal trauma, doing interviews also led to anxieties and confrontations with my own trauma. In 2011 and the years that followed when I conducted interviews for this project, I struggled with the idea of researching the controversial and sensitive topic of genocide memory, a topic that is directly linked to my own community and evokes personal memories, trauma, and pain. As I collected the stories of others, including those of children killed or children left orphaned, and engaged in discussions on the violence that people endured—especially those discussions held in areas where Rwandans congregate to commemorate—I was (re)traumatized and sometimes struggled to reconcile my own personal memory with that of others. Before starting this research, I had already been diagnosed with trauma-related symptoms in 2005, and these became worse when I lived through the 2007–2008 postelection violence in Kenya. I realized that my symptoms, like a lack of sleep, loss of appetite, and increased anxiety, were sometimes worsened in the research journey. But through speaking with respondents and attending commemorations, I realized I was not alone, and that was comforting. In some cases, some of my respondents experienced worse symptoms than I did, especially those who had lost family members in the war or genocide. I also admired those who managed to think through their complex family histories and continue to lead their normal lives. I envied some compatriots who were too young to remember or were from privileged families of Rwandans who escaped and did not see any dead bodies or those who returned from the diaspora and could afford to ignore commemorations or these difficult questions. As a researcher, I had to come to terms with these differences among Rwandans as a reality in postgenocide Rwanda.

However, the process of researching "the wounds of the other" crystalized my own.[9] The research journey constantly revealed my own connections to the histories of violence that I was investigating.[10] At the same time, the process itself was healing because it showed me that I had resources that I could rely on. In a couple of instances, I employed an experienced community psychologist who understood Rwanda's context to come and give ideas to community members I was working with on how to manage our anxieties. For me as a researcher, I had the privilege of affording care, including on-campus psychologists at my research institutions and those I paid privately to help me manage my life and what I was learning. The research experience ended up being restorative and productive. It was only after writing this book that I finally fully understood the point feminist scholars make about our life experiences determining what we study, the way we analyze it, the concepts and theories we choose, and the importance we give to each of these aspects.[11] I also realized that many academic controversies that are considered methodological are actually related to positionality, and that our position influences how we transmit knowledge to the world. Indeed, studying debates on reflexivity in research has allowed me to carry out the difficult task completing the writing this book.

Notes

1. Paul Tiyambe Zeleza, "Reckoning with the Pasts and Reimagining the Futures of African Studies for the 21st Century," *African Peacebuilding Network APN Lecture Series* 4 (2019), https://www.semanticscholar.org/paper/Reckoning-with-the-pasts-and-reimagining-the-of-for-Zeleza/f60a31b198a1cd865a221b0a4e0940f8578e1e11, 4. Paul Zeleza has also addressed certain challenges African scholars faced after independence, and that those on both the continent and outside it continue to face today. See Paul Tiyambe Zeleza, "Manufacturing and Consuming Knowledge," *Development in Practice* 6, no. 4 (1996): 293–303.
2. David Mwambari, Barney Walsh, and 'Funmi Olonisakin, "Women's Overlooked Contribution to Rwanda's State-Building Conversations," *Conflict, Security & Development* 21, no. 4 (2021): 475–499.
3. Lyndsay McLean Hilker, "Rwanda's 'Hutsi': Intersections of Ethnicity and Violence in the Lives of Youth of 'Mixed' Heritage," *Identities* 19, no. 2 (2012): 229.
4. This is also discussed elsewhere; see David Mwambari, "Local Positionality in the Production of Knowledge in Northern Uganda," *International Journal of Qualitative Methods* 18 (2019): 3.
5. Josephine Beoku-Betts, "When Black Is Not Enough: Doing Field Research among Gullah Women," *NWSA Journal* 6 (1994): 413–433.
6. Phillip L. Hammack, "Narrative and the Politics of Meaning," *Narrative Inquiry*, 21, no. 2 (2011): 313.
7. Chilisa Bagele, *Indigenous Research Methodologies* (Thousand Oaks, CA: Sage, 2019).
8. See Andrea Purdeková and David Mwambari, "Post-genocide Identity Politics and Colonial Durabilities in Rwanda," *Critical African Studies* (2021): 1–19.

9. Mark Freeman, "Open Wounds: Discerning, Owning, and Narrating Deep History," in *Race, Rage, and Resistance* (New York: Routledge, 2019), 31.
10. Mark Freeman, "Discerning the History Inscribed Within," in *Handbook of Culture and Memory*, ed. Brady Wagoner (New York: Oxford University Press, 2017): 68.
11. See Brenda J. Allen, "Feminist Standpoint Theory: A Black Woman's (Re)view of Organizational Socialization," *Communication Studies* 47, no. 4 (1996): 257–271; And Julia T. Wood, "Critical Feminist Theories," in *Engaging Theories in Interpersonal Communication: Multiple Perspectives*, eds. Leslie A. Baxter and Dawn O. Braithwaite (Thousand Oaks, CA: Sage, 2008): 323–334.

Acknowledgments

It has been a decade since I first started wrestling with the questions and mnemonic dilemmas discussed in this book. The first 4 years were spent researching and writing a PhD thesis on the topic and the other 6 years wondering if I should rewrite it and turn into a book. It has been the toughest assignment of my adult life. As many writers mentioned to me, it is difficult to start and finish such a long-term project and even harder to work on a topic that is not only a passion but close to my heart. Therefore, it has taken a "village" to bring this project to completion. This includes academic colleagues, family, and relatives, as well as kind strangers who gave me a place to stay, paid for my travels, or fed me in many small towns, villages, and cities in Rwanda, Kenya, thirteen other African countries, the United States of America, Australia, three European countries, and two countries in Asia. In each of these places, I either attended a workshop, conducted an interview, or received training on different skills that allowed me to bring this project to completion. My acknowledgment is therefore insufficient, and I apologize for those who I will not mention by name.

This project was possible because of many Rwandans in Rwanda and the diaspora who generously supported this project in immeasurable ways. In Rwanda, I received support from a network of families, relatives, and friends who wish not to be named. They include genocide survivors, perpetrators who were released from prison, bystanders, and others who do not neatly fit in any of these categories, whose complexities and limitations I discuss in later chapters. I also received generous resources from artists, journalists, intellectuals, and many others. I am grateful to genocide memorial guides and leaders of community meetings on commemoration across Rwanda; government officials in different ministries and offices; Rwanda Patriotic Army (RPA) senior military individuals in and out of Rwanda; staff of the now-defunct National Commission for the Fight Against Genocide (CNLG); current and former Rwandan politicians and officials; staff of the National Unity and Reconciliation Commission (NURC); and former staff of the Institute of Research and Dialogue for Peace (IRDP). I appreciate assistance from the staff at the Kigali Library, Kigali Independent University (ULK), University of Rwanda Library, and the National Museum of Rwanda. I am grateful to a network of elders, men and women around Rwanda and the diaspora too numerous to mention. I thank the staff and youth who attended *Itorero* camps, and annual commemorations and shared their experiences. I am grateful to a network of clergy, especially in the Catholic and Anglican Churches of Rwanda, members of Rwanda's Muslim community, and members of Rwanda's traditional religious community. Individuals in these places were generous with information. They took interest in my topic; some allowed me to interview them, and others gave me their views or engaged me in extended discussions about their opinions or experiences in relation to the genocide master narrative. They gave me unrestricted access to their stories, lives, and documents even when it involved emotional outbreaks. This book is a product of hundreds of Rwandans who are alive and who have passed on and who most of all have shown courage in facing a past that is ever-present in their daily lives in order to build a peaceful present and future. I am grateful to a network of research facilitators and translators in Rwanda and the diaspora who used their knowledge and skills to help me produce this book. Given the sensitive nature of this topic, I only mention their initials. I appreciate those who were generous with their time throughout my doctoral studies and as I worked on this final book.

I wish to thank my PhD supervisor Dr. Roland Burke, whose research skills, generosity, intellect, and inspiration are the foundation for this work. Dr. Burke welcomed my project and sharpened my thinking around this topic and led me to complete my PhD thesis on time. In addition to Dr. Burke, I received unmatched support from other researchers in the history department at the School of Social Sciences, La Trobe University. They include Dr. Shannon Woodcock, Dr. Ian Coller, Dr. Claudia Haake, and Dr. Ben Silverstein who made my life in Melbourne intellectually rewarding, fun, and memorable.

I am grateful to Professor Molly Andrews, who played an important role in introducing me to Professor Jens Brockmeier. Professor Brockmeier took interest in my ideas in their initial stages and recommended literature that shaped my thinking on this topic. I also thank Professor Marc Freeman, the editor of this series, for the generous support, mentorship, and patience over many years of working on this book. I have received advice, wisdom, encouragement, and generous feedback from scholars around the world, both junior and senior. I wish to thank Professor Micere Mugo, Professor

Paul Zeleza, Professor Funmi Olonisakin, Professor Alao Abiodun, and Dr. Godwin Murunga, who have mentored and encouraged me not to abandon this project at many junctures when I experienced the challenges associated with such a long journey. Colleagues such as Professor Dr. Aymar Nyenyezi Bisoka, Dr. Erin Jessee, Dr. Fama Ali, Professor Freida Brown, Professor Dr. Koen Vlassenroot, Dr. Judith Verweijen, Dr. Esther Marijnen, Dr. Jeroen Cuvelier, Amb. Dr. Kikaya David, Dr. George Jones, Professor Horace Campbell, Professor An Ansoms, Dr. Elijah Munyi, Dr. Andrea Grant, Dr. Rachel Ibreck, and Dr. Joan Bryant Ms Shuvai Nyoni, Dr. Eka Ikpe, Dr. Barney Walsh, Dr. Wale Ismael have all supported different aspects of this project.

I am very grateful to those who read the manuscript and gave me feedback. These individuals invested their time, skills, and other resources to make this book accessible to readers. I mention some full names but use initials for those who wish to remain anonymous. I am thankful to Professor Beth Whitaker, Mr. Ishimwe, Professor Catherine Newbury, Professor Timothy Longman, Dr. Ljiljana Radonic, Dr. Wanjiru., Dr. Delia Wendel, and anonymous reviewers. While these individuals have read and strengthened my argument in different chapters, four individuals dedicated their time and language and editorial skills in Kinyarwanda, English, and French. These individuals deserve a special mention and appreciation, including Dr. Sarah Watkins, Dr. Sayra van den Berg, Ms. Sarah Welsher, and Mr. Bob Banning. I am exceptionally thankful to the Oxford University Press staff including Ms. Hayley Singer, Ms. Kate Brown, and the production team for their dedication and patience in this process.

Although I spent many years of my education as a self-funded and broke student, this research and my graduate studies that led to this project later received funding from various institutions, including a La Trobe University FFRS scholarship, a La Trobe University PRS (Australia), the *Fonds Voor Wetenschappelijk Onderzoek-Vlaanderen* (FWO Belgium), Syracuse University Pan African Studies Department Scholarship (USA), an African Leadership Centre research grant (Kenya), and the Council for the Development of Social Science Research in Africa (Senegal). I am grateful for institutional support through fellowships that allowed me to complete the manuscript, including Churchill College, Cambridge University (United Kingdom), and my friends and colleagues from the Department of Conflict and Development Studies, Ghent University (Belgium) and the African Leadership Centre, King's College London (United Kingdom), who were all flexible and supportive as I balanced teaching duties and completing this manuscript.

I am grateful for the friendships and support from around the world, especially of the following families and individuals: Families who hosted me in Australia, where I did my doctoral studies, include the Mlay, Costello, O'Callaghan, Duncan, Blundell families; Laura Meese; Dr. Thomas; Dr. Stewarts; Mr. Nyaligwa; Ms. Radwa; Mr. Ruingu; Emma and Bridgitte. Also, Sally and Dave Fullerton receive my thanks. Special thanks go to friends who have supported me from the start to the end of this project, including Kampayana and Mukawenda, Sarah and Edmund; Ariane, Marten; Stephanie, Mugeni, James, and Nelly; Clarisse, Seraphine and Samuel; Yvette, Kalkidan; Cyusa, Timothy; Kagenza, Nuwayo, Manasseh; Dr. Eva; Usanayo, the Kennedy, Schaeffer, Karemera, Price, Hutton, Twycross, Sindayigaya, Woods, Cote, Rajbans, Donaldson, Prevou, and Wexler families; and my siblings and relatives who stood by me for more than a decade of pursuing my studies. I thank my parents for raising me to be a thinker and surrounding us with books and asking us to write essays and book summaries during holidays. To members of my crew who rejoice and travel this life journey with me, thank you for your support; this is for you, the ABCs! For any good analysis and wisdom in this text, I thank these individuals; the mistakes are all mine.

Introduction

The Complexities of Living after Mass Violence

Agahinda k'inkoko kamenywa n'inkike yatoyemo—A hen's sorrow is well known where it pecks.

—Rwandan Proverb

A friend of mine asked me to accompany him to visit a young woman in her twenties named Kayitesi.* At the time, in April 2007, Kayitesi lived in rural Kigali with two siblings. Kayitesi's parents and many of her relatives were killed during the genocide perpetrated against the Tutsi in Rwanda in 1994. The genocide took place for about three months, between April and July, in the central and eastern African country of Rwanda when radical Hutu youth militias and Hutu political elites targeted and killed the Tutsi. The Hutus and some foreigners who protected the Tutsi or opposed the genocidal violence were also killed. The Rwanda Patriotic Front (RPF), which had attacked Rwanda in 1990 to repatriate themselves and their families from neighboring countries, won the war and stopped the genocide. I expected a genocide survivor like Kayitesi to be actively involved in official commemoration activities and endorse the master narrative that had evolved about the genocide—except Kayitesi was indifferent about the annual anniversary of the genocide. My friend and I discussed the ongoing genocide commemoration activities and how important it was to participate in them, but Kayitesi barely contributed to the conversation. At that time, I didn't yet know much about the complexity of the matter at hand, as I have come to understand over the years researching this topic.

Commemorations have been ongoing annually since 1995, starting in the month of April and ending in early July, but with varying intensity

---

* All names have been changed in the text to respect the privacy of respondents.

Navigating Cultural Memory. David Mwambari, Oxford University Press. © Oxford University Press 2023.
DOI: 10.1093/oso/9780190942304.003.0001

over the years. Surprisingly, there was an uneasiness about Kayitesi whenever the subject of the genocide or its commemoration was broached. After leaving her house, my friend also expressed his astonishment at Kayitesi's demeanor, which was a stark contrast to her usual opinionated personality. This encounter left me with some questions about genocide commemorations and people's responses to them. It is with those questions that took seed in my heart and mind that day in 2007 that my research on this subject was borne.

Two years later, in 2009, I met a young man named Hakizimana in a rural town in southern Rwanda during a visit to learn about my family history. After establishing that we were age-mates, we discussed our experiences in primary school in the 1990s during the civil war but before the Genocide Against the Tutsi [**] ravaged Rwanda. In what developed into a long conversation, Hakizimana told me his father was a Hutu serving a life sentence for murder and rape charges determined during *gacaca* proceedings. Gacaca courts were traditional courts with roots in the precolonial period and were used to settle family conflicts in Rwanda. They were revitalized in 2001 to address the legacies of the 1994 genocide. Hakizimana's father was among one of over one million Hutu men and women tried by these community courts. Hakizimana's father denied that a genocide had happened, instead seeing the events of 1994 as merely an extension of the civil war of the early 1990s. To him the RPF had attacked a peaceful Rwanda in 1990, and the genocide campaign was part of self-defense. He endorsed a dangerous narrative that the genocidal radical Hutu extremists had been promoting to incite Hutu violence against the Tutsi.

For his part, Hakizimana told me about his own experiences in the gacaca proceedings, the shame he felt about his father's crimes and those of other family members who were involved in the killing of the Tutsi in a village familiar to both of us. He also told me about how different he was from his relatives, evidenced by his involvement in reconciliation projects and genocide commemoration. Now in his late twenties, he had completed secondary school sponsored by the postgenocide government. Hakizima absorbed the

---

[**] Throughout the course of the book, I have elected to capitalize the events that together form the 1994 Genocide Against the Tutsis. This is an intentional contribution to the decolonial discourse and a purposive counterweight to the literature on mass violence that has privileged episodes of mass violence in the Global North, through capitalization (i.e., World Wars I and II), but in some cases does not accord violence in the Global South as worthy of similar recognition when local and international laws have recognized these historical events as significant and given them a particular definition. In Chapter 3 I explore and elaborate on the politics and evolution around these definitions).

teachings of the postgenocide government, despite his father's convictions to the contrary. He was applying to a training institution in order to secure a better job to support his mother and siblings and ensure their family did not sink into extreme poverty while their former breadwinner lived out the rest of his life in a nearby prison.

What was striking to me during our lengthy conversation was how Hakizimana spoke of his life transformation and his support for postgenocide government programs. He was indeed unlike his father, who expressed fear, bitterness, and thoughts of revenge against the postgenocide political class. The commemoration events that Hakizimana followed on the radio and participated in within his community were always accompanied by a narrative of Rwanda's past that contradicted the views of his father when Hakizimana visited him in prison. To me, Hakizimana seemed to genuinely endorse the official narrative in order to put the gravity of his father's crimes in perspective and strengthen his resolve to never participate in such atrocities if they were to happen again.

While Hakizimana's and his father's convictions remained constant for the five years we were in touch, Kayitesi's changed significantly. She, a Tutsi survivor of the 1994 genocide, began to question the official narrative about the genocide and instead denied—like Hakizimana's father—that a Genocide Against the Tutsi took place at all, considering her own experiences in light of the politicization of the hegemonic narrative. Kayitesi was a Tutsi who was in the survivor group, while Hakizimana was a Hutu and part of the accused group, and yet their views were the inverse of what one would expect from their lived experiences.

Over the years I have spoken with many more people, and while some of them held unwavering perspectives about the past and the master narrative, others have changed their views about the genocide and its narrative significantly over time. Some of my Rwandan interlocutors have continuously changed their positions vis-à-vis the postgenocide official narrative as it emerged, evolved, and became entrenched in the nearly three decades since 1994 and beyond. Hakizimana's and his father's positions didn't. The stories I heard from Kayitesi, Hakizimana and his father, and many other respondents ushered in the realization that researchers had yet to investigate the emergence, evolution, and plurality of responses to the master narrative in postgenocide Rwanda. Similarly, shifting individual responses to the master narrative revealed the need for closer examination of how this narrative is enforced by various actors in Rwanda and in the diaspora globally.

In this book, I examine these complexities around the postgenocide memory narrative. This work contributes to emerging literature that centers these neglected lived experiences from the Global South in memory studies. Dominant theoretical and methodological research in memory studies have largely focused their attention on empirical insights from the Global North without addressing the interconnections between the Global North and Global South lived experiences. Yet Global South lived experiences are critical sources of empirical knowledge through which new theoretical and methodological approaches can also be created. This book does exactly that: It shows how everyday ways of commemorating developed from within the lived experiences in the Global South. It simultaneously complements and challenges how political narratives about the past emerge, evolve, and are constructed to shape the present and the futures of societies and politics after mass violence.

This book maps and examines to the extent to which, and under what conditions, the master narrative of the Genocide Against the Tutsi has emerged, evolved, and been enforced as a hegemonic master narrative in Rwanda and worldwide. It also explores the plurality of responses to the postgenocide official memory and investigates the implications of these specific commemorations for larger questions about memory politics globally and in memory studies. In this book I address the following questions:

- How and why did memorializations of multiple narratives of the interrelated histories of violence in Rwanda emerge, evolve, and become enforced into a hegemonic master narrative of the Genocide Against the Tutsi over the first two decades after the 1994 genocide in Rwanda and beyond?
- How have memory channels such as language, art, literature, memorials, and the media been used in the construction and evolution of the hegemonic master narrative?
- How have individuals and groups used these same channels to respond to this hegemonic master narrative over time, and what factors influence shifts in these actors' relationships to the official memory in the two decades following this genocide?
- Last, what empirical, theoretical, and methodological insights can such an analysis of a Global South context such as Rwanda bring to memory studies and more broadly to humanities and social sciences research?

Throughout this book I distinguish between the concepts of the master narrative and the hegemonic memory, a distinction anchored in power and one that is necessary to make in order to fully grasp the evolutionary character of Rwanda's genocide memory politics in the last two decades.

Defining a Master Narrative and Hegemonic Memory in Postgenocide Rwanda

In her book *Narrative Imagination and Everyday Life*, Molly Andrews reminds us: "Stories—both personal and communal—are pivotal to the way in which politics operates, both in peoples' minds (how they understand politics and their place within and outside of the formal political sphere) as well as how politics is practiced."[1] Through the exchange of stories, a culture of commemoration emerges even as the "individual navigates the discursive waters of the master narrative and makes decisions about which aspects of them to appropriate and which to repudiate."[2] Furthermore, the stories allow us to construct narratives about experiences of violence.[3] Phillip Hammack writes that a master narrative "represents a collective storyline which group members perceive as compulsory—a story which is so central to the group's existence and 'essence' that it commands identification and integration into the personal narrative."[4] Building on the work of Andrews and Hammack, this book identifies and examines the discourses around the creation of a master narrative about the 1994 genocide. It traces the collective stories and personal narratives of Rwandans that inform and are shaped by the memory politics in postgenocide Rwanda. The master narrative of the genocide in Rwanda[5] emerged after the 1994 genocide and 1990 civil war. It evolved over time, created by a range of local and international actors engaged in debates on the construction of memory in the wake of the human calamity in Rwanda and its repercussions throughout the African Great Lakes region.

In addition, the book uses the terminology of the hegemonic memory. Berthold Molden asserts that a hegemonic master narrative "is built by prioritizing some memories over others according to the specific power constellations of a given society."[6] A hegemonic approach often excludes and silences alternative perspectives so that the excluded voice cannot even be "articulated" as a position against it. In the case of Rwanda, the postgenocide government insists on having the sole legitimacy and moral authority to define and interpret what happened during the genocide and thereby alienates any other narratives about this contested past. Their master narrative has become hegemonic and gives priority and weight to certain events and people over others and delinks histories that are otherwise connected. Through an analysis of new and repurposed vocabulary, memorials, films, literature, commemorative events that include displays of materials of memory, and artistic expressions, this book explores how various actors have enabled the master narrative of the 1994 genocide to turn into a hegemonic master narrative.[7] Actors like Hakizimana who support this hegemonic official narrative at the local level take it as "common sense"[8] or as an avenue to understand, commemorate, or speak about the violent past. Further political, social, and economic factors have elevated the master narrative of the genocide to hegemonic status globally. Other factors include the ability of the RPF elites to acquire and maintain power since 1994, mimicking and borrowing ideas on genocide representation and resources from international hegemonic Western approaches, an intense international lobbying campaign, and alienating and criminalizing alternative versions of the past that contradict the official narrative, among many others.

In this book, I argue that what has emerged as the master narrative and, over time, as the hegemonic memory of the Genocide Against the Tutsi was created out of earlier plural and fluid memorialization approaches, debates, tensions, contradictions, and contestations among local and international mnemonic actors in Rwanda and beyond. Mnemonic hegemony enhances "the ability of a dominant group or class to impose their interpretations of reality-or the interpretations that support their interests-as the only thinkable way to view the world."[9] In this book, I use hegemonic narrative to point to two different forms of hegemonic memory approaches that have emerged in the context of Rwanda. One is centered on "the best ways" to remember or how to remember more generally (Western hegemony), and the other is about the specific hegemonic narrative in Rwanda (what is silenced and what is advanced in postgenocide Rwanda).

Using interviews collected in Rwanda, participant observation carried out during genocide commemorations in Rwanda and around the world, as well as an analysis of artworks and secondary sources, this book centers the overlooked plural and contradicting voices of Rwandans whose lives have been shaped by political memory in the nearly three decades since 1994. Recentering the variety of Rwandan voices is vital to overcoming limitations in the current literature on postgenocide Rwanda; current debates on postgenocide memory practices tend to privilege the analysis of political actors of the RPF. In most cases the RPF elites are incorrectly discussed at times as a homogeneous group—or, indeed, as the only actors involved in the emergence, evolution, and enforcement of official memory.[10] There is less discussion on how other actors like ordinary Rwandans, artists, journalists, and international actors have influenced the current memory politics. Therefore, this book reveals that in the first two decades after the genocide there were, in fact, local and international actors who shaped memory politics in Rwanda through various avenues. While the government of Rwanda, which itself is not a homogeneous actor, has played a significant role in the construction and enforcement of the 1994 Genocide Against the Tutsis narrative, a multitude of other actors have also played varying roles, at different times, in these memory politics.

This book also demonstrates that shifts in individual and collective positions vis-à-vis the official narrative were not determined only by people's ethnic belonging or experiences during the 1994 genocide and 1990s civil wars. Rather, as my interactions with Kayitesi, Hakizimana and his father, and many others discussed in this book, show, there are other social, political, economic, and contemporary factors that influence these shifts. These factors have long been overlooked in scholarship on Rwanda's postgenocide memory politics.[11] Through the analysis of novel primary and secondary memory material sources, such as analysis of lyrics or on changes in colors and clothes used during commemorations to display messages and as parts of memorials, among others, this book contributes empirically to postgenocide literature on memory politics in postgenocide Rwanda as its first goal.

This book was further inspired by transcultural debates in memory studies that advocate for the decentering of hegemonic approaches in favor of those that consider plural perspectives about the past. It is for this reason that I advance *Agaciro*, a Kinyarwandan concept, with its multiple meanings (dignity, self-worth, and self-respect in relation to another's Agaciro) within this book. The Agaciro-centered approach or dignity approach developed in the next chapter and in the conclusion is essential to the Rwandan perspective about the cycles of collective thinking about life.[12] Thus this book makes an empirical, theoretical, and methodological contribution to mainstream literature on transcultural, multidirectional, and decolonial perspectives (developed in the next chapter) that has taken root in the past decade and which "critiques previous approaches that have privileged Eurocentric approaches to memory research."[13] It further influences emerging literature that explores the multiple meanings of dignity globally.[14] It emphasizes dignity as something that is fought for in different contexts and at different levels where hegemonic memory seeks to dominate how the memory of mass violence is practiced and studied. Thus a broader understanding of dignity provides an avenue to examine the interlinkages between what I discuss below as Champions, Fatalists, and Antagonists, a final goal of this book.

The book accomplishes these goals through chapters that examine how this master narrative evolved through annual themes, in local communities and changing public national commemorations activities, to memorials, and how actors like artists, journalists, politicians, and ordinary citizens endorsed or opposed the evolving master narrative.

Mapping the Master Narrative of the Genocide Against the Tutsi

The master narrative of the Genocide Against the Tutsi can be summarized in five key points. First, the 1994 genocide was planned by a small group of radical Hutu military officers and politicians and was preceded by other forms of violence: torture, imprisonment, harassment, and other killings that targeted the Tutsi in 1959, the 1960s, the 1970s, and the early 1990s. Second, the Tutsi were the main targets of the 1994 genocide in Rwanda, and some one million Tutsi were killed in one hundred days. Third, although there were a handful of Hutu who saved their Tutsi neighbors (with the Hutu individuals or their family members dying in the process), the Hutu as a social or ethnic group are guilty of participating either directly or indirectly in the killings that define the Genocide Against the Tutsi and who therefore must apologize. Fourth, the international community failed to do anything to save the Tutsi, especially the French, who in fact played an active role in supporting the genocidal junta. Finally, the Rwandan Patriotic Army (RPA)—and by association, the RPF—are the heroes who stopped the genocide and won the war. The master narrative of the genocide has emerged and evolved to set the parameters of what is permitted in public discourse on the genocide but also on Rwanda's and the African Great Lakes region's pasts in general. To map the plurality of responses to the master narrative, I develop a typology of responses that has evolved among Rwandans in public discourses on the past. It includes those who support, disagree with, or even completely reject the master narrative.

The first of these are *intore* or Champions of the master narrative. The Kinyarwanda word *intore* (also can be plural) is the closest term to identify Champions of the master narrative and commemoration. It has multiple meanings and has also changed to accommodate the creation of a master narrative. In precolonial Rwanda, the word referred to warriors who served the king, or *mwami*.[15] In contemporary Rwanda, it is used sometimes to refer to male traditional dancers. It is also used to refer to youth who attend government *itorero* camps (camps that were created to bring postgenocide youth from different backgrounds together to educate them about the master narrative and, like in Hakizimana's case, introduce them to other versions of history than those of their parents or relatives).[16] In addition, intore is also used in casual conversations to mean generally those who support or champion postgenocide government projects, including the master narrative of the genocide, without drawing parallels to other histories of violence of the 1990s.

They also include those who argued that commemorations were essential to reconstruction and reconciliation in Rwanda throughout the two decades following the genocide. These actors contended that commemoration entails, first, a duty for each Rwandan to restore dignity to genocide victims and, second, an occasion for civic education that is considered essential for fostering a peaceful future. The majority in this category are Tutsi survivors of the 1994 genocide and their allies in and outside of Rwanda. Among genocide survivors are Tutsi genocide survivors who never left Rwanda. Among those who align themselves with the category of genocide survivors, one may also find the RPF members and their families who were living in exile and returned to Rwanda after the war and genocide ended. As discussed the third chapter, the strict definition of "survivor" solidified over the two decades following the Genocide Against the Tutsi, and at the time of writing this book remains a volatile term itself. Per the Champions, it does not include the Hutus or foreigners who lost their relatives while protecting the Tutsi. As discussed in third chapter, those who oppose the master narrative argue that the current master narrative is too strong and harsh on the Hutus and not inclusive of all survivors of the events of April–July 1994. They argue that the definition of "genocide survivor" is limited and should be expanded. Thus, as research has shown, some insist on developing and telling alternative personal and family histories not included in the master narrative.[17] The Champions regard these arguments and actions as amounting to genocide denialism.

The Champions also include Hutu political elites who are members of the RPF or other political parties with close ties to the RPF, as well as independents in parliament and other institutions. Champions also include former pregenocide government officials, including even some who were accused of committing genocide or were high-ranking members of the defeated pregenocide army, but who have since defended the RPF's political agenda. A few examples can include Marcel Gatsinzi, a military official in both the pre-and postgenocide Rwandan army,[18] and Rucagu Boniface, who has been part of all three postcolonial Rwandan governments and has been accused of genocide but was never tried in court, as well as many others.[19]

It is critical to highlight that the Champions enjoy a potentially dangerous privilege within this typology of memory narratives. In describing the hegemonic power exercised by the largely Western doctrine of transitional justice, the Champions of transitional justice not only prescribe "what is good and necessary for societies emerging from violence to achieve repair and progress" but also importantly wield the power to diagnose populations, "defining who is good . . . as well as who is bad."[20] Champions of the master narrative equally hold this relational diagnostic power over not only determining the "correct" narrative of the past, but also designating individuals as belonging to either of the other categories, of *ibipinga* (antagonists) or *ntibindeba* (fatalists). This power asymmetry that advantages the Champions has significant implications for the social capital that they control, across all three groups, and also influences the fight for dignity, a relational concept that is presented throughout this book.

Second, in postwar and postgenocide Rwanda, *igipinga* (*ibipinga*, pl.), or the Antagonists, is a well-known derogatory term adapted into Kinyarwanda from the Swahili verb *kupinga*, meaning to discount, deny, or oppose. Antagonists are cast in official discourse as *abanzi b' igihugu*, or enemies of the country.[21] Anyone who opposed the government's reconstruction projects or voiced opposition to the master narrative belongs to this category. There are different kinds of opposition: one that calls for a stronger narrative of memory and another that calls for less. Individuals belonging to this group of Antagonists associate commemoration activities with anxiety, resentment, and fear. During my research, these were largely a segment of the Hutu community who were either coerced into participating in official commemoration or rejected the master narrative altogether for various reasons. Some Antagonists, especially those residing inside Rwanda, contested the master narrative through silence by boycotting commemorations and sometimes public attacks on memorials or people who were mourning. Such public displays of antagonism, when they happened, often occurred during the official commemoration period in April. They include those that Richard Benda identifies as "emerging generation" who were in their teens during the genocide, like Hakizimana and the "second generation" born after the official end of the genocide.[22] Theirs are dissident narratives, meaning those that deviate from the official narrative. It is equally potentially dangerous especially when used to campaign for violence as a means to challenge the current master narrative and political power.

However, depending on one's actions and how they are interpreted or perceived by Champions, a Tutsi genocide survivor could also end up in the Antagonist category if their actions or words question government programs or the master narrative parameters. For example, this was the case in discussions of high-profile court cases of the Rwigara family, who for many years supported the RPF but later fell out of favor with party elites.[23] This was also the case for Kizito Mihigo, whose story is discussed in Chapter 6. Mihigo was an influential Champion but came to be regarded as an Antagonist when he began to compose music that questioned the master narrative and was accused of associating with antagonistic and opposition groups. Champions have also declared many former members of the RPF in exile and its army Antagonists, including high-ranking generals like Kayumba Nyamwasa or RPF's former financial supporters, like the wealthy Tutsi entrepreneur Tribert Rujugiro.[24]

Finally, influenced by experiences like my encounter with Kayitesi and given the complexity and variety of responses to the master narrative, the third colloquial term is on the third group of *Ntibindeba*[25] or Fatalists of the genocide master narrative. In public discourse in Rwanda, Fatalists were discussed in Kinyarwanda as Ntibindeba, a term that when literally translated means "it's none of my business" or "this does not concern me." They are those who look away and prefer not to concern themselves with the affairs of commemoration in either support or disagreement. These include individuals who advocate for neither the genocide master narrative nor the counternarratives pushed by Antagonists. They do not want their experiences to be politicized. They do not hold a coherent position but, due to their personal pain or other reasons, simply wish to withdraw from the politics of memory.

In this book, I work with a set of colloquial terms from Rwandan discourse on these issues translated into English. These terms are used to make sense of categories of people in everyday discourse. This is an approach that seeks to nuance how actors are organized in this particular context and the fluidity of engagement with the master narrative as opposed to seeing them as rigid categories. The use of these categories is not to imply that I support these categories or consider them as fixed or all encompassing. These are political positionalities that cut across and include lay public, politicians, survivors, museum officials, members of the clergy, and others. They are analytical categories that help to structure an examination of the responses to memory politics in Rwanda. They are flexible and fluid, unlike the often applied but not-so-strictly lived trichotomy of survivors, perpetrators, and bystanders. Thus in expanding on the categories of Champions, Antagonists, and Fatalists this book contributes to debates that point out limitations of this trichotomy and argues for these simplistic categorical approaches to be redrawn to accommodate the complexity and fluidity inherent to the experiences of people that populate and move throughout them.[26] While the typology that I put forward throughout this book forms a necessary epistemological tool with which to map the memory politics of individuals' relationships to master and hegemonic memory, these three terms do not capture fully the specific dynamics of the aftermath of genocides and other types of mass violence.[27] This book agrees that just like "there are no tidy endings following mass atrocities,"[28] there is no tidy way of discussing the emergence, evolution, and categorization of the plurality of responses to how mass atrocities are remembered.

Reflections on Methodology, Life Narratives, and Written Sources

This book uses multiple sources, including interviews collected during research in Rwanda; participant observation in official commemorations in Rwanda and around the world; artworks; and other written and oral sources that are often overlooked in studies on Rwanda and memory studies in general.[29] This approach allows for the tracing of various actors shaping the emergence and evolution of official memory and responses to it. It also permits me to locate and analyze nuances around the use of language and the significance of cultural tools in the commemoration process.

The temporal frame of this research explores the emergence, evolution, enforcement, and responses to the 1994 genocide in Rwanda between 1994 and 2014. This 20-year time frame is significant because it allows for the excavation of the fluid, evolving, and transformational character of narrative production, transmission, and change over time. Significantly, however, while this research has been guided by this time frame, it has not been exclusively bound to it: As memories and narratives have continued to evolve, so has this research continued its engagement beyond 2014 and until the time of writing. I conducted research in Rwanda on the topic of commemoration and responses to it between 2011 and 2014 for a total of 12 months. In 2011 and 2012, I conducted interviews, and in 2013 and 2014, I focused on collecting gray literature (locally published books, pamphlets, and other publications not in circulation outside Rwanda), which are sometimes ignored in postgenocide literature. Respondents were adult men and women aged between 23 and 35, with the exception of community and religious leaders, who were between the ages of 45 and 75 at the time of the interviews. Although I collected many more interviews, I have drawn on forty-seven in-depth, semistructured interviews and three focus groups of twelve participants each for the analysis in this book. My research covered the districts of Ruhango, Nyamagabe, and Huye in the southern province of Rwanda; Bugesera in the eastern province; Musanze in the Northern Province; and Kigali, the capital. In 2014, two research associates and I conducted interviews with government leaders and other elites, including Christian and Muslim religious leaders who have played crucial roles in producing or responding to the master narrative. Additional stories were collected through informal conversations with middle managers of institutions that enforce the master narrative of genocide memory in Rwanda; research brokers familiar with commemoration; advisors to different commissions; teachers, survivors, those who, like Hakizimana's father, committed crimes during the genocide; and many others. This book is also based on participant observation and notes taken while I attended over a dozen commemorations across Rwanda and abroad among the diaspora, which were attended by hundreds of people. They included "naturally occurring conversations," which are treated as an important addition to formal interviews.[30]

Interviewing people in an overresearched context such as Rwanda and on a sensitive topic, such as the 1994 genocide, posed unique challenges and required reflection throughout the research and writing journey. Interviews are vulnerable to many factors, including false memory and asking respondents to recall exact dates or events that they sometimes wish to forget. There are also those who tell you "rumors" to evade the conversation or opt for silence.[31] There are also respondents such as orphans who were not yet born in 1994 or were young at the time of the genocide and do not have a full account of their family history.[32] I had to negotiate all these factors and many others in the research, analysis, and writing processes. To overcome any gaps in respondents' stories, I compared stories to each other and triangulated them with other sources, such as documentary evidence, secondary sources, and gray literature, to test validity.[33] I used ethnographic approaches to collect data, combined with sociological tools such as field research and textual analysis, especially in tracing the emergence and responses to official memory. I also used historical approaches to trace the evolution of commemoration across time and space.[34]

I collected local sources written in various languages, including Kinyarwanda, from local and international libraries, which are at the center of this book. It is often the case that Western scholars who work on Rwanda or in other postcolonial contexts overlook local researchers and overrely on Western knowledge, keeping their scholarly debates confined among each other. Olivia Rutazibwa asserts that this is how Rwandans are silenced about their own country. While commenting on knowledge production in postgenocide Rwanda she argues:

> Rwanda is silenced, in the sense that the experts are invariably of Western origin—even if they have not been allowed into the country in the last decade or more. When Rwandan sources are included—usually as informants rather than authors—they tend to be either cast as victims, corroborating the experts' analysis, or as partisans, too closely linked to the current regime to be trusted for objective information.[35]

It is for this reason that I collected the 47 oral interviews mentioned previously[36] to combine with conventional textual materials, including academic theses written by Rwandans in Rwanda or abroad who have examined related topics. Other sources include newspaper articles written by Rwandans accessed through libraries and both physical and digital Rwandan archives. In addition, I feature multiple voices of Rwandans through the use of Kinyarwanda proverbs, poetic artistic expressions, and other marginalized carriers of memory[37] to offer an alternative, decolonial approach to memory research. Epistemic decolonization is concerned with unsettling colonial approaches to how we construct knowledge. It is a "delinking from colonial matrix of power" in research and in other spheres of life.[38] It invites us to consider other approaches, like indigenization. Bagele et al. put it this way:

> Decolonisation is followed by indigenisation, where researchers invoke indigenous knowledge embodied in languages, proverbs, folktales, stories, songs, music, taboos, artifacts, cultural and lived experiences to envision new topics, themes, indigenous-centred conceptual frameworks, methods, processes and categories of analysis not easily obtainable from conventional methods.[39]

Thus, this work builds on the vital foundations of those who seek to decolonize methodological approaches used to study postcolonial contexts and conduct memory research in general.

I have employed a thematic analysis approach to select and analyze interviews with similar themes that addressed aspects of the emergence, evolution, or responses to the genocide master narrative. While I found significant support, this research was difficult on numerous levels not only for me, as a researcher, but also for my respondents.[40]

Case Selection

I have chosen to focus on the commemoration of the Tutsi killed during the genocide and not other unofficial memory practices in Rwanda for several reasons. First, the stories of the Tutsi as victims or survivors are central to the master narrative of the genocide that has shaped the fabric of postgenocide social, economic, and political life of all Rwandans. These annual events have allowed various actors to recalibrate the master narrative of the genocide reproduced throughout the country. The government has, in turn, used that master narrative that turned into a hegemonic narrative to shape its domestic and foreign policies as well as its engagement with the Rwandan diaspora. Second, it is the master narrative that, to a large extent, is internalized by Rwanda's youth, who comprise over 60% of the country's population born after the genocide.[41] Last, focusing on this one type of commemoration allows for an examination of how power is manifested through the emergence, evolution, enforcement, and responses to official memory. However, it is important to point to some of the limitations of this book.

First, the book does not examine alternative vernacular memory practices that have equally emerged and evolved and elicited responses in postgenocide Rwanda (I have written about this in previous work).[42] Second, the book does not address commemorations of the missing soldiers and civilians who died or went missing in the civil war and during the genocide and after. During my research, I was informed that vernacular commemorations existed and returned later to research them.[43]

A third limitation is that the book does not specifically engage with gendered aspects of the master narrative, although as research has shown, this is part of the postgenocide Rwandan memory landscape.[44] My intention was not to continue dominant practices in literature, especially in African contexts, that have often written women out of "historical accounts and political memory."[45] Rather, it is simply that this theme did not emerge often in my interviews at the time of researching this topic. However, throughout the book I constantly reference literature, including my own, that has applied gendered analyses to memory politics in Rwanda.[46] My intention is to provide analyses that show how one's gender, class, and ethnicity relate to the master narrative of the genocide.

Layout of the Book

This book is organized into nine chapters, including the introduction and three parts. The first three chapters introduce 1 the intellectual and historical foundations of the text. Here I provide a nuanced approach to studying memory politics both in Rwanda and globally. I develop analyses that advance evolving interdisciplinary debates in memory studies. These include discussions of the transcultural turn, technology turn, decolonial turn, and intergenerational memory politics in memory studies.

After the introduction, Chapter 1 focuses on major shifts in memory studies that have led to the transcultural and decolonial turns that have opened avenues for scholars to examine Global South contexts in memory studies. It is through examining these debates that Agaciro, or dignity, emerges as an alternative to current approaches. This chapter situates this book in the evolving debates within memory studies around decolonization and decentering Global North perspectives, to which this book hopes to contribute.

The second chapter provides a historical background of Rwanda. It focuses on the role of master narratives in governance and legitimacy and examines how previous master narratives evolved into hegemonic narratives and how these hegemonic narratives sometimes became dissident narratives through political developments. The chapter highlights the fluidity with which narratives have evolved from marginalization to dominance and then back again.

The next five chapters examine the emergence and evolution of the master narrative of the Genocide Against the Tutsi and how it turned into a hegemonic narrative. These chapters engage with evolving literature on hegemonic narratives and dissident or vernacular narratives in memory studies.

Chapter 3 shows how, immediately after the genocide and civil war ended in 1994, initial commemorations were mostly ad hoc or organized by local and nongovernmental actors. It analyses academic literature on that period, using primary sources to illustrate how the postgenocide government used the Holocaust "model"[47] of remembrance and other international reconciliation ideas to inspire its creation of the master narrative, over other local approaches presented at conferences in Rwanda by scholars and postconflict entrepreneurs who studied different contexts. The postgenocide government chose a foreign but universalized approach that was understandable to many people around the world—including Westerners—but that alienated Rwandan mourning practices. The chapter posits that language, speeches, themes, and other tools were used to create a master narrative both domestically and internationally. However, the chapter also shows how these innovations were the products of fierce debates among Rwandan political elites and how this period saw the rise of critics who resisted "the competitive memory" approach to representing the past both within and outside Rwanda. The chapter also employs the analytical categories of Champions, Antagonists, and Fatalists as a typological tool through which to systematically understand diversity and power in relation to genocidal memory politics among Rwandans. By identifying these actors and their relationships with the hegemonic memory narrative, and with each other, I challenge literature that centers the Rwandan government as the exclusive and most powerful creator and purveyor of memory and that ignores the agency of other local and international actors that have equally contributed to Rwanda's postgenocide official memory construction.

Chapter 4 then shows how the hegemonic master narrative gained prominence in Rwanda through the construction of physical symbols and through institutions and laws created to guard it from denialism. While physical symbols such as memorials might seem permanent, they also have evolved to serve different and sometimes contentious political, community, and individual purposes. They are also at the center of debates between local and international actors as well as among Champions, Antagonists, and Fatalists. In this chapter, I examine how some memorials emerged and evolved using the universalized Holocaust model and other international approaches to reconciliation and analyze the community-level official commemorations I observed during my fieldwork. I show how the master narrative was enforced during ceremonies and around memorials during the first two decades after the genocide. This is especially the case for the mainstream Kigali Genocide Memorial, which has become the center stage of genocide memory politics in Rwanda.

Chapter 5 examines how Rwandans have responded to the creation of the hegemonic master narrative. It looks at how Champions, Antagonists, and Fatalists emerged in response to the sorts of public ceremonies that I attended at the Amahoro Stadium in Kigali, in community commemorative events where survivor testimonies were shared around the country, and among the diaspora. It also examines how politicians and military officials played key roles in transmitting the master narrative of the Genocide Against the Tutsi. In addition, I discuss how attendance at commemorations was enforced among Champions, Antagonists, and Fatalists. I analyze commemorations organized at the family level and observe that while changes occurred at both the micro and macro levels, it is the micro-level commemorations that often produced the dissident narratives of Antagonists. These dissident narratives circulated, and their originators were sometimes severely punished. The chapter relies on transcultural literature in memory studies to show how the master narrative gained mobility not only using carriers, including physical symbols of memory, but also through Champions, Antagonists, and Fatalists, who developed memory narratives of events that happened within Rwanda and beyond its borders.

Chapter 6 builds on the previous chapter to provide concrete examples of this reward and punishment approach to enforcing the official narrative in the first 20 years after the genocide. It examines how three individual artists emerged as prominent Champions, Antagonists, and Fatalists, respectively.

One of them, Kizito Mihigo, was a genocide survivor who became an Antagonist; Edouard Bamporiki, who identified as being from a radical Hutu family, became a Champion. Dorcy Rugamba's artistic output categorized him as a Fatalist, speaking to both local and diaspora communities and to international audiences without capitalizing on genocide memory to pronounce a political position in support or against the hegemonic master narrative. This chapter brings a much-needed analysis of artists and art to memory studies, where such analyses have been historically neglected. It develops a nuanced discussion of postgenocide Rwanda to show that when it comes to youth, who are the majority in the country, it is not about their identity backgrounds. Instead, there are many other economic, social, and political factors that inform one's position as a Champion, Antagonist, or Fatalist, and that can shift one's position over time. This discussion contributes to growing debates in memory studies that challenge the concepts of perpetrators, survivors, and bystanders as fixed categories that explain people's relationship to mass violence. It also contributes to the evolving literature on intergenerational memory politics in the digital age.

Chapter 7 evaluates how various actors used the evolving media landscape to communicate their positions as Champions, Antagonists, or Fatalists. It shows how the government and its representatives rewarded Champions who used the media to spread the hegemonic master narrative globally and punished Antagonists through the implementation of genocide denial laws. This chapter argues that the media remains a crucial and influential space for narratives about the genocide—much like it was in promoting violence leading up to and during the 1994 genocide. It is a space where the malleability of the master narrative and its purpose are evident, as are its interactions with the dynamic landscape of the digital age. I rely on primary and secondary sources, including social media, to argue the wildfire nature of these evolving digital cultures—that afford the hegemonic narrative an opportunity to evolve further and spread but simultaneously threatens its very durability by making people vulnerable to "fake news" and the limits of enforcement. These questions are especially salient given that, as described in Chapter 2, previous master narratives in Rwanda emerged, evolved, and were enforced for a period of time but eventually became marginalized and considered dissident. This analysis contributes to emerging debates in memory studies, especially in an age of dissident and often decolonial movements that are using online spaces to challenge hardened hegemonic master narratives around the world, including in the Global North. These dissident narratives are sometimes silenced despite assumptions that democratic countries do not suppress dissident narratives.

Part 3 concludes the book with a single chapter revisiting the book's core arguments and then proposes opportunities for future research in Rwanda and beyond. I first show that an analysis of multiple sources over the first two decades after the genocide shows that Rwanda's approach to coming to terms with its violent past is characterized by contradictions. On the one hand, we see the construction of this master narrative using a competitive memory approach informed by Western practices of memory and reconstruction; on the other hand, we observe a parallel development of spaces such as localized vernacular practices and/or Gacaca, among others, that privilege Rwandan philosophies and approaches to mourning. I argue that when it comes to Rwanda's memory politics and especially current tense debates among memory actors in both Rwanda and among the diaspora, there are spaces that are crucial and must be developed to foster such debates into peaceful conversations. The book proposes an Agaciro (self-worth or dignity) approach from Rwandan philosophy that centers an understanding of dignity that is not about the individual's rights only but that relates to another's dignity and *utu* (or being).[48] It is a concept that makes space for compassionate discussion of what a dignity-centered approach in memory studies would mean for examining multiple narratives about past violent events, regardless of geography or a country's (un)democratic status. Such a dignity approach allows us to locate and study interlinkages between memory forms that emerge out of mourning experiences from the Global South with those in the Global North. It also allows us to interrogate the power dynamics between these different approaches in contexts where actors are crafting narratives about recent or distant violent histories. A relational dignity turn also advocates for each context to first look within its own history and philosophy for practices of coming to terms with the past. These localized forms of remembering should be included in what is referred to as universal or international practices of mourning.

Throughout this book, I use anecdotal evidence from my lived experience as a researcher witnessing the creation and evolution of the master narrative in not only Rwanda but also other countries where I lived and took part in commemorations before, during, and after this research. As discussed previously, reflexivity is important in research, and such anecdotal evidence can itself be translated into rich empirical analysis. Rwanda's case is important because a new generation of memory studies scholars themselves is increasingly realizing that contexts, experiences, concepts, and methodological approaches from the Global South have been overlooked.

The journey of writing this book has been a labor of both science and love. I invite you, the reader, to join me on this complicated but necessary journey through time, memory, people, and place, which has been equally painful, insightful, and cathartic for me.

Notes

1. Molly Andrews, *Narrative Imagination and Everyday Life* (London: Oxford University Press, 2019), 85–86.
2. Ibid.
3. Sara B. Cobb, *Speaking of Violence: The Politics and Poetics of Narrative in Conflict Resolution* (Oxford, UK: Oxford University Press, 2013), 81.
4. Phillip L. Hammack, "Narrative and the Politics of Meaning," *Narrative Inquiry* 21, no. 2 (2011): 311–318.
5. Richard Benda refers to it as the official metanarrative of the postgenocide; see Richard Benda, "Youth Connect Dialogue: Unwanted Legacies, Responsibility and Nation-Building in Rwanda" (working Paper 001, Aegist Trust, September 2017), https://www.genocideresearchhub.org.rw/document/youth-connekt-dialogue-unwanted-legacies-responsibility-and-nation-building-in-rwanda/. However, I find the master narrative is the one with clear vocabulary for this analysis.
6. Berthold Molden, "Resistant Pasts versus mnemonic hegemony: On the power relations of collective memory," *Memory Studies* 9, no. 2 (2016): 128.
7. Ernesto Laclau and Chantal Mouffe, *Hegemony and Socialist Strategy: Towards a Radical Democratic Politics*, 2nd ed. (London: Verso, 2014). See also: Derek Boothman, "The Sources for Gramsci's Concept of Hegemony", *Rethinking Marxism*, 20, no. 2 (2008): 201–215; and Norberto Bobbio, "Gramsci and the Concept of Civil Society," in *Civil Society and the State: New European Perspectives*, ed. John Keane (London: Verso 1988), 73–99.
8. Molden, "Resistant Pasts versus Mnemonic Hegemony," 128.
9. Molden, "Resistant Pasts versus Mnemonic Hegemony."
10. See, for instance, some of the literature that has emphasized the role of the government and ethnicity of Hutu and Tutsi rather than focusing on other factors that shape the emergence, evolution, and responses to the official memory. Erin Jessee, *Negotiating Genocide in Rwanda: The Politics of History* (New York: Springer, 2017); and Timothy Longman, *Memory and Justice in Post-genocide Rwanda* (New York: Cambridge University Press, 2017). See also Susan Thomson, *Rwanda: From Genocide to Precarious Peace* (New Haven, CT: Yale University Press, 2018).
11. See Note 10.

12. David Mwambari, "*Agaciro*, Vernacular Memory, and the Politics of Memory in Post-genocide Rwanda," *African Affairs* 120, no. 481 (October 2021): 613.
13. Astrid Erll, "Travelling Memory," *Parallax* 17, no. 4 (2011): 11.
14. Norman Ajari, *La Dignité ou la mort: Éthique et politique de la race*, (Empécheurs de penser rond, 2019), 12. For other writings on dignity, see Catherine Dupré, *The Age of Dignity: Human Rights and Constitutionalism in Europe* (New York: Bloomsbury Publishing, 2016), 16; Eleni Coundouriotis, "The Dignity of the 'Unfittest': Victims' Stories in South Africa," *Human Rights Quarterly* 28, 4 (2006): 842–867.
15. For precolonial use of *Intore*, see Thomas Riot, Herrade Boistelle, and Nicolas Bancel, "Les politiques d'itorero au Rwanda: Un dispositif éducatif et guerrier à l'épreuve de la reconstruction nationale," *Revue Tiers Monde* 228 (2016): 101–120. Also see Paul Rutayisire, "L'évangélisation du Rwanda (1922-1945) (PhD dissertation, Université de Fribourg, 1984).
16. On Ingando camps, see Andrea Purdeková, *Making Ubumwe: Power, State and Camps in Rwanda's Unity-Building Project* (New York: Berghahn Books, 2015). See also Simon Turner, "Making Good Citizens from Bad Life in Post-genocide Rwanda," *Development and Change* 45, no. 3 (2014): 415–433; and Chi Mgbako, "Ingando Solidarity Camps: Reconciliation and Political Indoctrination in Postgenocide Rwanda," *Harvard Human Rights Journal*, 18 (2005): 201.
17. See Benda, "Youth Connect Dialogue," 3.
18. Filip Reyntjens, *Political Governance in Post-genocide Rwanda* (Cambridge, UK: Cambridge University Press, 2013), 79.
19. Rucagu is one of the few politicians who have managed to navigate Rwanda's politics for many decades. His story of helping the RPF win control of the North is one of many that show why he is favored by the RPF leadership. See, Eugene Kwibuka, "Citizens Played Central Role in Defeat of Insurgency in Ruhengeri," *New Times*, September 23, 2023, https://www.newtimes.co.rw/section/read/220015. He is one of the prominent Hutu politicians who encouraged Hutus to ask for forgiveness for their role during the genocide. Archived newspapers from the 1990s highlight the following as evidence of his hatred against the Tutsi before the genocide: "Député Rucagu Boniface nous a écrit, les tutsis se passent pour être plus malins que les autres mais en réalité ce n'est que de la cruauté cachée" [Deputy Rucagu Boniface wrote to us, the Tutsis pretend to be smarter than the others, but in reality it is only hidden cruelty]. See Rucagu Bonifasi, "Depite Rucagu Yaratwandikiye. Tugerageza Kumenya Ubugoma N4amayeri Y4abatutsi. Umututsi Umuvura Ijisho Ryamara Gukira Akarigukanurira," *Kangura*, July 1993, https://genocidearchiverwanda.org.rw/index.php/Kangura_Issue_46. He is on the list of elite Hutus who were accused of the genocide. See Reyntjens, *Political Governance in Post-genocide Rwanda*, 79.
20. Sayra Adinda van den Berg Bhagwandas, "Rhetoric, Ritual and Reality: Understanding the Relationship between Ex-combatants and the TRC in Sierra Leone," (PhD thesis, University of Edinburgh, 2020), 114.
21. Allan Thompson, *Media and the Rwanda Genocide* (Ottawa, ON, Canada: IDRC, 2007), 88.
22. See Benda, "Youth Connect Dialogue," 3.

23. Awino Okech, "Gender and State-Building Conversations: The Discursive Production of Gender Identity in Kenya and Rwanda," *Conflict, Security & Development* 21, no. 4 (2019): 1–15.
24. Pritish Behuria, "Centralising Rents and Dispersing Power while Pursuing Development? Exploring the Strategic Uses of Military Firms in Rwanda," *Review of African Political Economy* 43, no. 150 (2016): 630–647.
25. The term was first used during the genocide by the then interim president Theodore Sindikubwabo as he argued for everyone to participate in the genocide. He claimed he did not want people who were not taking sides or claiming neutrality. See Liberata Gahongayire, "The Contribution of Memory in Healing and Preventing Genocide in Rwanda," *International Journal of Innovation and Applied Studies* 10, no. 1 (2015): 109. And see Jim Fussell, "Amagambo y'ngenzi [A Glossary of Important Words and Phrases]," *prévenirgénocideinternational*, http://www.preventgenocide.org/rw/amagambo2.htm. Retrieved September 2021. It has since been adapted into conversations when discussing those who are not interested in participating in commemoration.
26. Johanna Ray Vollhardt and Michal Bilewicz, "After the Genocide: Psychological Perspectives on Victim, Bystander, and Perpetrator Groups," *Journal of Social Issues* 69, no. 1 (2013): 1–15. See also Giorgia Donà, "'Situated Bystandership' During and After the Rwandan Genocide," *Journal of Genocide Research* 20, no. 1 (2018): 1–19; and Sara E. Brown, "Female Perpetrators of the Rwandan Genocide," *International Feminist Journal of Politics* 16, no. 3 (2014): 448–469. Finally, see Régine Uwibereyeho King and Izumi Sakamoto, "Disengaging from Genocide Harm-Doing and Healing Together between Perpetrators, Bystanders, and Victims in Rwanda," *Peace and Conflict: Journal of Peace Psychology* 21, no. 3 (2015): 378.
27. For the most recent intervention to challenge labeling of perpetrators, survivors, or bystanders, see Michael Rothberg, *The Implicated Subject* (California: Stanford University Press, 2020), 33; and Susanne C. Knittel and Sofía Forchieri, "Navigating Implication: An Interview with Michael Rothberg," *Journal of Perpetrator Research* 3, no. 1 (2020): 6–19.
28. Martha Minow, *Between Vengeance and Forgiveness: Facing History after Genocide and Mass Violence* (Boston: Beacon Press, 1998), 102.
29. Lee Ann Fujii, "Shades of Truth and Lies: Interpreting Testimonies of War and Violence," *Journal of Peace Research*, 47, no. 2 (2010): 231–241.
30. Andrews, *Narrative and Imagination*. On "naturally occurring" conversations, see Sabina Mihelj, "Between Official and Vernacular Memory," in *Research Methods for Memory Studies*, eds. Emily Keightley and Michael Pickering (Edinburgh: Edinburgh University Press, 2013), 60–75.
31. Lee Ann Fujii, "Shades of Truth and Lies."
32. See, for example, this story: J. Tabaro Mbonyinshuti and Irene Nayebare, "Genocide Survivor Reunites with Family after 19 Years," *New Times* (Kigali, Rwanda), June 1, 2013, https://www.newtimes.co.rw/article/93295/National/genocide-survivor-reunites-with-family-after-19-years.

33. Nancy Carter, Denise Bryant-Lukosius, Alba DiCenso, Jennifer Blythe, and Alan J. Neville, "The Use of Triangulation in Qualitative Research," *Oncology Nursing Forum* 41, no. 5 (2014): 545–547.
34. Wulf Kansteiner, "Finding Meaning in Memory: A Methodological Critique of Collective Memory Studies," *History and Theory* 41, no. 2 (2002): 179–197.
35. Rutazibwa, "Studying Agaciro," 292.
36. Isidore Okpewho, *African Oral Literature: Backgrounds, Character, and Continuity* (Bloomington: Indiana University Press, 2013). See also David Mwambari, "Can Online Platforms Be e-*Pana-Africana liberation zones* for Pan-African Decolonization Debates?" *CODESRIA Bulletin Online*, No. 5 (2021), https://kclpure.kcl.ac.uk/portal/en/publications/can-online-platforms-be-epanaafricana-liberation-zones-for-panafrican-and-decolonization-debates(9b329fbc-cd9b-4fd0-b8db-b703014e7032).html.
37. See Erll, "Travelling Memory," 11.
38. Walter Mignolo, *The Darker Side of Western Modernity: Global Futures, Decolonial Options* (Durham, NC: Duke University Press, 2011), xxvii–viii.
39. Bagele Chilisa, Thenjiwe Emily Major, and Kelne Khudu-Petersen, "Community Engagement with a Postcolonial, African-Based Relational Paradigm," *Qualitative Research* 17, no. 3 (2017): 327.
40. Though I do not disagree that there are serious challenges in doing research or accessing leaders in Rwanda articulated in the scholarly literature, there is a danger that younger scholars I engage with have adopted an attitude of resignation before even trying to interview or find information from official sources. This is a pattern that can result in producing information that misinforms international audiences, including future diaspora or Rwandan researchers. Indeed, as researchers we need to remember that humility is important, especially when probing people's lives to find stories that are private and often traumatizing to reveal, as was my experience. We therefore must be patient, devoting our time and making multiple visits if we really care about the context we are researching. At the same time, we must realize that the people we interview or are interested in, whether government elites, ordinary people, or others, have their own agency, interests, and anxieties, and we should respect their privacy.

    For works that detail individual accounts of experiences of doing research in Rwanda, see Yolande Bouka, "Nacibazo, 'No Problem': Moving Behind the Official Discourse of Postgenocide Justice in Rwanda," in *Emotional and Ethical Challenges for Field Research in Africa: The Story Behind the Findings*, eds. Susan Thomson, An Ansoms, and Jude Murison (New York: Palgrave Macmillan, 2013), 107–122; Susan Thomson, "Academic Integrity and Ethical Responsibilities in Postgenocide Rwanda: Working with Research Ethics Boards to Prepare for Reseach in Rwanda with Human Subjects," in *Emotional and Ethical Challenges for Field Research in Africa: The Story Behind the Findings*, eds. Thomson, Ansoms, and Murison, 139–54; and Olivia Umurerwa Rutazibwa, "Studying Agaciro: Moving Beyond Wilsonian Interventionist Knowledge Production on Rwanda," *Journal of Intervention and Statebuilding* 8, no. 4 (2014): 291–301. See also Jonathan Fisher, "Writing about Rwanda since the

Genocide: Knowledge, Power and 'Truth,'" *Journal of Intervention and Statebuilding* 9, no. 1 (2015): 134–145. For an examination of mutuality as a leadership concept, see Grace Elizabeth Thomas, "Re-imagining Framework for Leadership Analysis," *Leadership & Developing Societies* 5, no. 1 (2020): 69–73. For more on how ordinary Rwandans emerge into political elites and vice versa, especially women, see David Mwambari, "Women-Led Non-governmental Organizations and Peacebuilding in Rwanda," *African Conflict and Peacebuilding Review* 7, no. 1 (2017): 66–79.
41. United Nations Children's Fund (UNICEF). *UNICEF Annual Report 2013–Rwanda* (New York: UNICEF, 2013).
42. David Mwambari, "*Agaciro*," 611–628.
43. Ibid.
44. To consistently engage with gendered analysis, I bring into dialogue scholarship that has done so especially in Rwanda's context. See, for example, Jennie E. Burnet, *Genocide Lives in Us: Women, Memory, and Silence in Rwanda* (Madison: University of Wisconsin Press, 2012).
45. Sylvia Tamale, *Decolonization and Afro-feminism* (Ottawa: Daraja Press, 2020), 23; and also see Ayesha Iman, Amina Mama, and Fatima Sow, eds., *Engendering African Social Sciences* (Dakar, Senegal: CODESRIA Book Series, 1999).
46. See also the varied works that address one or another postgenocide memory politics and gender: Marie E. Berry, "From Violence to Mobilization: Women, War, and Threat in Rwanda," *Mobilization: An International Quarterly* 20, no. 2 (2015): 135–156; and Marie E. Berry, "When 'Bright Futures' Fade: Paradoxes of Women's Empowerment in Rwanda," *Signs: Journal of Women in Culture and Society* 41, no. 1 (2015): 1–27. I have also researched this for a number of articles. See David Mwambari, "Women-Led Non-governmental Organizations and Peacebuilding in Rwanda," *African Conflict and Peacebuilding Review* 7, no. 1 (2017): 66–79; and "Leadership Emergence in Postgenocide Rwanda: The Role of Women in Peacebuilding," *Journal of Leadership and Developing Societies* 2, no. 1 (2017): 88–104.
47. See Jinks, "Representing Genocide," 21.
48. Micere Mugo, *The Imperative of Utu/Ubuntu in Africana Scholarship* (Wakefield, QC: Daraja Press, 2021), 5.

1
Decolonial Approaches to Memory

When I started doing research in graduate school, I struggled to understand how certain accounts of Rwanda's past shaped what we learned in textbooks and what was left out. Wherever I studied, be it in Rwanda, Kenya, South Africa, the United States, Belgium, the United Kingdom, or Australia, Rwanda was always present as a topic on my syllabi. It was something of a relief when I started reading works that used memory studies perspectives as they were more relevant to my experience and research. Until recently, however, this interdisciplinary field has often overlooked memory practices in the Global South and instead privileged insights drawn mainly from Western societies.

Prior to engaging with questions of memorialization and master narrative in Rwanda, in this chapter I situate the book within the wider debates of the interdisciplinary field of memory studies, which is still evolving. As a place to begin for interested readers, I analyze key concepts and ideas that have informed the vast literature on acts of remembering the past, around the world. I first explore key debates that have shaped memory studies over the past decade, while highlighting key terminologies and ideas relevant to Rwanda in particular. I then argue that, given that the transcultural and decolonial turns have opened up an avenue for analyzing mnemonic experiences in the Global South, we must also develop and apply theoretical and methodological approaches derived from southern empirical insights,[*] which have been overlooked throughout the evolution of memory studies. Further on, the chapter contends that it is equally important to establish threads that connect postcolonial, postconflict, and postgenocide mnemonic processes in contexts such as Rwanda with mnemonic experiences ongoing in other societies. The *Agaciro* dignity turn, as I argue toward the end of this chapter and elaborate further in the conclusion of the book, can be a useful tool to examine the interlinkages between the memory claims of Champions, Antagonists, and Fatalists.

---

[*] Here southern pertains to the Global South.

The debates and definitions explored below have been influenced by the rise of Holocaust studies and to some extent literature on reconciliation politics developed for mostly Western publics, though some concepts are applicable to Global South contexts. There are many other practices, modes of conceptual thinking, and forms of knowledge produced in other languages on memorialization that are not included in this literature, especially those derived from the Global South and marginalized in the Global North. Thus this chapter serves to start a discussion to contextualize the book within the most known and used literature in postgenocide Rwanda. Thereafter, I build on this extant scholarship to argue for the adoption of approaches informed by lived experiences from the Global South. The decolonial approach is one grounded in ordinary people's memories, subaltern memories, gendered memories, and those more broadly from the underside of master narratives.

Understanding Key Concepts in the Literature

Remembrance of the dead is an almost universal feature of human society across time, culture, and geography.[1] Ancient and modern remembrance initiatives range from formal public events to private ones, at both the individual and collective levels.[2] Remembering the dead has been defined as "the act of gathering bits and pieces of the past, and joining them together in public" through these rituals.[3] Central to these practices is a seemingly universal human tendency seeking to revive past significant events and construct a coherent master narrative about the past and ourselves. "Collective remembrance" therefore "points to time and place and above all, to evidence, to traces enabling us to understand what groups of people try to do when they act in public to conjure up the past."[4] The process may include sending condolence messages, visiting grieving families, or visiting official memorials. Initiators of these rituals include individuals, families, communities, or governments and other institutions.

Memories of the past, whether individual or collective, cannot be imprisoned.[5] The past resists "efforts to make it over."[6] Remembrance serves to collectively acknowledge the past in the present, to satisfy a desire to honor victims of mass violence.[7] The transfer of the past can be a conscious process (through official and organized rituals), one that is conveyed subconsciously, or both.[8] To date, theories developed within memory studies[9] have tried to grapple with the question of "who remembers, when, where, and how?" and take into consideration the agency of different actors involved in the act of remembering.[10]

Creating master narratives that can evolve into hegemonic narratives, like the one examined in this book, is one of the many activities that engage powerful actors. These actors include political elites, government officials, survivors, international organizations, and other members of society. There are other "countless symbolic and material practices of commemoration, remembrance and historical self-reflection" that in different contexts "have taken on the forms of societal rituals, carried out by specialized professions and institutions."[11]

As James Young has pointed out, these institutionalized memories are continuously negotiated, and their meanings are determined by a wide-ranging audience.[12] Individual remembrance and collective acts of remembrance are co-constituted in a process by which individual memory is co-produced within collective acts of remembrance.[13] It is through this co-constitutive process that a collective memory emerges, vulnerable to many factors that shape its outcome.[14] These include who is remembering, individual memories of shared experiences, the state of a person's ability to remember, and who permits what is to be remembered or forgotten. Furthermore, what is remembered depends on the physical environment in which the acts of commemoration are reconstructed, for example, whether it is in the public— through overt memorials—or implicit, for instance through art.[15] It is in these environments that, as Pierre Nora states: "Memory crystallizes and secretes itself" over time.[16] Societies create monuments, museums, and sites, otherwise known as "lieux de memoire, and give them meaning that reminds traumatized communities of their past."[17]

Building on Maurice Halbwachs's concept of collective memory, Jan Assmann, among many others, introduces the notion of "cultural memory," denoting a collective construction of the past.[18] Cultural memory, according to Assmann, "is a struggle over power and who gets to decide the future."[19] He distinguishes this from "communicative memory." Communicative memory refers to that which "lives in everyday interaction and communication and, for this very reason, has only a limited time depth which normally reaches no farther back than eighty years, the time span of three interacting generations."[20]

Further, Aleida Assmann identifies four forms of memory that are useful for this book. The first is individual memory, which is what we rely on to make sense of our past and personal identity and what we reiterate when we tell stories about ourselves.[21] In defining her second category, that of group memory, she argues that individual memory interacts with the group memory of those who have experienced similar events. These can be not only friends and family members but also people of our generation we might not know but who have lived through similar events.[22] Aleida Assmann's third type of memory is political memory, introduced to build on Jan Assmann's earlier distinction, which dealt too little with political power and censorship. Unlike previous individual and group memory, political memory is mediated and "*trans*generational."[23] Finally, in defining cultural memory, Aleida Assmann writes of "memory that is defined by what is remembered and what is forgotten, excluded, rejected, inaccessible, buried."[24] Cultural memory "recognizes the agency that mobilizes and remobilizes memories rather than just the trajectories, materials and media of remembrance,"[25] even when this agency depends on institutions that regulate what is recollected.

However, as Ernest Renan pointed out in 1882, nations are built not only on what people have in common, but also what parts of the past they forget en masse.[26] Indeed, the insight that "whole societies may choose to forget uncomfortable knowledge" led to the concept of "social amnesia,"[27] referring to a social process in which members of a community disregard the uncomfortable events of their past and the victims of their past shameful actions.[28] Inevitably, the process of commemoration is a political process that produces a desired outcome, including the creation of a master narrative about the past.

Exploring Debates on the Transcultural, Prosthetic Memory, and Decolonization Perspectives in Memory Studies

The field of memory studies was created through interdisciplinary collaborations with contributions from sociologists, historians, anthropologists, psychologists, and scholars from other fields.[29] Its large body of literature is dedicated to examining how societies remember or forget their pasts after experiencing mass violence and how these processes of remembering and forgetting affect those involved.[30] In the 1980s, interest in this field gained momentum to a large extent in Western universities, leading scholars to speak of a "memory boom" as having revived the "cult of memory."[31] The field's foundations are traced to examining commemorations of wars that involved Western powers, including Holocaust memory.[32]

Edward Said asserted that memory studies rose to prominence in the twentieth century "at a time of bewildering change, of unimaginably large and diffuse mass societies, competing nationalisms, and, most important perhaps, the decreasing efficacy of religious, familial, and dynastic bonds."[33]

However, critics point to limitations within the field. For example, some argue that scholars have focused on analyzing the commemoration of heroes who tended to be white and male while ignoring, for instance, women's experiences during violence.[34] These criticisms inspired debates in memory studies that led to a shift from remembering heroes to remembering victims. The original approaches were highly gendered and racialized.[35] Sara McDowell's research on commemorations in Northern Ireland explains that women were ignored because memorialization ceremonies focused on "dead men," often combatants.[36] Others show earlier scholarship lacked engagement with ordinary peoples' experiences, especially minorities' experiences in Western societies.[37] Other criticisms center on the fact that examined contexts often involve wars and other large-scale conflicts rather than famines, epidemics, and natural disasters.[38] Studies have also pointed to methodological gaps in memory studies given that mainstream literature relies heavily on Western institutionalized archives and photography that ignores marginalized groups' (race, gender, or disability, e.g.) experiences and promotes Western powers' hegemonic master narratives.[39] The resistance to such approaches goes beyond academic debates, and, as we were reminded recently through movements like the #RhodesMustFall, #BlackLivesMatter, and many other vernacular practices that may not become global, these questions about the past and who is included or excluded in its memorialization matter in everyday life.

Thus, to address these gaps, recent scholarship has been concerned with examining the transnational and transcultural aspects of memory. These ideas were preceded by the recognition of the transmission of Holocaust memory in different contexts and for many reasons. Daniel Levy and Natan Sznaider's analysis of Holocaust memory in Germany, Israel, and the United States contextualizes this as cosmopolitan memory, "one that does not replace national collective memories but exists as their horizon."[40] Yet, the Holocaust "paradigm" and World Wars I and II remembrances do much more than exist on the horizon of other cultural mourning practices.[41] In the case of Rwanda, the master narrative has acquired hegemonic status through affiliation with the Holocaust memory already in circulation globally and to some extent liberal peace and reconciliation ideals.

The above themes are explored further in this chapter but before I move on to analyze those, I first explore the "transcultural turn" "and "decolonial turn" that have evolved in memory studies and are important for examining Rwanda's postgenocide context.

Transcultural Perspectives: Opening Avenues

The recent generation of transcultural scholars represents a departure from "old-fashioned" approaches that promoted a "container-culture."[42] Astrid Erll, building on Wolfgang Welsch's writings, argues that transcultural "describes phenomena which reach across and eventually, as a result of the contemporary process of globalization—also beyond cultures."[43]

Equally, in his generative work *Multidirectional Memory: Remembering the Holocaust in the Age of Decolonization*, Michael Rothberg advanced three important arguments to critique memory studies.[44] He argues against what he calls a "competitive memory" approach, the idea that when two different remembrances of the past interact in public they must compete for attention and cannot coexist.[45] Rather, he asserts that different pasts can borrow from each other through negotiation and cross-referencing. Second, he builds on previous arguments to show that these memories are not separable, but rather relate in different ways as they evolve and—to use Erll's phrasing—travel across "time, space, and mnemonic communities."[46] Finally, Rothberg argues that group identities do not simply exist; they are formed over time, shaped by power and the interests of various actors, in some ways complementing each other. Rothberg's work shows that memorialization of the Holocaust or the two world wars need not marginalize other types of mass violence, such as colonialism or slavery in public remembrance. Building on this insight, parts of this book examine how Holocaust representation and world wars commemoration models of the past traveled to Rwanda.[47] It notes the contradictions and interlinkages within the Rwandan context that, on the one hand, embrace this international model and allow donors to co-fund and shape aspects of local commemoration,[48] but simultaneously limit Western commemorative practices' impact on justice by instead recreating earlier, indigenous Rwandan systems of jurisprudence. Thus, the book also examines Rwandans' responses to the travels of the master narrative and the outcome of these contradictions inherited from such hybrid models.

Further, the book utilizes Marianne Hirsch's concept of postmemory, acknowledging that experiences of the past travel to generations who might not have lived through the events being remembered.[49] Through examining experiences of her own, Hirsch argues that the "generation after" also suffers from transmitted traumas and narratives, and that these constitute legitimate memories on their own.[50] These memories gain momentum and in some ways even replace memories of those who lived in the "era of memory."[51] Eva Hoffman asserts that in fact the "paradoxes of indirect knowledge haunt many of us who come after."[52] Some of the youth who I interviewed for this book constitute this group of young Rwandans who consider themselves guardians of the genocide memory and Champions of the master narrative. They assert its importance in shaping how the past is understood in present and future politics. But in this context, their activism and remembrances come into conflict with those Antagonist youth who did not experience directly but have inherited stories of other histories of violence that unfolded before and after the genocide. They equally consider themselves guardians of those dissident narratives and unrecognized memories. In the middle are the Fatalists, who for many reasons do not concern themselves with the past. Online platforms constitute a prime carrier of these perspectives—sites with transformative potential in political and epistemic decolonization.[53]

Online Memory Making: Opening Communities

Alison Landsberg's concept of "prosthetic memory" offers an avenue to understand how new technologies are transforming cultural memory. It refers to a "new form of public cultural memory" that "emerges between a person and a historical narrative of the past at an experiential site such as a movie theatre or museum."[54] Landsberg further writes:

> In the process that I am describing, the person does not simply apprehend a historical narrative but takes on a more personal, deeply felt memory of a past event through which he or she did not live. The resulting prosthetic memory has the ability to shape that person's subjectivity and politics.[55]

Like Rothberg, Landsberg argues that through these processes memories no longer belong to only one group—as in, the Holocaust does not belong only to Jews, or memories of slavery only to African Americans—but instead can be acquired by anyone through technological means.[56] The narratives about the past are made possible and mobile by capitalist advancement and commodification of cultures in a globalized world.[57] A recent phenomenon that has accelerated the growth of such prosthetic memories is the use of social media in commemoration processes. For instance, studies that have looked at the use of social media by marginalized communities' commemorations—such as those of South Africans through the #RhodesMustFall or African Americans through the Black Lives Matter movement—show that Twitter has become a powerful tool to mobilize global communities around pasts of Black death that had been previously confined to local communities. The "born digital" generation in Rwanda and its diaspora, as Yvonne Liebermann calls them, have used social media to make visible their positions, whether as Champions, Fatalists, or Antagonists. Technological tools have facilitated dissident narratives emergence in public.[58] In Rwanda, one reason for this phenomenon is the relative success of Rwanda's Vision 2020, promoting a technologically connected Rwanda.[59] Another is that the youth are the majority in Rwanda. Of this group, the majority are under 26, which is to say, born after the genocide. This demographic is increasingly using social media to express their views on politics and life in general.[60] This generation learned only what is permitted by the master narrative and does not engage critically with some sources.[61] Some are in the diaspora due to the massive migration of Rwandans around the world in the 1990s. They live in countries that do not teach Rwandan history, and therefore the internet serves as not only the main teacher about their origins, but also a platform where myths circulate, histories of their violent pasts compete, and power relations are negotiated. While it is true that the majority of Rwandans do not live their lives on social media, their lives are nevertheless shaped by interactions on these platforms.[62]

Online platforms also make possible analysis on how the memorialization approaches of the Holocaust and the world wars have traveled to Rwanda and shaped its national memory culture after the genocide. These spaces have also broken barriers that previously allowed the government to police the master narrative and curb antagonism around it, and they have become one of the factors that inspire individuals to shift from Champions to Antagonists or Fatalists explored in later chapters.

Decolonial Turn: Contesting Power

The decolonial turn debates are relatively new in memory studies, but they have been circulating in postcolonial scholarship for decades.[63] In introducing her book *Decolonization and Afro-Feminism*, Sylvia Tamale reminds us to delve into the history of any concept with which we wish to engage. She argues that: "No situation, concept or person can ever be fully understood without probing their histories."[64] Thus, before I explain the value of employing a decolonial lens in memory studies, it is important to briefly discuss decolonization in social sciences and humanities more generally.

Decolonization denotes a multilayered process of liberation from the political, economic, and epistemological constructs of the colonial project. Colonial modes of thinking are not "neutral or natural," but loaded with political meaning.[65] Decolonization, according to Walter Mignolo, is "delinking from the colonial matrix of power."[66] These, as Sabelo Ndlovu-Gatsheni argues, are the "invisible power structures that sustain colonial relations of exploitation and domination long after the end of direct colonialism."[67] One of the ways colonialism is sustained is through knowledge production establishing a world order that centers European and North American thought "as human heritage rather than a [mode of] thought from one geographical centre."[68] Thus calls for the decolonization of memory practices and discourse around them are meant to question why Western forms of remembering and "various forms of knowledge and knowing"[69] about the human past have been elevated as universal models. Coloniality has adapted over time through globalization. Hence within the decolonial turn in both social sciences and the humanities, scholars speak of interrogating the "global coloniality" of "matrices of power and technologies of subjection that produced African subjectivity as that of a being constituted by a catalogue of deficits and series of 'lacks.'"[70]

First, a decolonial lens challenges approaches that continuously privilege analysis of the postgenocide government in Rwanda to have participated in the emergence, evolution, and enforcement of the hegemonic master narrative. Analysis of the 20 years of creation and evolution of the master narrative in Rwanda amply evidences the plurality of actors that have participated in this, even if official actors have had strong control of the emergence of the hegemonic memory. Right after the genocide, civil society efforts to learn from other models of remembering the past—other than those developed in the Global North—while also developing conflict resolution mechanisms were not implemented. Human rights groups and other actors organized a conference in Kigali to learn from other contexts, like those in Afghanistan, Argentina, Bosnia, Cambodia, Chile, Palestine, and South Africa. The government, however, failed to act on the findings of this conference.[71] Other efforts that were disregarded include those of the national Parliament, which recommended constructing a memory culture drawing on Rwanda's existing mourning practices.[72] Instead, the government, wishing to draw inspiration from Holocaust remembrance in the Western world, invited Belgian historian Jean-Philippe Schreiber to Rwanda as a consultant on commemorative practices.[73]

Thereafter, subsequent meetings and conferences in Kigali gravitated toward an approach modeled on Holocaust remembrance, which followed a script of genocide commemoration recognizable to Western, rather than Rwandan, publics. This approach attracted Western organizations, genocide scholars, and other "well-meaning outsiders"[74] who supported the construction of memorials based on a commemoration culture that in many cases felt foreign to Rwanda's cultural mourning practices. Foreign governments, organizations such as the Aegis Trust and Clinton Foundation, and many other individual donors have supported the construction of the genocide narrative.[75] The master narrative of the genocide in Rwanda has also gained global mobility through "dark tourism."[76] Tourists who visit the memorials all transmit what they learn from those spaces to their communities back home through narratives of their own. Furthermore, the master narrative of the genocide, or sections thereof, is often used to warn of mass atrocities in international forums like the United Nations and African Union, and to justify certain initiatives like peacekeeping interventions in peace and security discourse.[77] The phrase "never again" in international diplomacy has come to be intimately associated with the events of the 1994 Genocide Against the Tutsi and often used as a tool to mobilize Western publics[78] and leverage diplomatic action in favor of Global North political agendas.[79] Through these exchanges of influence, various actors shape and transmit the master narrative according to the needs of their audience—which are all too often international institutions, rather than survivors or those experiencing the violence.

Second, a decolonial lens allows, as I argue throughout this book, for the examination of responses to two forms of hegemonic master narratives. One attempts to establish a Western model of commemorating the past, and the other is about a specific hegemonic master narrative in Rwanda that silences other practices of memory. Beyond Rwanda's context, recent global protests like Rhodes Must Fall or Black Lives Matter have shed light on vernacular narratives that have been silenced within democratic countries and Western institutions and have not received enough attention in memory studies. They have illuminated what postcolonial scholars have always argued: Even the multiculturalism that politicians talk about seems to be a façade.[80] Thus, a dignity turn approach can be used in memory studies to examine everything from movements promoting dissenting narratives among the marginalized in whatever context, whether in Rwanda or for racial justice efforts in the United States or involving Indigenous initiatives in Canada and Australia.[81] The dissenting narratives that have been fighting for prominence in politics and knowledge production in memory studies and beyond exist in relation to the Western hegemonic master narratives that are closely linked to settler societies' colonial pasts and presents.[82]

These vernacular narratives are rooted within societies where memory studies theorists live and work. Yet, because most of these influential scholars are trained in Western epistemologies, such vernacular narratives from the Global South remain largely invisible. Additionally, where the epistemic and empirical value of Global South narratives are recognized, they remain largely overlooked in academia because they are considered inaccessible. Countries like Belgium, Britain, France, and Germany, for example, sideline commemorations of their colonial crimes, as these events do not fit comfortably within the official master and hegemonic narratives they adopt and promote for themselves. Activists and scholars have pointed out that the master narratives within Western democracies rarely include critical analysis of colonialism and enslavement, and certainly not from the perspective of the colonized and enslaved.[83] This erasure happens in public discourse as well as in curricula, where official histories are passed on across geographies and between generations. It is not only governments that perpetuate these master narratives. Revelations in the wake of protests by Indigenous groups in Canada, for instance, demonstrate that the Catholic Church—one of the world's most powerful entities, which many assume to be a moral guardian—has concealed heinous crimes of its priests for many decades and covered up sites in Canada where Indigenous children were killed.[84] These silences and open secrets have also informed mnemonic cultures in Argentina, Sri Lanka, Peru,[85] and Bosnia.[86] Thus, both Western and non-Western governments as well as powerful institutions have promoted master narratives of their pasts while deliberately ignoring and even silencing dissident narratives.

Consequently, in decolonial thinking, questions on memory politics should be discussed as not only a problem in postcolonial contexts, but also an aspect of dealing with the past across diverse contexts that resulted in the oppression of those who are not included in official remembrance models. Mahmood Mamdani is correct in warning that:

> Powerful epistemic forces in the world today seek to make history go away and to replace it with a universal impulse called human rights. Human rights denies the existence of history, instead looking only to the here and now and asking who did what to whom, so that perpetrators may be punished and victims vindicated.[87]

The "powerful epistemic forces" Mamdani writes about include those in memory studies that argue that the Holocaust and two world wars commemoration approaches travel as an international or universal model promoting human rights in non-Western contexts.[88] In Western democracies, state-centered approaches are shaped by power relations, often sidelining and silencing the memories of marginalized groups whose experiences do not conform to local master narratives. Similarly, meanwhile, in postcolonial contexts like Rwanda, such state-centered approaches can create a "hierarchy of suffering."[89] Yet, unlike other studies on postgenocide Rwanda that center the Rwandan government as the main agent of memory,[90] this book attempts to include other actors—especially global elites and local Champions—involved in the emergence, evolution, enforcement of, and responses to the hegemonic master narrative.

Agaciro: A Dignity-Centered Turn

In charting a way forward, we must go beyond dominant assumptions that prevail in Western scholarship and instead turn to identifying and examining principles of an "Agaciro-centered approach" that respects everyone's "right to be human."[91] This is a different approach to dignity as this understanding does not center on an individual's right but rather a collective way of thinking about life and death. It is about respecting another's "utu" (or being) and thinking about life in relation to the other. Micere Mugo refers to this concept of utu as a transformation concept rooted in philosophies of the Global South. Mugo further reflects on John Mbiti's phrase "I am because you are and since you are, therefore I am."[92] While cautioning against romanticizing collective societies, Mugo calls on us to reflect on what these philosophies of individuals existing in relation to the other mean for scholarship. In this book and elsewhere in my work discussed below, I develop an understanding of the Agaciro-centered approach as that focused on not only the dignity of the self but also the dignity of the other. The decolonial turn emphasizes the voice of the people themselves. This perspective agrees with that of Norman Ajari, who analyzes the struggles of Afro-descendants in France, builds on postcolonial scholarship to assert that dignity is the product of struggle.[93] It is a fight over power dictating how we study and craft narratives about the past that shape present and future societies.

In earlier work on vernacular memory of the missing in postgenocide Rwanda, I show how respondents in Rwanda deploy Agaciro to engage in vernacular memory for themselves and their missing loved ones. Such vernacular avenues become avenues to resist the silencing of the master and hegemonic narrative of the genocide.[94] I therefore build on this work in the conclusion of this book to argue that the "dignity turn" can work on different levels of analysis and practices. In Rwanda's context, it can allow us to locate relationships between official and vernacular memory approaches. On the global level in literature, this dignity-centered approach offers an avenue to overcome the limitations inherent within Western models fixed on hegemonic narratives. It presents an opportunity to embrace plural approaches to memory practice and scholarship in what is termed as "universal" or "international" approaches to understanding the past. It locates relationships between different approaches to studying the past and interpretations of what we term as vernacular or hegemonic in global discourses. It promises to unsettle colonial durabilities that have continued to influence Rwandans' everyday lives and those of others.[95]

Before delving into this new approach, however, in the next chapters I examine various aspects of the master narrative: its emergence and evolution and how people responded in this tense and multiphase process. The next chapter examines the trajectory of master narratives in Rwanda's history and politics and elaborates how these narratives have shifted from hegemonic to dissenting narratives. Then in further chapters, I examine responses to the hegemonic master narrative.

Notes

1. Edward S. Casey, *Remembering: A Phenomenological Study* (Bloomington: Indiana University Press, 1987), 11. See also Susannah Radstone, ed., *Memory and Methodology* (Oxford, UK: Berg, 2000). For debates on the question of death and the dead in Judaism and the Christian tradition, see Terence L. Nichols, *Death and Afterlife: A Theological Introduction* (Ada, MI: Brazos Press, 2010).
2. Marita Sturken, *Tangled Memories: The Vietnam War, the AIDS Epidemic, and the Politics of Remembering* (Berkeley: University of California Press, 1997), quoted in Jeffrey K. Olick and Joyce Robbins, "Social Memory Studies: From 'Collective Memory' to the Historical Sociology of Mnemonic Practices," *Annual Review of Sociology* 24 (1998): 111.
3. Jay Winter and Emmanuel Sivan, eds., *War and Remembrance in the Twentieth Century* (Cambridge: Cambridge University Press, 1999), 1.
4. Jay Winter, introduction to *Remembering War* (New Haven, CT: Yale University Press, 2008), 3.
5. Liz Ševčenko and Maggie Russell-Ciardi, "Sites of Conscience: Opening Historic Sites for Civic Dialogue, Forward," *Public Historian* 30, no. 1 (2008): 9. For work on individual memory, see Henri Bergson, *Matter and Memory* (1912; repr., Hong Kong: Casimo Classics, 2007).
6. Michael Schudson, "The Present in the Past versus the Past in the Present," *Communication* 11 (1989): 105.
7. Ereshnee Naidu and Cyril Adonis, *History on Their Own Terms: The Relevance of the Past to a New Generation* (Braamfontein, Johannesburg: Center for Study of Violence and Reconciliation, 2007), 18.
8. Carole L. Crumley, "Exploring Venues of Social Memory," in *Social Memory and History: Anthropological Perspectives*, eds. Jacob J. Climo and Maria G. Cattell (Lanham, MD: Rowman Altamira Press, 2002), 39.
9. "Memory" is treated by a vast literature as it has been discussed in different contexts. For example, Pierre Nora discusses the distinction between memory and history in "Between Memory and History: *Les Lieux De Mémoire*," *Representations* 26 (Spring 1989): 7–24. A social perspective on memory has been offered by Peter Burke, "History as Social Memory," in *Memory: History, Culture and the Mind*, ed. Thomas Butler (Oxford, UK: Basil Blackwell, 1989), 97–113; and Olick and Robbins, "Social Memory Studies." On the culture of trauma, see Jeffrey K. Olick, Vered Vinitzky-Seroussi, and Daniel Levy, eds., *The Collective Memory Reader* (Oxford, UK: Oxford University Press, 2011). On the cultural dimension of memory, see Jan Assmann, *Cultural Memory and Early Civilization: Writing, Remembrance, and Political Imagination* (Cambridge: Cambridge University Press, 2011). Many others have offered various perspectives. All recognize the importance of official commemorations. Noa Gedi and Yigal Elam, "Collective Memory—What Is It?," *History and Memory* 8, no. 1 (1996): 30–50.
10. Winter, introduction to *Remembering War*, 3.

11. Jens Brockmeier, "Remembering and Forgetting: Narrative as Cultural Memory," *Culture & Psychology* 8, no. 1 (2002): 17.
12. James Edward Young, *Writing and Rewriting the Holocaust: Narrative and the Consequences of Interpretation* (Bloomington: Indiana University Press, 1988).
13. Jan Assmann, "Communicative and Cultural Memory," in *Cultural Memories: The Geographical Point of View*, eds. Peter Meusburger, Michael J. Heffernan, and Edgar Wunder (Dordrecht, Netherlands: Springer, 2011), 15–29.
14. Nora, "Between Memory and History," 8.
15. Steven Hoelscher and Derek H. Alderman, "Memory and Place: Geographies of a Critical Relationship," *Social & Cultural Geography* 5, no. 3 (2004): 347–355.
16. Nora, "Between Memory and History," 7.
17. Ibid. Italics in original.
18. Assmann, "Communicative and Cultural Memory," 43.
19. Alexandra Barahona de Brito, Carmen González-Enríquez, and Paloma Aguilar, eds., *The Politics of Memory: Transitional Justice in Democratizing Societies* (Oxford, UK: Oxford University Press, 2004), 38.
20. Assman, "Communicative and Cultural Memory," 111.
21. Aleida Assmann, "Memory, Individual and Collective," in *The Oxford Handbook of Contextual Political Analysis*, eds. Robert E. Goodin and Charles Tilly (Oxford, UK: Oxford University Press, 2006), 211–212.
22. Assmann, "Memory, Individual and Collective," 213–214.
23. Ibid., 215.
24. Ibid.
25. Rick Crownshaw, ed., *Transcultural Memory* (New York: Routledge, 2016).
26. Ernest Renan, *What Is a Nation?(1882)* (New York: Routledge, 2002), quoted in Homi K. Bhabha, ed., *Nation and Narration* (New York: Routledge, 2008), 8–22. See also Paul Connerton, "Seven Types of Forgetting," *Memory Studies* 1, no. 1 (2008): 59–71; and Marc Augé, *Oblivion* (Minneapolis: University of Minnesota Press, 2004).
27. Stanley Cohen, *States of Denial: Knowing about Atrocities and Suffering* (Cambridge, UK: Polity Press, 2001), 138.
28. Ibid.
29. Henry L. Roediger III and James V. Wertsch, "Creating a New Discipline of Memory Studies," *Memory Studies* 1, no. 1 (2008): 9–22.
30. Maurice Halbwachs, "The Social Frameworks of Memory," in *On Collective Memory* (Chicago: University of Chicago Press, 1992), 35–189; Richard Terdiman, *Present Past: Modernity and the Memory Crisis* (Ithaca: Cornell University Press, 1993); Jay Winter, *Sites of Memory, Sites of Mourning: The Great War in European Cultural History* (Cambridge: Cambridge University Press, 1998); Jeffrey K. Olick, "Collective Memory: The Two Cultures," in *The Collective Memory Reader*, eds. Jeffrey K. Olick, Vered Vinitzky-Seroussi, and Daniel Levy (Oxford, UK: Oxford University Press, 2011), 333–348.
31. Concerning the memory boom, see Olick, Vinitzky-Seroussi, and Levy, *Collective Memory Reader*, 14; and concerning the "cult of memory," see Duncan Bell, ed.,

Memory, Trauma and World Politics: Reflections on the Relationship between Past and Present (Basingstoke, UK: Palgrave Macmillan, 2006), 25.

32. Olick, Vinitzky-Seroussi, and Levy, *Collective Memory Reader*, 29. However, Andreas Huyssen points to the limitation of the Holocaust as an instigator of interest and links memory politics to human rights as well. See Andreas Huyssen, "Trauma and Memory: A New Imaginary of Temporality," in *World Memory: Personal Trajectories in Global Time*, eds. Jill Bennett and Rosanne Kennedy (Basingstoke, UK: Palgrave Macmillan, 2003), 8.

33. Edward W. Said, "Invention, Memory, and Place," *Critical Inquiry* 26 (2000): 179. For a similar discussion, see Andreas Huyssen, *Twilight Memories: Marking Time in a Culture of Amnesia* (New York: Routledge, 1995).

34. To support this thought, see also Sherna Berger Gluck and Daphne Patai, eds., *Women's Words: The Feminist Practice of Oral History* (New York: Routledge, 1991).

35. See Didier Fassin and Richard Rechtman, *The Empire of Trauma: An Inquiry into the Condition of Victimhood* (Princeton, NJ: Princeton University Press, 2009).

36. Sara McDowell, "Commemorating Dead 'Men': Gendering the Past and Present in Post-conflict Northern Ireland," *Gender, Place and Culture: A Journal of Feminist Geography* 15, no. 4 (2008): 340.

37. Rogers Brubaker and Margit Feischmidt, "1848 in 1998: The Politics of Commemoration in Hungary, Romania, and Slovakia," *Comparative Studies in Society and History* 44, no. 4 (2002): 700.

38. For example, see Anne Eyre, "Remembering: Community Commemoration after Disaster," in *Handbook of Disaster Research*, eds. Havidán Rodríguez, Enrico L. Quarantelli, and Russell Dynes (New York: Springer, 2007), 441–455.

39. Claudia Rankine, "The Condition of Black Life Is One of Mourning," in *The Fire This Time: A New Generation Speaks about Race*, ed. Jesmyn Ward (New York: Scribner, 2019), 145–155.

40. Daniel Levy and Natan Sznaider, "Memory Unbound: The Holocaust and the Formation of Cosmopolitan Memory," *European Journal of Social Theory* 5, no. 1 (2002): 93.

41. Rebecca Jinks, *Representing Genocide: The Holocaust as Paradigm?* (London: Bloomsbury, 2016), 21.

42. Levy and Sznaider, *Memory Unbound*, 88.

43. Astrid Erll, "Travelling Memory," *Parallax* 17, no. 4 (2011): 8.

44. Michael Rothberg, *Multidirectional Memory: Remembering the Holocaust in the Age of Decolonization* (Berkeley, CA: Stanford University Press, 2009).

45. In certain instances, it is not so much that one prefers the competitive memory approach, but rather is forced into it when it is the prevailing situation in that particular context. Some agree this is a major problem. This is the case in Rwanda's context, where memories of Tutsi victims are always pitted against those of Hutu killed in other eruptions of violence. I revisit this in the Conclusion.

46. Erll, "Traveling Memory," 9.

47. Jinks, *Representing Genocide*, 29.

48. Annalisa Bolin, "Imagining Genocide Heritage: Material Modes of Development and Preservation in Rwanda," *Journal of Material Culture* 25, no. 2 (2020): 196–219.
49. Marianne Hirsch, *Family Frames: Photography, Narrative, and Postmemory* (Cambridge, MA: Harvard University Press, 1997).
50. Ibid.
51. Eva Hoffman, *After Such Knowledge: Memory, History, and the Legacy of the Holocaust* (New York: Public Affairs, 2007).
52. Ibid., 25.
53. David Mwambari, "Can Online Platforms Be e-Pana-Africana Liberation Zones for Pan-African and Decolonization Debates?," *CODESRIA Bulletin* 5 (2021): 5.
54. See Alison Landsberg, *Prosthetic Memory: The Transformation of American Remembrance in the Age of Mass Culture* (New York: Columbia University Press, 2004), 2.
55. Ibid.
56. Ibid.
57. Ibid., 18.
58. Yvonne Liebermann, "Born Digital: The Black Lives Matter Movement and Memory after the Digital Turn," *Memory Studies* 14, no. 4 (2020): 3.
59. An Ansoms, "Striving for Growth, Bypassing the Poor? A Critical Review of Rwanda's Rural Sector Policies," *Journal of Modern African Studies* 46, no. 1 (2008): 1–32.
60. Youth are using social media especially in urban areas to discuss topics that were previously not discussed in public. See Andrea Purdeková and David Mwambari, "Post-genocide Identity Politics and Colonial Durabilities in Rwanda," *Critical African Studies* 14, no. 1 (2021): 1–19. And also Tugce Ataci, "Narratives of Rwandan Youth on Post-genocide Reconciliation: Contesting Discourses and Identities in the Making," *Journal of Youth Studies* 25, no. 10 (2021): 1–18. And Andrea Mariko Grant, "Bringing the Daily Mail to Africa: Entertainment Websites and the Creation of a Digital Youth Public in Post-genocide Rwanda," *Journal of Eastern African Studies* 13, no. 1 (2019): 106–123.
61. David Mwambari and Sarah Schaeffer, "Post-conflict Education: The Case of History Curriculum in Post-genocide Rwanda," in *Contemporary Issues in African Studies: A Reader*, eds. Ernest E. Uwazie and Chaunce Ridley (Dubuque, IA: Kendall Hunt, 2011); and Elisabeth King, "From Data Problems to Data Points: Challenges and Opportunities of Research in Postgenocide Rwanda," *African Studies Review* 52, no. 3 (2009): 127–148.
62. See Eric Sibomana and Brooker Chambers, "Remembering from a Distance: Genocide Commemoration in Rwanda and COVID-19," *Society Pages*, April 6, 2021, https://thesocietypages.org/Holocaust-genocide/remembering-from-a-distance-genocide-commemoration-in-rwanda-and-covid-19/.
63. Jill Jarvis, *Decolonizing Memory: Algeria and the Politics of Testimony* (Durham, NC: Duke University Press, 2021), 2.
64. Sylvia Tamale, *Decolonization and Afro-Feminism* (Ottawa: Daraja Press, 2020), 1.
65. Jarvis, *Decolonizing Memory*, 2.

66. See Walter Mignolo, *The Darker Side of Western Modernity: Global Futures, Decolonial Options* (Durham, NC: Duke University Press, 2011), xxvii–viii.
67. Sabelo Ndlovu-Gatsheni, "Coloniality of Power in Development Studies and the Impact of Global Imperial Designs on Africa" (inaugural lecture delivered at the University of South Africa, Department of Development Studies University of South Africa, Pretoria, October 16, 2012).
68. Sabelo J. Ndlovu-Gatsheni, *Epistemic Freedom in Africa: Deprovincialization and Decolonization* (New York: Routledge, Taylor & Francis Group, 2018).
69. Ibid., 5.
70. Sabelo J. Ndlovu-Gatsheni, *Empire, Global Coloniality and African Subjectivity* (New York: Berghahn Books, 2013), 4.
71. Rémi Korman, "L'État Rwandais et la mémoire du génocide," *Vingtième siècle. Revue d'histoire* 2 (2014): 87–98.
72. Rémi Korman, "Commémorer sur les ruines. L'État Rwandais face à la mort de masse dans l'après-coup du génocide (1994–2003)" (unpublished PhD dissertation, École des hautes études en sciences sociales, 2020).
73. Korman, "L'État Rwandais et la mémoire du génocide," 96.
74. Elizabeth Jelin, "Silences, Visibility and Agency: Ethnicity, Class and Gender in Public Memorialization," *ICTJ Research Brief* (June 2009), cited in Eva Willems, *Open Secrets and Hidden Heroes: Violence, Citizenship and Transitional Justice in (Post-)Conflict Peru* (doctoral dissertation, Ghent University, 2019), 30.
75. See Annalisa Bolin, "Imagining Genocide Heritage: Material Modes of Development and Preservation in Rwanda," *Journal of Material Culture* 25, no. 2 (2020): 196–219.
76. Sarah Kenyon Lischer, "Narrating Atrocity: Genocide Memorials, Dark Tourism, and the Politics of Memory," *Review of International Studies* 45, no. 5 (2019): 805–827.
77. David Mwambari, "Emergence of Post-genocide Collective Memory in Rwanda's International Relations," in *Beyond History: African Agency in Development, Diplomacy, and Conflict Resolution*, eds. Elijah Munyi, David Mwambari, and Aleksi Ylönen (London: Rowman & Littlefield International, 2020): 119.
78. Ibid.
79. Ibid.
80. Paul Gilroy, *Postcolonial Melancholia* (New York: Columbia University Press, 2005), 1.
81. Frances Peters-Little, Ann Curthoys, and John Docker, *Passionate Histories: Myth, Memory and Indigenous Australia* (Canberra: ANU Press, 2010).
82. Mahmood Mamdani, *Neither Settler nor Native* (Cambridge, MA: Belknap Press of Harvard University Press, 2020).
83. See Rothberg, *Multidirectional Memory*.
84. See James Gallen, "Jesus Wept: The Roman Catholic Church, Child Sexual Abuse and Transitional Justice," *International Journal of Transitional Justice* 10, no. 2 (2016): 332–349. On the revelation and publicizing of concealed memory of Indigenous children in Canada: Associated Press, "More Graves Found at New Site, Canadian Indigenous Group Says," NPR, July 1, 2021, https://www.npr.org/2021/07/01/1012100926/graves-found-at-new-site-canadian-indigenous-group-says?t=1625388369719.

85. Willems, *Open Secrets and Hidden Heroes*, 188.
86. Marita Eastmond and Johanna Mannergren Selimovic, "Silence as Possibility in Postwar Everyday Life," *International Journal of Transitional Justice* 6, no. 3 (2012): 502–524.
87. Mamdani, *Neither Settler nor Native*, 21.
88. See, for example, Michael Rothberg, *The Implicated Subject* (Palo Alto, CA: Stanford University Press, 2020).
89. Paul Gilroy, *The Black Atlantic: Modernity and Double Consciousness* (New York: Verso, 1993); or Rothberg, *Multidirectional Memory*, 5.
90. See, for instance, Erin Jessee, *Negotiating Genocide in Rwanda: The Politics of History* (New York: Springer, 2017); Timothy Longman, *Memory and Justice in Postgenocide Rwanda* (New York: Cambridge University Press, 2017); and Nicole Fox, *After Genocide: Memory and Reconciliation in Rwanda* (Madison: University of Wisconsin Press, 2021).
91. Gilroy, *Postcolonial Melancholia*, 29.
92. Micere Mugo, *The Imperative of Utu/Ubuntu in Africana Scholarship* (Ottawa: Daraja Press, 2021: 5.
93. Norman Ajari, *La Dignité ou la mort: Éthique et politique de la race* (Empécheurs de penser rond, 2019), 12.
94. David Mwambari, "Agaciro, Vernacular Memory, and the Politics of Memory in Postgenocide Rwanda," *African Affairs* 120, no. 481 (2021): 611–628.
95. Colonial legacies and colonial durabilties in the postgenocide Rwanda have gained attention recently. See, for instance, in Education, Michael Schulz and Ezechiel Sentama, "The Relational Legacies of Colonialism: Peace Education and Reconciliation in Rwanda," *Third World Quarterly* 42, no. 5 (2020): 1052–1068; and in identity politics, Purdeková and Mwambari, "Post-genocide Identity Politics," 1–19.

2
Rwandan Narratives and Rwandan Pasts

One of the most challenging tasks I have found in my teaching and research career is recounting Rwanda's past. It is a complex and sensitive endeavor to explore Rwanda's past because—as in many postcolonial contexts—histories are in large part written by outsiders who in most cases do not speak Kinyarwanda or have not lived among Rwandans long enough to appreciate the cultural nuances that inform our lived experiences. This is further complicated given those who construct curricula and who construct official history through institutions tend to gravitate toward a version of events that is convenient for their current politics and future aspirations.[1] As such, one of the first questions I grappled with in and out of classrooms around the world where I have spoken or taught about Rwanda is always where to begin. Where does history start for a country and a people that boast thousands of years passing on historical knowledge mostly through oral literature and, later, with the arrival of Europeans, written accounts?[2] As this chapter explores briefly, each actor who takes on the role of retelling or examining how past events construct present and future politics insists on a particular master narrative that in some instances turns into hegemonic narratives. Yet intervening events, including violence and genocide, have turned past hegemonic narratives into dissident narratives in some instances. This is one of the reasons I started the book by discussing my positionality, given I am also taking on a role constructing knowledge about this messy past. I am aware that my approach might not be accepted by all readers familiar with Rwanda.

This chapter argues that in order to understand the emergence, evolution, enforcement, and responses to the current master narrative of the genocide, it is important to locate present-day tensions into a *longue durée* (a longer historical timeline than immediate human memory) analysis of previous master narratives in Rwanda and how they relate to power, violence, and marginalization. This allows us to explore the malleability of master narratives, including those that became hegemonic narratives at one point in history, and how actors have manipulated these narratives to serve their interests and agendas. To locate these shifts and changes both official and unofficial discourses on the past, this chapter draws on a variety of resources, including written and oral historical accounts in an attempt to overcome methodological limitations that often rely exclusively on written accounts of this complex past.[3] I take, for example, knowledge passed on through folklore, proverbs, and other Rwandan cultural carriers that are often alienated in studies on Rwanda. When combined with analysis of written sources, this broader interrogation provides an avenue to get closer to Rwandans' complex lived realities. Such a methodological approach allows us to put into dialogue previously neglected and underutilized sources with mainstream ones and construct knowledge that is valuable in this book.

Rather than simply giving a chronological account of events and actors, I briefly highlight how I have learned about the politics of both "official" and unofficial narratives at different points of Rwanda's past, depending on the political class in power and their foreign allies. I endeavor to identify key versions of historical master narratives that emerged, actors who shaped these narratives in each historical era, and their significance to constructing Rwanda's past and current politics. I argue that these competing narratives have not only shaped politics and conflicts over time but also manifested political legitimacy for different actors and groups throughout Rwanda's history.

Learning Narratives of Rwanda's Pasts through Oral Tradition and Historians

The first place I learned contradicting versions of Rwanda's pasts is through *inanga* (a large, tough, zither instrument), formal education, and my interactions with elders—both men and women—from the time I was a very young boy. Inanga is guitar-like music composed to accompany long, lyrical poetry that narrates memorable events. It is used to pass on both official oral narratives of major events for Rwandans and stories of ordinary Rwandans—both men and women—who became famous warriors or who led unconventional lives that challenged societal norms or values or are especially entertaining. I grew up listening to them on the radio, and later, when they became available online, they accompanied me throughout my travels and studies around the world. The tensions in Rwanda's pasts are even present in this description: official narrative histories interwoven with tales of those who challenged norms and became famous for it.

One famous inanga, *Rukara rwa Bishingwe* (Rukara, son of Bishingwe), tells the story of a man from what is now northern Rwanda, who was an arrogant, proud warrior during the nineteenth century. He led armies that challenged Rwanda's monarchy, which was based in present-day southern Rwanda.[4] As David Newbury has argued, there were regional differences in what is now the state of Rwanda.[5] Under the reign of Cyilima Rujugira (ca. 1738–1765), the royal court expanded its power toward the southern region.[6] Among major developments of the nineteenth century was the further increase of stratification in the society, which became even more pronounced under King Kigeli IV Rwabugiri's (ca. 1863–1895) reign. Power was centralized around the few political elites who had influence at the royal court in territories it controlled, but not the northern region.

At the time, present-day northern Rwanda was not fully integrated into the kingdom and had varying ties to what scholars refer to as the Central Court.[7] Rukara, whose father Bishingwe was from a famous warrior lineage, led armies that had protected their region from invaders, including incursions from the Central Court.[8] The story holds that the warrior king Rwabugiri negotiated with Rukara and other factions in the north to make Rukara into an army commander while Rwabugiri was visiting the region.[9] Rukara is also famous for having challenged a white missionary for overstepping his role in preaching Christianity to engaging in political matters.[10] The dispute resulted in death for both of them, though in different circumstances. Another example of a famous inanga is that of *Rwanyonga and Rwabugiri* by Apploinaire Rwishyura, who tells the story of an ordinary warrior who challenged Rwabugiri on his warrior tactics and manhood.[11]

Both inanga and repeated warrior stories recounted in these oral histories are significant when learning about Rwanda's past.[12] They contradict both the current official narrative that portrays precolonial Rwanda as a peaceful and unified monarchy that was interrupted only by violent European colonization, and the concept that genocidal violence was due to "tribal hatreds."[13] Both narratives oversimplify precolonial Rwanda's complex social relations, which were at different points peaceful and also characterized by violence in the precolonial kingdom and in the Great Lakes region more broadly.[14] A brief discussion of precolonial Rwanda's monarchy can help illuminate this complexity.

Rwanda's precolonial monarchs were, first and foremost, ritual practitioners whose reigns were classified as cowherd kings, fire kings, warrior kings, or peaceful kings.[15] When ruled by warrior kings, Rwanda knew wars, especially wars of expansion both within the borders of present-day Rwanda and into contemporary Democratic Republic of Congo (DRC), Uganda, and Burundi.[16] They attacked to either defend their territory or expand the central kingdom.

Expansion wars began with arrival of Ndori, who is believed to have established the Central Court around 1650.[17] He introduced a professional military loyal to the Central Court, created structures of governance, and established an economic and political elite. He, in collaboration with other local kings, forced Rwandans to "trad[e] political submission for military protection."[18] One of the earliest master narratives was created under the Nyiginya dynasty, which he founded through his clan. It held that the mythical *Gihanga*—the creator—had fallen from heaven and had three children: Hutu, Twa, and Tutsi.[19] This narrative asserted that the Nyiginya kings were divine.[20] Yet other sources show Rwanda evolved out of wars of conquest, especially by King Rwabugiri. The Kinyarwanda language and religions united inhabitants of different regions over time, slowly knitting together a shared culture with regional variations. Viewed from this perspective, inanga poetry on Rwanyonga confronting Rwabugiri was heroic, as was Rukara's negative attitude toward the Central Court before being promoted and uniting with Rwabugiri. These stories demonstrate the process of state building in the centuries prior to colonization.

Second, inanga and the story of Rukara and his armies equally challenges the simplification of the history of the Central Court during Rwanda's Second Republic (1973–1994). When I was in primary school in the 1980s, we were told stories of a powerful central kingdom led by Tutsi kings and powerful queen mothers who oppressed and killed Hutu and Twa. In one of the popular myths widely circulated during this period, the Queen Mother Kanjogera requested a spear to put into a newborn Hutu boy every morning when she woke up.[21] There is no doubt that Kanjogera was one of the most ruthless and powerful queen mothers in Rwanda, but most of her recorded political violence was actually to fight her enemies within the royal court and other aristocrats; no evidence exists of this targeting of Hutu children.[22] This story was told in pregenocide Rwanda to alarm Hutu about historical oppression under monarchical rule. These were not completely without factual basis: Rwabugiri had intensified taxation and class divisions that impoverished many Rwandans in the late nineteenth century before Europeans arrived, as had his predecessor Gahindiro (reign ca. 1820 to ca. 1841).[23] It is said Rwabugiri once declared: "The Hutu could farm for themselves by night, since by day they would have to work for the courageous Tutsi."[24] Narratives of Hutu oppression evolved and circulated from vernacular narratives into the official discourse of Rwanda's past during both the first (1962–1973) and second (1973–1994) postcolonial republics. These stories circulated, for example, through the songs of Simon Bikindi that were performed in official government ceremonies in the 1980s.[25]

Third, the inanga of men from different parts of Rwanda whose armies resisted the Central Court challenge historical accounts that Rwanda was one, unified entity in which first the Twa, then the Hutu, and then the Tutsi migrated.[26] Rwanda was not always one territory with one king.[27] Rather, independent kingdoms existed in present-day Rwanda and were at times antagonistic to the Central Nyiginya Court until the early decades of the twentieth century.[28] These kingdoms were not always led by the Central Court and did not organize power and relationships with their inhabitants in the same ways.[29] Neither did Rwandans migrate as Twa, Hutu, and then Tutsi, but rather as families and other kinship groups from other parts of Africa in search of land and cattle grazing and settled in different parts of modern Rwanda. There were mostly Tutsi and fewer Hutu chiefs who were influential in the communities they led. Relationships among ordinary Rwandans of lower-class Hutu, Tutsi, and Twa were complex as they were tied around *ubuhake*, a type of patron-client relationship, but there was no large-scale political violence based on Hutu, Tutsi, or Twa labels as was the case in postcolonial era.[30]

This short discussion of precolonial Rwanda challenges the postgenocide official narrative of a peaceful Rwanda to show the negative impact of colonial rule. While it cannot be denied that colonial agendas sought to reconstruct Rwandan identity and had profound negative long-term effects on Rwandans that led to violence, including the 1994 genocide, it is also true there were tensions among Hutu, Tutsi, and Twa prior to arrival of colonialists, as well as tensions between people and groups within these categories. These tensions were largely based on class and access to power and land and varied depending on the leadership style of each king and political class but did not lead to large-scale violence as they did once colonial powers imposed their own interpretations. Regional wars existed, and some of the precolonial tensions among ruling elites influenced late colonial and postcolonial Hutu-sponsored narratives to eliminate Tutsi from Rwanda, which eventually led to genocidal violence.

From these inanga and other sources, in precolonial Rwanda the master narrative was constructed by advisors to the monarchy in a secretive process, but was communicated through poetry, songs, warrior panegyrics, and inanga. Yet vernacular narratives—sometimes antagonistic toward those in power—were communicated through similar means. Popular media in any historical era were used to communicate and debate the past and present, including asserting and challenging the legitimacy of political authorities.

Colonial Master Narratives

Unlike other African countries allocated illegally to European colonialists during the Berlin Conference of 1884–1885, Rwanda and other neighboring countries in the Great Lakes were allocated to Germany at the Brussels Conference in 1890, though the first Europeans arrived in Rwanda in the 1870s. The colonial administration of German East Africa initially supported the monarchy led by the Queen Mother Kanjogera as a coruler with her son, Musinga.[31] The Germans upheld the master narrative of royal court elites as superior to the majority of ordinary Rwandans.[32] They also supported the long-standing military campaign in the north, including defeating the northern armies to whom Rukara belonged that had resisted submitting to Central Court control, especially after Rwabugiri's death in 1895. However, their introduction of Christianity to ordinary men and women shifted loyalty from the Central Court to Europeans and, combined with questions of legitimacy raised by Kanjogera's coup in 1896 (this coup was for Kanjogera to ensure her son was the one who became king and not a son of the other queens),[33] the influence of the Central Court began to wane in the first decades of the twentieth century.[34]

Twa, Hutu, and Tutsi existed and showed differences in status, from types of labor to land allocation to ritual participation. Colonialism imposed something different, transforming these status variations into inflexible ethnic categories. After World War I, the Belgians were allocated Ruanda-Urundi when German territories in East Africa were divided up among victorious European powers. For the three decades that followed, Belgians worked largely with the Tutsi-led monarchy to expand their rule, imposing an ethnic hierarchy and introducing an even more punitive system of corvée labor (forced or extractive labor) against the poor. Like the Germans before them, the Belgians became influential in almost all aspects of Rwandan life. Christian missionaries introduced education that favored elites affiliated with the Central Court and nobility. They reinforced Tutsi as "supreme humans" and declared them as "a European under a black skin."[35] Class divisions increased with the introduction of new crops such as coffee and tea. Rwandans migrated in increasing numbers to neighboring countries given famine, such as a severe one like Ruzagayura, Rumanura, that had struck Rwanda at different periods.[36]

Yet it was Belgium's introduction of race science that would most alter the master narrative and reshape social understandings of Hutu, Tutsi, and Twa. During research for my master's thesis on a visit to Butare (Huye) in 2009, a historian I had been interviewing took me to a small house in the middle of a scientific research center just opposite the University of Rwanda. The house was full of dust, and the researchers had just opened it after years of disuse. A few men and women unpacked some cracked skulls with numbers that corresponded to a card used by colonial-era scientists to determine who was Hutu, Tutsi, and Twa. In the main building, long tableaux were still hanging with the names of scientists involved in these eugenics experiments that had taken over Europe and the United States. This experience was deeply troubling and also fundamental in my research life.[37] The Belgians gave each inhabitant of Rwanda Hutu, Tutsi, or Twa identity cards (introduced in the 1930s)[38] that determined one's livelihood. Through their colonial experiments they divided up families, including my own.

Elders I spoke with told me how helicopters and colonial administrators arrived in the 1950s to oversee the distribution of identity cards.[39] They gave me examples of their family members who were told they would become Tutsi or Hutu, even though they shared lineages with each other. My own elderly relatives confirmed the same. I flew to German and Belgian colonial archives and these same skull experiments, and craniofacial and nose measurements, were a reality.[40]

By the 1930s, the Central Court realized what was happening, and Musinga tried to resist colonial rule even though he—and even more, his mother—had earlier collaborated. In 1931, Musinga and Kanjogera were forced to abdicate and were replaced with King Rudahigwa, Musinga's son. Rudahigwa was friendly to the Belgians and converted to Catholicism in 1943. Yet, the Belgian scientific and social experiments in the service of establishing and maintaining governance and political demand had a massive and long-lasting impact among Rwandans. They planted seeds for future violence. The system of ethnicity they created was one of the main underpinnings for the

1994 genocide and 1990s civil wars. The Belgians constructed Hutu, Tutsi, and Twa as political identities. A new master narrative was created that cast the Hutu as indigenous and Tutsi as foreign occupiers—not much different from European colonizers.[41] It was, as Jean Paul Kimonyo wrote, the "overworked historical memory" that produced Rwanda's history.[42]

It was this master narrative combined with long "mythico-histories"[43] about the oppression endured by Hutu ancestors under the royal court, as well as historical amnesia about other kingdoms, that led to the most controversial events and debates about Rwanda's recent history among Rwandans and scholars alike. For some, the Hutu elites were responding to the concerns of the ordinary people.[44] Others argue it was about power and early development of anti-Tutsi ideology.[45] Regardless of their motivations, Hutu elites contested attempts by Rudahigwa in 1959 to abolish ethnic identities and for Rwandans to unite around their king. For these elites, such attempts meant that the historical symbol of power for the royal court, *Ingoma Kalinga* (the royal drum Kalinga), would remain and become a symbol of the newly independent nation. Joseph Habyarimana Gitera, a prominent member of Hutu political party *Association pour la promotion de la masse* (APROSOMA), rejected this idea. He argued the drum was decorated with the genitalia and heads of conquered kings from the north, which by the 1950s was understood as the "Hutu" north.[46] These events are rightly discussed in the present postgenocide official master narrative as some of the reasons that led to the two postcolonial, Hutu-led republics casting Tutsi as not Rwandan and therefore targets for liberation violence in their own master narratives.

Narratives of Liberation and Oppression

In 1959, various incidents culminated into what was called *Rubanda nyamwishi*—majority ordinary people protests—even though in reality it was instigated by and benefited a small group of Hutu elites. However, unlike other decolonization movements in Africa, the initial violence was not directed toward the Belgians, but rather against royal elites and other Tutsi, including poor Tutsi from clans that had not benefited from royal political power. This "social revolution" was led by educated Hutu men. They upheld and reinforced the emerging master narrative of Tutsi as aliens and themselves as the rightly indigenous Rwandans. New Hutu elites mobilized and organized the masses under the "Bahutu Manifesto," not a "Rwandan Manifesto."[47]

The events of 1959 are controversial and divisive in both narratives of Rwandans and scholarly literature. Prior to the genocide in 1994, most scholarship recognized these events of 1959 and the 1960s as a "social revolution"; however, after the genocide scholars also started to shift their position on this master narrative. In the postgenocide period, scholars problematized this framing as having given social and economic benefits to a few Hutu men but deepened tensions among the majority of Rwandans. The events of 1959 included looting and burning of Tutsi homes, which escalated along with other types of anti-Tutsi violence in 1960–1965. The anti-Tutsi sentiments followed armed attacks from outside Rwanda by Rwandans (mostly Tutsi) who had been forced into exile. These attacks from outside the country were the result of displacement and insecurity within those other countries, and do not excuse the violence against Tutsi within Rwanda. Tutsi families were killed and displaced, with many fleeing to neighboring countries and increasing the numbers of these refugees. Others fled to Europe and North America. These massacres created the foundation for long-term future violence.[48] For some, it is this violence against Tutsi—massacres, burning of houses, and being forced to flee—that marks this period, rather than the celebration of a social revolution of decolonization. My interest is in how these events of 1959—the revolution and massacres occurring simultaneously—reinforced a master narrative based on colonially constructed identities and which facilitated future violence and political contestations, while also transforming the previous master narrative—that of a unified monarchy—into a dissident one, most prominent among those Tutsi who fled into exile between 1959 and 1973.[49]

From 1959, the Belgians organized elections, and Hutu won and celebrated their victory over both the monarchy and colonial rule. However, during the 1960s the government of Hutu elites orchestrated killings of Tutsi families and forced thousands into exile. This included many of the families who are political elites in postgenocide Rwanda, some of whom were also political elites during the monarchical period. From the 1960s to the 1990s, Tutsi in Rwanda were treated as increasingly dangerous aliens according to Mamdani:

> Hutu and Tutsi had, under colonialism, become synonymous with an indigenous majority and an alien minority, decolonization was a direct

outgrowth of an internal social movement that empowered the majority constructed as indigenous against the minority constructed as alien.[50]

President Grégoire Kayibanda, a Hutu from the south, ruled until the 1973 coup. Northerners led by Juvénal Habyarimana captured power without much violence and added another regional aspect to the master narrative and politics of identity in Rwanda. While Tutsi were still foreign to the northerners, Hutu from the south were classified as *Abanyenduga*, "those from Nduga," who were perceived as friendly to Tutsi. The royal court had been headquartered for hundreds of years in Nduga, a region in southern Rwanda. The Habyarimana government, made of mostly Hutu elites from the north, upheld and reinforced Hutu, Tutsi, and Twa colonial political identities and deepened divisions.[51]

The Hutu hegemonic memory narrative was based largely on not only victimhood but also victory over the oppressive Tutsi monarchy. They repeatedly reinforced the mythical numbers of 84% Hutu, 14% Tutsi, and 1% Twa. These mythical colonial numbers would circulate in conversations among Rwandans and in scholarly literature and helped justify development agendas, sustaining Habyarimana because he represented the majority. Hutu pride was coupled with northern pride. In the 1970s and 1980s, Tutsi insurgency decreased, and although Tutsi were discriminated against professionally, in social life, and in education, systemic killing subsided.[52] In early 1990, the Rwanda Patriotic Army (RPA)—a militia based out of Uganda made up of mostly Tutsi refugees—launched a major attack, and a civil war ensued. It was an army largely led by descendants of Tutsi nobility who fled in 1959 (including some Hutu politicians who fled Rwanda after falling out with Habyarimana) who claimed they wanted to liberate all Rwandans from a government they saw as repressive. Peace negotiations were organized by the United Nations and the Organization of African Unity (OAU), but war continued in the north and western part of Rwanda.

This summary of Rwanda's postcolonial history demonstrates some important continuities and ruptures in Rwandan political culture. First, a favorable master narrative has emerged with each government that has ruled Rwanda, and some cases acquired hegemonic status surrounded by tensions. Central Court members glorified themselves and their armies when they conquered new territories or defended Rwanda in major attacks. Boasting of killing one's enemy was symbolized by the castrated body parts of defeated monarchs hung on the royal drum. This symbolism was a major part of creating a king's master narrative. They celebrated the victory of battles won. The master narrative was rarely a tool to mourn their dead soldiers or victims of the violence. This would change later in postgenocide Rwanda.

The master narrative under Belgian colonial rule emphasized the superiority of Europeans and therefore sought to scientifically prove that their Central Court collaborators were superior as well, justifying their rule. Yet this same master narrative labeled the Tutsi "foreigners" or "aliens." Postcolonial Hutu political elites from the south used the same narrative to capture power initially through political elections and violence. Once Hutu military elites from the north transformed the master narrative to center northerners, even Hutu from the south and those from mixed backgrounds were alienated and distanced from meaningful political and social roles. Thus, these narratives that emerged to mobilize and politicize Rwanda's pasts created an environment that allowed for the 1990s civil war, which took its heaviest toll on Hutu from the north.[53] It is also these same narratives that made a Genocide Against the Tutsi possible and the spurred the regional wars that followed in the DRC. What was an official narrative for the Central Court became a dissident narrative and part of vernacular memory for Tutsi once they opposed a Belgian administration, and then later during the First and Second Republics, most especially for those living in exile. Historicizing narratives in Rwanda allows us to see how these histories are occasions for seeking legitimacy, contesting political power, and in some cases justifying violence and the creation of new master narratives.

As we have seen with ingana poetry, and later with the Hutu uprising in 1959 and the 1990 attack by the RPA, at different times political elites mobilized the masses to violently attack or challenge that era's master narrative. The group seeking power uses their own dissident narrative to justify their actions, centering that narrative once they achieve power. While past narratives were mostly about claiming and boasting a ruler's victory, postgenocide elites have used Tutsi victimhood, Hutu-as-perpetrators, and RPF victory to create a master narrative that has turned into a hegemonic memory. According to the current official narrative, the genocide started in the 1950s; it was just not called such due to prevailing master narratives of Hutu elites who ruled Rwanda at the time. Yet again, through various channels ordinary people have evolved with the current master narrative and responded to it in myriad ways explored in this book.

Evolution of the Master Narrative of the 1994 Genocide against the Tutsi

On April 7, 1994, that unforgettable day, I was a teenager living in the southern part of Butare town. We woke up to news that President Habyarimana had been killed in a plane crash the previous night. As a young man growing up mostly naïve of the past and contemporary politics or history, I had no idea how the story we heard on the radio, accompanied by strange classical music, was about to transform my life, our families, our country, the Great Lakes region, and international relations. As I would come to learn 10 years later, the killings and targeting of Tutsi in Rwanda commenced many decades before that momentous morning. Like the genocide we were about to live through, and were lucky to survive, previous killings in the 1960s and onward were grounded in shifting political contexts.[54] Like many Rwandans, including Hakizimana and Kayitesi mentioned in the Introduction, the Genocide Against the Tutsi and the mnemonic politics that have evolved with it have shaped my worldview, interests, devotion to research, and career for many years.

In early July 1994, the RPA and its political wing, the Rwanda Patriotic Front (RPF), won a war it began in October 1990 and ended the Genocide Against the Tutsi. Different Tutsi-led insurgencies like the RPA had been fighting what they saw as both an ideological and liberation struggle through attacks against the then-*Forces Armées Rwandaises* (FAR). Their zeal to take up arms was informed by "a lively historical memory."[55] Difficult life in exile, especially in Uganda, influenced their dreaming of a peaceful Rwanda.[56] These narratives that circulated in refugee camps and in exiled Tutsi communities in Burundi, DRC, Kenya, Tanzania, and other countries around the world inspired the RPF to attack Rwanda and defeat two well-armed and trained groups and the military. The ruthless, radical Hutu youth militias were many and exercised influence in different parts of the country. They included the *Interahamwe* ("those who attack together") of the *Mouvement Républicain National pour la Démocratie et le Développement* (MRND), and *Impuzamugambi* ("those who have the same goal"), led by the *Coalition pour la Défense de la République* (CDR). The equally youthful RPF leaders and RPA soldiers saw themselves as liberators of a country that, for some, their ancestors once inhabited and ruled. On the other hand, Hutu politicians capitalized on 1959 and 1960 anti-Tutsi narratives to mobilize ordinary Rwandans against the RPA. They considered the RPA attack as a foreign (Tutsi) assault on a sovereign country, inspiring fear of those who they said wanted to return to rule over the "indigenous" Hutu and Twa.

When the RPA and their families returned, instead of finding *igihugu cy'amata n'ubuki*, a country of milk and honey, as their refugee narratives romanticized, they inherited a country overwhelmed by death from the civil war (1990–1993) and the genocide (1994).[57] From north to south, west to east, there were bodies of dead babies, mothers, fathers, men young and old, raped women, and wounded elders hiding in bushes. Bodies floated in rivers and lakes, lay on hills and in valleys, and decomposed in city restaurants and shops and in remote places.[58] At some point after the killing, the bodies were in houses and prisons, hanging in broken-down cars, abandoned on roadblocks, and lying in football stadiums, hotels, and banks; funeral homes were full to capacity.[59] The country was littered with bullet shells, bomb remains, discarded machetes, and nail-covered bloody wooden clubs. The landscape abounded with the detritus of death. After the genocide, Rwandans—already divided on ethnic lines and class—were further divided morally, into broadly defined groups. Each group emerged with a different interpretation of the past.

In his memoir *Ma mère m'a tué*, Albert Nsengimana tells a chilling account of how his mother took him and his brothers to the killers. He managed to escape, but his brothers were killed by his uncle.[60] Stories of such cruelty have continued to emerge, revealing the extent to which the genocide was intimate and, in some contexts, a family affair. After such a significant loss of life in Rwanda, ordinary Rwandans and politicians began the difficult task of rebuilding a broken society from scorched earth and broken bodies.[61] Rwandan society in general was traumatized.

Debate on Tensions in National Politics Immediately Following the Genocide

In Rwanda, the official commemoration period begins on April 7 and runs through June 30.[62] During the 3-month mourning period, the famous words of Spanish philosopher George Santayana are featured in speeches and discussions: "Those who cannot remember the past are condemned to repeat it."[63] Over the past two decades, Santayana's words have provided the justificatory shorthand for the organization of official remembrances of the Tutsi. As official government rhetoric and Champions of the master narrative often emphasize, these official remembrances serve purposes that include fostering peaceful coexistence among all Rwandans, but Rwandans have widely differing views about the master narrative.

Tensions among divergent communities concerning the genocide and its commemoration first emerged within months of its end, on October 1, 1994. The RPF wing of the government organized a national victory celebration, which was the same date they had launched their first attack into Rwanda in 1990.[64] The festivities were held, but only RPF and RPA members[65] identified with the celebrations. The RPA members included refugees who fled to neighboring countries in the 1960s and other waves of exiles, and also those who joined secretly in the 1990s in Rwanda itself. Some were already in Rwanda because the Arusha Accords permitted a group of RPA soldiers to be based in the Parliament in Kigali.[66] Among this mixed group, there were some who were less enthusiastic to celebrate due to personal loss. Community leaders such as clergy and human rights activists had instead begun organizing informal commemorations at the local level.[67] They argued that society could not "just go on," and it was not a time to celebrate, as Rwanda had just lost hundreds of thousands of its people.[68] Among the known pioneers of these initiatives was human rights activist Alphonse-Marie Nkubito.[69] Nkubito, a former prosecutor in pregenocide Rwanda and minister of justice at the time, did not participate in any public celebrations organized by the RPF.[70] Instead, he and others organized a mass memorial at a Catholic church in Kigali to mourn the dead.[71] Although it was not widely attended, Nkubito's actions served as a public statement about a divided leadership and marked the first public declaration of the need to memorialize the dead.[72] A now-senior Catholic priest that I spoke with during the course of my research revealed that Nkubito's mass—although a significant event given his position in national politics at the time—was not the first public one.[73] As both a Tutsi and clergy, he told me that he and other clergy were invited to regions around Rwanda by their followers who had lost people in the civil war and genocide. He told me:

> As Catholic leaders we were also shocked on what happened in the genocide. Even for those of us who were mourning our beloved relatives, we continued to organize mass in remote places wherever our followers were. I went everywhere in different regions to bury people. We used the normal scriptures and prayers to pray for them and bury them mostly in their

homes as we had always done. We did not seek permission or ask why the person died. Hutu or Tutsi we prayed and buried them.[74]

The Catholic Church was one of the most powerful institutions that remained in Rwanda after the genocide; yet as the priest told me, they too knew how much credibility they lost among Rwandans with so many people being killed in their churches.[75] They rarely made public announcements and continued to read mass even though there were differences among them; many of the Hutu priests who endorsed radical Hutu ideology had fled the country. Thus, the remaining clergy—Tutsi and Hutu alike—read mass for anyone who died while clergy were fighting their own traumas and facing personal tragedies, mourning colleagues, and for some the guilt of doing little to save their Tutsi neighbors.

In addition to these informal commemorations or burials carried out by church leaders, there were other private initiatives. In his work, Rémi Korman has discussed the case of Anne-Marie Kabatende asking for help directly from the then-Minister of Labor and Social Affairs Pie Mugabo for support to bury her family.[76] She also sought support from international organizations like her employer, the United Nations Children Fund (UNICEF) and, since the rotting corpses were deemed a public health crisis, the World Health Organization (WHO). Both supported the reburial of her family on November 13, 1994.[77] Others who did not have such connections buried their dead using local materials, possibly following a small ceremony where prayers were often exchanged with the priest.[78] Others could not find their dead to bury them because the bodies were disposed of so carelessly, dumped into mass graves. The possibility of burying the dead was limited. For those who managed to find their dead, some ceremonies were supported by the local government without having to oblige any policies that would dictate later commemorations. It was from these activities in rural and urban Rwanda that contemporary official commemorations emerged. The new political elites took note of these mourning practices. Toward the end of 1994, the government delineated a set of priorities for memorialization activities that included a project on peace and democracy education and the declaration of a "year of tolerance" in 1995.[79]

What began as spontaneous or in response to "survivors' intrinsic concerns" and grassroots people-directed initiatives became a centralized and well-crafted master narrative that guided commemorations in the decades to come.[80] Something unprecedented that was a genocide had happened. At first these localized practices were mobilized but as soon as international actors, including transitional justice practitioners, scholars, and Holocaust experts, an international dimension of shaping memory emerged and started to dominate local practices. From July 1994, the postgenocide government embarked on a major transition and reconstruction process with many economic, social, and political priorities, including the removal of rotten, unburied bodies in hidden and public places. The government encountered a set of divisive challenges, including how to deal with the ongoing consequences of genocide and civil war and mitigating environmental hazards that resulted from bodies deteriorating and being eaten by dogs.[81] Civil society efforts to draw lessons on how to come to terms with past mass violence from Chile, Argentine, Palestine, South Africa, and Bosnia experiences were ignored.[82] Debates in Parliament to elevate one symbolic monument in the middle of Kigali were never implemented. Instead, the government invited a Belgian scholar to help them shape a narrative that drew inspiration from the Holocaust model given its global hegemonic status and emphasis on genocidal violence toward a particular people.[83] A key conference was organized in 1995 that brought together academics from Rwanda and outside as well as journalists and politicians to discuss the 1990s civil war and 1994 genocide.[84] From these events and conversations, political elites—especially those in the influential RPF—recognized the power of constructing a master narrative that borrowed and mimicked the globally recognized Holocaust representation of genocides. They also had historical precedent for that.[85] Every single one of these RPF leaders—as well as those in the country who had survived—knew the power of those narratives not as an abstract concept, but through their own lived experiences. Capturing the narrative was a matter of survival for the country. The power to interpret recent events in Rwanda's history was not only a preoccupation of scholars or educators but also a national security issue, despite their varied opinions on what master narrative to create between the mostly Tutsi RPF members of government and pregenocide Hutu politicians who were part of the government of national unity.

This is when the earliest voices of Champions of the master narrative of genocide memory emerged. Tutsi survivors in particular insisted it was important to acknowledge that there was an organized massacre intended to exterminate one group of people—the Tutsi—and that this was a culmination of previous killings and not a result of the RPF rebellion or civil war.[86] Failing to acknowledge this would allow victims of the recent genocide to be forgotten, much as victims of the previous massacres of Tutsi in the 1950s, 1960s, and 1970s had been largely forgotten and ignored by institutions of power, including government and education.[87] In addition, the government, survivors' association groups, and sympathizers insisted that it was more important to apply the definition of *genocide* set forth by the United Nations convention and to give due weight to the organization and scale of the Genocide Against the Tutsi—and to the genocide's effect on Tutsi survivors—than to remember the victims of the civil wars and other 1990s conflicts in Rwanda.

One survivor of the 1959 massacres explained that after 1959, a Tutsi who remained in Rwanda had difficulty engaging in social interactions with their Hutu neighbors, especially during the First Republic under President Grégoire Kayibanda.

> The Tutsi had no right to demand the commemoration of those they lost [in earlier massacres].... You [Tutsi] were obliged to put yourselves in front of the person who had killed as if nothing happened. Then, after a few years, they committed genocide.[88]

The advocacy to protect the memory of the Tutsi also allowed for the government to set up specific programs and budgets to establish genocide survivors' funds, create nongovernmental organizations that focused on the welfare of Tutsi survivors, and enact laws to protect genocide memory against the genocide denial that would soon emerge. Furthermore, commemorations were a potent avenue for promoting national unity and a means of helping survivors re-establish their lives or reintegrate into their communities according to the rhetoric of the government.

In the early postgenocide period (1994–2001), the story of an African country miraculously reborn from its violent past spread widely through Africa and beyond, eliciting ferocious debates for those interested in Rwanda and postconflict Africa more generally. Western governments gave a large amount of aid to finance this miracle out of guilt (as some argue) for failing to intervene to end the genocide.[89] Yet the narrative of successful rebirth was met with criticism, especially among exiled Rwandan politicians and international analysts, including researchers, human rights activists, and local and international journalists. They argued that while the donors were appeasing their guilt, the new emerging elites had political reasons to prioritize the master narrative as an important and sensitive pillar of their reconstruction agenda and one to mobilize finances from donors.[90] There was power and legitimacy in remembrance, but applying a hierarchy to that remembrance—official/institutionalized versus private/informal—led to further power. There was power in grievance and victimhood. Legitimacy was based on not only direct power, but also the coercive power of a story of victimhood or martyrdom.[91] This is, as mentioned previously, a departure from previous historical eras in which only strength and violence were celebrated.

Conclusion

As we have seen in this chapter, master narratives in Rwanda that acquired hegemonic master narrative status in earlier historical eras were not permanent. They changed over time, and in some instances the political actors who shaped them were forced to leave Rwanda, taking their now-dissident narratives with them. In the case of the RPF, they were able to return and build on earlier generations' ideals to reconstruct a master narrative of the genocide. Through campaigns mobilizing local, regional, and international support, they turned the master narrative of the Tutsi into a hegemonic narrative over the 20 years after the genocide. It became a narrative that is both believable and constantly rehearsed in all kinds of international forums despite opposition to it or some aspects of it.

If analyzed though the context of previous master narratives, it is unique in the sense that it bears contradictions, as on one side it uses cultural space like gacaca to transmit memory locally but at the same time is inspired by the Holocaust "paradigm," whic egh gives it global mobility and influence. Thus, the history of Rwanda confirms that indeed historical master narratives that emerge, evolve, and are enforced by powerful elites can turn into dissident narratives depending on the power of those actors who respond and their allies who support them. The historical analysis approach allows finding the moments of disruptions to particular narratives and power relations that determine its durability. The next chapter allows us to see how the affiliation with the Western approaches to memory construction has allowed the national collective memory in Rwanda to emerge into a hegemonic master narrative in Rwanda and around the world.

Notes

1. Rwandan historians writing the official history of Rwanda acknowledged this manipulation of history by different generations of political elites and scholars. See Deogratias Byanafashe and Paul Rutayisire, *History of Rwanda: From the Beginning to the End of the Twentieth Century* (Kigali, Rwanda: National Unity and Reconciliation Commission [NUCRC], 2016), 3, 19–20.
2. Written works on Rwanda's recent history and politics vary but are mostly written by Western-based scholars, journalists, and policymakers. For the first 20 years after the genocide, anglophone scholarship on postgenocide Rwanda tended to dominate the debates more than Francophone or knowledge produced by Rwandans, including those few who write in Kinyarwanda. The large number of existing works is also written by men for both Rwandans and non-Rwandan scholars. There are many works, and this list is not exhaustive: concerning those who view postgenocide Rwanda as a success story, see Stephen Kinzer, *A Thousand Hills: Rwanda's Rebirth and the Man Who Dreamed It* (Hoboken, NJ: Wiley, 2008). Kinzer, through interviews with mostly RPF elites and President Kagame, presents an account of a Rwanda imagined and built by former refugees from Uganda. Similar accounts are presented in Philip Gourevitch, "The Life After: Fifteen Years after the Genocide in Rwanda, the Reconciliation Defies Expectations," *New Yorker*, May 4, 2009, http://www.newyorker.com/magazine/2009/05/04/the-life-after. Gourevitch, like Kinzer, documents RPF as the savior of Rwandans, saviors who have achieved much in a short time. See also Philip Clark, *The Gacaca Courts, Post-genocide Justice and Reconciliation in Rwanda: Justice without Lawyers* (Cambridge: Cambridge University Press, 2011). Also see Caroline Sinalo, *Rwanda after Genocide: Gender, Identity and Post-traumatic Growth* (Cambridge: Cambridge University Press, 2018). Although Rwandans have not written much on the postgenocide period, some of their works even about the genocide inform us about how and why the master narrative has evolved as it has because these few intellectuals write and influence ideas in postgenocide Rwanda.

    Apart from Jean Paul Kimonyo's work on postgenocide Rwanda, there are few Rwandans who have contributed to this debate due to various factors. Some have to do with the political, social, and economic realities of a postgenocide society, while others have to do with how long it took to train people to write given many scholars or researchers fled the country, were killed, or had other, more pressing preoccupations. Those who returned and started writing there were mostly writing about the genocide and coming to terms with it and relearning their country. This includes Paul Rutayisire, who wrote on local experiences of genocide. See Paul Rutayisire, "Approche locale du génocide, la région de Nyarubuye," *Vingtième Siècle, Revue d'histoire* 122, no. 2 (2014): 37. Antoine Mugesera has focused on Tutsi experiences under the two previous republics in Kinyarwanda and in French. For example, see Antoine Mugesera, *Imibereho y'abatutsi mu Rwanda 1959–1990: itotezwa n'iyicwa bihoraho* (Kigali: Les Editions Rwandaises, 2015). Théoneste Rutagengwa is another and has written with Timothy Longman. See Timothy Longman and Théoneste Rutagengwa, "Memory and Violence in Postgenocide Rwanda," in *States of Violence: Politics,*

Youth, and Memory in Contemporary Africa, eds. Donald L. Donham and Edna G. Bay (Charlottesville: University of Virginia Press, 2007), 233. Charles Mironko is also notable: "Igitero: Means and Motive in the Rwandan Genocide," *Journal of Genocide Research* 6, no. 1 (2004): 47–60.

A new generation of scholars has also written on trauma, including a collaborative and insightful article on how genocide survivors experience trauma during commemorations. See D. Gishoma, J. L. Brackelaire, N. Munyandamutsa, J. Mujawayezu, A. A. Mohand, and Y. Kayiteshonga, "Supportive-Expressive Group Therapy for People Experiencing Collective Traumatic Crisis during the Genocide Commemoration Period in Rwanda: Impact and Implications," *Journal of Social and Political Psychology* 2, no. 1 (2014): 469–488. Gishoma's PhD thesis, Darius Gishoma, "Crises traumatiques collectives d'ihahamuka lors des commémorations du génocide des Tutsi: Aspects cliniques et perspectives thérapeutiques" (PhD, Université de Louvain, 2014), https://dial.uclouvain.be/pr/boreal/fr/object/boreal%3A143580/datastream/PDF_01/view , is also well researched and authored by a Rwandan researcher. The work of Chantal Ingabire is further important on trauma experienced by Rwandans in the genocide. See Chantal Marie Ingabire, Grace Kagoyire, Diogene Karangwa, Noella Ingabire, Nicolas Habarugira, Angela Jansen, and Annemiek Richters, "Trauma Informed Restorative Justice through Community Based Sociotherapy in Rwanda," *Intervention* 15, no. 3 (2017): 241–253. Jean Damascène works on the church and also how genocide denialism informs debates on the roots of the genocide and how it is remembered. See, for example, his works on the church: Jean Damascène Bizimana, *L'église et le génocide au Rwanda: Les pères blancs et le négationnisme* (Paris: Editions L'Harmattan, 2001).

In the diaspora, we can reference the works of researchers who are originally from Rwanda, such as Rutazibwa, "Studying Agaciro." My own article on music and commemoration is also part of a further chapter in this book. See David Mwambari, "Music and the Politics of the Past: Kizito Mihigo and Music in the Commemoration of the Genocide against the Tutsi in Rwanda," *Memory Studies* 13, no. 6 (2019): 1321–1336. Some of this work is critical of the government's project and its effect on Hutu diaspora narratives of victimhood and memory. See also Claudine Kuradusenge, "Denied Victimhood and Contested Narratives: The Case of Hutu Diaspora," *Genocide Studies and Prevention* 10, no. 2 (2016): 59–75.

There are also those deemed critical by the RPF or that are silenced in Rwanda, including, just to name a few: Scott Straus and Lars Waldorf, eds. *Remaking Rwanda: State Building and Human Rights after Mass Violence* (Madison: University of Wisconsin Press, 2011). Then there are those that examine memory politics, such as the following: On the first 10 years after the genocide, see Claudine Vidal, *La commémoration du génocide au Rwanda. Violence symbolique, mémorisation forcée et histoire officielle*, vol. 44, no. 175 (Paris: Éditions de l'École des hautes études en sciences sociales, 2004). On inconsistency of memory, see René Lemarchand, ed., *Forgotten Genocides: Oblivion, Denial, and Memory* (Philadelphia: University of Pennsylvania Press, 2011). On early collective remembrance, see Catharine Newbury and David Newbury, "A Catholic Mass in Kigali: Contested Views of the

Genocide and Ethnicity in Rwanda," *Canadian Journal of African Studies [La Revue canadienne des études africaines]* 33, no. 2–3 (1999): 292–328. On handling human remains, see Rémi Korman, "Mobilising the Dead? The Place of Bones and Corpses in the Commemoration of the Tutsi Genocide in Rwanda," *Human Remains and Violence: An Interdisciplinary Journal* 1, no. 2 (2015): 56–70; and Rachel Ibreck, "A Time of Mourning: The Politics of Commemorating the Tutsi Genocide in Rwanda," in *Public Memory, Public Media and the Politics of Justice*, eds. Philip Lee and Pradip N. Thomas (Hound Mills, UK: Palgrave Macmillan, 2014), 98. On the politics of the past in mourning, see Anna-Maria Brandstetter, *Contested Pasts: The Politics of Remembrance in Post-genocide Rwanda* (Wassenaar, Netherlands: NIAS, 2010). On remembering and forgetting, see Susanne Buckley-Zistel, "Remembering to Forget: Chosen Amnesia as a Strategy for Local Coexistence in Post-genocide Rwanda," *Africa* 76, no. 2 (2006): 131–150. On remains, see Sara Guyer, "Rwanda's Bones," *Boundary 2*, 36, no. 2 (2009): 155. On women's experiences of remembering, see Burnet, *Genocide Lives in Us*. On individual and collective narratives, see Jessee, *Negotiating Genocide in Rwanda*. On memory and rendering justice, see Longman and Rutagengwa, *Memory and Justice in Post-genocide Rwanda*. On remembering and state-building, see Andrea Purdeková, *Making Ubumwe: Power, State and Camps in Rwanda's Unity-Building Project* (New York: Berghahn Books, 2015); Jens Meierhenrich, "Topographies of Remembering and Forgetting," in *Remaking Rwanda: State Building and Human Rights after Mass Violence*, eds. Scott Straus and Lars Waldorf (Madison: University of Wisconsin Press, 2011), 283. See also Nigel Eltringham, "The Past Is Elsewhere," in *Remaking Rwanda: State Building and Human Rights after Mass Violence*, eds. Scott Straus and Lars Waldorf (Madison: University of Wisconsin Press, 2011), 269–282.

These scholars include some of the most experienced researchers on Rwanda from across disciplines who are also considered as mainstream Western "experts," for instance, René Lemarchand, see *The Dynamics of Violence in Central Africa* (Philadelphia: University of Pennsylvania Press, 2009), "Genocide, Memory and Ethnic Reconciliation in Rwanda," *L'Afrique des Grands Lacs: Annuaire*, 2006–2007 (2007): 21–30, and "A History of Genocide in Rwanda," *Journal of African History* 43, no. 2 (2002): 307–311. Also see Gerard Prunier, *Africa's World War: Congo, the Rwandan Genocide, and the Making of a Continental Catastrophe* (Oxford, UK: Oxford University Press, 2009)). In addition, see Filip Reyntjens, "Constructing the Truth, Dealing with Dissident, Domesticating the World: Governance in Post-genocide Rwanda," *African Affairs* 110, no. 438 (2011): 1–34, *The Great African War: Congo and Regional Geopolitics, 1996–2006* (New York: Cambridge University Press, 2009), "Rwanda, Ten Years On: From Genocide to Dictatorship," *African Affairs* 103, no. 411 (2004): 177–210. Also Timothy Longman, *Christianity and Genocide in Rwanda* (Cambridge: Cambridge University Press, 2011)); plus Susan Thomson, *Rwanda: From Genocide to Precarious Peace* (New Haven, CT: Yale University Press, 2018, and *Whispering Truth to Power: Everyday Resistance to Reconciliation in Postgenocide Rwanda* (Madison: University of Wisconsin Press, 2013). For the politics of reconciliation and peace featured in literature in urban planning after the

genocide, see Delia Duong Ba Wendel, *"Duture Neza, Duture Heza": Planning and Building a "Liberal Peace": The Wiley Blackwell Companion to Cultural and Social Geography*, eds. Jamie Winders and Ishan Ashutosh (New York: Wiley Blackwell, forthcoming 2022): 13.
3. Funmi Olonisakin, Alagaw Ababu Kifle, and Alfred Muteru, "Shifting Ideas of Sustainable Peace towards Conversation in State-building," *Conflict, Security & Development* 21, no. 4 (2021): 1–22.
4. Jean de la Croix Tabaro, "Know Your History: Rukara, an Icon of Resistance to Colonialists," *New Times* (Kigali), October 22, 2014, https://www.newtimes.co.rw/section/read/182210.
5. David Newbury, "Precolonial Burundi and Rwanda: Local Loyalties, Regional Royalties," *International Journal of African Historical Studies* 34, no. 2 (2001): 255–314.
6. John Keith Rennie, "The Precolonial Kingdom of Rwanda: A Reinterpretation," *Transafrican Journal of History* 2, no. 2 (1972): 11–54.
7. David S. Newbury, "The Clans of Rwanda: An Historical Hypothesis," *Africa* 50, no. 4 (1980): 389–403.
8. On Inanga, see Jos Gansemans, *Les Instruments De Musique Du Rwanda: Etude Ethnomusicologique* (Tervuren, Belgium: Musée royal de l'Afrique centrale, 1988).
9. Richard Batsinduka, "The Rwanda Conflict," in *Regional and Ethnic Conflicts: Perspectives from the Front Lines*, eds. Judy Carter, George Emile Irani, and Vamik D. Volkan, 133-158 (Hoboken, NJ: Taylor and Francis, 2015).
10. Warren Weinstein, "Military Continuities in the Rwanda State," *Journal of Asian and African Studies* 12, no. 1–4 (1977): 48–66.
11. David S. Newbury, "Les Campagnes de Rwabugiri: Chronologie et Bibliographie," *Cahiers d'études africaines* 14, no. 53 (1974): 181–191.
12. Jan Vansina, *Oral Tradition as History* (Madison: University of Wisconsin Press, 1985).
13. David Newbury and Catharine Newbury, "Bringing the Peasants Back In: Agrarian Themes in the Construction and Corrosion of Statist Historiography in Rwanda," *American Historical Review* 105 (2000): 832-877.
14. Gillian Mathys, "Bringing History Back In: Past, Present, and Conflict in Rwanda and the Eastern Democratic Republic of Congo," *Journal of African History* 58, no. 3 (2017): 465–487.
15. Christopher C. Taylor, "Kings and Chaos in Rwanda: On the Order of Disorder," *Anthropos* (2003): 41–58.
16. Alexis Kagame, *Un Abrégé De L'histoire Du Rwanda* (Butare, Rwanda: Editions universitaires du Rwanda, 1972). See Vol. 1, 212–14, and Vol. 2, 22–35. See also Kagame's *Les Milices Du Rwanda Précolonial* (Brussells: Académie royale des sciences coloniales, Classe des sciences morales et politiques, 1963), 155–157.
17. Royal chronology is a matter of significant debate. See David Newbury, "Trick Cyclists? Reconceptualizing Rwandan Dynastic Chronology," *History in Africa* 21 (1994): 191–217; John Keith Rennie, "The Precolonial Kingdom of Rwanda: A Reinterpretation," *Transafrican Journal of History* 2, no. 2 (1972): 11-54; and John Keith Rennie, "The Banyoro Invasions and Interlacustrine Chronology" (PhD dissertation, University of California, Los Angeles, 1973); also Jan Vansina, *Antecedents to Modern Rwanda: The Nyiginya Kingdom* (Oxford, UK: James Currey, 2005).

18. Vansina, *Antecedents*, 47.
19. Kagame, *Abrégé*, Vol. 1.
20. Vansina, *Antecedents*, 56–57.
21. Ibiro by'amakuru muli Prezidansi ya Republika, "Ingingo z'Ingenzi mu Mateka y'u Rwanda" (Kigali, Rwanda: President's Office, 1972). Original text: "Umugabekazi nawe yali afite ububasha bwo kwica. Nka Nyirayuhi yali afite inkota ye yitwaga ruhuga, yavuga ati ruhuga ifite inyota, bakazana umwana w'umushishe bakamwuhira amata, yamara kumwuzura inda, akayimushinga akamuhagukiraho." As cited in Peace Uwineza, Elizabeth Pearson, and Elizabeth Powley, *Sustaining Women's Gains in Rwanda: The Influence of Indigenous Culture and Post-genocide Politics* (Washington, DC: Hunt Alternatives Fund, 2009), 12. On the Twa origin, see Jérémie Musilikare, *La Vie Des Pygmées Batwa Au Rwanda* (Paris: L'Harmattan, 2015).
22. Sarah E. Watkins and Erin Jessee, "Legacies of Kanjogera: Women Political Elites and the Transgression of Gender Norms in Rwanda," *Journal of Eastern African Studies* 14, no. 1 (2020): 84–102.
23. Sarah Elizabeth Watkins, "Iron Mothers and Warrior Lovers: Intimacy, Power, and the State in the Nyiginya Kingdom, 1796–1913" (PhD, University of California, Santa Barbara, 2014), http://gateway.proquest.com/openurl?url_ver=Z39.88-2004&rft_val_fmt=info:ofi/fmt:kev:mtx:dissertation&res_dat=xri:pqm&rft_dat=xri:pqdiss:3637516.
24. Vansina, *Antecedents*, 192.
25. David Mwambari, Alfred Muteru, Barney Walsh, Irenee Bugingo, Thomas Munyneza, and Funmi Olonisakin, *Trajectories of State Building and Peace Building in Rwanda. Reframing Narratives of Statebuilding and Peacebuilding in Africa* (Nairobi, Kenya: African Leadership Centre, 2016), http://hdl.handle.net/10625/56347. See also James E. K. Parker, *Acoustic Jurisprudence: Listening to the Trial of Simon Bikindi* (Oxford, UK: Oxford University Press, 2015); and Jason MacCoy, "Making Violence Ordinary: Radio, Music and the Rwandan Genocide," *African Music: Journal of the International Library of African Music* 8, no. 3 (2009): 85–96
26. For more on migration patterns in Rwanda, see David Newbury, *Kings and Clans: Ijwi Island and the Lake Kivu Rift, 1780–1840* (Madison: University of Wisconsin Press, 1991), especially 92–93, 105–106.
27. This is further evidenced in recently republished works of Emmanuel Ntezimana, who traced Hutu kingdoms. See Françoise Imbs and Florent Piton, "*Emmanuel Ntezimana (1947-1995). Etre historien et citoyen engagé au Rwanda* (Toulouse, France: Presses universitaires du Midi, 2021). And, equally, the existence of Hutu kings (Abami) is explored by Marcel d'Hertefelt and André Coupez, *La royauté sacrée de l'ancien Rwanda: texte, traduction et commentaire de son rituel* (Tervuren, Belgium: Koninklijk Museum voor Midden-Afrika-Musée royal de l'Afrique centrale, 1964).
28. Alison Des Forges, *Defeat Is the Only Bad News: Rwanda under Musinga, 1896–1931* (Madison: University of Wisconsin Press, 2011). See also Newbury and Newbury, "Bringing the Peasants Back In" and Catharine Newbury, *The Cohesion of Oppression: Clientship and Ethnicity in Rwanda, 1860–1960* (New York: Columbia University Press, 1994).

29. Des Forges, Defeat is the Only Bad News
30. Mahmood Mamdani, *When Victims Become Killers: Colonialism, Nativism, and the Genocide in Rwanda* (Princeton, NJ: Princeton University Press, 2002). Scholarship on ubuhake is various and contentious. For more, see Jacques Maquet, *Le système des relations sociales dans le Ruanda ancient* (Tervuren: Musée Royal du Congo Belge, 1954). Vansina discusses ubuhake in the context of centralization: Vansina, *Antecedents*, p. 123. A nuanced discussion of this can be found in Gillian Mathys, "People on the Move: Frontiers, Mobility and History in the Lake Kivu Region, 19th-20th Century" (PhD thesis, Ghent University, 2014), https://biblio.ugent.be/publication/5705875
31. Watkins, "Iron Mothers and Warrior Lovers," 180. See also Julius Adekunle, *Culture and Customs of Rwanda* (Westport, CT: Greenwood, 2007).
32. Adekunle, *Culture and Customs of Rwanda*.
33. On Kanjogera's reign and violence, see David Mwambari, Barney Walsh, and 'Funmi Olonisakin, "Women's Overlooked Contribution to Rwanda's State-Building Conversations," *Conflict, Security & Development* 21, no. 4 (2021): 475–499.
34. Ian Linden and Jane Linden, *Church and Revolution in Rwanda* (Manchester, UK: Manchester University Press, 1977). See also Watkins, "Iron Mothers and Warrior Lovers"; and Des Forges, *Defeat Is the Only Bad News*.
35. Mamdani, *When Victims Become Killers*, 88. See also Edith R. Sanders, "The Hamitic Hypothesis: Its Origin and Functions in Time Perspective," *Journal of African History* 10, no. 4 (1969): 521–532.
36. Dantès Singiza, La famine Ruzagayura (Rwanda, 1943–1944): Causes, conséquences et réactions des autorités" (PhD dissertation, Université de Liège, Belgium, 2011); Johan P. Pottier, "The Politics of Famine Prevention: Ecology, Regional Production and Food Complementarity in Western Rwanda," *African Affairs* 85, no. 339 (1986): 207–237; Bernard Lugan, "Causes et Effets de La Famine 'Rumanura' Au Rwanda, 1916–18," *Canadian Journal of African Studies [Revue Canadienne Des Études Africaines]* 10, no. 2 (1976): 347–356, https://doi.org/10.2307/483837.
37. See David Mwambari, "Inventing Ethnicity: The Malleability of Identity in Rwanda" (MA thesis, Syracuse University, 2010).
38. On identity cards, see Florent Piton and Nora Bardelli, "Papers to Ward Off the Threat: Identity Cards, Documentary Uncertainty, and Genocide in Rwanda," in *Identification and Citizenship in Africa*, eds. Séverine Awenengo Dalberto and Richard Banégas (Routledge, 2021), 144–159.
39. Conversation with a Rwandan elder, New York, NY, 2009.
40. For more details on this study and its findings, see Mwambari, "Inventing Ethnicity."
41. Mamdani, *When Victims Become Killers*, 34.
42. Jean-Paul Kimonyo, *Transforming Rwanda: Challenges on the Road to Reconstruction* (Boulder, CO: Lynne Rienner, 2019, 14.
43. Liisa H. Malkki, *Purity and Exile: Violence, Memory, and National Cosmology among Hutu Refugees in Tanzania* (Chicago: University of Chicago Press, 2012).
44. Linden and Linden, Church and Revolution in Rwanda. See also Emmanuel Ntezimana, "Histoire, culture, et conscience nationale: le cas du Rwanda des origines à 1900. Pt. 1," *Études rwandaises* 1, no. 4 (1987): 462–497.

45. Jean Demascène Bizimana, *L'Eglise et le genocide au Rwanda: Les Peres Blancs et le negationnisme* (Paris: Éditions L'Harmattan, 2001).
46. United Nations Visiting Mission to Trust Territories in East Africa, *Report on Ruanda-Urundi* (New York: United Nations, 1960).
47. Mamdani, *When Victims Become Killers*, 104. See also René Lemarchand, "Rwanda: The Rationality of Genocide," *Issue: A Journal of Opinion* 23, no. 2 (1995): 8–11. Also see Florent Piton, "II/Le Rwanda indépendant (1959–1990)," in *Le génocide des Tutsi du Rwanda*, ed. Florent Piton (Paris: La Découverte, 2018), 33–66.
48. Mamdani outlines these different interpretations of events of 1959. See *When Victims Become Killers*, 104. Kimonyo also gives it another interpretation. See Jean-Paul Kimonyo, *Rwanda's Popular Genocide: A Perfect Storm* (Boulder, CO: Lynne Rienner, 2015).
49. Gérard Prunier, *The Rwanda Crisis: History of a Genocide* (New York: Columbia University Press, 1995).
50. Mamdani, *When Victims Become Killers*, 30.
51. Christopher C. Taylor, *Sacrifice as Terror: The Rwandan Genocide of 1994* (New York: Routledge, 2020).
52. Kimonyo, *Rwanda's Popular Genocide*.
53. Malkki, *Purity and Exile*. Jennie Burnet also uses the concept in the context of Rwanda's history. See Burnet, *Genocide Lives in Us*.
54. For discrimination and killings of Tutsi in Rwanda, both Mugesera and Kimonyo have shown that Tutsi faced many injustices decades before the genocide. See Antoine Mugesera, *Les conditions de vie des Tutsi au Rwanda de 1959 à 1990: Persécutions et massacres antérieurs au génocide de 1990 à 1994: Essai* (Kigali: Izuba Éditions, 2014); and Kimonyo, Rwanda's Popular Genocide. See also Newbury and Newbury, "A Catholic Mass in Kigali."
55. Kimonyo, *Transforming Rwanda*, 77.
56. See: Prunier, *The Rwanda Crisis*, 66; also cited in Longman and Rutagengwa, *Memory and Justice in Post-genocide Rwanda*.
57. Longman and Rutagengwa, *Memory and Justice in Post-genocide Rwanda*.
58. For detailed accounts of the genocide in different parts of Rwanda and the overwhelming presence of death, see André Guichaoua and René Dégni-Ségui, *Rwanda, de la guerre au genocide. Les politiques criminelles Au Rwanda (1990–1994)* (Paris: La Découverte, 2010); and African Rights, *Rwanda: Death, Despair, and Defiance* (London: African Rights, 1995). Many works have been written on the genocide in the last two decades, notably Prunier, *The Rwanda Crisis*; and Alison Liebhafsky Des Forges, *"Leave None to Tell the Story": Genocide in Rwanda* (New York: Human Rights Watch, 2014). While Prunier gives context, including an analysis of the Rwanda Patriotic Front's history, Des Forges's work includes many detailed accounts from genocide survivors, other Rwandans with diverse experiences, and other voices that were influential in the genocide. Other scholars have studied the genocide and international community, notably Linda Melvern, *A People Betrayed: The Role of the West in Rwanda's Genocide* (Cape Town: New Africa Education, 2001) and *Conspiracy to Murder: The Rwandan Genocide* (London: Verso,

2006); as well as Roméo Dallaire, *Shake Hands with the Devil: The Failure of Humanity in Rwanda* (New York: Carroll & Graf, 2005). Patrick de Saint-Exupéry has analyzed the role of France in *L'inavouable: La France au Rwanda* (Paris: Arènes, 2009); and countless survivors' autobiographies detail the genocide and its manifestation in specific locations. See, for example, Yolande Mukagasana, Patrick May, Anna Cinzia Sciancalepore, and Lisa Foa, *La morte non mi ha voluta* (Molfetta, Italy: La meridiana, 2008); and Immaculée Ilibagiza and Steve Erwin, *Left to Tell: Discovering God Amidst the Rwandan Holocaust* (Carlsbad, CA: Hay House, 2006), among many others.

59. Straus, *The Order of Genocide*, 115–118. He estimates that prisons held 175,000–210,000. However, Carina Tertsakian argues that the exact number of those in prisons is unknown. Her research on prisons shows that according to July 2009 government records, 38,000 prisoners were accused of genocide and 23,000 of common crimes. See "'All Rwandans Are Afraid of being Arrested One Day': Prisoners Past, Present, and Future," in *Remaking Rwanda: State Building and Human Rights after Mass Violence*, eds. Scott Straus and Lars Waldorf (Madison: University of Wisconsin Press, 2011), 210–220. This number had decreased since 2004, when the majority of those in prisons were genocide suspects. The *Christian Science Monitor* put the number at an estimate of 15,000 to 20,000, mostly Hutu, and reported that the government at the time estimated that a total of 30,000 to 100,000 had committed genocide crimes. This implied many more were outside prison or were in refugee camps in neighboring countries, especially then-Zaire. See Robert M. Press, "In Rwanda's 'Slave Ship' Prison, Life Is Grim for Suspected Killers," *Christian Science Monitor*, November 1994, https://www.csmonitor.com/1994/1118/18011.html.

60. Albert Nsengimana, *Ma mère m'a tué: Survivre au genocide des Tutsis au Rwanda*, romans édition (Paris: Hugo Document, 2019). The various roles women played in the genocide and postgenocide and postwar periods have been documented. See, for example, Adam Jones, "Gender and Genocide in Rwanda," *Journal of Genocide Research* 4, no. 1 (2002): 65–94; Marie E. Berry, *War, Women, and Power from Violence to Mobilization in Rwanda and Bosnia-Herzegovina* (Cambridge: Cambridge University Press, 2018); and Donatilla Mukamana and Petra Brysiewicz, "The Lived Experience of Genocide Rape Survivors in Rwanda," *Journal of Nursing Scholarship* 40, no. 4 (2008): 379–384. Also see Jennie E. Burnet, "Gender Balance and the Meanings of Women in Governance in Post-genocide Rwanda," *African Affairs* 107, no. 428 (2008): 361–386; as well as Erin Jessee, "Rwandan Women No More: Female Génocidaires in the Aftermath of the 1994 Rwandan Genocide," *Conflict and Society* 1, no. 1 (2015): 60–80; or Erin Jessee and Sarah E. Watkins, "Good Kings, Bloody Tyrants, and Everything in Between: Representations of the Monarchy in Post-genocide Rwanda," *History in Africa* 41 (2014): 35–62.

61. I have given an account of challenges Rwandans and the new political leadership faced in two previous published papers see: Further, see David Mwambari, "Women-Led Non-governmental Organizations and Peacebuilding in Rwanda," *African Conflict and Peacebuilding Review* 7, no. 1 (2017): 66–79, and "Leadership Emergence in Post-genocide Rwanda," *Leadership & Developing Societies* 2, no. 1 (2017): 88–104.

62. In earlier years, official commemorations were held from April 1–14; however, as survivors sought to influence state policy on commemoration, they also argued for a change of dates; through their influence, the remembrance days were changed to, and still remain, April 7–13. See Philibert Gakwenzire, "Contribution à la gestion de la mémoire du génocide des Tutsi du Rwanda en 1994" (MA, Université Senghor, 2005), 6.
63. George Santayana, *Reason in Common Sense: Volume One of the Life of Reason* (New York: Dover, 1980), 284.
64. See details on these developments in Newbury and Newbury, "A Catholic Mass in Kigali."
65. I use "returnees" instead of Tutsi because even though Tutsi dominated the RPF, Hutu dissidents like former president Pasteur Bizimungu and Kanyarengwe and many others were declared enemies of former president Juvénal Habyarimana. Prunier, in *Rwanda Crisis*, estimates that about 500,000 returnees migrated to Rwanda after decades in exile. These returnees had left Rwanda as children or were born in exile from parents who left Rwanda in 1959 and during the 1960s massacres.
66. David Mwambari, Barney Walsh, and 'Funmi Olonisakin, "Women's Overlooked Contribution to Rwanda's State-Building Conversations," *Conflict, Security & Development* 21, no. 4 (2021): 475–499.
67. In Kabgayi, for example, the priests of the Catholic Church gathered to commemorate their Hutu bishop colleagues and innocent civilians who had been killed by the RPF. See Paul Lewis, "Rebels in Rwanda Said to Slay 3 Bishops and 10 Other Clerics," *New York Times*, June 10, 1994, http://www.nytimes.com/1994/06/10/world/rebels-in-rwanda-said-to-slay-3-bishops-and-10-other-clerics.html.
68. Newbury and Newbury, "A Catholic Mass in Kigali."
69. Ibid.
70. Ibid.
71. Ibid.
72. This was not the first time Nkubito protested an action by his country's government. Prior to the genocide in the 1990s, Nkubito had opposed the Habyarimana government on a number of human rights abuses. See Allan Thompson, ed., *The Media and the Rwanda Genocide* (London: Pluto Press, 2007), 319.
73. Interview with Catholic priest, Brussels, Belgium, 2017.
74. Interview with Catholic priest, Brussels, Belgium, 2017. Interviews were conducted in Kinyarwanda and translated by the author unless otherwise noted.
75. For a detailed account of the Catholic Church in Rwandan history, see Jean Damascène Bizimana, *L'église et le génocide au Rwanda: Les pères blancs et le négationnisme* (Paris: Editions L'Harmattan, 2001). Also see Paul Rutayisire, *La christianisation du Rwanda (1900–1945): Méthode missionnaire et politique selon Mgr Léon Classe* (Fribourg, Switzerland: Éditions Universitaires Fribourg, 1987); and Timothy Longman, *Christianity and Genocide in Rwanda* (Cambridge: Cambridge University Press, 2011).

72 NAVIGATING CULTURAL MEMORY

76. Rémi Korman, "Le Rwanda face à ses morts ou les cimetières du génocide," in *Génocides et Politiques Mémorielles*, ed. F. Blum (Paris: Centres d'histoires sociales du XXe siècle, 2011), 1–4.
77. Korman, "Le Rwanda face à ses morts ou les cimetières du génocide."
78. For more stories about these ad hoc and early informal burials, see Korman, "Le Rwanda face à ses morts ou les cimetières du génocide" and Darius Gishoma, "Crises traumatiques collectives d'ihahamuka lors des commémorations du génocide des Tutsi: Aspects cliniques et perspectives thérapeutiques" (PhD, Université de Louvain, 2014), http://hdl.handle.net/2078.1/143580. http://worldcat.org.
79. Gishoma, "Crises traumatiques collectives d'ihahamuka lors des commémorations du génocide des Tutsi," 50–51.
80. Rachel Ibreck, "The Politics of Mourning: Survivor Contributions to Memorials in Post-genocide Rwanda," *Memory Studies* 3, no. 4 (2010): 339. For the evolution of the Rwandan Patriotic Front and President Paul Kagame, who emerged as the most influential leader in postgenocide RPF affairs, see Colin M. Waugh, *Paul Kagame and Rwanda: Power, Genocide and the Rwandan Patriotic Front* (Jefferson, NC: McFarland, 2004).
81. One of those challenges was how to render justice to victims of the genocide and at the same time rebuild the country, as well as embark on reconciliation programs. Although many publications that have attempted to explain these challenges, one volume includes essays that explain the magnitude of problems that Rwanda faced after the genocide and how the new government went about resolving these issues. The essays are from various perspectives. See Philip Clark and Zachary D. Kaufman, eds., *After Genocide: Transitional Justice, Post-conflict Reconstruction and Reconciliation in Rwanda and Beyond* (Oxford, UK: Oxford University Press, 2013).
82. Korman, "L'État rwandais et la mémoire du génocide."
83. Korman, *Commémorer sur les ruines*.
84. Helen Dumas and Rémi Korman, "Espaces de la mémoire du génocide des Tutsi au Rwanda," *Mémoriaux et lieux de mémoire, Afrique contemporaine* 238, no. 2 (2011): 11–27.
85. The borrowing or having foreign ideas influence construction of official and political narratives about the past are not unique to Rwanda or the Holocaust model. For instance, North Korean artists, architects, and construction workers have been involved in shaping and building many monuments in over 17 African countries through the Mansudae project. See Meghan L. E. Kirkwood, "Postindependence Architecture through North Korean Modes: Namibian Commissions of the Mansudae Overseas Project," in *A Companion to Modern African Art*, eds. Gitti Salami and Monica Blackmun Visonà (Chichester, West Sussex: Wiley Blackwell, 2013): 548–571.
86. The previous governments had overlooked the memory of victims of 1950s–1990s killings of Tutsi that included many of the new RPF family members. See Marcel Kabanda, "Droit des archives et droits de l'homme," *La Gazette des archives* 206, no. 2 (2007): 97–105.
87. For example, Tutsi believe that the 1994 genocide originated from a 1959 massacre of Tutsi, but Hutu claim this event was a social revolution that ended the Nyiginya

kingdom's rule. The 1959 massacre was followed by other killings in the 1960s and 1980s. For more on the circumstances of the 1959 killings of 10,000–20,000 Tutsi and on anti-Tutsi sentiments, see Prunier, *Rwanda Crisis*, especially Chapter 1.

88. Rachel Ibreck, "The Politics of Mourning: Survivor Contributions to Memorials in Post-genocide Rwanda," *Memory Studies* 3, no. 4 (2010): 330–343.

89. *Le Monde*, October 26, 1996, as quoted in Filip Reyntjens, "Constructing the Truth, Dealing with Dissident, Domesticating the World: Governance in Post-genocide Rwanda," *African Affairs* 110, no. 438 (2011): 1–34.

90. See Johan Pottier, *Re-imagining Rwanda: Conflict, Survival and Disinformation in the late Twentieth Century* (Cambridge: Cambridge University Press, 2004). And "the genocide credit" refers to the fact that the RPF continually praises itself for stopping the genocide when the international community failed to act. See, for example, Reyntjens, "Rwanda, Ten Years On." Paul Kagame had responded to those who advanced a "genocide credit" narrative arguing there were malicious given RPF members in government were also genocide survivors. See Paul Kagame, *Paul Kagame's Speech at the 7th Anniversary of the Genocide in Rwanda at the Nyakibanda Memorial Site* (Rukumberi, Rwanda: Government of Rwanda, 2001).

91. For a discussion of different ways Power works within the leadership process, see Grace Elizabeth Thomas, "Re-imagining Framework for Leadership Analysis," *Leadership & Developing Societies* 5, no. 1 (2020): 69–73. And, for Rwandan dialogue on this topic, also see RwandaTV, *Inama y'igihugu y'umushyikirano | Day 2–14 Ukuboza 2018*," YouTube video, December 23, 2018, 5:01:40, https://www.youtube.com/watch?v=7hYFz398Do4&ab_channel=RwandaTV.

3
Shaping the Emergence and Evolution of the Genocide Master Narrative

Intimba ntibuza intore guhamiriza—Sorrow may not prevent a dancer from performing.

—Rwandan Proverb

One of the many jobs I had growing up in Kenya was as a tour guide. It was always important to show tourists sites of mass violence at slavery or colonial memorials throughout East Africa and the Great Lakes region. However, what began as a trade of survival soon became a fascinating topic of study. I ended up developing an interest in learning about how different actors approached these memorializations, whether it was as remembering slavery in Ghana or lynching in the United States. It was even more intriguing to visit and observe how memorials that remembered terrorist attacks in Nairobi, Brussels, New York City, and Garissa University in Kenya have all emerged to construct particular narratives about these events in my lifetime. Yet whether it was visits to war memorials, rituals of remembering among indigenous communities in Canada and Australia, or learning about memorialization culture around German cities and towns, nothing was as intense for me as those events and spaces that memorialized the Genocide Against the Tutsi.

It always felt like memorials and memorialization in other contexts were less present in everyday life than in Rwanda during the first two decades after the genocide. Postconflict African countries in particular have adopted different strategies to deal with the past. Some choose to organize public and politicized memorials of past violence, like Rwanda and South Africa; others have chosen more vernacular and private ceremonies, like in the Democratic Republic of the Congo (DRC), Uganda, and Burundi. These countries' approaches, while having unique characteristics, have less national and international activities like those created for and in Rwanda.

Over the past decade I have had the privilege of participating in genocide commemorations as they emerged and evolved in rural Rwanda, Kigali, and the diaspora. It has been both challenging and rewarding to learn and write about how a particular society tries to come to terms with such horror and how champions claimed these sites important as they emerged. From participating in private acts of remembering in Ruhango district in southern Rwanda, going to a large national remembrance that was held in a large stadium in Kigali for years or in cities around North America; in Melbourne, Australia; or in Nairobi; at the United Nations (in Nairobi and New York headquarters); or in Brussels, I have seen firsthand how various actors shape their local commemoration events. It was intriguing to observe that while they each were unique in terms of their program of events, they all had someone—whether an individual or group or Rwandan embassy staff—who were connected to political actors in Kigali who gave guidelines on the main theme of that given year. In this way Kigali-based Champions were involved in the co-creation of the master narrative at the local, national, and international levels, reinforcing emerging terminologies and vocabularies to use. However, there is little research that examines how these networks of actors emerged and evolved across different geographies and how these relationships formed over time, giving mobility to the master narrative of the genocide as it emerged into a hegemonic narrative around the world. We are yet to understand how Champions, Antagonists, and Fatalists interact during commemorations, and why some like Kayitesi, discussed in the Introduction, shift their positions to support or contradict the master narrative.

This chapter asks how the creation or repurposing of vocabulary, themes, and language in general was used in the emergence and evolution of a master narrative of the genocide memory in postgenocide Rwanda and in the diaspora. It also examines to what extent political events of a given commemoration year shaped how language tools evolved and what tensions these evolutions caused between various actors, including Champions, Antagonists, and Fatalists, as well as foreigners interested in commemoration in Rwanda. Finally, this chapter asks how the master narrative of the genocide memory emerged and evolved through these webs of relationships across local, regional, and international contexts and who the involved actors were in shaping giving hegemonic status to this master narrative.

This chapter explores varied local and international actors who shaped the emergence and evolution of official memory institutions, laws, and the discourses around the master narrative in the first two decades after the genocide. It argues that there is a need go beyond current literature that focuses only on the role of the government. The chapter finds that while government political elites were always influential, they were not alone, and neither were their perspectives homogeneous. It shows their monopoly was mostly in guiding the implementation process of the master narrative and ensuring the sustainability of the master narrative, employing resources, and relying on partnerships to turn it into a hegemonic narrative in Rwanda and globally. Political actors also provide oversight and ensure dissenting narratives around these commemoration events around the world are suppressed and Antagonists are punished.

The first part of this chapter explores how Champions created themes or new vocabulary or changed the meaning of existing words, as well as involving institutions and laws to propel and sustain a master narrative on the genocide memory. Second, it illustrates how different actors enabled the master narrative to evolve and travel from domestic to international platforms and gained hegemonic memory status itself. Throughout its analysis of primary and secondary data, including both scholarly and artistic accounts of the genocide—such as Allison Des Forges's *Leave None to Tell the Story*, or films such as *Hotel Rwanda*—that was geared toward popularizing the 1994 genocide to Western publics, the chapter examines how these tools shaped the emergence and evolution of this master narrative and the kind of responses generated among Rwandan communities in both the country and abroad, among Rwandans and foreigners alike. It finds that over the years, themes, vocabulary, and speeches were developed for multiple purposes as different actors collaborated to rebuild Rwanda. While in some instances national and official commemoration days became platforms to address Western actors, especially those who still refused to acknowledge that a genocide took place in Rwanda, such as France, official commemorations, themes, and vocabulary also evolved over time to become platforms that set the tone for domestic commemorations explored in the next section.

Setting the Tone for Domestic Commemoration

As discussed in the previous chapter, the Genocide Against the Tutsi in Rwanda followed the killing of President Juvénal Habyarimana on April 6, 1994, a Hutu elite who rose to power through a coup d'ètat in 1973. On the night of his death, Hutu youth militias associated with the political parties Mouvement Dèmocratique Républicain (MDR) and Mouvement Républicain National pour la Démocratie et le Développement (MRND), as well as some individuals in the military, targeted mostly Tutsi but also killed Hutu, Twa, and those of mixed heritage who did not support their plan to exterminate the Tutsi. Policies and institutions were introduced over time as the master narrative evolved to protect the genocide memory.

The evolution of a master narrative of the genocide during commemoration was accompanied by semantic innovation and set the tone for other justice processes in the gacaca system of domestic justice and the International Criminal Tribunal for Rwanda set up in Arusha, Tanzania, in 1994. Some new words were crafted, and existing words acquired new connotations to articulate what was unfolding. For example, the verb *kwibuka* (commémorer; "to commemorate") meant "to remember" in Kinyarwanda, French, and English (respectively) prior to the genocide. Although its meaning was not changed, the term was highly popularized in the postgenocide period, to the extent that the word is now synonymous with commemoration rituals. It also plays a central role in the ways people express themselves while performing the ritual. For instance, survivors commonly begin a sentence with the phrase *ndibuka*, meaning "I remember," then pronounce the name or names of victims. The term takes on several meanings during commemorations. Ibuka, an imperative form of *kwibuka* is also the name of an influential survivors' lobbying group. The Kinyarwanda name for "A Walk to Remember"—an annual event organized by youth in Kigali that takes place at the beginning of the April mourning period—is *urugendo rwo kwibuka*.

In early commemoration, the Kinyarwanda word used was *umurambo*, which meant "the dead body," but to honor and distinguish genocide victims the word used in official memory became *umubiri* meaning simply "a body." So, one would say we found "a body" rather than we found "a *dead* body" if new massacre sites were found. Also, it was preferred to say "bodies of survivors are buried in this memorial," rather than "dead bodies are buried in this memorial." This means they cannot be reduced to a corpse.

In 1995, activities to bury the dead officially were already in progress around Rwanda, namely, in the municipalities of Mugina and Ntongwe and many other areas in the country.[1] Debates were mostly on the correct way to bury such bodies in Rwandan culture and who should take part in such ceremonies. The speech of the Ibuka director at the time, Jean-Pierre Dusingizemungu, in 2012 shows the intensity of emotion that these debates elicited even 18 years after the killings. He asked:

Would it have been better for the survivors to remain silent? In what way did they have to talk about the facts to the limit of the imaginable? To leave the bodies in the open air, in the latrines or in the middle of a church, would it have been less violent? To not bury the bodies, it would have allowed better healing of wounds. To bury but without inviting the family to the exhumation of bodies and the burial of one of their own, would that have been more beneficial to them? In another context (any country in Europe), can the burial of the body of a loved one, disfigured or shredded as a result of a traffic accident, be experienced as nonviolent for family members who must recognize the body? Unfortunately, in commemorations there is a first violence inherent in the genocide itself, which remains almost inevitable.[2]

The burying of bodies and cleaning the country after such mass deaths was not the only challenge for survivors or the government. In the aftermath of the genocide, state actors, ordinary citizens, and international stakeholders focused on many challenges, especially restoring security and managing large-scale humanitarian assistance.[3] The government could barely pay its employees or fund the priority sectors needed to restore "normalcy."[4] Therefore, prior to 1995, organized and official national commemoration events were not prevalent. Nonetheless, in Kigali religious leaders held a ceremony at Rebero in 1995, a site that includes memorials of twelve senior politicians who were killed for their fight against the genocide, including Hutu politicians like former Prime Minister Agathe Uwilingiyimana.[5] As Rémi Korman has argued, this 1995 commemoration struck a reconciliatory tone in referring to the killings as *Itsembabwoko n'Itsembatsemba* or "genocide and ethnic cleansing" to include those Hutu who died protecting their Tutsi neighbors. The speakers emphasized that the international community was to blame for not ending the genocide.[6] There were no official delegations from outside Rwanda except for a handful of diplomats representing their own countries and human rights organizations.[7] This would change in later commemorations when diplomats and non-Rwandan guests started attending commemorations. Thus, in early years, most commemorations organized were more individual and informal. Government actors, ordinary citizens, and international stakeholders were focused on restoring security and managing large-scale humanitarian assistance,[8] and the new fragile government could not coherently promulgate any official theme or organize a national commemoration.

However, in 1996, after the conference at which a deliberate choice was made to draw inspiration from a Western model to construct Rwanda's commemoration culture (discussed in a previous chapter), themes for each commemoration event started to emerge and became central to forming the master narrative for each commemoration. The 1996 theme was *Twamagane ubutegetsi bubi, dushimangira ubutabera twimakaza umuco w'amahoro n'ubwumvikane*, or "Shun bad governance, emphasizing justice and a culture of peaceful understanding in Rwanda." During this period, organizers of the commemoration attempted to steer collective sentiment toward unity and reconciliation, and the theme particularly targeted those harboring an intense desire for vengeance and retribution.[9] Although this strategy was arguably a reasonable and necessary response to the precarious and polarized environment inherited by political authorities at the time, it nonetheless marked an effort—even at this early stage—to shape how, and what, people should remember as part of building a master narrative of the genocide. This was largely due to not only challenges of revenge killings inside the country but also challenges that refugees, including former army officials and those who committed genocide who were outside Rwanda, paused to the new government and Rwandans in general.

> In 1996, 1997, 1998, 1999, not as many people attended the commemorations as they do today (...) The country was not well organised back then; therefore, the people were not in a place where they could make room for their emotions. People had survived the genocide but hadn't gotten to terms with the fact that they had literally escaped death. Some people were still searching for family members who might have survived. All those who had fled the country had not yet returned home. The entire country was not yet stable, there wasn't much life, which didn't give the permission to people and society to think about their psychological and emotional needs. Gradually, people started to find out more about whether family members had survived or not, new houses were built in urban areas, children went back to school, adults started to find employment, survivors found each other and set up community organisations, basically gradually life picked up again.[10]

Beth Whitaker's research into experiences of Rwandan refugees in Tanzania and the DRC showed that "between July and September 1994, more than one million Rwandans crossed the border into Congo (then Zaire)."[11] She writes that:

> Throughout 1995, international negotiations emphasized immediate repatriation as the only solution to the refugee situation. Despite hopes that refugees who had not committed crimes in Rwanda would filter back home, hard-liners in the camps intimidated their neighbors and prevented them from repatriating. In light of this challenge, regional states accepted the principle advocated by the RPF [Rwanda Patriotic Front] government that suspected perpetrators of genocide (génocidaires) and intimidators in the camps should be separated from "innocent refugees." International support to facilitate that process was not forthcoming, however, and there was little progress toward repatriation.[12]

After warning the international community of the untenable situation in Congo, Rwanda took action, and in October 1996, the first Congo war broke out. An estimated "600,000 refugees fled back into Rwanda and another 300,000 headed west into the dense forests of central Congo."[13] In December 1996, hundreds of thousands of mostly Hutu refugees followed as they began to return from Tanzania.[14] In most cases, the Tanzania government forced refugees to return to Rwanda. In 1995–1998, prisons reached peak capacity, hosting approximately 130,000 prisoners, mostly Hutu, accused of genocide crimes.[15] There was fear that the insurgency in the north would escalate into another civil war or that ethnic animosity would intensify.[16] The RPA (Rwandan Patriotic Army) became the Rwanda Defense Force (RDF), replacing the pregenocide army it defeated. As the now official army of the government of Rwanda, it relentlessly fought the *abacengezi* ("infiltrators"), who included former army officials from the FAR (Rwandan Armed Forces, many of whom actively participated in the genocide) who would attack at night and during the day. As one study has noted: "The civilian population was frequently caught in the crossfire between RPA and insurgency forces."[17] Eventually, the RDF won the war, and former Forces Armées Rwandaises (FAR) fighters—those who had served the genocidal government—returned to the DRC.

Before 2000, Rwanda's borders were not entirely secure. Many people lived in fear of returning to war or genocide. Regardless of each person's ethnic and migration background, the majority of Rwandans were traumatized, and the overall sociopolitical climate was rampant with fear and mistrust among various ethnic groups and political elites. Genocide survivors were still stitching their lives together after reappearing from hiding. Tutsi specifically were recuperating from literally decades of violence, rape, exile, discrimination in everyday life, and then a genocide. Young RPA soldiers included traumatized Tutsi survivors charged for killing Hutu neighbors whenever they found their relatives dead. In this period of insecurity, revenge killings were rampant in some regions of Rwanda.[18]

Those refugees who had recently returned, especially from DRC, had to put their lives back together. This included reclaiming property that had been taken over by those who remained in Rwanda, including both their own relatives but families of the RPA, who had come back to Rwanda from exile neighboring countries and believed the majority of Hutu refugees in Zaire would not return. As one of my interviewees, who was among those who returned after being separated from his family in Zaire, told me, they received news of the second Congo war (1998–2003), which prevented them from returning to Zaire, instead forcing them to face the challenges of reintegrating themselves into the new Rwanda.[19]

In the early 2000s, these former refugees were rebuilding their lives, learning to live under the rules of the RPF-led government while fearing for their loved ones who were being forced deep into Congolese forests and facing starvation and death.[20] They also feared the RPF government because they had been fed a steady diet of narratives that emphasized how evil and exploitative the "Tutsi" monarchy was. But there were also other factors that informed their fear. Some Hutu had returned from refugee camps with stories of RDF's violence in DRC against refugees and former Interahamwe, as well as Congolese, documented in memoirs like the life histories of former refugees (i.e., that of Marie Béatrice Umutesi[21]) or journalists' accounts.[22] Rumors spread around Rwanda that any Hutu risked being accused of the genocide and facing imprisonment, especially during the official commemoration period.[23] Stories of April 1995 killings of refugees in Kibeho camp, which targeted Hutu suspected to have participated in the genocide, all informed these fears[24] (I come back to this in the next chapter). These included the stories and rumors of reported killings of bishops and priests in June 1994 by the RPA soldiers.[25]

All these complexities among Rwandans was met with the determination of the new government to rebuild and continue to prioritize genocide commemoration and creating a master narrative despite leading a divided society. The theme of 1997 was announced by the committee of

Champions: *Turwanye itsembabwoko n'itsembatsemba, duharanira kugaruka ku muco mwiza w'abanyarwanda* or "Let's fight genocide and ethnic cleansing and restore positive Rwandan cultural values." The focus was on Rwandans' shared culture. Thus the nation-building master narrative began, including the creation of new vocabulary to define the events of 1994. *Itsembabwoko n'itsembatsemba* (genocide and ethnic cleansing) referred to killings of Tutsi; and massacres, meaning moderate Hutu who were killed in the genocide. These terms were distinct from *Jenoside* (genocide) in Kinyarwanda, illustrating these linguistic challenges. One of my interviewees, Senga, who worked on different memorials around the country from 2004 to 2014, explained that:

> The concept was created from the English term to link what happened in Rwanda to other global phenomena of genocide. This was also at a time when [genocide] deniers were on the rise and many [Hutu] politicians left Rwanda with an excuse that the government had become authoritarian [and would persecute them as genocide deniers or as genocide suspects].[26]

Darius Gishoma agrees and argues that the word *Jenoside* was introduced as an addition to the Kinyarwanda lexicon. The word suited the master narrative. As commemoration became more organized, institutionalized, and internationalized, the term was embedded in the new 2003 constitution.[27] This term was easier to remember and recognize in comparison to *itsembabwoko* ("extermination of an ethnic group"). Later, it would also narrow down the group of victims who were to be remembered in this master narrative. It allowed for the easy connection of the Rwandan tragedy to the Armenian genocide, the Holocaust, and other genocide master narratives globally. Members of survivors' organizations and the government in Rwanda implanted their master narrative into global commemoration culture and international public memory.

Then, in 2008, after much debate, the term itself evolved even further to name who exactly was being remembered. The new legal term then became *Jenoside Yakorewe Abatutsi*, or "the Genocide Against the Tutsi."[28] Other terms were deemed too ambivalent and could easily be exploited by genocide deniers. For those who asked for changes, the argument was that, according to the International Convention on Genocide, for crimes to be described as genocide, killings must have targeted a particular group. Hence, for Rwanda, the Tutsi were the targeted "ethnic" group. The International Convention lists criteria for genocide, including the following: "(a) Killing members of the group; (b) Causing serious bodily or mental harm to members of the group; (c) Deliberately inflicting on the group conditions of life calculated to bring about its physical destruction in whole or in part; (d) Imposing measures intended to prevent births within the group."[29] These were all features of what was done to victims of the genocide who were Tutsi. This phrase, "Genocide Against the Tutsi," remains one of the most contentious terms in discussions among Rwandan opposition and exiled politicians and academics who disputed the single focus on Tutsi victims.

International Actors' Endorsement of a National Policy

Unlike the three prior remembrances of 1995, 1996, and 1997, the official 1998 commemorations featured visits by two important international political figures to Rwanda who occupied powerful offices during the genocide. First, U.S. President Bill Clinton landed at the Kigali airport on March 25, a few weeks before April 7, which is recognized as the first day of the genocide and its subsequent commemorations. This was the first time a US Air Force craft carrying an American president had landed in Rwanda. In Clinton's speech, he acknowledged the killing of Tutsi and politically moderate Hutu. His speech was well received and was commended for its inclusive language. "I have," Clinton intoned, "come today to pay the respects of my nation to all who suffered and all who perished in the Rwandan genocide"—at which point he was interrupted by applause in recognition of this important statement.[30]

President Clinton's words legitimized the memorialization project that was starting to take shape and elevated its global significance.[31] He also legitimized the fragile postgenocide government, which was composed of a few unknown former RPA rebel leaders. He stated in his speech: "Mr. President, to you, and to you, Mr. Vice President, you have shown great vision in your efforts to create a single nation in which all citizens can live freely and securely." The vocabulary "the Rwandan genocide" he gave visibility would later be repeated by scholars, journalists, and then eventually rejected by Champions of the master narrative and replaced by the Genocide Against the Tutsi instead of the Rwandan Genocide.

On May 7, a second important visitor arrived in Kigali. It was a few weeks after the April commemoration when former United Nations Secretary General Kofi Annan visited Rwanda on his first of many trips to follow. Unlike President Clinton, who remained at the airport, for security reasons

Secretary General Annan came into Kigali and addressed the Rwandan Parliament.[32] First, even though he acknowledged the genocide and to some extent endorsed the master narrative that was developing, Annan did not praise the RPF like Clinton did. Annan's language was perceived by RPF leaders as arrogant and lacking in empathy. Second, he refrained from acknowledging personal responsibility as former head of UN peacekeeping operations during the period of the genocide, an omission that was surely inflammatory to some political elites who were his audience.[33] As a fellow influential African serving as head of peacekeeping operations at the United Nations, his decision to order the withdrawal of peacekeepers in the middle of a genocide in an African country generated widespread resentment among RPF politicians.[34]

However, Joseph Sebarenzi, then-speaker of Parliament, points to other reasons in his memoir *God Sleeps in Rwanda: A Journey of Transformation*.[35] He writes, for instance, that the United Nations was not supportive of the RPF or Tutsi survivors even after it was evident a genocide took place but instead shifted international attention to Hutu refugees in the Congo. Thus, because of the nature of his interaction with Parliament, Annan's remarks were not as readily mobilized to bolster the evolving master narrative like Clinton's. Nevertheless, his high-profile visit played a major role in the internationalization of the master narrative in the period that followed, with much of the international media coverage dominated by the discussion of Annan's previous culpability.

Unlike President Clinton, who received a warm welcome to Rwanda and would later visit many times, Secretary General Annan's subsequent visits to Rwanda were met with hostility from government officials. Even after the genocide, his rhetoric and actions were antagonistic to the RPF and therefore failed to make meaningful contributions to the master narrative aside from attracting international media whenever he visited Rwanda. Additionally, it was more strategic to endorse an American president who had more power than Annan and could be more useful in providing aid, championing Rwanda in the international community, and legitimizing the new government.

Confronting Domestic Political Realities and Actors

Between 1994 and 2008, two important shifts occurred. The first was that the international community's attention progressively shifted from the

Congo to Rwanda as an influx of refugees returned to Rwanda. Instead of seeking revenge, with the exception of a few, the majority of survivors turned to local courts. Since Rwanda had a very weak judicial system, those seeking justice in genocide-related affairs eventually organized grassroots courts, initially on their own or through religious organizations, which later evolved into government-run gacaca courts.[36] As discussed previously, Gacaca courts had been revamped from platforms to resolve family and community disputes to modern, localized courts in which the local population was trained to listen to serious genocide crimes in public and sentence those found guilty.

Second, on a local level, many feared that the informal memorials that had already been constructed would be destroyed, and that more survivors would be killed given the people who committed the genocide were still living among survivors or had returned from Zaire.[37] The fresh memories of recent ethnic cleansing did little to ensure peace. With this in mind, the 1999 commemoration's theme was more assertive: *Turasaba ko abicanyi bahanwa bakanabuzwa gusibanganya ibimenyetso* or "We request that killers face justice and be restricted from erasing evidence." The theme's tone suggested that the government wanted to appear responsive to the concerns of a restless and impatient survivor community. Survivors were frustrated due to the slow process of the courts, which were overwhelmed because there were few legal resources.[38] In this period, debates also started to emerge on who exactly was a genocide survivor and what surviving meant in the context of genocide commemorations. Thus, a new word was introduced into Kinyarwanda. *Abacitse ku icumu* or *abarokotse*/rescapés/genocide survivors: The loose literal translation of the Kinyarwanda term is "those who escaped the spear." In earlier commemorations, *Abarokotse* or "those who were saved" was used. It then evolved into *Abacitse ku icumu rya Jenoside yakorewe abatutsi*, which can be translated as "those who were saved from the spear of the genocide perpetrated against the Tutsi," but in English most still use "survivors of the Genocide Against the Tutsi."

When used in English, French, or Kinyarwanda, "survivor" refers to Tutsi who were not killed but were targeted in 1994 and survived. The term is ambiguous sometimes in its use as one is not sure if it also refers to RPA families who lost loved ones in the genocide or simply to Tutsi who were in Rwanda before 1994.[39] This singling out of victims has been rejected by numerous academics and Antagonists of the master narrative. Anna-Maria Brandstetter argues that in the use of "survivor" to single out Tutsi, "dynamics of violence during the genocide are blended out." As a result, she argues: "Gradually some nuances are being added to the simplistic equation: Hutu = *génocidaires* and Tutsi = *rescapés*," or survivors.[40]

In 2000, Speaker of Parliament Joseph Sebarenzi, a Tutsi survivor, resigned, along with President Pasteur Bizimungu, one of the few high-ranking Hutu in the RPF, the latter citing "personal reasons."[41] The parliament elected the vice president, Paul Kagame, as the new president. As Joseph Sebarenzi would write later in his autobiography, Kagame's influence was increasing, and he was consulted on all major policies, including what Sebarenzi and some politicians regarded as Parliament business.[42]

During the commemoration period of 2000, the theme sent an explicit political message to those like Sebarenzi and other Tutsi or Hutu politicians who were starting to express different opinions than the RPF leadership. It said: *Twamagane uwo ariwe wese ushaka kwibagiza no gupfobya itsembabwoko n'itsembatsemba*, which can be summarized as "Resist anyone with revisionism."[43] Broadly, the "anyone" category included even elite Hutu politicians like Bizimungu, survivors like Tutsi politicians such as Joseph Sebarenzi, and others who were questioning the RPF's agenda. The limits of that dialogue were carefully constrained—the permissible range of speech on memory was tactically limited and hegemonically "closed." Politicians could and should speak, but only to reinforce the approach that had already been established.

Sebarenzi's approach and vision of rebuilding Rwanda contradicted that of the RPF elites who returned from outside the country.[44] He was not alone in this observation. Some of the pregenocide opposition politicians and ordinary Rwandans, including survivors and moderate Hutu, had suggested developing a national framework for reconstruction, one that allowed both Hutu and Tutsi, as well as Twa and other genocide victims, to be remembered and fostered a national dialogue on other war crimes committed during the 1990s. However, the RPF perceived this idea as a potential trap for its military officers who killed people in different contexts right after the genocide or during the 1990s war.[45] In their speeches, politicians like Sebarenzi would often speak of reconciliation and talk about the genocide like an ordinary crime or use words like "intambara" to mean the war and ramp all killings together, therefore deeming them equal. Some even outrightly refuted that there had been a genocide despite evidence provided by human rights organizations and other investigators. It was a fragile period when multiple voices could eventually make the genocide an ordinary crime of war. But survivors and the government disagreed with this kind of speech. This kind of approach to reconciliation contradicted their experiences of trauma, threatening the single master narrative of the genocide which was slowly evolving and gaining new vocabulary to become the monolithic narrative that Champions of the master narrative envisioned. Hence, the term *gupfobya/denegation*/denial. Denial is also explained as to have *ingengabitekerezo ya jenoside* or "genocide ideology."[46] While some of the recorded actions of denialism in earlier commemorations were obvious, they increasingly became subtle and more complex to identify.[47] They employ a competitive memory approach that gives each person the right to remember. As I show further in Chapter 4, Antagonists are diverse in opinion, and their vision of memory and reconciliation contradicts that of Champions.

In 1998 and 1999, important meetings took place in the president's office. It was these consultative meetings where many ideas—including economic plans in Vision 2020 that would be used to rebuild the country and ideas in it—emerged, as well as outlines for the gacaca courts. The meetings, chaired by President Bizimungu and attended by Rwandans from all walks of life, put forward a document that emphasized all challenges that Rwanda had at the time. Chief among them were disputes over identity and competitive memory narratives of the roots of the violence that had taken place in the 1990s and who should be held accountable.[48]

With the political changes brought about through the exit of Sebarenzi and imprisonment of President Bizimungu on corruption charges, the tone of themes also evolved. These two and other politically moderate Hutu, including Seth Sendashonga, who was murdered in Kenya in 1998, constantly challenged the creation of the master narrative. But by 2001, the RPF had gained even more power, appointing whoever agreed with their vision and especially those who were willing to endorse the master narrative regardless of background. To win hearts and minds, the RPF always distributed power and leadership positions as recommended by the Arusha Peace Agreement, which was signed in August 1993 to help end the civil war.

Thus, the theme for 2001 was *Twibuke itsembabwoko n'itsembatsemba twubaka igihugu cyacu*, or "Let us remember genocide and ethnic cleansing while building our country." The tone changed from a focus on apparent sources of historical unity, like cultural values, to a more forward-looking and action-oriented emphasis. Then, in 2003 the theme refocused its attention on the politics of elections. Jean Paul Kimonyo reflects on the politics of this period:

By mid-2003, Rwanda went through a period of increased political tension. An important part of the international community had criticized the new constitution and the way it had been drafted, especially via a process that, they felt, restricted freedom. On the eve of the presidential and legislative elections that followed the adoption of the constitution, a political campaign organized by RPF supporters had ended with the dissolution of the historic MDR and suspension of several local NGOs [nongovernmental organizations] because of their promotion of ethnic division.[49]

The banning of such an important political party that advanced division politics did not go unnoticed. The RPF government risked losing legitimacy and an important election. That year, the government was mobilizing all possible resources to win the elections. As one of my interviewees, Kayihura, explained, the commemoration that year was a balancing act between acknowledging the needs of survivors and using nonpersecutory language to attract Hutu votes. Alongside the 2003 elections was a referendum that established a new constitution on May 26. The new constitution gave strong legal backing to the National Unity and Reconciliation Commission (NURC) as the legal body orchestrating discussions of alternative versions of memory. The 2003 theme was: *Twibuke itsembabwoko n'itsembatsemba dushyigikira ibikorwa byose by'ubumwe n'ubwiyunge* or "Let us remember genocide and ethnic cleansing by supporting all activities of unity and reconciliation." This theme, like others preceding it, targeted Rwandans and was concerned with internal politics. However, in the years that followed, themes began to target outsiders and reach outward to a regional and global audience.

Internationalization of Commemoration and Global Outreach

By 2004, Rwandans were familiar with the April 7 ceremonies and first-week activities; hence, more localized commemorative efforts started to materialize. Additionally, other independent international initiatives emerged around the 10-year anniversary and had a significant impact on the global focus of the campaign. For example, the Kigali Memorial Museum and similar memorial sites opened around the country, and two books about the genocide published in 1999 received global attention. The books—one authored by American journalist Philip Gourevitch and the other by renowned

Rwanda scholar Alison Des Forges—popularized the genocide and Rwanda among elite and middle-class Americans and Europeans.[50] Besides her outstanding research in *Leave None to Tell the Story*, Des Forges was credited with having insisted that the word *genocide* was necessary for giving an accurate account of what had happened in Rwanda in 1994. While Des Forges was very familiar with Rwanda and her book went on to become an important reference for scholars and policymakers because of its detailed accounts of how the genocide unfolded in cities and small towns, with specific names of killers and victims included in some sections and documenting RPA's killings in the 1990s on one hand; on the other hand, Gourevitch's work received both praise and criticism. Gourevitch's book, *We Wish to Inform You That Tomorrow We Will Be Killed with Our Families*, became popular among nonspecialist Western college students but received criticism from scholars.[51] The book became famous for giving gruesome details and created an image that associated Africa with death and terrible violence, especially for American audience. But for scholars who were familiar with Rwanda's complex history, it was a book that lacked substance. For example, political scientist René Lemarchand wrote that it lacked historical clarity and context for why the genocide happened and the way it unfolded.[52] In Bert Ingelaere's opinion, it was not balanced and gave a one-sided view of the multilayer violence that surrounded the genocide.[53] These were two different books with different styles but both popularized the genocide to different local, regional, and international audiences.

In addition to these books, scholarship on Rwanda increased. The growing body of popular scholarship drew attention to the genocide experience in Western public discourse. However, it was not until the release of the Hollywood film *Hotel Rwanda* (2004) that the official genocide memory evolved into a regional and global phenomenon.[54] *Hotel Rwanda* is a fictional story based on real events that showed how a hotel manager had used his network to protect mostly the Tutsi elites who had fled to the hotel in Kigali. His hotel had been under protection of the United Nations force. Although the government eventually rejected the narrative of *Hotel Rwanda* and the political activism of its main character, Paul Rusesabagina, that resulted from his fame, the movie nevertheless marketed the master narrative to the United States first and to the world more generally. The "Hollywood effect" generated by these prominent works popularized the genocide narrative and introduced another perspective that diverged from the master narrative once dominated by the RPF, survivors, and international political and humanitarian actors. Nevertheless, the government capitalized from this public relations blitz by countering the events propagated in the movie and advancing its own master narrative among an enthralled international audience. These were days when, as I have argued elsewhere, Rwanda started to use the master narrative to shape its international relations.[55]

In Rwanda, the master narrative evolved complemented by the establishment of systematized and institutionalized annual ceremonies and memorials around the country that enthusiastically put bones on display. The internationalization agenda was reflected in the commemoration theme of April 2004: *Twibuke kandi duhashye burundu Jenoside dukoresheje ubufatanye nyakuri bw'abatuye isi yose* or "Let's remember and boldly fight genocide through true cooperation with world citizens." A similar message was repeated in 2005's theme: *Twibuke Jenoside turwanya ingengabitekerezo yayo mu Rwanda no mu mahanga* or "Let us remember the genocide by fighting its ideology in Rwanda and internationally." The themes referred to the events of 1994 as genocide, not ethnic cleansing. At this time, international campaigns against genocide were increasing because of the genocide in Darfur.[56] The Rwandan government played a significant role in prompting discussions at the United Nations and African Union that aimed to stop the genocide in Darfur before it could claim victims on the same scale as in Rwanda. The Rwandan government sent the first African Union troops to Darfur in August 2004.[57] Thus, the theme reflected Rwanda's plans to become a leading actor in the global fight against genocide.

If the books and literature that were published popularized the genocide among elites around the world, *Hotel Rwanda*, and the much less known but equally successful *Sometimes in April*, delivered the genocide to ordinary citizens around the world in their cinemas and living rooms. The Hollywood effect achieved much more than what journalists reporting the genocide in 1994 managed to accomplish when everyone turned away from the news on Rwanda. For example, during graduate school at Syracuse University, I regularly went to the Library of Congress in Washington, D.C. The two elderly women who worked at the front desk asked where I was from. When I said Rwanda, one got up and gave me a hug and said she was sorry that the world did nothing in Rwanda. At first, I was puzzled as they assumed that I was a genocide survivor who somehow made it to America. In homes where I visited American or British friends, individuals often looked for an opportunity to ask about my family and what side we were on. In these instances, the narrative of the genocide had been brought to ordinary peoples' attention, and survivors and Rwandans in general became evidence of that genocide. But this was not the case while requesting a visa to the United States. Once, in Nairobi, I was asked for extra clearance because I had said I was born in Rwanda, and according to this official anyone born in Rwanda had to be investigated for ties to fugitive political elites who were migrating using fake names in Belgium, the United Kingdom, France, and the United States.

However, the publicity also attracted unwanted attention. Sceptics of the RPF's program, including human rights organizations and media representatives, increasingly gained visibility in the worlds of journalism and academia that strive for so-called balanced reporting or objectivity in research (these tensions are explored in Chapters 4 and 6).

Local Discussion of Reconstruction

Unlike the 1999 theme, the 2006 theme indicated that gacaca was experiencing substantial difficulties in its implementation. It argued for the support and cooperation of witnesses and the general public: *Twibuke Jenoside twitabira inkiko Gacaca kandi tugira ubutwari bwo kuvugisha ukuri no guhangana n'ingaruka zayo* or "Let us remember the genocide by supporting gacaca courts with courage to speak the truth about the genocide and facing its consequences." In this period, survivors were being killed or intimidated. The lack of provision for witness protection induced some to avoid gacaca court proceedings. Like commemoration activities, gacaca courts were indigenous initiatives that later became de facto law and were co-opted into legislation. This shift attracted attention from analysts, who were both critical and laudatory.[58] In 2007, as both praise and criticism for the gacaca courts increased, the theme for commemoration responded with: *Twibuke Jenoside twita ku bacitse ku icumu, duharanira ubutabera* or "Let us remember the genocide by caring for survivors and supporting justice." The 2008 theme was *Twibuke Jenoside duhashya ingengabitekerezo yayo, twite ku bacitse ku icumu kandi duharanire iterambere* or "Let us remember the genocide by fighting genocide ideology, caring for survivors and supporting development." This explicit focus on survivors reflected continuous dilemmas embedded in earlier themes, such as the genocide denial aspect addressed in 2000 and 2002. The forward-looking, development-oriented themes established were also sustained. In the 2009 theme, *Twibuke Jenoside yakorewe Abatutsi, turwanya ipfobya n'ihakana byayo, twubaka igihugu cyacu* or "Let us remember the Genocide Against the Tutsi, fight genocide denial and negationism, build our country," the tone became more pointed. Similarly, in 2010, 2011, and 2012, the commemorations' rhetoric now emphatically and explicitly defined *Tutsi* as the victims worthy of remembrance.[59]

The 2010 theme, *Twibuke Jenoside yakorewe Abatutsi turushaho gufatanya mu guhangana n'ihungabana* or "Let us remember the Genocide Against the Tutsi while increasingly confronting trauma," focused on healing memories of those who suffered from trauma. The 2007, 2008, and 2010 themes considered survivors' plight, but the themes advanced in subsequent years inspired a new kind of language that could help describe what survivors were experiencing. Jean Paul Kimonyo notes in 2010 the police reported a significant reduction in acts of violence against survivors.[60] The word *ihahamuka*/traumatism/being traumatized evolved from another word, *ihungabana* or traumatized as well, but *ihahamuka* has deeper meaning. Internationalization also introduced new ideas and words to confront the realities of trauma. In Rwanda, there had not been a context or any local words to express such trauma since it was traditionally dealt with informally and was not professionally diagnosed. The emergence of the term *ihahamuka*,[61] "to be traumatized," marked a breakthrough in the public understanding of post-traumatic disorder (PTSD).

Darius Gishoma's research on trauma during commemoration has showed that in earlier events, trauma was more on an individual level and not a collective. Some of his interviewees talked about signs of trauma in early years leading up to 2010 commemoration theme.

> I witnessed these mental crises for the first time a while before I began my work in mental health. I remember the very first time I came across such matter; it was in 1996 during the month of April in Gisenyi in a place called Nyundo. Like any other survivor, I was taking part in a commemoration day of the Genocide. During a survivor's testimony of what happened in Nyundo, a young lady started to scream to the extent that her screams interrupted the testimony. She was saying that the *Interahamwe* were attacking them, she wanted to escape, she screamed; these are similar signs to what we are currently experiencing. The only difference with the crises of today is that it only concerned a handful of people. That day, I remember that it

was only that young lady who had that reaction. It wasn't much of a collective experience as it is today. (DJ, 31 years old, psychiatric nurse, contributor since 2004)[62]

Traumatic episodes were few, but even then, from 2002 to 2004, the government started taking notice and ensuring there were psychiatrists at commemorations to help those who might experience trauma.[63] Gishoma further observes:

> This has become a public health issue so much so that in 2006, the government's administration had to come up with some sort of strategies in order to tackle this phenomenon when dealing with what I would call "epidemic mental crises" in schools. Consequently, everyone becomes mobilised, the police are mobilised, the politicians are fully engaged, those in the health sector are also mobilised. We are very aware that it has become a national issue. (BR, 48 years old, psychiatrist, contributor since 2002)[64]

He concludes that: "In retrospect, when I think about the mental crises of 2005, 2006, 2007, 2008, 2009, it is evident that from the year 2008 and 2009, there is some stability."[65]

The progress in those years all led up to the 2010 commemoration theme above that focused on trauma.

However, in 2011 and 2012, the themes became more inward looking. For example, the 2011 theme was *Kwibuka Jenoside yakorewe Abatutsi: Dushyigikire ukuri, twiheshe Agaciro* or "Let us remember Genocide Against the Tutsi: supporting the truth, giving ourselves dignity." The 2012 theme was *Twigire ku mateka, twubake ejo hazaza* or "Let us learn from our history to build a better future." With this theme, the RPF began to leverage its competence as a manager of the state and the economy as a source of its legitimacy and authority, rather than citing its older role as the liberators and saviors of the state.[66] The twentieth commemorative theme was "Remember, unite, renew." Discussion in forums focused on a controversial *Ndi umunyarwanda* ("I am a Rwandan") program, which emphasized commonalities among Rwandans, language, customs, and traditions but at the same time was used as a platform to generalize genocide guilt to Hutu communities and not individuals.[67] The policy of *Ndi Umunyarwanda* became more deeply embedded as part of the government agenda and discussion publicly in 2014 toward rebuilding national identity.[68]

Actors Who Influenced the Master Narrative in Commemoration and Regional Dynamics

As discussed previously in this chapter, the government meeting of ministers adopts a new theme every year and communicates it through the Ministry of Culture and Sports.[69] La Commission Nationale de Lutte contre le Genocide (CNLG), popularly known as the National Commission for the Fight against Genocide, is one of the central parastate organizations involved in the planning of the commemoration events with survivor organizations. This is evident in reports that announced the nineteenth theme of commemoration. After a cabinet meeting on February 5, 2013, Minister of Sports and Culture Protais Mitali announced the theme: *Twibuke Jenoside yakorewe Abatutsi duharanira kwigira* or "Let us commemorate Genocide Against the Tutsi as we strive for self-reliance."[70]

During the nine years from 2004 to 2013, four of eight official ceremonies were held in the Kigali National Stadium. However, none of the eight were held in the north of the country. A number of factors contributed to this resistance of what they regarded as a Tutsi-led government's policies, including a complex history of northern Rwanda in Rwanda's past dating back to the precolonial kingdoms. As Catharine Newbury, Gerald Prunier, and other scholars of Rwandan history have argued,[71] the kingdoms that existed in present-day northern Rwanda were not under the control of the central kingdom of the Nyiginya dynasty until after the arrival of the Europeans.[72] There were some small principalities (e.g., Bushiru), but large areas were not under centralized control of the type found in the Nyiginya Kingdom. Hutu in this region were independent, unlike other conquered regions, which were subject to the rule of the monarch. Furthermore, Hutu in the north held influential positions in the Habyarimana administration of 1973–1994 (after a coup against Grégoire Kayibanda from the south of Rwanda) because the second president himself was from the same region. The anti-Tutsi sentiments that existed before the genocide in the north increased when the RPF won the civil war and took power from the Hutu-dominated pregenocide government. After the genocide, the northern part of Rwanda became synonymous with genocide denial, and from 1997 to 2000, areas in the north were the main sources of insurgency by former government soldiers attacking Rwanda from refugee camps in the DRC.[73] In some instances, the northerners were imprisoned due to their questions about the plight of their relatives killed during the RPF attacks in the region. An example found in Bert Ingelaere's research shows that at a 2006 local commemoration in the Ruhengeri area: "A number of inhabitants were put in prison after asking when justice would come for family members who were lost in the period between October 1990 and April 1994 as well as during the war with the infiltrators after the 1994 genocide."[74]

These are some possible explanations why few commemoration ceremonies were held in the north and the general resistance to government programs in earlier periods. In fact, one researcher found that usage of the term *genocide* in the north is also associated with a different period of violence by youth even many years after a campaign to popularize the master narrative. Yuko Otake's study of Rwandans in the north gives accounts of how silences around their suffering during the *Abacengezi* or insurgency period of 1997 influences their thinking decades after.[75] Richard Benda's research into young Rwandans also showed that when it came to conversations about the past held all over Rwanda, the northern youth believed the genocide was against the Hutu and confused the war against insurgency that killed many of their relatives with the genocide.[76] Thus, they formed different narratives that deviated from the master narrative based on the version of history their parents told them. Their beliefs were different from Hakizimana's resistance to his father's instructions. This distinguishes the northerners' experiences of commemoration and genocide memory from mnemonic experiences in other regions of Rwanda.

In an effort to target and influence those who disagree with the master narrative, the cabinet of the Government of Rwanda announced that commemoration ceremonies would be brought to the local level in 2013.[77] Two interviewees explained this move. One of the interviewees gave several reasons:

> The first was to make commemoration a citizen-centered ritual and make every citizen feel involved, even those who were not able to get where commemoration was held. The second was to encourage participation by involving both social groups (ethnic groups) since commemoration was, for some, for survivors and others felt less concerned with participation. Before this policy, local security personnel used to intervene in order to force the population to massively participate.[78]

During earlier commemorations I attended, there were uniformed police present during the commemoration as it was, for instance, in 2011 in a community in Kigali. On some evenings, a local official went around with a loud microphone asking people to attend the evening vigil. When we arrived at the site, we found the police seating people and maintaining order. Yet, in subsequent commemoration events, only senior police officials attended the commemoration, and order was kept by a neighborhood watch-type group that was not armed. This change intrigued me. My research associate explained the change based on his experience researching genocide memory-related topics and observing commemorations around Rwanda and in prisons:

> In my opinion, as it was a duty for National Police initially, the use of DASSO (District Administrative Security Support Organ) serves as an indicator of the politics of decentralization of commemoration. Hence, the rigidity has been also decentralized and consequently encouraged citizen participation. Likewise, decentralization reduces a sense of shame and fear on former perpetrator and their family members who could at the beginning dodge commemoration ceremonies for that. But since decentralization, fear and shame slowly got off as they join their village-mates. Again, decentralization brought shame for those who do not show up among others at commemoration site in a village. The person wonders how others may perceive him/her once he/she skips commemoration ceremonies. This positive fear and shame was cultivated by the politics of decentralization of commemoration ritual.[79]

That displayed crucial elements of how hegemonic memory works. There were also policy reasons for this shift. When the decentralization began in 1999, it was not only for commemoration functions, but also mostly for all other services that were brought closer to the people and encouraged participation and inclusion in the reconstruction process. This was one of the key elements that the Bizimungu presidency contributed to the evolution of the master narrative.[80]

Beginning in 2013, the minister of sport and culture, who was at the time a genocide survivor himself, Mitali Protais announced that the national commemoration event, to be held at Amahoro National Stadium in Kigali, would take place once every 5 years. This changed the practice completely. Then-Minister Mitali was quoted as saying: "As usual, the commemoration week will be held from April 7 to April 13. However, there won't be a commemoration ceremony at Amahoro Stadium; we want the commemoration week to be more people-centered, which is why we have chosen to hold it at the village level."[81] He also announced that the colors that symbolized the mourning period would be changed from purple to gray. He explained that research showed that Rwandan culture favored gray for purposes of mourning. Among other reasons discussed in Chapter 4, the color gray, which symbolized ashes, was used by Rwandan ancestors to express sadness.[82]

These themes, commemorations, and other mourning practices had powerful implications for the emerging country and master narrative. They evolved into forums where actors representing the state, parastate organizations, and NGOs exercised immense influence and played a personal role—reawakening and amplifying, with metronomic regularity each April, great personal distress, anger, and sadness among Champions, Antagonists, and Fatalists. They touched on, and engaged with, individual memories that remain truly traumatic. It is probably unavoidable, but it was also potentially risky. No matter how carefully crafted, this became a dangerous space for state and nonstate actors to operate. As Antagonists increased their resistance to language and themes that excluded their individual memories and experiences, new laws were created to protect the master narrative and its affiliated institutions.

National Policies, Institutions, and Laws to Protect Commemorations and Genocide Memory

When the RPF established its government of national unity, it appointed a Hutu who had also gone into exile in Uganda. President Pasteur Bizimungu (who had worked as a senior manager in the MRND government in the 1980s) led Rwanda from July 19, 1994 to March 23, 2000. A few weeks before the commemoration of April 2000, Bizimungu resigned, and his vice president Paul Kagame, who wielded significant influence within the RPF and disagreed with Bizimungu, became president.[83] One of Bizimungu's last actions before leaving the government was to oversee the law that established a commission that would play an important part in the evolution of the master narrative.[84] The postgenocide government created the NURC and later, the CNLG to deal with consequences of genocide and civil war. The CNLG, formed to focus specifically on genocide-related matters, partnered with newly created survivors' NGOs and built on previous individual and nongovernmental efforts to construct an official genocide memory, but one that emphasized remembering genocide victims.

Darius Gishoma noted that various memory institutions were then created to promote and protect the master narrative.[85] A phalanx of new laws was also created to guard the master narrative and memory of the genocide. The NURC was one of the first agencies to be charged with fostering long-term peacebuilding and coexistence among Rwandans. Part of its work was to reconcile Rwandans, a goal also expressed in the Arusha Peace Agreements of the 1990s.[86] The NURC was first created in March 1999, and the national parliament mandated its presence into legislative law.[87] The NURC selected six themes considered critical to evaluating progress on unity and reconciliation among Rwandans. One of the six pillars was "understanding the past," which includes organizing memory into a master narrative.[88] However, as the past became even more important and the influence of survivors' organizations and lobby groups increased, the government agreed to create another institution, CNLG, charged with a sole task of further developing the master narrative and guarding it at the same time. Over time, the CNLG evolved into the most central formal body, organizing or present in the majority of commemorations around the country and focusing on all activities having to do with the genocide.

Over 18 years later, parliament adopted other laws to complement NURC and CNLG's work; for example, law No. 33 bis/2003 of September 6, 2003, "Repressing the Crime of Genocide, Crimes Against Humanity and War Crimes"; law No. 18/2008 of July 23, 2008, relating to the punishment of the crime of genocide ideology; and law No. 7/2001 of December 18, 2001, for suppression and punishment of the crime of discrimination and sectarianism.[89] The antidenial law is often used to deal with those who disrupt the functioning of commemoration. It empowers law enforcement to confront "any person who will have publicly shown, by his or her words, writings, images, or by any other means, that he or she has negated the genocide committed, rudely minimized it or attempted to justify or approve its grounds."[90] In the period of 1994–2012, there 243 people found guilty and were sentenced to 10 to 20 years in jail according to this law. General Prosecutor Martin Ngoga argued that the laws were adopted as part of international practice in connection with other legal instruments, such as those that guard against the denial of the Holocaust or those used in state campaigns to fight racism.[91] Lars Waldorf noted the range of denial activities that took place as the fifteenth commemoration approached.[92] He writes:

Every April, the designated month of mourning and commemoration, there are vivid reminders that unrepentant genocidaires still live among the survivors. In April 2008, someone threw a grenade at the country's main genocide memorial and museum, killing one of the guards. The previous April, a radio talk show caller expressed the need to "finish the job." At the same time, negationist propaganda is preached by genocidaires across the border in eastern Congo or on trial at the ICTR [International Criminal Tribunal for Rwanda], as well as by some Rwandan exile groups in Europe.[93]

Yet it was also argued that these laws became tools to repress political opposition from emerging or debating Rwanda's different versions of pasts openly. Scholars cite the case of Victoire Ingabire, who was arrested after making what Rwanda's government considered efforts to bring out competitive memory narrative or "moral equivalency."[94]

These parastate institutions and laws worked alongside other NGOs. The most recognized and prominent is Ibuka (whose name means "to remember" in Kinyarwanda), a lobby group whose activities, unlike those of other organizations, extend to the Rwandan diaspora. Ibuka was founded by a group of survivors immediately after the 1994 genocide in Belgium, after which it was started in Rwanda. Its main work is to provide for genocide survivors through its vision, which "is that Rwandan society should be a place where the memory of the genocide is preserved and where all the genocide survivors are socially included, financially able and live with full dignity."[95] The United Nations and other governments have recognized Ibuka, as it often writes to foreign governments and the United Nations on matters concerning accused perpetrators in the diaspora and reacts publicly to the ICTR's case proceedings. Another NGO, AVEGA Agahozo, brings together over 25,000 widows of the genocide.[96] Similarly, the Genocide Survivors Students Association (also known in French as Association des Étudiants et Éleves Rescapés du Genocide, or AERG) brings together young survivors. It is represented in over 20 universities and institutes and has a presence in over 300 secondary schools in different parts of the country.[97] Although it is not stated in their policies, survivors' organizations are perceived locally as organizations composed of Tutsi who survived the genocide and whose relatives were killed.[98] While, for example, Ibuka works with the NURC and CNLG to organize official opening and closing national commemoration ceremonies, the AERG, AVEGA Agahozo, and others who joined Ibuka are involved in local official commemorations throughout the 3-month annual remembrance period.[99]

Allowing these NGOs to operate and address the needs of survivors was part of the inherent politicization of genocide memory discourse and set the distinction between perpetrator and victim.[100] However, this is not the reality among all ordinary Rwandans. Yuko Otake points to her research findings, which showed that:

> In reality, amongst grassroots citizens, ethnic identity did not necessarily decide who became victim or perpetrator. Social dynamics shaped by diverse forms of identity and personal circumstances, such as kinship, friendship, personal desire and conflict, complexly intertwined toward perpetration and survival. Thus, simplistic classifications of Tutsi victims and Hutu perpetrators, or vice versa, do not appropriately reflect the grassroots reality.[101]

In addition to these organizations, other stakeholders are involved directly and indirectly. They include local and international governments, NGOs, academics, and private-sector groups that finance and participate in the annual official remembrance. The most influential non-Rwandan organization is the United Kingdom and Rwanda–based Aegis Trust, which has been responsible for financing and maintaining official memorials since 2004. As we will see in the following chapters, Aegis has also provided expertise in shaping the master narrative for Rwandans and non-Rwandan visitors to the Kigali Memorial Center. Although the government has evolved into the key keeper and director of collective memory, the commemorative community, both in Rwanda and internationally, consists of numerous and varied stakeholder groups, made up of a wide range of people whose involvement is influenced by their own individual or families' memories for younger generation.

The theme "building our country" in 2001 was promulgated in the context of large inflows of international aid, which was increasingly being poured into the country.[102] Before that, most of the funds raised in Western countries and organizations just after the genocide were used in Zaire to solve the humanitarian crisis caused by the high number of refugees exiled in DRC.[103]

Foreign organizations, such as the World Bank, DFID (Department for International Development, now Foreign, Commonwealth & Development Office [FCDO]), Aegis Trust, USAID (United States Agency for International Development), and many other international donor agencies began operating in Rwanda. By 1995, they increasingly started to turn their attention to survivors and those who stayed behind in Rwanda. A significant portion of foreign aid supported the rehabilitation of some genocide memorials and the articulation of a coherent collective narrative that continued to evolve and feature in commemorations.[104]

Memorialization and *Urwanda Rushya*—New Rwanda

The formalization of memory in postgenocide Rwanda evolved in parallel to the definition of the "new Rwanda" and the articulation of RPF's vision. As espoused in the proverb *Intimba ntibuza intore guhamiriza*, loosely translated "sorrow may not prevent a dancer to perform," the new Rwanda began to form; with the exception of the country's name, most of other national symbols changed. The new constitution, adopted in 2003, was accompanied by new national symbols: a new flag, coat of arms, and national anthem. National holidays were swapped and given new meaning. For instance, Liberation Day, celebrated on July 4 to celebrate the victory of the RPF, replaced Independence Day, which had been observed on July 1 to mark Rwanda's independence in 1962. The various commemorative and celebration dates, symbols, institutions, policies, and laws all contributed, quite intentionally, to the new Rwanda imagination. Dates mattered in the new Rwanda. The master narrative has evolved in such a way that April 7, 1994, has been established as the beginning of the genocide; the killing is said to have lasted for 100 days. A date to celebrate Rwandan heroes (mostly those who were part of the RPF, like Fred Gisa Rwigema, and other politicians who opposed the genocide, such as former Prime Minister Uwilingiyimana Agathe) has been added to the calendar on February 1. The RPF is credited with creating a new beginning on July 4, 1994, by saving Rwanda. Official commemoration periods have evolved into periods where parastate institutions could preach a version of the "past" that they deem conducive for generating reconciliation among the "new Rwandans." In the new Rwanda, asserts Buckley-Zistel: "There is a deliberate, public rewriting of history as part of the government effort to unite the country."[105]

In the first two decades, the creation of this new Rwanda, the RPF and its international partners relied on an official master narrative to imagine and develop a new country. For example, the master narrative often featured speeches to attract Western aid to contribute to the reconstruction process and investment. This is noticeable in all the major speeches delivered by Rwandan officials and foreign actors with a vested interest in Rwanda. Regardless of the place, space, audience, or timing of the presentations, the memory of the Genocide Against the Tutsi features in the introduction. The past became a cornerstone for contemporary politics and future planning in every aspect of the country.

During the first 20 years, the creation of annual themes, genocide-specific terminologies, institutions charged with managing memory, and wide-scale events have ingrained powerful and sacred rituals of remembrance. They were protected by the constitution of the new Rwanda and could not be criticized or questioned.[106] Consequently, opposition politicians, especially those self-identifying as Hutu, as well as ordinary Rwandans, were restricted from contributing to certain national matters if their contribution sought to bring out competitive memories to the master narrative. Therefore, official memory has gradually but continuously developed into a "forced" selective narrative.[107] The current state of commemoration activities is in many ways different from those that individual organizers like Nkubito, Sibomana, and other ordinary Rwandans had started to develop in 1995. In postgenocide Rwanda, as Timothy Longman showed, the new government developed a new historical narrative for ordinary, mostly rural, Rwandans—which by definition became the official historical narrative—in order to give shape to the very concept of a nation.[108]

Conclusion

This chapter has attempted to map out key events surrounding the evolution of different pillars of the master narrative and commemoration. It has shown that there were certain events that influenced how different actors participated in creating the master narrative and have been overlooked in existing studies on postgenocide Rwanda. It documented how early commemorations were not aligned with the master narrative and how they eventually converged. It showed that to communicate the goals and meanings of each commemoration activity, remembrance themes were created and often corresponded to the mood in the country. Alongside these themes, the chapter has shown that a vocabulary also emerged for how to talk about the Genocide Against the Tutsi. Within that process, institutions and laws were created to guard the master narrative from genocide deniers and revisionists. It is through analyzing these vocabularies and discourses around the master narrative that we capture how many actors with varied personal and political interests shaped the emergence, evolution, and response to the master narrative. Both Antagonists and Champions took the comparative memory approach, with Antagonists seeking moral equivalency of memorialization of different pasts, and the government and Champions of master narrative fighting back to protect the sanctity of annual commemoration. It is through these relationships that the master narrative has gained prominence in national, regional, and international contexts and emerged as a hegemonic master narrative of Rwanda's past. From these events and discourses around them we learn that memory is multidirectional, and its travels do not depend on a linear process; rather, it is one that is shaped by interests and power, and the process is even more complicated and multifaceted for those actors like genocide survivors, whose lived experiences are closely linked to events being remembered. Further chapters examine why certain actors shift positions from Champions to Antagonists or vice versa or from Fatalists to Champions or Antagonists.

The next chapter examines how Champions', Antagonists', and Fatalists' actions and response to the official master narrative as it emerged into a hegemonic narrative. It looks at the shifts over time and various factors underlying their actions.

Notes

1. Rémi Korman, "L'État rwandais et la mémoire du génocide commémorée sur les ruines (1994–1996)," *Vingtième Siècle. Revue d'histoire* 122, no. 2 (2014): 89.
2. Darius Gishoma, "Crises traumatiques collectives d'ihahamuka lors des commémorations du génocide des Tutsi: Aspects cliniques et perspectives thérapeutiques" (PhD, Université de Louvain, 2014), http://hdl.handle.net/2078.1/143580..
3. Immediately after the genocide, humanitarian assistance efforts focused on camps of refugees in Zaire and not survivors or other Rwandans in the country. This was largely as a result of international media focusing on two million refugees that crossed into neighboring countries, especially into Zaire. For a comprehensive discussion of the humanitarian assistance—including its scale—and of the politics of the countries and organizations involved, see Anne Mackintosh, "The International Response to Conflict and Genocide: Lessons from the Rwanda Experience Edited by David Millwood," *Journal of Refugee Studies* 9, no. 3 (1996): 334; and Korman, "L'État rwandais et la mémoire du génocide," 90.
4. Korman, "L'État rwandais et la mémoire du génocide," 90.

5. Ibid.
6. Ibid., 91.
7. Ibid., 91.
8. See Note 3.
9. Martin Ngoga, "The Institutionalization of Impunity: A Judicial Perspective of the Rwandan Genocide," in *After Genocide: Transitional Justice, Post-conflict Reconstruction and Reconciliation in Rwanda and Beyond*, eds. Philip Clark and Zachary D. Kaufman (Oxford: Oxford University Press, 2013), 321–322. The reconstruction narrative has also been characterized with skeptism on the official statistics of Rwanda's recovery. See An Ansoms, Esther Marijnen, Giuseppe Cioffo, and Jude Murison, "Statistics versus Livelihoods: Questioning Rwanda's Pathway Out of Poverty," *Review of African Political Economy* 44, no. 151 (2017): 47–65.
10. Gishoma, "Crises traumatiques collectives," 159.
11. Beth Whitaker, "Refugees and the Spread of Conflict: Contrasting Cases in Central Africa," *Journal of Asian and African Studies* 38, no. 2–3 (2003), 214.
12. Whitaker, "Refugees and the Spread of Conflict."
13. Ibid.
14. The *New York Times* published a story that described resistance in camps and reported that thousands refused to return and instead went toward the south, into Zimbabwe, Zambia, Malawi, and other countries, fearing that they would be killed if they returned to Rwanda. Some feared facing justice and spread rumors to encourage others to follow them. See James C. McKinley Jr., "Tide of Rwanda Refugees Flows Back to Tanzania Camps," *New York Times*, December 14, 1996, http://www.nytimes.com/1996/12/14/world/tide-of-rwanda-refugees-flows-back-to-tanzania-camps.html?pagewanted=all&src=pm.
15. Carina Tertsakian, "'All Rwandans Are Afraid of Being Arrested One Day': Prisoners Past, Present, and Future," in *Remaking Rwanda: State Building and Human Rights after Mass Violence*, eds. Scott Straus and Lars Waldorf (Madison: University of Wisconsin Press, 2011), 212.
16. See Richard Orth, "Rwanda's Hutu Extremist Genocidal Insurgency: An Eyewitness Perspective," *Small Wars & Insurgencies* 12, no. 1 (2001): 76–109.
17. Burnet, *Genocide Lives in Us*, 71.
18. See Buckley-Zistel, "Remembering to Forget," 137.
19. See also Beth Elise Whitaker and John F. Clark, eds., *Africa's International Relations: Balancing Domestic & Global Interests* (Boulder, CO: Lynne Rienner Publishers, 2018).. See especially chapter 7 on the regionalization of conflict.
20. For more on Congo Wart, see Filip Reyntjens, *The Great African War: Congo and Regional Geopolitics, 1996–2006* (New York: Cambridge University Press, 2009); or René Lemarchand, *The Dynamics of Violence in Central Africa* (Philadelphia: University of Pennsylvania Press, 2009); and Thomas Turner, *The Congo Wars: Conflict, Myth, and Reality* (New York: Zed Books, 2007).
21. Marie Béatrice Umutesi, *Surviving the Slaughter: The Ordeal of a Rwandan Refugee in Zaire* (Madison: University of Wisconsin Press, 2004).
22. See, for instance, Howard W. French, *A Continent for the Taking: The Tragedy and Hope of Africa* (New York: Vintage, 2007).

23. David Mwambari, "Agaciro, Vernacular Memory, and the Politics of Memory in Postgenocide Rwanda," *African Affairs* 120, no. 481 (2021): 623.
24. Des Forges, *Leave None to Tell the Story*, 546–547.
25. Ibid., 547.
26. Senga, interview with the author in Kigali, Rwanda, June 2014.
27. See Assumpta Mugiraneza, "Les écueils dans l'appréhension de l'histoire du génocide des Tutsi," *Revue d'histoire de la Shoah* Janvier–Juin (2009): 190.
28. Erin Jessee who conducted fieldwork in this period, notes seeing changes even among guides at memorial sites. See Erin Jessee, *Negotiating Genocide in Rwanda: The Politics of History* (New York: Springer, 2017), 69.
29. See United Nations, *Convention on the Prevention and Punishment of the Crime of Genocide* (New York: United Nations, 1960).
30. In this video, now available on the internet, then-President Bizimungu is seen starting applause to encourage the audience to acknowledge this moment in history, perhaps showing that some negotiations concerning what the United States should acknowledge may have taken place before the speech. See Ikaze Iwacu, "Bill Clinton Visits Rwanda—March 26, 1998," YouTube.com, 2013, https://www.youtube.com/watch?v=avJr2qRbPcQ&ab_channel=IkazeIwacu.
31. On the impact of Clinton visit to Rwanda, see Paul Williams, *Memorial Museums: The Global Rush to Commemorate Atrocities* (Oxford, UK: Berg, 2007), 80.
32. By the time Kofi Annan was visiting, the United Nations had established the International Criminal Tribunal for Rwanda (ICTR) to deal with first-class crimes committed during the genocide. However, the ICTR itself has been criticized for its slow pace, requiring large amounts of funds, and not persecuting RPF crimes.
33. For full discussion on why this mission failed, see Jason A. Edwards, "The Mission of Healing: Kofi Annan's Failed Apology," *Atlantic Journal of Communication* 16, no. 2 (2008): 88–104. Annan gives his own account in his 2012 memoir: Kofi A. Annan and Nader Mousavizadeh, *Interventions: A Life in War and Peace* (New York: Penguin, 2013).
34. On Peacekeepers, see Wouter Reggers, Valérie Rosoux, and David Mwambari, "In Memory of Peacekeepers: Belgian Blue Helmets and Belgian Politics," *International Peacekeeping* 29, no. 2 (2022): 1–24.
35. Joseph Sebarenzi and Laura Mullane, *God Sleeps in Rwanda: A Journey of Transformation* (Oxford, UK: Oneworld, 2009). In Chapter 7, where Sebarenzi discusses both Clinton's and Kofi Annan's visits and interprets their reception by RPF elites, he argues that while the RPF applauded Clinton, they refused to meet Annan at a reception and instead asked Sebarenzi to receive him as head of Parliament. Annan was perceived as if he did not cooperate.
36. *Gacaca* courts are community courts established in 2001 to deal with the bulk of genocide cases in the aftermath of the Genocide Against the Tutsi in Rwanda. They were adopted from an ancient practice in Rwanda, according to which community members formed an informal court to deal with family and social conflicts in communities. The process relies on elders and those considered people of integrity in the community, not lawyers and judges. Most analysts have noted that this process was severely hampered by lack of resources (i.e., the country had only ten lawyers and

very weak judicial institutions) for trying cases and also by lack of political will. See, for example, Filip Reyntjens, "Rwanda: Genocide and Beyond," *Journal of Refugee Studies* 9, no. 3 (1996): 240–251.

37. Philip Clark gives an example of gacaca that is perceived by researchers to have been dictated from high-ranking government elites. However, in the following article he shows how gacaca evolved out of debates and also highlights, by documenting his extensive fieldwork, how citizens have participated in the implementation of gacaca justice: "Bringing the Peasants Back in, Again: State Power and Local Agency in Rwanda's Gacaca Courts," *Journal of Eastern African Studies* 8, no. 2 (2014): 193–213.

38. According to an Amnesty International report, *Rwanda—Gacaca: A Question of Justice* (London: Amnesty International, International Secretariat, 2002), Rwanda had only ten qualified lawyers in the country.

39. Lemarchand and Niwese, "Mass Murder, the Politics of Memory and Post-genocide Reconstruction," 83.

40. Brandstetter, *Contested Pasts*, 14.

41. After his resignation, Bizimungu was a free man until 2004, when he was arrested and given a 15-year sentence in what was perceived as a politically motivated case. He had fallen out with high-ranking RPF colleagues over cabinet positions and was also accused of plotting to destabilize the nation. However, after serving only 3 years of his sentence, he was released through a presidential pardon on April 6, 2007. See Arthur Asiimwe, "Rwanda's Ex-President Freed from Prison," *Reuters (Kigali)* April 6, 2007, https://www.reuters.com/article/us-rwanda-president/rwandas-ex-president-freed-from-prison-idUSL0650070720070406.

42. Sebarenzi, a Tutsi survivor and, from 1997 to 2000, speaker of Parliament, then explains that he increasingly became frustrated. (Sebarenzi's autobiography offers the best published account of this period, especially Chapters 8, 9, and 10.) When he resigned as speaker in 2000, he fled Rwanda. He explains in his autobiography that he found it hard to establish an independent parliament because the RPF dismissed his claims and maintained he was an extremist. He also found it difficult to negotiate and work with the then-vice president, Paul Kagame, who was the "man" behind the scenes and had a lot of power and influence. See Sebarenzi and Mullane, *God Sleeps in Rwanda*.

43. The Rwandan government enacted a number of laws after the genocide, proscribing "genocide ideology," "genocide minimization," and "negationism." See Constitution of the Republic of Rwanda, supra note 4; "Law No. 33bis/2003, Repressing the Crime of Genocide, Crimes against Humanity and War Crimes, art. 9," Official Gazette of Rwanda, November 1, 2003; and "Law No. 18/2008, Relating to the Punishment of the Crime of Genocide Ideology," Official Gazette of Rwanda, October 15, 2008.

44. Joseph Sebarenzi and Laura Mullane, *God Sleeps in Rwanda: A Journey of Transformation*.

45. For a detailed analysis of complexities of Kibeho camp killing, see Kimonyo, *Popular Genocide*, 101–103; and outside Rwanda in refugee camps in DRC, see Prunier, *Africa's World War*, 37–67.

46. Also see Jean Paul Kimonyo, *Transforming Rwanda: Challenges on the Road to Reconstruction* (Lynne Rienner, 2019), 190.

47. Kimonyo, *Transforming Rwanda*, 193. Tom Ndahiro offers a good analysis in "Genocide-Laundering: Historical Revisionism, Genocide Denial and the Role of the Rassemblement Républicain pour la Démocratie au Rwanda," in *After Genocide: Transitional Justice, Post-conflict Reconstruction and Reconciliation in Rwanda and Beyond*, eds. Philip Clark and Zachary D. Kaufman (Oxford: Oxford University Press, 2013), 311–320.
48. See minutes in this document: Office of the President of the Republic, *Report on the Reflection Meetings Held in the Office of the President of the Republic from May 1998 to March 1999*, Kigali: Republic of Rwanda, 1999. https://repositories.lib.utexas.edu/bitstream/handle/2152/4907/2378.pdf;sequence=1.
49. Kimonyo, *Transforming Rwanda*, 195.
50. This was evidenced by various stories published in high-profile newspapers, such as Marc Lacey, "10 Years Later in Rwanda, the Dead Are Ever Present," *New York Times*, February 26, 2004. http://www.nytimes.com/2004/02/26/world/10-years-later-in-rwanda-the-dead-are-ever-present.html. See also "Rwanda Marks Genocide Anniversary," *One-Minute World News*, BBC, April 6, 2004. http://news.BBC.co.uk/1/hi/world/africa/3602859.stm. Many TV programs reflected a similar growth in international attention toward the memory of the Rwandan genocide; for example, the much-viewed PBS *Frontline* episode "Ghosts of Rwanda" premiered on April 1, 2004 (excerpts can be watched at http://www.pbs.org/wgbh/pages/frontline/shows/ghosts/video/).
51. Philip Gourevitch, *We Wish to Inform You That Tomorrow We Will Be Killed with Our Families: Stories from Rwanda* (London: Picador, 1998).
52. Lemarchand, *The Dynamics of Violence in Central Africa*, 88.
53. Bert Ingelaere, "Do We Understand Life after Genocide?: Center and Periphery in the Construction of Knowledge in Postgenocide Rwanda," *African Studies Review* 53, no. 1 (2010): 41–59.
54. The *Hotel Rwanda* narrative was at first well received in Kigali, but the government soon learned that the man behind it, Paul Rusesabagina (the hotel manager who protected refugees in his hotel), was working with the Rwandan diaspora, which had been forced into opposition, and that he was going around the United States constructing a narrative different from the memory being systematized. He was fought at every level and labeled as a genocide denier. However, the systematization of official memorialization still benefited from *Hotel Rwanda*. Members of the public rarely examined these sorts of debates. Other movies, though not very popular, such as *100 Days* (2001) and *Sometimes in April* (2005), also contributed to this internationalization.
55. David Mwambari, "Emergence of Post-genocide Collective Memory in Rwanda's International Relations," in *Beyond History: African Agency in Development, Diplomacy, and Conflict Resolution*, eds Elijah Munyi, David Mwambari, and Alexi Ylonen (London: Rowman & Littlefield International, 2020), 118-137.
56. It is disputed in literature whether these were genocidal killings; see Mahmood Mamdani, *Saviors and Survivors: Darfur, Politics, and the War on Terror* (New York: Pantheon, 2009).

57. See "Rwandan Soldiers Arrive in Sudan," in *One-Minute World News*, BBC, August 15, 2004, http://news.BBC.co.uk/2/hi/africa/3562096.stm.
58. For a critical perspective, see Jennie E. Burnet, "The Injustice of Local Justice: Truth, Reconciliation, and Revenge in Rwanda," *Genocide Studies and Prevention* 3, no. 2 (2008): 173–193. For a more recent assessment of the gacaca courts after their closing. See also Clark, *The Gacaca Courts,* and Lars Waldorf, "Rwanda's Failing Experiment in Restorative Justice," in *Handbook of Restorative Justice: A Global Perspective*, eds. Dennis Sullivan and Larry Tifft (London: Routledge, 2006), 422–434.; Anuradha Chakravarty, *Investing in Authoritarian Rule Punishment and Patronage in Rwanda's Gacaca Courts for Genocide Crimes* (Cambridge: Cambridge University Press, 2016); and Bert Ingelaere, *Inside Rwanda's Gacaca Courts: Seeking Justice after Genocide* (Madison: University of Wisconsin Press, 2018).
59. The shift in language to naming Tutsi reflects emphasizes one of the International Convention's criteria for describing an action or event as genocide: Killings must have targeted a particular group. Hence, for Rwanda, the Tutsi were the targeted "ethnic" group. Other criteria of the International Convention include the following: "(a) Killing members of the group; (b) Causing serious bodily or mental harm to members of the group; (c) Deliberately inflicting on the group conditions of life calculated to bring about its physical destruction in whole or in part; (d) Imposing measures intended to prevent births within the group." See United Nations, *Convention on the Prevention and Punishment of the Crime of Genocide* (New York: United Nations, 1960).
60. Kimonyo, *Transforming Rwanda*, 77, 194.
61. See Naasson Munyandamutsa, Paul Mahoro Nkubamugisha, Marianne Gex-Fabry, and Ariel Eytan, "Mental and Physical Health in Rwanda 14 Years after the Genocide," *Social Psychiatry and Psychiatric Epidemiology* 47, no. 11 (2012): 1753–1761; also Darius Gishoma and Jean-Luc Brackelaire, "Quand le corps abrite l'inconcevable, comment dire le bouleversement dont témoignent les corps au Rwanda?" *Cahiers de psychologie clinique* 30, no. 1 (2008): 159–183.
62. Gishoma and Brackelaire, "Quand le corps abrite l'inconcevable, comment dire le bouleversement dont témoignent les corps au Rwanda?", 158.
63. Ibid., 158.
64. Ibid., 161.
65. Ibid., 161.
66. Esther Marijnen and Jaïr der van Lijn, "Rwanda 2025: Scenarios for the Future Political Stability of Rwanda," in *Rwanda Fast Forward Social, Economic, Military and Reconciliation Prospect*, eds. Maddalena Campioni and Patrick Noack (London: Palgrave Macmillan, 2012), 13–28.
67. For politics of reconciliation and experiments of Rwandan government, see Andrea Purdeková, *Making Ubumwe: Power, State and Camps in Rwanda's Unity-Building Project* (New York: Berghahn Books, 2015), especially 11–15.
68. See Kwibuka's *New Times* article on the framing of this discussion: Eugene Kwibuka, "What Does 'Ndi Unuyarwanda' Mean to You?" *New Times (Kigali)*, December 3, 2013, http://www.newtimes.co.rw/section/article/2013-12-03/71264/.

69. " Genocide commemoration week taken to village level." https://www.newtimes.co.rw/article/87822/National/genocide-commemoration-week-taken-to-village-level.
70. Republic of Rwanda, "The 19th Commemoration of the 1994 Genocide against Tutsi Will Be Marked in Each Umudugudu Village under the Theme 'Let Us Commemorate the Tutsi Genocide as We Strive for Self Reliance'," 2013, https://web.archive.org/web/20130218063625/http://www.gov.rw/The-19th-Commemoration-of-the-1994-Genocide-against-Tutsi-will-be-marked-in-each-Umudugudu-village-under-the-theme-Let-us-commemorate-the-Tutsi-Genocide-as-we-strive-for-self-reliance.
71. Catharine Newbury, *The Cohesion of Oppression: Clientship and Ethnicity in Rwanda, 1860–1960* (New York: Columbia University Press, 1994); Prunier, *Rwanda Crisis*.
72. Dixon Kamukama, *Rwanda Conflict: Its Roots and Regional Implications* (Kampala, Uganda: Fountain, 1998), 9. See also Alison Liebhafsky Des Forges, *Defeat Is the Only Bad News: Rwanda under Musinga, 1897–1931* (Madison: University of Wisconsin Press, 2011). Also relevant is René Lemarchand, *Rwanda and Burundi* (London: Pall Mall, 1970).
73. For more context on various factors that caused the Congo wars between 1994 and 2004, see Timothy Raeymaekers and Koen Vlassenroot, *Conflict and Social Transformation in Eastern D R Congo* (Ghent, Belgium: Academia, 2004). See also Macharia Munene, "Mayi Mayi and Interahamwe Militias: Threats to Peace and Security in the Great Lakes Region," in *Civil Militia: Africa's Intractable Security Menace?*, ed. David J. Francis (Burlington, VT: Ashgate, 2005), 251–280.
74. Bert Ingelaere, *Inside Rwanda's/Gacaca/Courts: Seeking Justice after Genocide* (Madison: University of Wisconsin Press, 2016), 109–110.
75. Yuko Otake, "Suffering of Silenced People in Northern Rwanda," *Social Science & Medicine* 222 (2019), 172.
76. Richard Benda, *Youth Connekt Dialogue: Unwanted Legacies, Responsibility and Nation-Building in Rwanda* (working paper 001, Nottingham, UK: Aegis Trust, September 2017), https://www.genocideresearchhub.org.rw/document/youth-connekt-dialogue-unwanted-legacies-responsibility-and-nation-building-in-rwanda/
77. Jean de la Croix Tabaro, "Genocide Commemoration Week Taken to Village Level," *New Times (Kigali)* February 8, 2013, https://www.newtimes.co.rw/article/87822/National/genocide-commemoration-week-taken-to-village-level.
78. Interview with a member of the committee that was involved in early debates and worked in security in the first two decades Kigali, Rwanda, January 3, 2020.
79. Interview with R. A., January 3, 2020, Nairobi, Kenya.
80. Aloisea Inyumba, "Restoring Human Dignity and Reconciling the People of Rwanda," *JENdA: A Journal of Culture and African Women Studies* 10 (2007).
81. Ibid.
82. This switch of colors of mourning is further explored in Chapter 4, on materials of memory. See also Ange de la Victoire Dusabemungu, "It's Grey Not Purple for Genocide Commemoration," IGIHE, August 2, 2013, https://en.igihe.com/news/it-s-grey-not-purple-for-genocide-commemoration.

83. For more on the Bizimungu presidency, see Reyntjens, "Constructing the Truth," and Kimonyo, *Transforming Rwanda*, 164–165, talks about his appointment and reasons for tensions within the RPF. Kimonyo's arrest and release are also detailed.
84. Inyumba, "Restoring Human Dignity."
85. See Note 13.
86. Kigero Muhire, "Analyse de la commémoration du génocide des Tutsis dans le contexte socio-politique du Rwanda: 'Cas du District de Gasabo'" (BA, Université Nationale du Rwanda, 2011), 69.
87. National Unity and Reconciliation Commission, *Rwanda Reconciliation Barometer* (Kigali: Republic of Rwanda, 2010). For a critical perspective on reconciliation and state building see also Purdeková, *Making Ubumwe*.
88. Republic of Rwanda, *Rwanda Reconciliation Barometer*, 10.
89. Jessee, Erin, and David Mwambari. "Memory Law and the Duty to Remember the '1994 Genocide Against the Tutsi' in Rwanda." In *Memory Laws and Historical Justice: The Politics of Criminalizing the Past*, pp. 291–319. Cham: Springer International Publishing, 2022.
90. For a discussion of these laws, see Martin Ngoga, "Why Rwanda Needs the Law Repressing Genocide Denial and Ideology," *Umuvugizi (Kigali)* June 4, 2011, https://umuvugizi.wordpress.com/2011/06/04/why-rwanda-needs-the-law-repressing-genocide-denial-and-ideology/.
91. Ibid.
92. For a detailed study of genocide denial laws and genocide denial politics, Lars Waldorf provides the most balanced and detailed account of how these laws evolved and why, as well as the politics around them. His research is based on fieldwork carried out in Rwanda. See Lars Waldorf, "Revisiting Hotel Rwanda: Genocide Ideology, Reconciliation, and Rescuers," *Journal of Genocide Research* 11, no. 1 (2009): 101–125. See also Kimonyo, *Transforming Rwanda*, 181–191.
93. Waldorf, "Revisiting Hotel Rwanda," 102.
94. See Waldorf, "Revising Hotel Rwanda," 106, and Jessee, *Negotiating Genocide in Rwanda*, 52. The debates on freedom of speech in postgenocide Rwanda were especially brought into international discourse in 2010, when American lawyer Peter Erlinder was prosecuted, convicted, and imprisoned by the Rwandan government. He had previously been at ICTR in the defense team for one of the genocide suspects, and he had come to Rwanda to defend an opposition politician named Victoire Ingabire, who was accused under the denialism law. Erlinder was the first non-Rwandan to receive this verdict.
95. See Ibuka's strategic plan for 2011–2015 in "Ibuka Strategic Plan, 2011–2015," Ibuka Survivors Fund, http://survivors-fund.org.uk/wp-content/uploads/2011/11/IBUKA-Strategic-Plan-2011-2015.pdf; there are other websites for Ibuka's association in different countries, like the one in Rwanda (https://ibuka.rw) or in Belgium (https://ibuka.be).
96. See "What We Do: Avega Agahozo," SURF (Survivors Fund), accessed August 16, 2012, https://avega-agahozo.org/about/#:~:text=What%20We%20Do,including%20peace%2Dbuilding%20and%20reconciliation.

97. Ibid.
98. For another survivors' organization, see Ibuka's website: "Memoire & Justice," Belgium, Ibuka Belgique, http://www.ibuka.be/.
99. On a recent field trip in 2011 and 2012, I attended two of these kinds of events. They were organized by AERG in universities, and the organizers used the opportunity to create awareness of the plight of survivors, especially young orphans. It was well attended, and participants used videos, music, and other activities discussed in further chapters to pass on different messages, including educational ones.
100. Republic of Rwanda (RoR), "Law N° 02/98 of 22/01/1998. Establishing a National Assistance Fund for Needy Victims of Genocide and Massacres Committed in Rwanda between 1 October 1990 and 31 December 1994," 1998, accessed April 1, 2019, http://www.refworld.org/cgi-bin/texis/vtx/rwmain/opendocpdf.pdf?reldoc=y&docid=52df99854.
101. Otake, "Suffering of Silenced People in Northern Rwanda," 172.
102. On aid politics in Rwanda, including budget cuts and how it shaped Rwanda international relations, see Haley J. Swedlund, *The Development Dance: How Donors and Recipients Negotiate the Delivery of Foreign Aid* (Ithaca, NY: Cornell University Press, 2017). On how funding was driven by outsiders, see Barbara Oomen, "Donor-Driven Justice and Its Discontents: The Case of Rwanda," *Development and Change* 36, no. 5 (2005): 887–910. On history of aid in Rwanda more generally, see Peter Uvin, *Aiding Violence: The Development Enterprise in Rwanda* (Boulder, CO: Kumarian Press, 1998).
103. Kimonyo, *Transforming Rwanda*, 103.
104. The United Kingdom's Department for International Development has been one of the major funders to restore the Ntarama Church Memorial for the preservation of skulls and bones. See "UK International Development Minister Lynne Featherstone Visits Ntarama Genocide Memorial Site," GOV.UK, June 2, 2014, https://www.gov.uk/government/news/uk-international-development-minister-lynne-featherstone-visits-ntarama-genocide-memorial-site.
105. Buckley-Zistel, "Remembering to Forget," 133.
106. For counternarratives and how laws are applied to punish those who question official remembrances, see Chapters 4, 5, and 6 in this book.
107. Susanne Buckley-Zistel, "Development Assistance and Conflict Assessment Methodology," *Journal for Conflict, Security and Development* 3 (2003): 1.
108. Timothy Longman, *Memory and Justice in Post-genocide Rwanda* (New York: Cambridge University Press, 2017).

4
Imprinting the Land with the Materials of Memory

> Everybody wants a memorial. . . . But the whole country can't be covered with memorials. We're a small country. We can't live with that kind of chaos.
>
> —Idelphonse Karengera[1]

During my research in Rwanda in 2009, I finally worked up the strength to visit our former home in what was known in pregenocide Rwanda as Butare préfecture, later renamed Huye district in southern Rwanda. Butare has remained the name of the main town in the district. Its border with Burundi allowed many people to cross and escape death—at least those who had the means and information, which was not our family. For a while Butare town in particular was a safe haven for many who fled the genocidal killings or in fear of the Rwandan Patriotic Army (RPA) attacks pursuing the Forces Armées Rwandaises (FAR), who pushed toward the south once they lost Kigali.[2] However, when the Minister for Family Welfare Pauline Nyaramasuhuko arrived in Butare from Kigali fleeing the RPA, she replaced Mayor Jean Baptiste Habyarimana, who had resisted participating in the genocide, with a Hutu radical, Sylvain Nsabimana. Butare had boasted of hosting many Tutsi, including the academic elite, as it was a university town and many who were in mixed marriages with Hutu. At different points between April and July, we in the south were caught in between bombs, grenade attacks in the night from the RPA trying to capture the city, and killings with machetes in the early mornings from the radical Hutu youth groups.

During my research visit, I longed to trace and retrieve my individual memory of my childhood in Butare. It was a hard place to go to and reflect on how lucky we were to escape. Not far from our former neighborhood is a genocide memorial where some of my childhood friends are buried. We were fortunate to escape death at many roadblocks with the assistance of many friends, who sacrificed their lives to get us out of town. Stories told at memorials in this particular neighborhood were the most disturbing in my research, and I did not include them in my dissertation or this book. The names of killers, rescuers, and those of my childhood friends—victims—are still difficult to think through.[3]

One of the memorials I visited many times during my frequent visits to Rwanda, and where I attended commemoration, was constructed next to a familiar road. The road is reminiscent of the proverb *Inzira ntibwira umugenzi*, meaning "the pathway does not warn the traveler what lies ahead." It was the road we took to school, to town, and to church with friends during my childhood, and it was the same road we used to flee in 1994. It was the road on which I had seen the first body of a dead person, killed in a car accident. As a child coming from church one Sunday in 1993, it was a brutal, memorable place. Then the genocide happened, and there were more dead bodies on the same road, this time of innocent victims of the genocide, including my classmates and former neighbors. The walk past the university was no longer the same. It was no longer the university where I spent my childhood dreaming that I too would study one day. A memorial with remains of professors, students, and other Tutsi, Hutus who attempted to rescue the Tutsi who were killed in this part of Butare was built near a place that had a deadly roadblock. Images of not only the accident but also those roadblocks haunt me to this day as do many others, including some of my interlocutors during this research.[4] Memorials of the genocide are one of the most noticeable features of the postgenocide Rwandan landscape, everyday reminders to Rwandans of this violent past and that deep-seated undeniable reality that no Rwandan is immune to the legacies of the 1994 genocide.

This chapter demonstrates how physical space in postgenocide Rwanda was used to inscribe symbolic representations of the master narrative of genocide memory that furthered its institutionalization and it becoming a hegemonic master narrative imprinted in Rwanda's hills. It explores how genocide memorials lie at the heart of creating cultural memory where individual and social memory converge to allow the master narrative to emerge, evolve, and travel to different generations and geographies. I argue that the physical manifestation of memory, due to its tangible and visible nature, has afforded the master narrative more durability and permanence than laws, annual commemoration themes, and rituals. I also argue, however, that the permanence of these physical symbols is only in appearance because the physical materials of memory and their meaning have changed over time.

First, I trace the emergence of memorials after the genocide and the manner in which they evolved and were inscribed—and re-inscribed—onto the Rwandan physical landscape. Second, I examine the creation of the Kigali Genocide Memorial (KGM) and how the master narrative was advanced within it. The KGM remains one of the most prominent national memorials, visited by thousands of Rwandan and international guests each year. Third, I consider other commemoration sites, such as Bisesero, Murambi, Rebero, Nyamata, Ntarama, Nyarubuye, and Nyanza-Kicukiro, whose scope and influence evolved substantially over time and whose statuses were elevated to parallel that of the KGM. Finally, I highlight the surfacing tensions between the needs of Champions, Fatalists, and Antagonists in the process of changing physical materials of memory. The complex interactions between government, community, and memorial space point to the "untidiness" of the symbolic, physical representation of memory and to contradictions that threaten the purported permanence of memorial sites after the mass atrocities.

Materials of Memory after Mass Atrocities

Memorials, monuments, museums, banners, and colors have become important means through which commemoration of mass atrocities and disasters in many societies are commemorated, in Western countries especially.[5] For example, governments, religious institutions, individuals, and the general public in Europe and the United States and later in other parts of the world[6] have used materials of memory to remember fallen soldiers in the world wars and victims of the Holocaust for decades.[7] A more recent example is the construction of United States' 9/11 memorials in New York, which have received international recognition.[8] In many societies, materials of memory are employed through communal activities to enact rituals for remembrance.

Some of the literature on mass atrocities claims that images, symbols, and narratives used in memorialization promote master narratives and occupy an important place in the recovery of post–mass atrocity societies.[9] These needs include the need to mourn collectively for victims of a nation, and they play a crucial role in allowing memories to travel to a younger generation continually haunted by the legacies of a violent past.[10] A society that has suffered mass atrocities often addresses these needs so that citizens can work through their trauma and tap into the bounds needed to rebuild the nation, although this is not always the case given the same processes can lead to many becoming disillusioned and not interested, like the Fatalists in this study.

Unlike cemeteries, which tend to be for private visits and came to be perceived as sites for private spaces for familial visits, memorials and other materials of memory serve many purposes, both private and public. They include education, collective mourning, and engaging outsiders who might even disagree with the master narrative promoted in such sites through dark tourism.[11] Physical symbols and spaces of memory are crucial in shaping individual and collective imagination of the past and in constructing a community's future after mass atrocities.[12] In recent years, there has been an increase in the construction of memorials commissioned with remembering the atrocities of a nation's recent past, including the genocides in Rwanda, Cambodia, and Bosnia; the violent repressions in Argentina and Chile; and the wars of liberation in Bangladesh, Israel, and Palestine.[13] These relatively recent memorials have generated spaces that not only welcome citizens to gather in order to ritualize the victims of those mass deaths but also have resulted into controversies and conflicts. However, these sites used to uphold and represent certain memories paradoxically serve to disremember and exclude other histories of violence that might have unfolded in the same period and space but for political reasons are left out of the official memory.[14] For example, Canada, the United States, and Australia have erected many monuments to honor their Anglo-Saxon founding, mostly white men, but few are for Indigenous leaders who were mostly displaced for the sake of new European immigrants. Both democratic and less democratic societies tend to use materials of memory to represent a partial memory or to tell one story while repressing others.[15] The evolution of the memorials after the genocide in Rwanda mimicked these global practices as recognizable symbols and part of a script with "free-floating, abstract cultural conception of what 'genocide is,' and how it happens."[16] They replaced Rwanda's cultural practices of mourning the dead in some cases. In other instances, local cultural tools were employed to make them acceptable to Rwandans and foreigners alike.

Debates on the Function of Rwanda's Memorials

Scholars studying Rwanda have asked many questions about memorials and the rituals surrounding them. Burial processes are among the most controversial and puzzling in this context. The method that was adopted to keep bones in memorials was foreign to Rwandan cultural practices.[17] Before genocide memorials became part of Rwanda's landscape, there were few sites where one could learn about past violence. For instance, there were human remains displayed in the cultural museum in Butare. These were mostly for political Rwandan leaders and even then a very limited number.

To some extent Rémi Korman, Claudine Vidal, and Valerie Rosoux's works, mostly published in French, have been ignored in the anglophone literature that evolved after the tenth commemoration of the genocide.[18] Through their research, nevertheless, the details of this sensitive process, of the myriad ways in which survivors negotiated with the government concerning the presence of dead bodies, and how memorials evolved are well documented. These early works in French also contain interviews with actors, including government elites, survivors, and international figures who were more responsive in this earlier period before the master narrative unfolded. From Rémi Korman, for instance, we learn that right after the genocide, civil society actors not only explored with other models of remembering the past but also focused on what that memorialization could mean for reconciliation and reconstruction. They invited researchers working on Chile, Argentine, South Africa, Cambodia, and Bosnia,[19] but political elites ignored their recommendations. In another instance, we learn from the same author that parliamentarians also tried to propose one memorial in the center of Kigali and debated on what was appropriate within Rwandan culture to represent such genocide atrocity. They thought about one memorial in the city of Kigali that symbolized the memory of genocide survivors but debates did not go very far. This is because the Rwanda Patriotic Front (RPF) political elites in the new government did not consider their input as important.[20] Instead, their interest was to align with a more prominent narrative that was recognizable globally: the Shoah. It was for this reason that they solicited support and ideas from scholars of the Holocaust from outside Rwanda to help them shape an agenda that would lead to creation of the master narrative of the genocide. The first documented visitor to arrive in Rwanda with that mission was the Belgian historian Jean-Philippe Schreiber.[21] His recommendations to construct a culture of memorialization that borrowed from the Shoah were taken seriously and implemented over time, unlike the ideas from civil society and Parliament.

These earlier nuances are often ignored in anglophone literature on the commemoration of the genocide in Rwanda. Yet, they show how the focus on the government as the sole or the most powerful actor, as depicted by most scholars, overlooks the role played by foreigners in constructing the master narrative and its rise to hegemonic status. In these earlier processes, we learn that political elites within the postgenocide government exercised influence over the process of constructing the master narrative but not exclusively. The foreigners who aligned with the vision of the Rwandan postgenocide elites also played important roles in shaping the master narrative and its rise to hegemonic status. Apart from a handful of Tutsi survivor organizations, in most cases other civil society organizations who were deemed critical of the master narrative exercised limited power to shape the rise of the master narrative. Other scholars have argued that challenges are neutralized through a combination of coercion and co-optation.[22]

In the anglophone scholarship, Rachel Ibreck, Erin Jessee, and Timothy Longman's work stands out as they examine how memorials help construct a selective and highly politicized narrative about the genocide. Memorials such as those in Nyamata, Ntarama, Nyarubuye, Bisesero, Gisozi, and Murambi are central to debates surrounding the evolution of the master narrative, even though most research has focused on the Gisozi memorial. International and Rwandan organizations were involved in a complex and sensitive process of exhuming bodies, burying bones, and creating memorials. They often were burying anonymous victims, to the displeasure of many survivors.[23] These tensions were even clearer in 1995, right after the genocide.[24] At the time, Rwandans were "pretend[ing] to live together."[25] For Susanne Buckley-Zistel, Rwandans had "chosen amnesia" as a mechanism for community members to coexist regardless of their association with the genocide violence and civil war that had just ended.[26] Yet, there were many divisions in the postgenocide society, including on issues including selective representation in construction of the memorials.[27] For instance, there were disputes about whose body remains were buried in rivers and other special sites.[28]

Contrary to research that pointed to divisions among the postgenocide society, the divisions were often underplayed in national studies on reconciliation. For instance, the National Reconciliation Barometer argues that commemoration activities and memorials have been a crucial component of national healing and reconciliation. Through annual reports, the National

Unity and Reconciliation Commission (NURC) asserted that memorials and the practices around them help promote healing, education for younger generations, reconciliation, forgiveness, justice, and social cohesion.[29] They also serve as evidence to the younger generation of what happened and to the international community of its initial indifference to the genocide.[30] Rwandan researchers such as Philibert Gakwenzire and Célestin Kanimba agree with NURC and show the importance of memorials in eradicating denialism.[31] In addition, Darius Gishoma's research asserts that while survivors exhibit trauma when visiting memorials, this is also part of the healing process.[32]

Whichever position one takes, most will agree that the evolution of these sites has transformed and changed Rwandan society and its landscape significantly. The evolution of these memorials is part of everyday life for Rwandans, and the discourses around them have produced tensions among Champions, Fatalists, and Antagonists, like the physical manifestations of memory and other materials—such as banners, colors, and flames—suffuse the entire physical landscape.

Formalization of Materials of Memory in Postgenocide Rwanda

Memorials for Various Purposes, Addressing Various Needs

Prior to the genocide, *urwibutso* was used casually in Rwanda to mean a souvenir or a "monument."[33] Graves were referred to as *imva*. There were not, however, many physical public memorials to which these terms could be applied—none, for example, for the massacres of the 1950s–1990s or for past presidents and local heroes. In other African countries, such memorials were much more common. The construction and evolution of memorials in Rwanda not only introduced new physical structures into the country's landscape, but also popularized the term urwibutso.[34] Memorials have since evolved into respected spaces that are protected by national laws.

Immediately after the genocide, memorials were mostly constructed in areas where mass atrocities were carried out, like the memorial in Butare mentioned previously in this chapter, or where mass graves already existed. Their placement followed the vicious logics of the genocide itself, with no design other than concentration of the visible deaths. In most cases, survivors initiated these memorials and the government completed them. Later,

CNLG (La Commission Nationale de Lutte contre le Genocide [National Commission for the Fight against Genocide]) was put in charge of building official memorials and establishing laws that protect them.[35]

For the larger, better-known memorials, the government received financial assistance from international partners such as the British government through the Department for International Development (DFID); the Aegis Trust, also based in the United Kingdom; and the Rwandan diaspora. The government allocated the land for mass graves, international partners brought experts to organize disinterred bones, and after 2004 survivors' communities increasingly took charge of maintaining the memorials.[36] The memorials were to serve a variety of functions for survivors, including education. Champions of the master narrative wanted to rebury their dead with dignity, given that their bodies had been left in public in an undignified manner. Champions also wanted to create spaces to remember their dead and to give those spaces a permanent role in their lives and community.

However, with an increase in funding after the tenth anniversary from the government and other international stakeholders, the memorials addressed a variety of needs beyond those of survivors. This included teaching history to youth, providing civic education for adults, fighting genocide ideology, and promoting trauma tourism. The first memorials were criticized by some as haphazard initiatives of individuals before the government and international organizations brought in funding and organization.[37] The very disparagement of the effect behind the need to memorialize the loved ones as illegitimate was revealing—sentiment proved as good an organizing principle as any for commemorating the murder of loved ones. Notwithstanding the real significance of this sentiment, however, physical memorials evolved over time into organized institutions that are now central to the master narrative of genocide memory—just as the commemoration rituals discussed in the previous chapter evolved.[38]

It is estimated that Rwanda has around five hundred memorials,[39] and each district has at least one.[40] However, the list of memorials has also changed as a few were chosen as UNESCO World Heritage sites in 2018. Only four were listed by UNESCO: Nyamata, Murambi, Bisesero, and the Kigali Memorial Centre.[41] While the first three were massacre sites turned into burial places after the genocide, the KGM became the most prominent memorial given its location in the capital.

Several memorials also exist in remote sites in districts countrywide. There are also those dedicated to particular groups, such as the memorial for the Belgians killed in 1994 in Kigali while protecting former Prime Minister Agathe Uwilingiyimana. In addition to the memorials within Rwandan borders, several memorials have been constructed on small, unique sites outside Rwanda. These include the Lake Tanganyika memorial in Ggaba, Uganda, a site where many bodies were recovered, and a monument to remember the victims of the genocide in Rwanda in Woluwe St. Pierre, in Brussels, Belgium.

The memorials evolved alongside other physical materials that are used during commemoration and displayed at memorials throughout the year. These include banners that have different themes and colors as mentioned in the previous chapter.[42] In addition, a flame on a stand is lit at the entrance of the KGM for one hundred days, the entire mourning period. These physical materials are key as they are the visible, tangible symbols of memory displayed for Rwandans and the outside world to see.

Materials as Tools of Memory and Central to the Master Narrative

During my research from 2011 to 2014, from early April to the end of June, I found the banners that are displayed all over Kigali and in different parts of Rwanda very striking. The cloth banners are often displayed on government buildings, banks, shopping malls, and road signs, in both rural and urban spaces. For the first 18 years, a background cloth of purple dominated, on which words were displayed in white for high contrast, ensuring the text's visibility. When the mourning period ends, banners continue to be displayed on memorial sites countrywide, although not in notable public spaces. While the banners are used for the general purpose of popularizing the theme each year, they are displayed on memorial sites throughout the year to identify them. In this sense, the banners can be understood as a physical symbol that differentiates a genocide memorial from a "normal"/regular graveyard. Annalisa Bolin references a CNLG document asserting their utility:

> CNLG documentation states that it is "necessary that Genocide signs be protected" due to their importance in teaching both Rwandans and foreigners about the genocide and countering genocide ideology and denial.[43]

Three changes show how the Catholic influence was apparent in the first 20 years of commemoration and how these three aspects were changed to reduce the power these symbols had on the master narrative. While some decisions caused tensions, others were not publicly disputed by any Catholic or other church leaders.

First, the transformation of Nyamata, Ntarama, Kibeho, and Nyundo churches into memorials resulted in tensions in the early period after the genocide, even for some Champions of the master narrative.[44] These four sites were turned into memorials after a heated dispute between the government, which sought to create these memorials, and the Catholic Church, which wanted to retain their churches. This disagreement first surfaced during the construction of memorials in Kibeho. In April 1995, a group of RPA soldiers attacked the Kibeho camp of the internally displaced majority Hutus.[45] Thousands were killed according to Australians who were part of the UN mission for Rwanda.[46]

In his book *Rwanda's Popular Genocide*, Jean Paul Kimonyo explains the complexity of the Kibeho camp. He first gives details of the exodus of refugees to neighboring countries and gives about "600,000 as a number for IDPs [internally displaced persons] to Gikongoro Prefecture, 800,000 to Cyangugu and 300,000 to Kibuye," who all left for Zaire in July and in August.[47] He continues:

> After this exodus, the former Zone Turquoise continued to accommodate between 280,000 and 350,000 IDPs who were living in 38 camps. The Camp in Kibeho along with surrounding area, held 100,000 IDPs and Ndago camp 60,000. As soon as the RPA took control of the region at the end of August, violent incidents broke out between RPF soldiers and the IDPs. Some of these displaced persons would go out of the camps in order to assassinate genocide survivors in the vicinity before returning to their base. Most of the camps in the former Zone Turquoise, especially at Kibeho, were controlled by groups still committed to the genocidal project. These gangs recruited and provided military training inside the camps and prevented other IDPs from leaving. This armed opposition was to end nine months later in an especially violent manner during the massacre at Kibeho camp.[48]

Allison Des Forges also detailed other killings that individual battalions in the RPA committed in various regions of Rwanda. The reasons for killing varied, including targeting those suspected to have participated in the genocide, targeting specific politicians, and self-defense.[49] As discussed previously, the Kibeho violence has become a key source of tension for Antagonists of the master narrative. However, while Kibeho remains a thorn in the RPF's side, it is also a place of hope and faith in postgenocide Rwanda. Kibeho is also the place where it is said the Virgin Mary appeared on November 28, 1981, according to testimonies from three women who were present—Alphonsine Mumureke, Nathalie Mukamazimpaka, and Marie Claire Mukangango. It is telling that such a place, where a respected religious symbol of mercy, love, and grace in Catholicism appeared was also the place of controversial killings, destruction, and genocide. Even with such tragedy and tensions, it has continued to enjoy popularity and become a place for prayer, forgiveness, and home to many.[50]

My interviewee told me that "survivors fought for the dignity of the loved ones. It was a long case that resulted in Ministry of Justice intervening to put an end to the disputes. Similar tensions developed between survivors and local administrators in Nyundo and Gikongoro Parish."[51]

To resolve the tension in Kibeho, an interviewee who worked at the Kibeho memorial as a researcher told me, they divided the church into two sections. When asked about refugees who died in Kibeho, his response was complex and had a warning. He asserted:

> Kibeho is controversial? RPF was hated and there were acts of resistance. . . . Kibeho was considered by Hutu radicals as a place Tutsis were taking refugee to attack the Hutus. Many people who talk about it don't know the details or give right facts. Kibeho is sensitive as it is a location that some of those who reject commemoration use as a site for double genocide comparing the genocide killings of 1994 to those of RPF destroying the refugee camp in 1995.[52]

As the Rwandan priest told me, Catholic leaders in Rwanda took time to reflect on their position, their priests, and their actions during the Genocide Against the Tutsi.[53] Like them, the Vatican, including the Pope, kept silent or denied any wrongdoing whenever confronted by international media.[54] Pope John Paul II, who visited Rwanda just before the genocide and a month before the RPA attacked, refused to acknowledge the role of the Catholic Church or its priests in the genocide. This resistance produced a complicated relationship between the government, survivors, and the church in general, and sometimes generated outright hostility during the mourning period in particular.[55]

A second change that raised tensions among Rwandan society and survivors was the change of the color of remembering from purple to gray. An interviewee who was involved in the committee that advised on these decisions in the early 2000s gave reasons for the thinking around changing the color at the time:

> It was a big debate amongst Champions that the Catholic Church was having a monopoly over ownership of commemoration symbols. As advisors of CNLG we agreed that the Genocide Against the Tutsi affected Rwandans of different faiths not just Christians. We had been using purple as the color of remembrance without giving it much though because it was done that way for majority victims who were Christian. The same thing with the symbol of the Cross that had been put on memorials. When we debated, we wanted to remove this Christian aspect and make commemoration neutral.[56]

Changes in color used during commemoration did not cause as much tension. The government representative explained that the change was necessary to distinguish with colors used in burials for Christians. In other words, it was to confirm that genocide commemorations were for every Tutsi victim regardless of their religious affiliation. CNLG advisors and survivors' associations recommended the changes to the government, which adopted the changes. They then had to discuss it with Catholic leaders to ensure it did not increase the already existing tensions around other issues relating to the genocide.

In discussing the changes publicly, then-CNLG Executive Secretary Jean de Dieu Mucyo asserted: "We searched for information from people who are knowledgeable in Rwandan traditions like intellectuals and elders in order to choose what colour use during the week of mourning." He continued: "We realized that, traditionally, Rwandans were mourning their beloved ones by putting wood ashes upon their heads."[57] In addition, Ibuka's president, Dr. Jean Pierre Dusingizemungu, argued: "There is no reason why this colour [purple] should be used in the mourning week while there is another one that connects better with our traditional mourning events."[58] Their comments were consistent with those previously made by the minister of sports and culture, who had emphasized a focus on community-centered commemorations in order to "eventually create ownership of the commemoration activities."[59]

Although no public criticism, either spoken or written, from Rwandans or outsiders appeared in the months following the decision, I followed discussions and rumors in small groups of friends during my visit to Rwanda in 2013. Some interviewees I spoke to suspected that it was a money-making gimmick intended to benefit certain entrepeneurs given all the materials around memorials, T-shirts worn at commemorations, and other materials that had to be reprinted. Others saw the reasons as neutral. Notwithstanding these privately expressed doubts, in April 2013 the color change took effect, and this changed the way people often reacted to materials of memory. Gray seemed lighter and seemingly did not convey the same intensity, depth of sorrow, or darkness of mood that purple commanded. In many ways, the fact that Catholic Church leaders endorsed the new color and did not contest it—at least publicly—showed that relations between the government and the Catholic Church were improving. Indeed, religious leaders from Catholic, Anglican, and Muslim communities were becoming supporters of the master narrative and other government initiatives generally after many years of pursuing them. By 2014, when I was concluding my first phase of research, many masses I attended announced the program and activities of local commemoration during their gatherings. The master narrative and commemoration were starting to become part of national cultural practices with religious leaders' and other social influencers' endorsement. The church pulpits became the most effective mobilizer for the master narrative given the spiritual and moral force they still command among Rwandans despite the churches' reputation that was damaged in the genocide.

A third significant innovation around commemoration that reduced the influence of the Catholic Church was replacing the cross—that predominantly Christians identified with—with the flame, seen as a neutral symbol of hope for the future. Flames of remembrance were probably adopted from non-Rwandan practices since they have historically had no relevance in Rwanda. A flame is usually lit at the start of the mourning period on April 7 and stays at the KGM until the end of the commemoration period in July. When I visited other memorials around the country, I did not see a flame being lit in the same way and with the same meaning. Instead, the flame would be passed on like the Olympic torch in different parts of the country just before the commemoration period. At best, it resembled the Jewish practice of lighting a memorial candle on the anniversary of a death and perhaps also those used at various shrines of remembrance around the world.[60] Thus, over time with these changes of symbols more Christian leaders became part of Champions of the master narrative or at least sympathetic to commemorations.

Formalizing Memorial Sites

Kigali Genocide Memorial

Memorial museums emerged out of a paradigm shift within societies from celebrating past triumph to reflecting honestly on past grief and coming to terms with less honorable histories.[61] Unlike other memorial sites in Rwanda, the KGM is a memorial museum that adheres to international standards. Its knowledge preservation and data storage resemble those of the United States Holocaust Memorial Museum in Washington, DC; the United Kingdom's Beth Shalom Holocaust Center; and the Yad Vashem in Jerusalem.

The KGM is located in the Kigali neighborhood of Gisozi in the Gasabo District. It is perhaps the most important memorial that Champions have established, with a clear goal of making a particular narrative of memory permanent. A statement on the KGM's website reads:

> The Kigali Memorial Centre was officially opened on the 10th Anniversary of the Rwandan Genocide, in April 2004. The Centre is built on a site where over 250,000 people are buried. These graves are a clear reminder of the cost of ignorance. The Centre is a permanent memorial to those who fell victim to the genocide and serves as a place for people to grieve those they lost.[62]

By establishing it in such a central location, the government aimed to distinguish this museum/memorial site from other sites around Rwanda. KGM represents a static version of the genocide narrative and memory as it was articulated in the early 2000s, when that memory was already relatively stable. Unlike earlier ad hoc, spontaneous memorials, the KGM was created de novo under state directive at a moment when what was to be commemorated was already very clearly, officially codified. Its organization and methodical curatorship stand in a kind of symmetry with the government's narrative. The KGM is central to Rwandan postgenocide politics. It is also a prominent feature associated with the experience of visiting in Rwanda for large numbers of international guests. Since its opening in 2004, each dignitary who visits Rwanda visits the KGM. Many groups of Rwandans also organize visits. The highest number of guests usually come between April and June. However, fewer foreigners visit the KGM in April, perhaps because they fear being entrapped in violent outbreaks that occasionally manifest during commemoration ceremonies—as observed in 2008 and 2009 at the KGM itself—or are afraid to express their own sorrow in front of survivors during such a vital period.[63] The distribution of visitors fluctuates according to these annual patterns, but over the years the number of visitors has progressively increased, and the number of visitors remain substantial across the year; they are not merely a transient phenomenon confined to the peak commemoration period in April.

Following Bill Clinton's and Kofi Annan's first visits in 1998, discussed in a previous chapter, the 1994 genocide in Rwanda gained renewed national and international attention. At the same time survivors, in the new government, were lobbying for a memorial in a central location. During my visit in 2011, a genocide survivor informed me that Gisozi was one of the first locations in Kigali to be liberated by the RPF in 1994.[64] The KGM occupies dual significance in RPF mythology as it is both a site of victory and a site of tragedy, a space to commemorate military liberation and to grieve the killing of Tutsi that was ended by the RPF's victory.[65]

Although it is not officially documented, the Kigali residents that I spoke to informed me that the former mayor of Kigali, Théoneste Mutsindashyaka, spearheaded the construction of the KGM. Mutsindashyaka, one of the most influential genocide survivors, held key positions in postgenocide Rwanda.[66] The site was selected in 1999 when Marc Kabandana was the mayor of Kigali; however, the actual work on the building started in 2000 and was designed by a Rwandan architect.[67] While the work commenced as a national project, it evolved into an international partnership that combined elements of local and international commemoration rituals. In 2001, the new mayor, Mutsindashyaka, along with other government officials, approached the Aegis Trust, a British nongovernmental organization, to partner with Rwandan actors in constructing and maintaining the KGM.[68]

As mentioned previously, one of the first prominent visitors to the KGM was Kofi Annan. Kofi Annan was a controversial personality in postgenocide Rwanda given he had been the head of UN peacekeeping operations that the RPF elites argued had failed to prevent and stop the genocide. His first official visit was therefore not a coincidence but he was also not the most wanted state guest to visit Rwanda. He did not receive a warm welcome also for his second visit in 2001. RPF political elites in the government did not like his criticism of their postgenocide government's approach to rebuilding Rwanda.[69] It is during this second tour of Rwanda that he visited the KGM as the first prominent international personality to visit the newly constructed memorial center. Since then, many other prominent guests would arrive to Rwanda and often start with a visit to the KGM. It became the flagship memorial. It remains the centerpiece of the master narrative and commemoration. A brief description of the KGM is important to show how the master narrative is discussed among its different visitors and guides.

KGM Tour
Much has been written about the KGM, so I will not go into significant detail but focus on key aspects that show its evolution.[70] For the purpose of showing shifts and evolving discourses on the master narrative, there are two sections of the KGM analyzed in this part of the chapter. The first is the outside area, including the "memorial gardens," other small buildings surrounding the main exhibition building, and the space around the main building. The second part, the main exhibition building, has three permanent exhibitions: the exhibition on the 1994 genocide that showcases a brief background of relevant Rwandan history; the children's memorial; and a third section dealing with genocidal violence around the world.[71] The following description of the center (both outside and inside) shows how the effects of the interactive experience coincide with and sustain a particular historical narrative.

Discourse of the Master Narrative at the KGM
In 2004 when I did my first of many visits to the KGM, visitors were welcomed by a guide who introduced the place and could also provide a guided tour. It's a modern brick house that resembles those that were built around Kigali after the genocide, surrounded by beautiful manicured gardens. Downhill from the main building are mass burials covered in cement. There are offices of museum officials and a library at the back. The first thing that a visitor sees when they enter the main exhibition about the genocide is troubling because of its graphic nature and content. Along the corridor, machetes, stories of horror, UN failure, and the RPF narrative of ending the war are told to cement the pillars of the master narrative. Images of machetes, old guns, and other crude tools used in the genocide are on display at the beginning of this section. Bleak photos of the corpses of children, women, men—some of them clearly rotting—as well short film clips of the actual killing of Tutsi

in 1994 inexorably remind the visitor that the Hutu were the perpetrators, feeding on colonial era theories of ethnic divisionism.[72]

However, it is the last section that I think shows the extent the KGM cements this master narrative to anyone who visits. It is located upstairs and cannot be seen while visiting other sections. As one of my interviewees noted, even if visitors approach the first sections with skepticism of the master narrative, by the time they reach this Children's Memorial most refrain from commenting. On the wall, a life-size photo of each Tutsi child is displayed. These are children that were killed during the genocide. Each photograph is accompanied by the child's name and their favorite food. The intensity of this exhibit derives from the juxtaposition of these details, evoking the children's innocence, with the graphic descriptions of how they were killed. The exhibit illustrates that genocide not only destroys the present generation but also brutally obstructs the dreams of the next generation. This exhibit is the last of the three inside the KGM main hall.

The sheer immensity and immediacy of the horror seems to subdue any critical engagement. One of the guides told me that he observes different reactions to this section:

> For Rwandans, you see them becoming very silent and you can almost deduce with certainty those who were forced to visit. The section forces perpetuators to experience the atrocities that they continue to ignore or dismiss as mere propaganda, while some genocide survivors find it difficult to relive these memories and either walk out or experience deep sorrow. In either case, as a guide, my job is to give them time and comfort them where possible.[73]

This section is the most divisive in the memorial. It evokes different reactions from Rwandans who visit. While Champions find this section factual proof in support of their argument about why these permanent exhibitions should exist alongside seasonal rituals of remembering, Antagonists believe it resembles the manipulation of history. For some Champions, Fatalists, and Antagonists, the KGM's exhibits are spaces that provide evidence of how the genocide happened, who did the killing, who died, and survivors of those atrocities. It can be a place of shame for visitors like Hakizimana, mentioned in the Introduction, whose father is in prison for the genocide. In other parts of the tour, the exhibition leaves an indelible impression that the Hutu and

Belgians are responsible for the politicization of identity in Rwanda and therefore the Genocide Against the Tutsi.

Of the other two exhibitions located on different floors, the first covers genocidal violence in Kosovo and Bosnia and master narratives of genocides from elsewhere. The master narrative around the KGM is put into dialogue with other master narratives from around the world of similar crimes. This exhibit, comprising mostly photos accompanied by short narrations of the events, is meant to contextualize the unique circumstances that allow a crisis to be identified as genocide globally. The exhibition focuses on similarities between the Rwandan master narrative encountered downstairs and other genocides that shaped the course of history. It also shows that this event is not unique to Rwanda but is a global phenomenon that is possible whenever a political crisis is pushed to extremes and hate imbues a society.

The outside of the KGM tour is a space for learning and reflection. The center has a growing library of archives concerning the genocide and the periods before and after it. When I visited toward the end of 2012, it was still a work in progress but nonetheless intended to create a space for debate—within limits. Given the threat of genocide denialism, those who oversee the debate that is "performed" are likely not to allow anyone to venture beyond the permitted master narrative that emphasized the suffering of Tutsi. This is one site where comparative memory narratives are disputed, policed, and prohibited.

The outside gardens of graves and the memories affiliated with them have engendered a permanent narrative that is illegal to tamper with. As a space established in the capital city Kigali, it will be difficult for future governments to neglect or destroy without provoking a political crisis. This is because alternative versions of the past (i.e., discussions about Hutu who died in the genocide or in other violence around the genocide) are strictly prohibited. As discussed elsewhere, the laws concerning this and other official sites have evolved to criminalize anyone who attempts to discuss alternative versions of the past.[74] This was the case for Victoire Ingabire, an opposition politician who on his return to Rwanda from the diaspora gave a speech asking when Hutu victims will be included in the official site. She was arrested and imprisoned following the speech.[75]

The guides are mostly genocide survivors. They communicate a well-curated master narrative bolstered by personal experience to guests. I noticed when I visited with Rwandans, alone, or with foreigners, guides tailor the depth, style, and explanations depending on the visitor.[76] Senga, one of the guides, explained the difference:

> When we are guiding Rwandans it's different than when it's foreigners. For Rwandans they might know the events of 1990s we are talking about because they also lived them if they were in Rwanda. In that case we mostly reference and look for their approval, or even some contribute in agreement. They rarely start a debate if they disagree; they keep quiet. Then the foreigners or even Rwandans from the diaspora, especially those who do not know much, we give them details. We don't skip any information and encourage them to read. These are the ones who usually want to know if we were in the genocide or if our families are buried here. And so, you share and explain what happened, but we don't give the whole individual story because it is too long and can take away from the tour.[77]

Senga explained the complex relationship between the individual story of a guide and what they tell a group of Champions, Fatalists, or those they suspect of being Antagonists in a group. It was clear the stories that guides tell align with the master narrative. When examples are given using their own survival stories, they choose parts that agree with the master narrative.

As he told me, international visitors are also different. Some have a better understanding of Rwanda's history; others do not, like tourists who come to Rwanda primarily for its wildlife and natural environment—notably its remarkable gorillas—but are encouraged to visit the KGM.[78] Most tour companies include the KGM in their itinerary of visiting Kigali before or after other activities. Annalisa Bolin asserted that some visitors also have their own motives and expectations when visiting the KGM.

> Visitors expect the site to provide a particular lesson; while the expectation may be for education, if that lesson does not appear, the humanitarian sentiment may thus arise to take the place of what visitors have not learned.[79]

Others are researchers or travel writers who then request more detailed and timely tours and may even contract with the guides to meet outside the KGM to hear more comprehensive stories. After visiting the KGM, visitors become channels to spread the master narrative within their respective domestic areas. Most diplomats who arrive in Rwanda on a tour of duty or for short visits start or end their visits at the KGM.[80]

In retelling their stories of visiting Rwanda or the KGM, both Rwandans and foreigners allow the master narrative to travel. Inevitably, some give it their own meaning, even to the extent of refuting what is told to them by guides. As mentioned above, some African writers who visited Rwanda in 1998 reflected years later on how they saw the shifts and changes around memorials 16 years after the genocide. One of them observed:

> The landscape of memory in Rwanda, 16 years after the genocide, was bound to have changed, both on the private and public levels. In what way is the memory of the survivors intertwined with that of those who returned to the country after the genocide? As time passes, memories become more and more subjective and selective. In addition, the number of Rwandans who have direct recollections of the events is diminishing. But it is the nature of collective memory to be written and rewritten by decision-makers in an attempt to cement it in the national psyche.[81]

Thus, the permanent exhibitions and graves are important not only in cementing the narrative in the physical space in Kigali but also in serving as an international conduit for the dissemination of the master narrative.

Permanence and Mobility of Other Regional Memorials

After the genocide, memorials were privileged to avoid having private graves, as the numbers of deaths were overwhelming. As the clergy referenced in the previous chapter told me, whenever they went to pray for victims, they buried them mostly in their homes. However, as people searched for their own/loved ones/relatives, communities throughout Rwanda created new mass graves whenever bones or remains of victims were found in groups. An interviewee who worked for the commission told me some memorials, such as Bisesero, Murambi, Rebero, Nyamata, Ntarama, and Nyanza-Kicukiro, initially were designated for victims who lived in their neighborhoods. These memorials differ from the KGM in two ways. First, ordinary Rwandans created some of the sites. Second, initially they were bone memorial sites, where bones were gathered and given the respect denied to the individual victims following their deaths. Educational museums were established at some of them only recently. Dumas and Korman write that the first memorial was created in Mugonero in western Rwanda and the only one that made direct reference to

Tutsi victims until 2009.[82] Save for this memorial, their original meaning has evolved, and their status and meaning in society continued to change over time. A document at the KGM published in 2010 singles out these memorials as key sites for future development. "It is hoped," the document asserts, "that Rwanda will develop seven key sites into meaningful memorial centres."[83]

At first, some of these sites were inundated with corpses and the desiccated bones of victims that could not be identified. Emmanuel Murangira, a well-known survivor and guide at the Murambi Memorial, has reflected on his experience after the genocide. He returned in 1995 and was welcomed by a nongovernmental group that was then called Amagaju. Some of its members were former refugees of previous massacres against Tutsi in 1959, the 1960s, and 1973; others were survivors of the 1994 genocide.[84] Amagaju helped Emmanuel re-establish his life until the government appropriated commemoration activities in 1996; the group also established a fund to assist other survivors.[85] Emmanuel lost his wife and children in the genocide. As he reconstructed his life, he found it important and comforting to help others find their relatives, and his testimony offers an analysis of the early years when memorials were created:

> I helped ten people to locate their relatives. All of these people were refugees from 1959 who were searching for their relatives. I helped them to locate the bodies [remains]. Often, I would ask people about different incidents [in order to ascertain] where the victims may have been killed or buried. At Murambi, there were four places [mass graves] where the dead were buried by machines [tractors].[86]

In a project "Through a Glass Darkly: Genocide Memorials in Rwanda," Jens Meierhenrich and his team sought to map out memorials in Rwanda.[87] They have documented both the local memorials that have been replaced over time and the big national memorials. When starting the project in 2010, the team noted the large number of visitors who traveled to Rwanda and visited genocide memorials in schools, churches, and hospitals where remains are buried.

Murambi Memorial is one such memorial that has welcomed many visitors. It is located in the Southern Province at a destination where the government had originally planned to build a technical school.[88] Constituting a part of Zone Turquoise, it also served as a temporary station for French troops.[89] Emmanuel continued:

> There is a problem with how many people were buried at Murambi because the bones of many were destroyed and mixed up [as a result of being moved by Caterpillar tractors]. The common grave [which contains the bones from the four original mass graves] in front of the memorial contains about forty-five thousand [remains]. In the classrooms [where skeletons of the dead are laid out on low tables and are covered with lime], there are no less than five thousand victims.[90]

Emmanuel's testimony explains why there was a need to establish selected sites for memorials instead of having mass graves everywhere. Similar testimonies of survivors who manned the sites show that after the government took over memorialization, individual survivors started burying and reburying the bones of their dead. This was the case when policies changed and survivors were asked to take bodies of their loved ones previously buried in their fields and rebury their dead in public memorials. A writer who visited Murambi in its early days reflected years later:

> When we went to Rwanda in 1998, the sites of genocide which we visited housed the remains of the dead as they had been found on location or around the buildings where the victims had taken refuge. Some bodies had also been disinterred.[91]

The human remains and shocked visitors inspired a Senegalese novelist, Boubacar Boris Diop, to title his book *Murambi, le livre des ossements* or *Murambi, the book of bones* in which he tells complicated stories reflecting his visit to Murambi.

Since 2004, many of these memorial sites have attracted a lot of attention and are managed under nationwide campaigns to ensure their sustainability. This meant more financing from the government of Rwanda and international aid institutions. In describing one of these sites, Meierhenrich and his research team have shown its transformation over the years. They noted that in the last 15 years, under the direction of an architect and curators, shelves full of bones, skulls, and other neatly organized remains replaced the disorganized artifacts of the genocide, such as piles of stained clothes that were dispersed all over the church after the genocide. Furthermore, researchers observed that in Ntarama, for instance, where the remains of a demolished church now stand, an "imposing British-funded steel structure [hovers] over the complex's remains."[92]

As observed in other divided societies, there is controversy on how to memorialize victims of mass violence. "Disagreement," Meierhenrich and team observed, "exists concerning the *purpose* of remembering the dead of the genocide as well as over appropriate *ways* of doing so."[93] For instance, the RPF and returnee Tutsi elites use the master narrative of the genocide to communicate the genocide story to the outside world and in some cases disagree with some survivors who object to key features of the master narrative, especially its use of displaying of skulls, bones, and other personal items.[94] Thus, two groups of people contest for ownership over these remains to serve different interests.

Discourse on Other Memorials around the Country

Since 2004, ten years after the genocide, some survivors have buried and reburied their loved ones more than twice. As my interview with Alice revealed, this can happen unexpectedly after survivors have "moved on," and the changes brought by local government can affect one's private mourning or healing process. Alice reflected on her and her family's experience:

> When I was about fifteen years old, in 2001, we went with our family to Nyamata to bury remains of our relatives. However, we were informed that only those of our uncles had been found but not grandparents and two aunts. We had to spend the night washing their skulls, preparing where to bury them. I watched from a distance as men and women with white gloves were collecting them and my mum was being asked to identify her brothers. Some survivors accepted to take part in washing the body remains of their relatives and others refused due to trauma. She identified her brother by looking at his teeth and shirt he was wearing. This went on for hours and when it was almost evening, mum could not do it anymore. She had never cried or talked much about her relatives but after identifying three uncles, she fainted and we had to take her to hospital. We were worried; we thought she was dead too.

Alice's story suggests that individual families have a very physical connection to the remains. She explained that her family buried their uncles after two days of identifying them before returning to Kigali. She remembers that many family members and friends from Kigali and the village where they were burying their loved ones came to show support. But just a couple of years later the family received news that as part of commemorating the tenth anniversary of the genocide, the government had found a new site in Ruhango town where they would bury all victims from sectors nearby. In 2001, they had buried their relatives in a nearby mass grave, but now they had to exhume the bodies *again*. This time Alice was mature and was asked to participate.

> It was terrible. We had started our new lives in Kigali. Mum was working as a nurse and I was in university now with my older brother. We talked about our father and uncles who were killed and kept their photos in the house but thought we had to move on. Mum had even reduced the times she used to go and put flowers on the graves. However, when the news came that we had to go back and exhume their bodies and rebury them we resisted at first. Then we were told it was very important and the government had asked all survivors to rebury their relatives in similar places. On that day I cried more than I have ever. We removed their remains again, which had deteriorated, but this time we did not wash them or take long like in 2001. We simply removed them and put them in new caskets and took them in a car for a ceremony to the mass graves in the compound of Nyamata Church. There were other families who had also brought their relatives' remains.[95]

Their bodies were found in a terrible state and recovered from where they had been killed.[96] The reburying happens not only in national memorials such as Nyamata, the KGM, or the other five, but also in other, local memorials. Nyamasheke Memorial is one of the earliest local memorials that are documented as having been built by survivors. It is located in the western part of Rwanda and has over 44,000 bodies. In 2012, it was reported that over 20,000 additional bodies were transferred to Nyamasheke from other, informal memorials in the same region.[97] The construction of Nyamasheke Memorial, built in 2012, is estimated as having cost 120 million Rwandan Francs (around USD 188,000). The funds were drawn from the local community; the Ministry of Youth, Sports, and Culture; the Ibuka association; and near the end, from international stakeholders.[98] Unlike other memorials, Nyamasheke is not centrally located; hence, it does not receive many visitors. It is jointly maintained by the local government and a survivors' association.[99]

Nyamasheke is an example of the hundreds of undocumented, community-driven memorials, pioneering through local initiative rather than state imperative.[100] These memorials are of significant value for the people who live close to them and the few visitors who come from farther away.[101] They are often not well fenced and are located near fields and neighborhood pathways (called *inzira ya kinyarwanda*, a term for a small pedestrian road in rural Rwanda). Unlike the nationally demarcated ones, local memorials tend to spill into the everyday lives of ordinary Rwandans by maintaining a visible presence in these local communities. Even in cases where they have not been well maintained, local people tell stories about them. They are easily differentiated from local cemeteries because they are marked with banners—often old but sometimes new—and with flowers, depending on the time of year. Local communities know that laws protect these memorials and that there are consequences for disrespecting them, unlike for cemeteries, which are not supervised. Conversations about memorials can happen during formal events, like during the monthly community service called *umuganda* when community members come together to do maintenance or other work on these sites. Such conversations can also happen in informal settings. Senga reflected on his experience as a guide in rural areas and his interactions with these sites:

> When I travel up country, I sometimes like to walk. Sometimes I walk by a small memorial and wonder who is buried in it. This happens when I am not prepared. Maybe going to see my cousin and having a conversation about school, then we see a memorial and we start discussing about the genocide. It is hard to ignore because we have both been affected. This happens especially in rural areas, where I pass the small memorials that are sometimes hidden in a forest.[102]

More recently, however, these small and unknown memorials have been the center of debate. One group of survivors I spoke to opposed the CNLG's suggestion that they rebury their loved ones in larger mass graves. In an interview with the local daily *New Times* on April 17, 2012, the CNLG's Mucyo argued that smaller memorials should be grouped together to ease their maintenance, and local authorities as well as community members should actively consider the memorial's maintenance a priority through the year[103]: "It shouldn't be looked at as a responsibility of the government only; every Rwandan should have a stake in the maintenance of the memorial sites."[104] Ibuka's president,

Dr. Jean Pierre Dusingizemungu, agreed with Mucyo's position on the importance of having fewer memorial sites to ease management. Aware of the controversy around such a move that can potentially retraumatize survivors and their local communities, he commented: "This is something that can only be done through mutual understanding with genocide survivors because it involves moving the remains of their relatives to another location."[105]

Contrary to the CNLG's position, the AERG's first vice coordinator, Jean Luc Mwizerwa, argued that instead of abolishing the small memorials and nationalizing them, the CNLG should encourage more people to maintain these local sites and support their efforts. Jean Luc emphasized the need for every Rwandan to own the bodies of victims in memorial sites.[106] He asserted that all memorials, whether small or big, should receive the same attention from the CNLG. Memorials, whatever their shape or size, contribute to the institutionalization and nationalization of the master narrative in very powerful ways given their visibility in the hills. Rwandans interact with them as a reminder of a past some want to forget, challenge, or endorse.

These sites, materials, and the discourses around them have evolved into the most strategic space in Rwanda to not only fix a master narrative of the past for generations to come but also transmit memory. They allow the stories told and kept in the various museums and memorials to travel to visitors in the present and with guides as interpreters of the past as well as the technology to conceive them and to shape future dialogue. The master narrative is not only mobile in the making of current memory but also travels to the "postmemory" future when horror such as that of 1994 will be unimaginable. To use Jan Assmann's concept, the KGM serves as a space that enables narratives around the master narrative of the Genocide Against the Tutsi from "commemorative memory," that which is shared by contemporaries through rituals and narratives and as the bearers of those memories die, transmit it to generations to come.[107]

Conclusion

In this chapter, I have shown that although sites and materials of memory give the impression that they are permanent and unchanging, in the case of Rwanda's first 20 years they were malleable. The chapter has demonstrated that through this evolution, certain policy decisions were made for memorials and commemoration to become more inclusive, at least religiously. While some policies, such as transforming churches into memorials, resulted in tensions in the early years; by 2014, at the end of the 20 years this book is focused on, relations with the Catholic Church, which initially resisted the master narrative, started to shift. Thus, over time both Christian and non-Christian leaders moved from Antagonists to Champions of the master narrative. This is exemplified by the silence—at least in public—of Catholic clergy on changing the official color of mourning from purple to gray. In addition, from a discussion in which survivors disagreed with local authorities on commemoration burial versus conservation of bones and bodies of their victims, relations improved especially after the creation of CNLG and as Ibuka became more accepted. The majority of survivors moved from Antagonists or Fatalists to become Champions who supported the construction of memorials and narratives around them. Deeper analysis of these shifts are discussed in the chapter that follows. Through analysis of stories that capture diverse experiences at the local level, this chapter has traced how individuals' interactions with memorials evolved over the years.

Examining these nuances shows that the shape and color of memory change over time, just like the perspectives about them. They are not permanent and depend on powerful political actors who dedicate resources and then use them for particular purposes to advance both personal and political needs of actors. Political actors can repurpose them and reshape them over time and dictate how they are perceived and their social and political significance. These are powerful sites where the master narrative not only gained power and visibility but also turned into a hegemonic narrative by borrowing from a globalized model like the Shoah while alienating other alternatives or plurality, such as those that were suggested by civil society and Parliament mentioned in a previous section.

The next chapter examines these relationships that are shaped around commemorative events, memorials, and other avenues and the varied response from Rwandans with assorted positions about the emergence and evolution of the master narrative.

Notes

1. Marc Lacey, "10 Years Later in Rwanda, the Dead Are Ever Present," February 26, 2004, https://www.nytimes.com/2004/02/26/world/10-years-later-in-rwanda-the-dead-are-ever-present.html.

2. See also Alison Liebhafsky Des Forges, *Leave None to Tell the Story: Genocide in Rwanda* (New York: Human Rights Watch, 2014); and Longman, *Christianity and Genocide in Rwanda*.
3. For more on Pauline Nyiramasuhugo and her role in Butare and her prosecution at the International Criminal Tribunal for Rwanda (ICTR), see Carrie Sperling, "Mother of Atrocities: Pauline Nyiramasuhuko's Role in the Rwandan Genocide," *Fordham Urban Law Journal* 33, no. 2 (2006): 637–664.
4. One interviewee explained how he worked in a restaurant in town during the genocide and would see dead bodies at that same site near the university. He explained the trauma it has left him, and how whenever he passes there now he remembers the dead bodies and dreams about them. Interview, respondent in Butare, January 2012.
5. See from history, Pierre Nora's key work on spaces of remembering (*Between Memory and History*). In sociology, Barbara A. Misztal, Theories of Social Remembering. See also Susan A. Crane, *Museums and Memory* (Palo Alto, CA: Stanford University Press, 2000).
6. For more on these practices, see Williams, *Memorial Museums*.
7. Marcel Berlins, "Victims of the Holocaust Get a Memorial Day. Victims of Other Atrocities Do Not. Isn't It Time We Dropped the Whole Idea?" *Guardian*, September 14, 2005, https://www.theguardian.com/theguardian/2005/sep/14/features2.g2.
8. See Haidy Geismar, "Building Sites of Memory: The Ground Zero Sonic Memorial Sound Walk," *Fabrications* 15, no. 2 (2005): 1–13.
9. Jeffrey K. Olick and Joyce Robbins, "Social Memory Studies: From 'Collective Memory' to the Historical Sociology of Mnemonic Practices," *Annual Review of Sociology* 24, no. 1 (1998): 105–140.
10. Barsalou and Baxter, *Urge to Remember*, 4. See also Astrid Erll, "Travelling Memory," *Parallax* 17, no. 4 (2011): 4–18.
11. See Wilde, "Chile's Memory and Santiago's General Cemetery."
12. Louis Bickford, Patricia Karam, Hassan Mneimneh, and Patrick Pierce, *Documenting Truth* (New York: International Center for Transitional Justice, 2009), https://www.ictj.org/sites/default/files/ICTJ-DAG-Global-Documenting-Truth-2009-English.pdf.
13. Lisa M. Moore, "Recovering the Past, Remembering Trauma: The Politics of Commemoration at Sites of Atrocity," *Journal of Public & International Affairs* 20 (Spring 2009): 213–244.
14. Jay Winter, "Sites of Memory and the Shadow of War," in *Cultural Memory Studies*, eds. Astrid Erll and Ansgar Nünning (Berlin: de Gruyter, 2008), 61–76.
15. Herman Wouk, *War and Remembrance* (Boston: Little, Brown, 1978).
16. Rebecca Jinks, *Representing Genocide: The Holocaust as Paradigm?* (London: Bloomsbury, 2016), 29.
17. See, for example, Rémi Korman, "Mobilising the Dead? The Place of Bones and Corpses in the Commemoration of the Tutsi Genocide in Rwanda," *Human Remains and Violence: An Interdisciplinary Journal* 1, no. 2 (2015): 56–70; and Rémi Korman, "L'Etat Rwandais et la mémoire du Génocide commémorée sur les ruines (1994–1996)," *Vingtième Siècle. Revue d'histoire* 122, no. 2 (2014): 87. Also see Rémi Korman,

"Bury or Display?: The Politics of Exhumation in Post-genocide Rwanda," in *Human Remains and Identification: Mass Violence, Genocide, and the "Forensic Turn,"* eds. Élisabeth Gessat-Anstett and Jean-Marc Dreyfus (Manchester, UK: Manchester University Press, 2017), 203–220. Also see Rémi Korman, "Le Rwanda face à ses morts ou les cimetières du génocide," in *Génocides et Politiques Mémorielles*, ed. F. Blum (Paris: Centres d'histoires sociales du XXe siècle, 2011), 1–4; among many others. See also Annalisa Bolin, "Dignity in Death and Life: Negotiating Agaciro for the Nation in Preservation Practice at Nyamata Genocide Memorial, Rwanda," *Anthropological Quarterly* 92, no. 2 (2019): 345–374.

18. These works on the early evolution and nature of the master narrative include Claudine Vidal, *La commémoration du génocide au Rwanda. Violence symbolique, mémorisation forcée et histoire officielle*, Vol. 44, no. 175 (Cahiers d'Études Africaines, 2004); or see also Valérie Rosoux, "Rwanda, la mémoire du génocide," *Etudes* 390, no. 6 (1999): 731, and others.

19. Rémi Korman, "L'État rwandais et la mémoire du génocide," *Vingtième siècle. Revue d'histoire* 2 (2014): 87–98.

20. Rémi Korman, *Commémorer sur les ruines. L'État rwandais face à la mort de masse dans l'après-coup du génocide (1994–2003)* (unpublished PhD dissertation, EHESS, 2020).

21. Ibid.

22. See, for instance; Timothy Longman, "Limitations to Political Reform: The Undemocratic Nature of Transition in Rwanda," in *Remaking Rwanda: State Building and Human Rights after Mass Violence*, eds. S. Straus and L. Waldorf (Madison, WI: Wisconsin University Press, 2011), 25–47, 28; and Filip Reyntjens, "Rwanda, Ten Years on: From Genocide to Dictatorship," *African Affairs* 103, no. 411 (2004): 185.

23. Erin Jessee, "Promoting Reconciliation through Exhuming and Identifying Victims of the 1994 Rwandan Genocide," *Africa Initiative Discussion Paper Series* 2, Paper 4 (2012), https://strathprints.strath.ac.uk/48263/1/CIGI_AI_Policy_Brief_2.pdf

    On funding of construction of memorials, see also Rachel Ibreck, "International Constructions of National Memories: The Aims and Effects of Foreign Donors' Support for Genocide Remembrance in Rwanda," *Journal of Intervention and Statebuilding* 7, no. 2 (2013): 149–169. See also Boubacar Boris Diop, *Murambi: The Book of Bones* (Bloomington: Indiana University Press, 2006).

24. Longman, *Memory and Justice*, 1–11.

25. Ibid., 331.

26. Susanne Buckley-Zistel, "Remembering to Forget: Chosen Amnesia as a Strategy for Local Coexistence in Post-genocide Rwanda," *Africa* 76, no. 2 (2006): 131–150.

27. See Buckley-Zistel, "Remembering to Forget"; Jennie E. Burnet, "The Injustice of Local Justice: Truth, Reconciliation, and Revenge in Rwanda," *Genocide Studies and Prevention* 3, no. 2 (2008): 173–193; Michel S. Kamanzi, "Rwanda: Quelle réconciliation?" *Études* 400, no. 5 (2004): 581–586; René Lemarchand, "Genocide, Memory and Ethnic Reconciliation in Rwanda," *L'Afrique des Grands Lacs: Annuaire* 2006-2007 (2007): 2–30.

28. Jens Meierhenrich, "The Transformation of Lieux de Mémoire: The Nyabarongo River in Rwanda, 1992–2009," *Anthropology Today* 25, no. 5 (2009): 13–19.

29. National Unity and Reconciliation Commission, *Rwanda Reconciliation Barometer* (Kigali: Republic of Rwanda, 2015), 24.
30. Ibid.
31. Gakwenzire, "Contribution à la gestion de la mémoire"; and see Célestin Kanimba, "Préservation de la mémoire du génocide: Rôles, actions et stratégies," *Etudes Rwandaises* September (2005): 128–147.
32. Darius Gishoma, "*Crises traumatiques collectives d'ihahamuka lors des commémorations du génocide des Tutsi. Aspects cliniques et perspectives thérapeutiques*" (PhD dissertation, Louvain-la-Neuve, Université Catholique de Louvain, 2014).
33. See "Institute of National Museums of Rwanda," http://www.museum.gov.rw/index.php?id=2.
34. On tensions around pregenocide monuments such as that of Dominique Mbonyumutwa, see Emmanuel Rutayisire, "RDF Defends War Memorial Monuments at Parliament," *The East African (Nairobi)*, July 18, 2014, https://www.theeastafrican.co.ke/rwanda/News/RDF-defends-war-memorial-monuments-at-parliament/1433218-2389352-12463aw/index.html. The house where Belgian soldiers were killed has been sealed off and is at times visited by United Nations or Belgian officials. For instance, see "Pictures of the Day: 9 April 2019,", *The Telegraph*, April 19, 2019, https://www.telegraph.co.uk/news/2019/04/09/pictures-day-9-april-2019/, Accessed March 10, 2023. On the twentieth commemoration, the government opened a new museum and memorial park in Mulindi. See David Nkusi, "The Historical Significance of Mulindi Museum," *New Times* (Kigali), September 20, 2014.
35. See Hélène Dumas and Rémi Korman, "Espaces de la mémoire du génocide des Tutsis au Rwanda," *Afrique contemporaine* 2 (2011): 11–27; and Véronique Tadjo, "Genocide: The Changing Landscape of Memory in Kigali," *African Identities* 8, no. 4 (2010): 379–388.
36. Ibreck, "Politics of Mourning," 8.
37. Ibid.
38. Jay Winter, *Sites of Memory, Sites of Mourning: The Great War in European Cultural History* (Cambridge: Cambridge University Press, 1998).
39. Ibid.
40. Ibid. Also see Bolin, "Dignity in Death and Life."
41. Athan Tashobya, "Genocide Memorials Inch Closer to Becoming UNESCO Heritage Sites," *New Times* (Kigali), April 6, 2018, https://www.newtimes.co.rw/news/genocide-memorials-inch-closer-becoming-unesco-heritage-sites.
42. Both purple and gray were still used in the April 7 commemoration of 2013.
43. Annalisa Bolin, "Imagining Genocide Heritage: Material Modes of Development and Preservation in Rwanda," *Journal of Material Culture* 25, no. 2 (2020): 196–219.
44. See "Pope Says Church Is Not to Blame in Rwanda," *New York Times*, March 21, 1996, https://www.nytimes.com/1996/03/21/world/pope-says-church-is-not-to-blame-in-rwanda.html. Yet both Christian institutions and individual church leaders participated in or influenced Hutu radicalism before and during the genocide. See, for example, Timothy Longman, *Christianity and Genocide in Rwanda* (Cambridge: Cambridge University Press, 2011); also Tharcisse Gatwa, *The Churches*

and *Ethnic Ideology in the Rwandan Crises, 1900–1994* (Oxford, UK: Oxford Center for Mission Studies, 2005).
45. On the Kibeho camp massacre, see also Gérard Prunier, *Africa's World War: Congo, the Rwandan Genocide, and the Making of a Continental Catastrophe* (Oxford, UK: Oxford University Press, 2008), especially see Chapter 2.
46. Australian War Memorial shows findings of this report and gives other references that cite the same number. See Australian War Memorial, "Rwanda (UNAMIR), 1993–1996," https://www.awm.gov.au/collection/U60680/, accessed March 10, 2023.
47. Jean-Paul Kimonyo, *Rwanda's Popular Genocide: A Perfect Storm* (Boulder, CO: Lynne Rienner, 2015), 102.
48. Ibid.
49. Ibid.
50. See Immaculée Ilibagiza and Steve Erwin, *Our Lady of Kibeho: Mary Speaks to the World from the Heart of Africa* (Carlsbad, CA: Hay House, 2012).
51. Ibid.
52. Interview, local researcher, Kigali, Rwanda, 2017.
53. Interview with priest, Kigali, Rwanda, 2017; see also Des Forges, *"Leave None to Tell the Story"*; and Longman, *Christianity and Genocide in Rwanda*.
54. Harriet Sherwood, "Pope Francis Asks for Forgiveness for Church's Role in Rwanda Genocide," *Guardian*, March 20, 2017, https://www.theguardian.com/world/2017/mar/20/pope-francis-asks-for-forgiveness-for-churchs-role-in-rwanda-genocide.
55. See Martin Kimani, "For Rwandans, the Pope's Apology Must Be Unbearable," *Guardian*, May 29, 2010, http://www.guardian.co.uk/commentisfree/belief/2010/mar/29/pope-catholics-rwanda-genocide-church. It is also important to note that President Kagame and the first lady, Jeanette Kagame, visited the Vatican, and Pope Francis offered what was judged to be an apology for what happened in 1994 and the role of the Church. See Sherwood, "Pope Francis Asks for Forgiveness."
56. Interview, Huye, Rwanda, April 2014.
57. Edwin Musoni, "Maintenance of Memorial Sites a Collective Responsibility—CNLG," *New Times* (Kigali), April 17, 2012, http://allafrica.com/stories/201204170166.html
58. Ibid.
59. Ibid.
60. See Ilana Bet-El and Avner Ben-Amos, "Holocaust Day and Memorial Day in Israeli Schools: Ceremonies, Education and History," *Israel Studies* 4, no. 1 (1999): 258–284.
61. Jeffrey K. Olick, *The Politics of Regret: On Collective Memory and Historical Responsibility* (New York: Routledge, 2007).
62. James M. Smith, *A Time to Remember: Rwanda: Ten Years after Genocide* (Retford, UK: Aegis Institute, 2004), 5.
63. This is from reflection notes from the field after talking with a Canadian resident in Kigali, who explained that some of his friends feared crying in front of survivors during commemorations. Yet most of the outsiders want to attend commemorations and find the stories extremely emotional (interview, Kimihurura residence, Kigali, Rwanda, April 2012).
64. Conversation with a genocide survivor, Kigali, Rwanda, December, 2011.
65. Ibid.

66. Conversation with a resident in Gisozi, Rwanda, August 2019. This resident had lived in Kigali since 1994 and followed how the memorial has evolved.
67. Ibid.
68. James and Stephen Smith, founders of Beth Shalom Holocaust Center, the only Holocaust museum in the United Kingdom, established Aegis Trust in 2000. KGM is one of their main projects. Aegis means "shield" or "protection." See Aegis, "Aegis Trust: What We Do," https://www.aegistrust.org/what-we-do/, accessed March 10, 2023.
69. Helen Vesperini, "Rwanda Warms to UN Chief," *BBC News*, September 4, 2001, http://news.BBC.co.uk/2/hi/africa/1524704.stm.
70. See Jennifer Yusin, "The Itinerary of Commemoration in the Kigali Memorial Centre: On Trauma, Time and Difference," *Culture, Theory and Critique* 57, no. 3 (2016): 338–356; Amy Sodaro, "Politics of the Past: Remembering the Rwandan Genocide at the Kigali Memorial Centre," In *Curating Difficult Knowledge: Violent Pasts in Public Places*, eds. Erica Lehrer, Cynthia E. Milton, and Monica Eileen Patterson (Basingstoke, UK: Palgrave Macmillan, 2011), 72–88; John Giblin, "The Performance of International Diplomacy at Kigali Memorial Centre, Rwanda," *Journal of African Cultural Heritage Studies* 1, no. 1 (2017): 49; Elisabeth King, "Memory Controversies in Post-genocide Rwanda: Implications for Peacebuilding," *Genocide Studies and Prevention* 5, no. 3 (2010): 293–309; Richard Sharpley and Mona Friedrich, "Genocide Tourism in Rwanda: Contesting the Concept of the 'Dark Tourist,'" in *Dark Tourism: Practice and Interpretation*, eds. Glenn Hooper and J. John Lennon (New York: Routledge, 2016), 146–158.
71. Smith, *A Time to Remember*.
72. The genocide was as brutal as the clubs and agriculture tools that were used. For an in-depth analysis, see Des Forges, *Leave None to Tell the Story*, 2014.
73. Anonymous interview, Kigali Memorial Center, Rwanda, April 2014.
74. Erin Jessee and David Mwambari, "Memory Law and the Duty to Remember the '1994 Genocide Against the Tutsi' in Rwanda," in *Memory Laws and Historical Justice. The Politics of Criminalizing the Past*, eds. Ariella Lang and Elaza Barkan (Cham, Switzerland: Springer, 2022), 291–319.
75. Ibid.
76. On the KGM visit and different experiences, see Erin Jessee, *Negotiating Genocide in Rwanda: The Politics of History* (New York: Palgrave Macmillan, 2019), 107–109; or Gretchen Baldwin, "Constructing Identity through Commemoration: Kwibuka and the Rise of Survivor Nationalism in Post-conflict Rwanda," *Journal of Modern African Studies* 57, no. 3 (2019): 355–375.
77. Interview with Senga, April 20, 2012.
78. For example, Rwanda's Development Board features Culture & Heritage activities on their tourism website. See Rwanda Development Board, "Culture & Heritage," https://www.visitrwanda.com/tourism/interests/culture-heritage/, accessed March 10, 2023.
79. Annalisa Bolin, "On the Side of Light: Performing Morality at Rwanda's Genocide Memorials," *Journal of Conflict Archaeology* 7, no. 3 (2012): 199–207.
80. For a discussion on high-profile diplomats and visitors of the KGM and their varied reasons for visiting, see Giblin, "The Performance of International Diplomacy," 2017.

81. Tadjo, "Genocide," 383.
82. Dumas and Korman, "Espaces de la mémoire du génocide des Tutsi au Rwanda," 19–20.
83. Fiona Gasana, "Gisozi Memorial Site: Voices of the Past Immortalized," IGIHE (Kigali), April 25, 2011, http://en.IGIHE.com/arts-culture/gisozi-memorial-site-voices-of-the-past.html.
84. Samuel Totten and Rafiki Ubaldo, *We Cannot Forget: Interviews with Survivors of the 1994 Genocide in Rwanda* (New Brunswick, NJ: Rutgers University Press, 2011), 90.
85. Ibid.
86. Ibid., 91.
87. Jens Meierhenrich, "The Transformation of *Lieux de Mémoire*: The Nyabarongo River in Rwanda, 1992–2009," *Anthropology Today* 25, no. 5 (2009): 13–19.
88. See also Shannon Scully, "The Politics of Memory and the Display of Human Remains: Murambi Genocide Memorial, Rwanda" (paper presented on Conflict, Memory, and Reconciliation: Bridging Past, Present and Future, Kigali, Rwanda, January 1, 2012).
89. Genocide Archive Rwanda, "Murambi Memorial," accessed April 20, 2012, https://genocidearchiverwanda.org.rw/index.php?title=Murambi_Memorial&gsearch=, accessed March 10, 2023.
90. Totten and Ubaldo, *We Cannot Forget*, 91.
91. Tadjo, "Genocide," 383.
92. Jens Meierhenrich and Martha Lagace, "Through a Glass Darkly: Genocide Memorials in Rwanda 1994-Present," 2020, http://maps.cga.harvard.edu/rwanda/home.html.
93. Ibid.
94. Ibid.
95. Interview with Alice, June 2012, Ruhango District, South Rwanda.
96. Burnet, *Genocide Lives in Us*, 105–107.
97. Ibid.
98. Ibreck, "Politics of Mourning," 8.
99. Ibid.
100. Ibid., 9.
101. However, given that the sites are not well maintained, they are also vulnerable to extreme weather conditions. See Athan Tashobya, "Genocide Memorial Sites in Sorry State, Says Report," *New Times* (Kigali), April 29, 2014, http://www.newtimes.co.rw/section/article/2014-04-29/74929/.
102. Interview with Senga, Ruhando and Kigali, April, 2012.
103. Musoni, "Maintenance of Memorial Sites a Collective Responsibility—CNLG."
104. Ibid.
105. Ibid.
106. Ibid.
107. See Jan Assmann, *Das Kulturelle Gedächtnis: Schrift, Erinnerung Und Politische Identität in Frühen Hochkulturen* (Munich: Beck, 1977).

5
Localizing Commemoration and Individual Responses to the Master Narrative

Akamarantimba kava mu muntu—the greatest sorrow healer comes from deep within.
Yes, that's how it is for us. The genocide lives in us.
—Donatia[1]

When I transitioned from being a tour guide to a researcher interested in memory, I changed from being the one who taught tourists to return to the role of a student of these events. The shift was significant as it allowed me to travel and study these events with more time to appreciate the complexity of these in their emergence, evolution, and contestations in response to them. Thus, when I went to visit the Bisesero Memorial in Kibuye in 2012, it was to listen to the guides, ask deeper questions, and reflect on how this site informed the kinds of knowledge that circulated about the genocide. On one of the days of my visit, I stayed at the memorial for many hours and returned to the guest house exhausted and partly frustrated. What was I to make of the hour's conversation I had just finished with a guide? Bisesero is in a remote place. When there were no visitors, the guide sat idle, waiting for someone to arrive so he could tell them what happened there in 1994. During our conversation he told me how people responded when they visited but also explained how those from the surrounding areas passed by every day and had conversations with him about ordinary life challenges and opportunities in their postgenocide rural area. He was clear: When it came to conversations about genocide history, there were divided opinions on memorials and on the evolving master narrative.[2]

This chapter explores how these responses mobilized individual and social memory and emerged in private settings, such as within families of survivors and public, state-sanctioned commemoration events. Unlike the political memory that unfolded systematically and in an organized manner as detailed in the previous chapters, private and public responses to the master narrative were mostly impromptu but rarely remained in private spaces.

This chapter further argues that Rwandans' experiences of the master narrative and political memory over the first two decades were characterized by diversity and plurality, despite the homogenizing efforts of the Champions of the master narrative who acted as custodians of the narrative. I contend that with individual memory and social memory such as those constructed at Bisesero by those locals who passed by, a number of sociopolitical factors intertwined to determine the nature of localized response to the hegemonic master narrative.

This chapter maps these various responses through activities taking place at the national, community, and family levels during the commemoration period.[3] It shows that commemorations and the master narrative evolved out of complex social interactions within society and between the state and society. This chapter argues that while some are explicit and clear in their engagement with the postgenocide master narrative and commemoration, the experience for many, if not most, is fluid and complex. This is a logical consequence of a genocide that was, in itself, never as simple as it was sometimes made out to be, as a binary opposition between perpetrators (Hutu) and victims (Tutsi). The broad groupings of Champions, Antagonists, and Fatalists define the dynamics of the debate around the master narrative and commemoration, but do not summarily categorize everyone. I also use Hutu, Tutsi, and Twa labels to help me discuss the variety of opinions and relationships to master narrative groups, but not to classify them as permanent or static, as their status is more complex than that. In the case of Rwanda, the predominant cultural memory and how the master narrative evolved privately and publicly inadvertently allowed individuals to assert their ethnic identity in some contexts,[4] despite an official ban on ethnicity in the country.[5] As a starting point, let us look at how the master narrative and commemoration are experienced publicly.

Public Discourses on Collective Commemoration

National Commemorations

On the morning of April 7, 2012, as I walked to the Amahoro Stadium in Kigali for the opening ceremony of the eighteenth official commemoration of the 1994 genocide, the streets were empty. The silence was disturbing. On the way, I noticed that shops were closed and very few cars were on the road, contrary to an ordinary business day. I joined hundreds of people coming from every direction to enter a stadium that would soon be filled to capacity.[6] In Kinyarwanda, *amahoro* means "peace." During the genocide, the stadium was one of the few safe places in Kigali to host hundreds of refugees under the protection of United Nations Peacekeepers.[7]

As we settled into our seats, people greeted each other in subdued tones with little facial expression or physical movements. It reminded me of the mood at the funeral of a good friend where strangers, acquaintances, family, and relatives gather to mourn a departed person. We heard the sound of a woman wailing loudly, as if she were under attack. Counselors on standby rushed to carry her out to a waiting ambulance. She, like many others, was carried out because the reawakening of memories prompted by the commemoration retraumatized her. The crowd looked around and tried to identify who was being carried out to receive treatment.

After a few minutes of listening to soft and slow Kinyarwanda commemoration music, laden with emotion and lament, we heard another loud cry; many more followed during the proceedings. The whole morning was an intense experience that lasted more than 2 hours. While some overwhelmed individuals were carried out, the majority stayed. They tried to manage their sorrow so that they could continue to follow the day's activities to honor their victims and for those in the official program to ensure events happened as planned. While survivors were central to this event, all other Rwandans and non-Rwandans from different walks of life were present and even participated. However, many people wailed repeatedly, punctuating the silence, and often strangers comforted each other as we were all united by the memory of a horrific past.

The most profound moment was when, in the middle of the ceremony, as a survivor recounted his testimony into the microphone, I saw tears flowing down the face of a male soldier sitting in front of me. His emotions were overpowering, defying the Kinyarwanda proverb, "*Amarira y'umugabo atemba ajya munda*" ("The tears of a man flow inwards"). The pain inflicted during these ceremonies transcends the boundaries of culture, physical strength, and social, gender, or professional status. However, while I tried to wipe my own tears, I noticed the woman next to me laughing. As I tried to identify anything that could possibly be humorous in this tense mood, I noticed she was simultaneously crying and laughing. She was giggling at the walking style of one of the singers. As she noticed some of us looking at her, I overheard her whisper to the person seating next to her: "*Turarira se ngo bagaruke?*" or, "Will our tears make them return?" Perhaps she was referring to her lost loved ones, but laughter can be a coping mechanism among victims of trauma as well.

Before the ceremony began, I observed the president and the first lady lay a wreath at the Kigali Genocide Memorial, as shown on a large screen in the stadium. I then started a conversation with a young man, Pierre, seated next to me, asking him if they would be coming to the stadium after that event. He confirmed with a simple yes. I learned later that Pierre was a survivor, and that it was his third time attending the ceremony at that particular stadium. As we continued to talk, he commented that ceremonies continue to develop into different experiences every year.[8] At this point, I confessed that even though we were speaking in Kinyarwanda, I was from the diaspora and asked him to elaborate on this observation. He explained how images of dead bodies used to be televised throughout the official remembrance period.[9] Pierre continued that people would be traumatized in their houses as well as in public spaces as they watched the footage or listened to the radio. This is a recurring story that I encountered during my travels around Rwanda. Although the visible intensity of peoples' trauma has been attenuated over time, surely it persists.

Pierre's stories explained how survivors face challenges when participating in such ceremonies, and that their presence and participation through music and testimonials are essential for such an event to take place.[10] Like the a Rwandan proverb put it, *Akamarantimba kava mu muntu* or "the greatest sorrow healer comes from deep within," and in these ceremonies survivors' sorrow, traumas, and stories are expressed publicly not only for their healing but also to give meaning to these annual public performances of the master narrative.[11] Yet, rituals like the one at the stadium and night vigils or walks to remember discussed in this chapter "replicate aspects of their [survivors'] traumatic experiences during the genocide"[12] for many reasons. For some, these events are important for personal healing, and for others they are an avenue to perform reconciliation, especially among Champions and Antagonists.[13]

In other public ceremonies over the years, April 7 speeches have been used as a platform, especially by the highest-ranking leaders of government, to comment on national economic recovery plans; Rwanda's relationship with difficult partners, such as France—which is accused of aiding génocidaires—and to discuss other pressing issues of that year. Sometimes, they comment on complex relationships with neighbors like the DRC (Democratic Republic of Congo) that still host members of the defeated pregenocide army and those in the diaspora-based opposition and other issues woven into the nation's annual themes.[14] Later that day in 2012, as I watched the evening news on the local television channels and listened to conversations where I was staying, I realized that similar ceremonies and messages were disseminated across all regions of the country, and the media broadcasted the messages for those who could not manage to physically attend the commemoration. These speeches informed the master narrative of the genocide being diffused to the public.

The annual themes inform and are an anchor to the conversations Rwandans have about the master narrative. I took Pierre's contact after the ceremony and interviewed him many times thereafter. In one of our conversations, Pierre, who was a second-year university student in 2012, told me that a few years earlier when he was still at secondary school, the official mourning period lasted longer and was more intense. He continued to give more examples of these changes he had seen throughout his lifetime. For example, in earlier years, no weddings were held in April or the month of May, but some people now organized them after the first week of mourning even though it remains a strange practice.

Nonetheless, that first week of mourning remains sacred, and all entertainment and other celebrations are banned nationally. For example, one local newspaper columnist's announcement in April 2012 caught my eye. This particular article detailed what was prohibited in this period: "All of Rwanda's schools, sports arenas, nightclubs and other entertainment outlets will be closed for a week. Everyone is expected to use the time to reflect on what happened in the country 18 years ago."[15] Jean de Dieu Mucyo, the executive secretary of CNLG (La Commission Nationale de Lutte contre le Genocide [National Commission for the Fight against Genocide]) in 2012, was quoted as saying: "During this period no person is authorized to perform marriages, and everyone should avoid the holidays [i.e., going on vacation] or any leisurely activity of its kind."[16] The observance of these dates is mandatory for all Rwandans regardless of what one thinks of the genocide and even applies to foreigners.[17] Even though I did not encounter any laws prohibiting any activities, it is socially expected that all who are in Rwanda will avoid them, and ignoring these expectations draws strong community opprobrium.

In the period leading up to the tenth anniversary of the genocide, commemorations intensified nationally and lasted several months. Commemorations gained popularity, and the official opening was fixed on April 7, a date that gave the master narrative more prominence in Rwanda's holiday calendar. Contrary to popular stories, especially by Antagonists, dates for commemorating other victims of the genocide also exist. For example, every year on April 13, most government officials remember Hutu politicians who were murdered for refusing to participate in the genocide.[18] On April 8, ten UN peacekeepers who died during the genocide are remembered.[19] These dates are as important as genocide laws, memorials, and any other symbol that gives meaning to the master narrative of the genocide and commemoration.

Over time, the number of official days to mark the opening of the genocide started to be reduced. In 2013, national events such as the one I attended in 2012 were localized to community-level commemorations, and a policy was communicated that, going forward, an official gathering would take place in the city every 5 years. This then communicated an effort to localize the master narrative and an important shift in diffusing commemorations.

Discourses around Community-Level Activities and Civic Education

Organization

Following the national opening ceremony held in Kigali and across other district headquarters on April 7, a week of community-level sessions was organized. Mainly intended to serve as civic education, these sessions occur in the afternoon and evening. In almost all thirteen public community events that I attended in different parts of the country, a government official attended to convey a government message that referenced the annual theme and reemphasized the master narrative. The officials reiterated the Rwandan Patriotic Army's (RPF's) vision for a peaceful, genocide-free

Rwanda, anchored in good governance and other stories that underpinned the master narrative of genocide.[20] In some cases, a military officer was present to promise security for survivors and other Rwandans.

Political messages are also conveyed publicly during the systematic civic education activities held in the first week of official commemorations. The government appointed and trained local leaders to engage in a public discussion on Rwandan history. Champions of the master narrative consider these platforms important opportunities to socialize the masses and shape youth perceptions of the past. Research has shown that survivors "are driven by grief and trauma and by a belief that safeguarding the memory of the genocide is an essential step towards political and social transformation in Rwanda."[21] April 7 itself is a national public holiday, but over the following days, public offices and businesses operate for half days. During this time, individuals are expected to attend afternoon community meetings for civic education, typically held in public spaces such as local schools, as well as evening gatherings in their neighborhoods that take the form of the traditional *ikiriyo* or "vigil," which is a time to mourn the death of a family member. For commemorations, it is organized on April 7 in preparation for the next day of commemoration activities. Given this is a new cultural ritual, aspects of planning require organizers to debate and improvise.

On April 12, 2012, I attended a community discussion in an afternoon session in the Kacyiru neighborhood in Kigali. The lessons had been detailed, printed, and passed on from one of the CNLG's central organizing committees.[22] In the meeting, facilitators continually referenced Western scholars' works to support their arguments or to criticize these same Western scholars for disseminating misleading stories about the genocide. The facilitators, some of whom were survivors, occasionally referred to their personal experiences, and if old enough, their experiences of other historical events in Rwanda, such as the 1959 massacres of Tutsi. I spoke with some of the facilitators, who informed me that they receive lesson plans produced by the CNLG and distributed through local governments. Local stakeholders, including sector leaders and Ibuka, select the most enlightened and mature people as conveners.[23] As in many other sectors in Rwanda, both men and women were represented on a panel. "It is a voluntary exercise," one woman answered when I asked why she participates every year. "It is considered an honour to be selected to participate as a leader."[24]

However, panelists also face complex challenges. In my informal discussions with a nationally acclaimed community activist, he confessed that when history is taught in community discussions, certain historical events are filtered out or are difficult to include. Though a survivor himself, he was concerned that as a convener he was deliberately imparting only partial knowledge to young people since further information is not part of the master narrative of the Genocide Against the Tutsi. Hence, to promote critical thinking, he expressed his concerns to organizers and requested that next time such lessons be subject to debate before they are delivered. He also explained to me that while it was difficult to encourage individuals to participate in public debate, most preferring instead to listen, occasionally someone would ask a question deemed out of "script" or based on counternarratives to the master narrative. He recalled one lively debate where a young man in attendance asked a controversial question about when those people whose relatives were killed during reprisal killings or other occurrences of violence during the 1990s civil war would be permitted to remember their loved ones. The panelist reported that he and his fellow panelists found a way to dismiss the question politely.[25] They asked the young man to approach them after the session for further discussion and noted that the end of that session was marked by uneasy silence.

Discourses Advanced through Storytelling and Testimonials

The evening gatherings that I attended in Kigali, Muhanga, Ruhango, and Huye were more informal and localized than the afternoon sessions.[26] Although children are welcome to attend the afternoon sessions, their participation is more evident in the evening as activities are more colorful, and storytelling takes center stage. Evening sessions are less discussion oriented, and civic education takes a different tone, with a focus on testimonials, music, and poetry. These sessions pivot on an amalgamation of survivors' testimonies, religious messages, and local government leaders' speeches. For example, in one of the ikiriyo (vigils) I attended, one speaker talked about the 1959 killings of Tutsi. The local government representative who spoke contrasted the current government's good governance with the bad governance of pregenocide leaders.[27] Then a representative of the police and military addressed the question of security for survivors and emphasized the police and military's commitment to protecting all Rwandans. The speeches in the evening were shorter and more relaxed. Throughout the evening a choir entertained the mourners with songs of lament that resembled those at funerals.[28]

In this ikiriyo, a survivor clergyman gave his testimony of forgiving Hutu, even those who had killed his father during the 1963 massacres.[29] He often referenced biblical passages to emphasize the importance of the ritual of remembering. He referenced Christ's words at the Passover supper before his death: "This is my body given for you; do this in remembrance of me." The clergyman asserted that there is a distinction between remembering as a Christian and as a non-Christian. He said: "Christians do not remember those who died to express anger or despair but to express hope and forgiveness."

Another survivor spoke of her journey and struggles with nightmares. She explained how she used to drink a lot of alcohol to forget and cope with past trauma. She concluded by echoing the clergyman's message, crediting God for her healing process. The Christian undertone is noticeable in many of the testimonials, especially when survivors speak of positive transformation after the genocide.

A Muslim leader informed me that most Muslims supported commemoration from the start and mobilized people to participate, though their reasons varied:

> The postgenocide government was the first of all the republics to honour and respect us as Muslims. Both Kayibanda and Habyarimana's governments were influenced by Catholic beliefs and so we were discriminated upon till the RPF brought the government of national unity. Muslims are always appointed into government positions. But also remember Muslims saved many people during the genocide. In most part Hutu Muslims refused to participate in the genocide. For us leaders we chose to encourage our followers to remember and take part in commemoration activities from early on.[30]

The master narrative has portrayed Muslims as heroes and rescuers during the genocide compared to Catholics and Christians in general. Two stories are part of the master narrative. One is that of Sula (Zula) Karuhimbi from Gitarama Province who died at age 106 in 2018. Her iconic story of saving Tutsi by hiding them in her home not only was told at the Kigali Memorial Center, where she was portrayed in a photo wearing hijab, but also was honored with Rwanda's highest medal *Indacyemwa*, meaning "righteous, unblamable." Her story is remarkable because she was an elderly woman who would have been an adult during PARMEHUTU's (Party of the Hutu Emancipation Movement's) radicalization period teaching Hutu extremist ideology in the late 1950s. She not only is a symbol of a rescuer, but also demonstrates that some Rwandan Hutu resisted the narrative of extremism for decades, through both the First and Second Republics.

The second story is that of Diagne Mbaye, a Senegalese military officer who was part of the UNAMIR (United Nations Assistance Mission for Rwanda) mission to Rwanda led by the Canadian General Roméo Dallaire. Unlike most peacekeepers, he defied UN orders and went on a solo mission to rescue Tutsi that eventually cost his life. As the tenth commemoration approached in 2004, his story was known to few but was publicized by the US Public Broadcasting Service (PBS) news show *Frontline*. The report cited those who knew him:

> From literally the first hours of the genocide, Capt. Mbaye simply ignored the UN's standing orders not to intervene, and single-handedly began saving lives. He rescued the children of the moderate Hutu Prime Minister Agathe Uwilingiyimana, after 25 well-armed Belgian UN peacekeepers surrendered their weapons to Rwandan troops. The Rwandan troops killed the Madame Agathe (and later, ten Belgian peacekeepers), while the unarmed Capt. Mbaye—acting on his own initiative hid the Prime Minister's children in a closet.[31]

Captain Mbaye's story was retold by a BBC reporter at the twentieth commemoration in 2014. Most documentations of his life emphasized the fact that he was Muslim. His story also became part of the master narrative when he was honored publicly among Rwandan heroes. His story has further been used in international forums to both recognize the reality of the genocide and to prove the failure of UN peacekeepers, regional organizations, and the international community at large.[32]

For most local commemorative events I attended, the program included Christian prayers. In addition to prayers, selected speakers for the 2012 commemoration I attended referenced the annual theme of 2012, affirming each other's speeches. They also encouraged survivors to tell their stories and to prevent becoming depressed by keeping each other company and ensuring that no one is alone during the commemoration period. Both the clergy and the woman mentioned above spoke of how testimonials should focus on hope, on working hard to survive, and on stories of success and recovery as opposed to past approaches ridden by anger, revenge, and contempt. The strong redemptive, recovery element of theology is well suited for the purposes of nation building.[33]

Localized Commemoration in Private, Public Institutions, and the Diaspora

Similar activities, though focused on more specialized groups and less structured, occurred during commemorations organized by private organizations.[34] The target audience was often the urban elites who could not manage to attend afternoon or evening public gatherings. The CNLG encouraged these gatherings, which were often organized to remember victims who were staff at foreign embassies, well-known private companies, or churches. Government affiliates reminded participants of the national annual theme. During the commemorations, Jean de Dieu Mucyo, the executive secretary of CNLG in 2012, asserted that all public and private institutions established after 1994 should be involved in commemorations. Previous to this statement, commemorations were mostly carried out in institutions that existed before the genocide and therefore had deceased staff to remember. Mucyo's argument was that institutions should not only remember staff but also allow current staff to participate collectively in this important national event.[35] Furthermore on April 5, 2012, he argued that foreigners who would normally leave Rwanda in April for their individual or family vacation should remain in the country and participate in national mourning events.[36]

Civic education sessions also extended to the diaspora. In Washington, D.C., commemorations included church ceremonies and testimonials and offered space for survivors to engage in political advocacy.[37] The Washington commemorations are distinct insofar as they are situated in a capital city where global politics takes center stage. Commemorations are used to highlight the plight of survivors and/or confront those who challenge the postgenocide government. The embassy of Rwanda in Washington often supports survivors' initiatives and ensure that the government's message is represented in those forums. In 2012, for example, the commemoration ceremony was organized by youth in the diaspora with the assistance of the Rwandan Embassy in Washington. While the leading organizers were survivors who were children during the genocide, other Rwandans joined them to organize the events. The events included a public lecture that brought together scholars of Rwanda, survivors, and other interested participants with a focus on fighting genocide denial outside Rwanda. The commemorative events also included a church service, a march to Capitol Hill, and political speeches that tied remembering to political messages emanating from the new Rwanda.

In these kinds of forums practiced in Belgium, Paris, Montreal, Darfur, Kampala, London, Nairobi, Stockholm, Johannesburg, and other places where Rwandans live in large numbers, individuals' experiences varied. Survivors were given priority, but non-Rwandans often also spoke about where they were when the genocide began and about the lack of international community action. Other non-Rwandans also participated in the United Nations' April 7 "Day of Remembrance," organized at UN offices in Nairobi and New York.[38]

However, it should be noted that for the first two decades examined in this book, the United Nations did not organize events around the same theme set in Rwanda as part of the master narrative. On April 7, during the first-week activities, and throughout the national mourning period, Champions of the master narrative, whether in Rwanda or in the diaspora, all argued that the commemoration period and mourning should lead all Rwandans to reconciliation. As one study concluded:

> Taking into account experience from other countries which have experienced genocide, we conclude that the preservation of genocide memory represents a fundamental basis for reconciliation; it allows people to learn from their history and offers the culprits an opportunity to meditate about the dimension of atrocities they did. In fact, it is in constructing cultural memory that Rwanda would envisage reconciliation.[39]

Jacqueline, a university student that I interviewed in 2011, feared that as commemorations continued to evolve, they would eventually lose meaning or come to an end:

> I fear that one day, there will be politicians who will say oh let's observe one minute of silence for the victims of genocide but continue with their lives. What will we do then? What will we tell our children about why we no longer remember their relatives?[40]

For now, commemorations are largely a space for mourning, healing, and conducting civic education and a time to pursue national reconciliation and quality national citizenship.

Responding to the Master Narrative through Private and Family Events

Private and noninstitutionalized settings provide a platform for people to respond to the master narrative. In these private spaces, individual, social, and political memory forms interact. These interactions between the mind of the individual, the monuments, and other nonsentient reminders of the past constitute what Jan Assmann called "communicative memory."[41]

Rwanda's postgenocide memorialization process includes contexts that provide for the evolution of a communicative memory. Scholars have pointed to the structure of Rwandan society before colonization as imagined through its own master narrative. Others argue that even the genocide itself was organized in these small units, which at times aligned with or defied government policy or the Arusha Peace process.

The family unit was completely ruptured during the genocide.[42] Apart from losing loved ones and in some cases never finding their remains, families were separated for a long period, both emotionally and physically.[43] In some cases, family members were reunited months and even years later, while others remain separated. Those who were separated had no chance to mourn, bury, or eulogize their dead collectively, a practice that is central to Rwandan mourning culture.[44] There are many rituals to be performed when someone dies.[45] Janet Jacobs has linked contemporary genocide commemoration rituals in Rwanda to ancestral practices of mourning in which the living gave gifts to the dead and asked for protection.[46] Longman and Rutagengwa showed that family members in postgenocide commemorations practiced a mourning ritual at burial sites, where they thanked the dead for looking after them by providing them with gifts.[47] Thus, family practices are rooted in indigenous belief systems fused with the Christianity introduced by colonialists in the twentieth century. Tutsi perceive the annual commemoration as some sort of replacement for what was not done for their family members immediately after the genocide.

During my research in April 2012, I had an opportunity to observe a family's commemoration. The family met at a house or public space, as they did for other social functions (e.g., weddings and funerals). Some activities resembled those in funerals, such as the ikiriyo, which involved relatives and family friends in the community. Yet, questions emerged during the planning as well. The first was whether they should allow a religious leader who had been tried in *gacaca* courts to lead the mass; should they rule him out even if he had been found innocent? A lively debate ensued, which ended with the decision that the religious leader would be allowed. The decision came after two members of the family used derogatory and insensitive language to express their anger amid a group that included several sympathizers who were not Tutsi survivors. One of the speakers regretted his anger toward the end of the meeting, and everyone reported that they "understood."

The second question pertained to the type of liturgies to be used. Traditional Catholic and Protestant leaders have not developed any documents that suit genocide commemorations, and the normal liturgies for the dead were deemed insufficient. The family resolved to create their own messages and report the program to the church leadership so that theologians could create relevant genocide-commemorative prayers for Christians. An interview with the Muslim leader mentioned previously confirmed they also did not have any specific prayers at the time for Muslims who were remembered during the genocide commemorations.

The family then grappled with who among them should give testimonies. It was agreed that one of the young survivors who witnessed the killing of the majority of his family should be the one to recount the story.

The last question was the family's consideration of whether they should thank individuals who hid their family's survivors. One member expressed concern that some of those who hid them were also killers, as was common during the genocide. The compromise on this issue was to buy individual gifts for whoever saved each person but to generally announce in public that survivors were thankful to the community that hid them. This would enable the survivors to avoid controversy since they planned to hold the commemorative events in the rural area rather than Kigali, where most of the survivors, perpetrators, and bystanders who would participate in this particular event coexisted.

Other issues to do with financial contributions and whom to invite were easily agreed on by family members. The fact that nonsurvivors should make it their duty to join in on family commemorations held by their friends was emphasized through the use of a Kinyarwanda proverb: *Ifuni ibagara ubucuti ni akarenge* or "One's feet are a small hoe that works the garden of friendship." By visiting each other, people strengthen friendships and relationships. Attendance, whether you are from a survivor or nonsurvivor family, was seen as a key duty and a building block of reconciliation and unity at the community level.

Participation in these events was not compulsory due to the mix of reactions that the event elicits from family members, especially those who are young and have no direct memory of the 1994 genocide. For instance, one of the older women organizers urged younger orphans and male youth who were children at the time of the genocide to go to work rather than come for family meetings. Many of these youth had been told and retold stories of the genocide and the death of their parents and chose to distance themselves from these experiences. However, in this particular family, which I followed for years, the youth organized the twentieth commemoration for their family members, perhaps because of the publicity surrounding youth engagement in national commemoration activities.[48] Family activities are not immune from the national ambiance surrounding commemorations.

However, as the discussion on the above questions demonstrated, remembrances in a collective or in a micro unit like a family could also become very complex. Individual family members were at different levels of healing, and that influenced debates on what kind of activities to plan, who should be invited, and who should be allowed to participate. For example, in this family, one man continually opposed participation of any Hutu in their community.

The group debated how much money should be allocated for such a ceremony. In the family whose planning meetings I observed, most members and close friends contributed freely and generously. However, there were also discussions on whether this money would have been better spent by paying university tuition fees for one of the family's survivors.

Given the dynamism of individual relations in postgenocide Rwanda, some topics are discussed with a sense of caution to avoid hurting new members of the extended family who might not come from a similar Tutsi background. Rwandans are conscious of silences that underpin the master narrative and commemoration. In a particular instance the young lady who was chosen to give her testimony was now married to a Hutu husband with whom she had children. He was present in these meetings and silent. His presence alongside several others who had married into the family reminded the Tutsi family members to cautiously deploy selective and respectful language. For example, they referred to the perpetrators of the genocide as *Interahamwe* to avoid generalizing all Hutu as perpetrators to ensure that survivors did not alienate their new family members. These other family members were also given various roles in the activities of the day.

By observing the commemoration activities in families for 3 years, I learned how individual, social, and political memory collide at the micro level just as they do at the national and community levels, though not with the same intensity. The experience and approach of family commemorative activity is different for each family, depending on whether there is any interest in organizing such an event; the capacity, including financial ability; how many people survived in that family; and many others. While some choose a religious-centered remembering approach, others choose to simply meet with friends at home in the evening as in the traditional ikiriyo held by community members. These functions evolved into different forms before national and community-level commemorations were institutionalized. Although it was beyond the scope of my research, in various discussions with interviewees I was informed that some Hutu also gather in their families to remember civil war victims, albeit lacking national recognition for these dead. These events are, of course, rarely organized in public like the planning activities I attended for commemorations of Tutsi victims.

People's Experiences of and Responses to Commemoration Activities

Champions of the Genocide Master Narrative

Both moderate and radical Champions of the genocide master narrative were involved in commemorations. Some were involved as members of the government, through the Ministry of Sports and Culture and the CNLG, which organize first-week activities from April 7 to April 13. Others were involved through Ibuka, a genocide survivors' association that oversees all further mourning activities until the official closing of the mourning period at the end of June. The Champions endorsed the master narrative publicly and spread it through their own localized commemorative events.

The Institute of Research and Dialogue for Peace (IRDP) conducted a countrywide study from 1995 to 2003 on citizens' sense of a duty to remember and asserted that:

> We have to remember that the requirement to preserve memory matches with Rwandan culture in which every Rwandese is required to provide decent burial to the deceased, as this is the case everywhere, but also to

observe a mourning period (*KWIRABURA, KWERA*, respectively, for mourning and end-of-mourning rites). Moreover, they have to remain spiritually in contact with their ancestors and other deceased relatives (*GUTEREKERA*).[49]

Similar sentiments were echoed in speeches on the first day of the remembrance period throughout Rwanda and during the weeks and months of commemoration. Emphasis was often laid on the importance of according Tutsi victims a dignified burial that they did not receive during the genocide. This was also confirmed in a separate study carried out from 2005 to 2011 on commemorations in Gasabo District. The study quotes an Ibuka representative urging genocide survivors not to forget, using a French translation of words written by Italian writer and Auschwitz survivor Primo Levi:

> Do not forget what happened, no do not forget it: guard these words in your heart. Think on it at home. In the street, when going to bed, when bathing, repeat it to your children. Or may your houses be destroyed, may illness strike you down, may your offspring turn their faces from you.[50]

Among the Champions, there was also another group of survivors who I identify as radicals, who consider commemoration a time to take action and revenge for their relatives. During my fieldwork in 2011, Kayihura, a young man in his late twenties, was one of the first people that I met in the Southern Province in rural Rwanda. He recounted to me his experience of his first commemoration in 1995:

> In 1995, I was a teenager and very active in my neighbourhood. We used to meet as young Tutsi in different houses and talk for hours about what had happened in the *intambara* [war]. At the time we did not call it genocide and we called ourselves *victimes* [victims]. Every other day we found an old friend who we thought had died or heard another story of someone who was killed. School resumed in 1995 and few of us attended. During the first commemoration in April 1995 our conversations intensified. We discussed a lot about taking action. How could we as young victims just sit and do nothing? We started to organize and distribute materials [printed materials] around with warning that we would take revenge and kill Hutu. We were very angry and very energetic. One day we heard that there were Interahamwe at *secteur* [the local sector station]; we went there and spent

hours negotiating with the RPA [Rwandan Patriotic Army] soldiers to give us a few of them so that we could "punish" them. We insisted and explained what they had done to us, but in their usual calm and soft voice, they [the RPA soldiers] told us "*ntabwo ari byiza*" [it was not a good idea]. We were very angry with this response but had to leave.[51]

Although some survivors I spoke to shared Kayihura's desire for revenge and unapologetically verbalized their hatred of Hutu, most admitted that these feelings were slowly diminishing over the years. The RPF has not sanctioned this kind of hatred, at least not in public, because vigilantism is a looming threat to the nation's stability and public order. Therefore, from this community of citizens we find that memory can be a site of division and conflict at all levels: the national, the community, and even into the most intimate space of the family.

Some Champions disagreed in early commemorations on how to bury their dead. In addition, there were tensions over what was required of survivors in the process of reconciliation and peacebuilding. While some argued for forgiveness, others rejected being coerced to forgive when they did not consider themselves ready to do so. For example, during the 2009 commemoration months, Jean Paul Samputu, a genocide survivor who was a famous singer before and after the genocide, started holding conferences and giving speeches to survivors about forgiveness. On April 14, 2009, BBC's Kinyarwanda and Kirundi section published a story in which it reported on a disagreement between Samputu and Ibuka's then-president Theodore Simburudari. Samputu had been spreading messages in his music and media on how he forgave those who killed his family and relatives and encouraged other survivors to do the same. Simburudari disagreed and said no survivor should be forced to forgive.[52] The BBC report explained that Samputu had called for a media conference to explain that he did not want to force anyone to forgive but wanted them to emulate his example because he believed it would free them. Samputu's comments were discussed in many forums in Rwanda and the diaspora. These discussions showed that genocide survivors were yet to deal with these traumas of the past, especially those who had not known where their loved ones were killed or buried. Although some Champions could be said to have embraced the proverb *Agahinda si uguhora urira*, or "sorrow does not mean keeping on whining," such social pressure to respond in particular ways to trauma, across identity categories, led some to become Antagonists of the genocide master narrative.

Antagonists of the Genocide Master Narrative

Anxious Communities
Here we look at actions in responding to the master narrative that Jean Paul Kimonyo identifies as "coerced obedience."[53] During the mourning period, Antagonists of the master narrative of the genocide are anxious or resist official memory publicly and privately. Although one cannot generalize the entire Hutu community, most people in this category are either former genocide convicts or persons who have been accused or suspected of participating in the genocide. It also often includes some (but not all) of their relatives or family members who are skeptical of the master narrative of the genocide or reject it altogether. Although fear and anxiety were more prevalent during the past years when gacaca trials were being held, they are still common among these communities. It was often during commemoration that their names were likely to be mentioned by a survivor who had never shared their stories. Hutu men in particular (though some women were included) feared commemoration gatherings because they risked being implicated in genocide crimes, which might lead to their prosecution in gacaca courts. Their fear was well founded because some Champions, especially radicals, took advantage of the large audiences rallied during commemorations to forge memories that erroneously implicated particular Hutu individuals.

This anxiety went beyond Rwanda to international Rwandan fugitives exiled in different countries. Every April, Champions use different forums to remind countries such as Zambia, France, and Belgium that they are providing a safe haven for genocide fugitives.[54] Consider President Kagame's statement on the eighteenth commemoration, which I attended at Amahoro Stadium: "There is little effort to apprehend them and when this happens it is a token meant to blind us and give us the impression that they are doing justice."[55] This signifies that the RPF, understandably, has yet to forget the international community's complicity in the genocide.

For the opening ceremony, everyone's participation is required. Though I did not find laws that punish those who do not participate, depending on one's personal or family story, appearing uninterested in ceremonies can have grave social repercussions and damage reputations. For instance, my interviewees told me that former prisoners or convicts, even if they were subsequently released, are expected to attend and show empathy. This affects even those in local government leadership positions, who have a responsibility to participate, especially as role models for communities. One interviewee, Aline, who came of age during this period of mourning, spoke of the dynamics surrounding participation:

> It's often at 6 a.m. when someone moves around with a loud voice amplifier announcing that everyone should come to the main place where we are meeting that day. Most people obey and those who do not (and are not survivors) are known or are not well perceived by the government or survivors. We all have to go but for survivors if we don't go no one will judge us as we are the ones who lost people.[56]

However, even with crowds of people in attendance at both the official ceremony on April 7 and the first week's afternoon and evening gatherings, it is difficult to assert that all participants agree on the narratives of official commemoration or even agree that the genocide took place. Some Antagonists perceive commemoration ceremonies as *une affaire des Tutsis où les Hutus ne s'y retrouvent pas*,[57] or, "It is a Tutsi affair or business in which Hutu do not find themselves represented." Darius Gishoma notes that participation in commemoration increased over time, and most Hutu considered commemoration of the genocide to be for Tutsi survivors.[58] This was one of the reasons commemoration activities were decentralized so that ordinary Rwandans could be part of the process and the events.

Therefore, it is possible that there are those who attend only as a sort of public repentance or performance, especially those who were accused in gacaca or were recently released from prison on suspicions of genocide denial. They want to be well perceived in society, especially if they or any of their relatives confessed to crimes and are repenting through community service.[59] To retaliate Kimonyo's argument mentioned at the beginning of this chapter, Antagonists—especially those in Rwanda—employ different strategies in the face of powers and laws supporting the master narrative they disagree with and challenge. "To gain access to certain privileges later," Kimonyo argues, "the dominated can feign overzealous obedience and employ strategies such as avoidance behaviour, manoeuvring, feet-dragging, pretended compliance with orders, work to rule, or passive sabotage."[60] This is true of Antagonists who are in Rwanda more than those who are outside, who employ "these strategies [as] part of a continuum that stretches between coerced obedience at one extreme and freely chosen course of action or open rebellion at the other."[61]

Yet their expressions of anxiety and alienation lead some Antagonists to engage in competitive memory activities that seek moral equivalency, which were on the rise between 1995 and 2014 and which translated into violence in Rwanda. For example, there were grenade attacks at the Kigali Memorial Center in 2008 and 2009, both during the commemoration period. In 2008, a guard was killed, and in 2009 one person was injured.[62] Both attacks reminded Champions, Antagonists, and Fatalists alike that there were alternative narratives about the genocide that induced some to remember while inducing others to disrupt the activities that honor a narrative with which they disagree.[63] For Antagonists, their actions in Rwanda and the diaspora are an avenue for them to "speak truth to power," with varied resistance strategies,[64] even when it is at the risk of being followed by the Rwandan government security agents.[65]

Antagonists' Comparative Approach to Critiquing the Master Narrative and Commemoration

The more radical among Antagonists argue that official memorialization is a "*Tutsification* of the genocide," a genocide that, in their judgment, never was, since they consider it to have been a civil war.[66] This is evident in various countermemory activities, which are often private, though in rare instances public. When such acts happen in public, they are more frequent during the commemoration period.

In most cases, such acts are carried out by adults who may have been released from prison or perpetrators displaying their trauma. However, these acts of sabotage are also more common among youth who were not yet born in 1994. According to a report produced by the CNLG and La Benevolencia in 2009, such acts of denial by younger people can often be a result of parents who socialize their children to believe that there was no genocide.[67] They interpret the 1994 events as a civil war that evolved out of the RPF's war in the early 1990s. Some parents advance a "double-genocide" narrative: one against the Tutsi in Rwanda and the other against the Hutu in Congo.[68] Others simply use vague words when discussing the events of 1994. They come up with various descriptions, consciously refraining from labeling the 1994 events a genocide. In a study carried out in rural former communes from 2001 to 2003, those Antagonists who were interviewed used a range of vocabularies when reciting their recollection of 1994. These included words like *ibyabaye* (happenings), *intambara yo muri 94* (war of 1994), *ubwicanyi* (killings), *amahano* (tragedy, horror), or *itsembatsemba* (massacres).[69] However, some used language that portrayed their consciousness of the official labeling of 1994 events as genocide. One interviewee said: "They have said it was a genocide and massacres, so I call it that as well."[70] These choices of words and actions are often what Champions look out for when trying to distinguish Antagonists of the genocide master narrative from the rest and accuse them of genocide denial.

Unlike Champions of the genocide master narrative who emphasize the historical hatred of Hutu toward minority Tutsi, the Antagonists prefer to situate the 1994 massacres in the context of elites competing for power on both sides. They discredit the mass participation of ordinary Hutu in the killing of Tutsi in 1994.[71] These two radical narratives oppose each other, and they are responsible for raising tensions through the 20 years of the evolution of the master narrative. To Antagonists, their oppositional narrative implies that they ought to organize remembrance activities that compete with the official ones. They typically organize such events outside Rwanda; those in Rwanda respond through attacking Champions and vandalizing genocide memorials.

The radicals also resist submission to the master narrative by disrupting official commemorations. Additionally, my interviewees told me stories of people who demonstrated "bizarre" behaviors during commemoration days or expressed hatred against survivors. For instance, a man once announced in his neighborhood that he would be remembering his dogs that died in the genocide in April. When confronted by local authorities, he did not deny it and therefore was arrested and charged with denialism for comparing Tutsi victims to dogs.[72]

Furthermore, radical Antagonists have tried to violently erase evidence of genocide. It is reported that such groups have killed survivors in rural areas to silence their testimonials. Such killings intensify during the commemoration period. A survey in 2009 found that 156 genocide survivors had been killed between 1995 and 2008.[73] These attacks give weight to the accusation that Antagonists of the genocide master narrative participate in commemoration ceremonies out of compulsion to *kurangiza umuhango*, or to get it over with. In interviews carried out by Longman and Rutagengwa, Hutu women confirmed that while Tutsi gather to commemorate, Hutu women prefer to continue their daily chores (like cultivating their fields).[74] One of the interviewees commented that this is because: "[Champions of the master narrative] commemorate the genocide of the Tutsi, but the experience of those who went to the camps [in Congo and in Kibeho] is put to the side."[75] However, in the diaspora, Antagonists do not participate in official commemorations or remain passive like those in Rwanda. Instead they respond by organizing their own commemorations on April 6. Their argument is that the first person to be remembered should be former President Habyarimana because the shooting down of his plane preceded the genocide.[76]

A particular group of moderate Antagonists gained increased publicity in 2012 and 2013. Mostly based in Europe and North America, they organized events under the theme "remember all," arguing against the privileging of only one form of memory in contemporary genocide commemoration. They protest a narrative that excludes their relatives or other victims killed in the 1990s civil war, especially in the northern city of Byumba; victims of the postgenocide 1995 Kibeho massacres; and those who died in refugee camps in the former Zaire.[77] Although they don't conduct public demonstrations on April 6 in Rwanda, a study conducted in 2007 in the Nyamagabe District in southern Rwanda showed that these views exist in Rwanda, especially for those who live near the site of the Kibeho massacre, and that these sentiments are often reiterated during April commemorations. The study concluded that the majority of interviewees were of the opinion that all victims, including their relatives who were killed in the Kibeho camp, should be commemorated.[78]

Although this study did not have any impact on how and what is remembered, it showed that among Antagonists, some do not necessarily object to the commemoration of Tutsi victims but have a different memory that they want to see officially expressed and institutionalized as well. These moderate Antagonists share platforms with radical Antagonists when it comes to competitive memory, and their positions have evolved over time. Some Antagonists' ideas have evolved to accept that there was a genocide that targeted Tutsi, and yet they also argue for official commemoration to include Hutu victims of the genocide and Rwandan victims of other killings outside the genocide. They use a competitive approach similar to that in early memory scholarship to assert their points, which Champions classify as a "double-genocide" thesis.

This tension between Champions of the genocide master narrative and Antagonists manifests itself in not only public spaces but also private ones. There are Hutu who become retraumatized or who torture survivors because of their own unsettled trauma and lack of opportunity to remember their civil war victims publicly. Thus, their frustrations culminate in revived anger during the commemoration period. This is often prevalent among Hutu and Tutsi friends and especially intense in mixed marriages. As one study has found, this complexity goes beyond an older generation to the new generation of postmemory.[79]

Fatalists of the Genocide Master Narrative

Some Fatalists of the genocide master narrative, either in public or in private, criticized the government's official commemoration and the effect that the mourning period had on their personal lives. Most of those who voiced their criticism publicly were Tutsi survivors like Kayitesi, whose silence left me with many questions when I visited her. Some were Hutu whose Tutsi spouses were killed in the genocide and often privately organized commemoration of their loved ones or attended other public commemoration but rarely gave testimonies.[80] Two years after concluding my study of the first 20 years, the RPF's vice president, former minister, and member of the East Africa Parliament Christophe Bazivamo, a Hutu political elite, was allowed to share his testimony publicly during commemoration,[81] although the trend did not continue.[82] He revealed how his Tutsi wife and their mixed children were killed during the genocide, and he mourned them publicly, which was rare for a Hutu to do during commemoration.

As Richard Werbner has argued, survivors demand the right to speak through "counterappropriations" of their memories whenever the state seeks to appropriate past traumas.[83] These survivors include, for example, women who were raped during the genocide. Some of these women gave birth or were infected with HIV.[84] In questioning official commemoration, these women argue that their children and illnesses are already a daily physical reminder of the genocide. They protest the public showcasing and appropriation of personal and private experiences (which are at times perceived as shameful) for purposes of state-dominated commemorations.[85] For them, official memorialization reconfirms what the Interahamwe spitefully presaged: "We will leave you to live so that you can die of sadness."[86] As one survivor woman reflected:

> I regret that I didn't die that day. Those men and women who died are now at peace whereas I am still here to suffer even more. I'm handicapped in the true sense of the word. I don't know how to explain it. I regret that I'm alive

because I've lost my lust for life. We survivors are broken-hearted. We live in a situation which overwhelms us. Our wounds become deeper every day. We are constantly in mourning.[87]

A member of Abasa, a women's group in Huye, was told that the mourning period is important as it allows space for reconciliation among Rwandans. She responded in objection: *"Nkuko inkovu y'umupanga cyangwa Sida wanduye muri icyo gihe itazakira kugeza gupfa, ni uko n'ubwiyunge butazabaho."* ("As a machete's scar on survivors will never be erased, and the AIDS virus inflicted on some survivors will never heal until death, likewise reconciliation will never happen.")[88] To her, reconciliation was nothing more than political rhetoric that did not have any tangible bearing on her life.

Hence, with deep, personal, unhealed psychological scars, some survivors feel used during commemoration. One of my interviewees, a university student survivor named Aline, explained this feeling to me:

In this world you have to be realistic. How else were they going to be heard? How would our stories be heard with all other issues and conflicts in the world? They had to make a clear and single story that could be remembered quickly. You have to consider that we are constantly appealing to these same *abazungu* (whites) that did nothing during the genocide."[89]

Despite her understanding of why a master narrative was necessary, she still refuses to participate in the events given the traumas they awaken. She explained that there were other survivors like her who choose to remember, but privately and informally, without the state and public's intervention.[90] Some of these individuals are struggling with their own traumas and/or were too young to have a memory of their family's genocide victims. During the first week of April 2012, I met Soso, a young lady in her twenties who was working and lived between Kigali and Rwamagana in the Eastern Province. Soso raised her siblings in a child-headed home outside Kigali and was a university student at the time of the interview. When in Kigali, Soso stays with one of her relatives, who shows extreme trauma symptoms, especially in April, and resents the mourning period. Soso told me:

I was very young in the genocide; I don't even know what my parents looked like. There are no pictures, everything in house was stolen and it was destroyed. I have asked my aunt many times if we can talk about them [parents] or organize a family commemoration for all our victims, but she keeps quiet whenever I ask. She drinks a lot of alcohol in April and makes a lot of jokes. How can I organize an event alone? My young siblings are asking me many questions and I don't know how to respond.[91]

Although Soso, like many survivors with similar experiences, has made strides and is focused on living and creating a better life for her siblings, she admits that the past is a continual burden.[92] She emphasized that her siblings ask many questions related to the past during the mourning period, to the point where it frustrates her. They see her as someone who is older and should have all the answers. She struggles because she herself would like to know and provide answers, but the only person who could help, her aunt, is too weak in April. These kinds of experiences disrupt the flow of life for survivors in April. Some cannot go to work or school; they do not want to be seen in public. Many survivors I interviewed mentioned how minor vestiges such as April rain, a graveyard, the announcement of someone's normal death, mention of names, a display of photos, or video footage on TV can abruptly resurrect deep-rooted traumas. April is a very sensitive and dreadful period for such individuals. It is a period when deep-seated sorrows surface and when silence is conspicuous among this population. Through the stories of Soso and that of the guard I met in Bisesero mentioned at the beginning of this chapter, it is clear the genocide "lives"[93] in Rwandans, and the evolution of the master narrative and commemoration of the Genocide Against the Tutsi sustains its contested memory among Champions, Fatalists, and Antagonists.

Conclusion

This chapter reveals that Rwandans' responses to the master narrative were diverse and complex during the first 20 years of the commemoration period. It showed that in the first 20 years of commemoration, whether it is in community-centered memorial events or public events, both tensions and agreements exist between not only Champions and Antagonists but also Fatalists. The responses not only contribute to the making of political memory, but also to the evolution of communicative memory.

For Champions of the genocide master narrative, official commemoration activities provided a platform to mobilize communicative memory relating to the master narrative and also diverged from it to evolve differently. Through civic education and other activities, some Champions found a purpose for the master narrative in healing and reconciliation processes. Antagonists of the genocide master narrative, by contrast, found the commemoration period a time of fear, anxiety, and frustration in their everyday interactions. That notwithstanding, Champions, Antagonists, and Fatalists have begun having conversations about contentious issues regarding the genocide and its commemoration.[94]

Members of each group shared certain characteristics, but there were embedded complexities and variances. Individuals could oscillate between affiliations depending on personal circumstances or other factors. Furthermore, there was a constant tension between the master narrative and individuals' personal memories. This was tension between the injunction to remember on the one hand, and the questions of how to remember, what to remember, or who should be remembered on the other hand. Equally, there were tensions between how individuals expressed their memories and how the memories of individuals were used to respond to the needs of the collective. However, they were overwhelmed by the sheer indoctrination of the master narrative, which made other tales very difficult to access and document. The next chapter examines how Champions, Antagonists, and Fatalists have used art and other avenues to transmit their responses to the master narrative as it gained more prominence in the country and around the world.

Notes

1. Jennie E. Burnet, *Genocide Lives in Us: Women, Memory, and Silence in Rwanda* (Madison: University of Wisconsin Press, 2012), 10.
2. There are spaces that allow memorialization outside the said official period. These include gacaca hearings, where participants collectively remembered and shared what happened. See Philip Clark, "Bringing the Peasants Back in, Again: State Power and Local Agency in Rwanda's Gacaca Courts," *Journal of Eastern African Studies* 8, no. 2 (2014): 193–213.
3. There is a growing literature that discusses commemoration and explores different related themes. See Susanne Buckley-Zistel, "Remembering to Forget: Chosen Amnesia as a Strategy for Local Coexistence in Post-genocide Rwanda," *Africa: Journal of the International African Institute* 76, no. 2 (2006): 131–150; Rachel Ibreck, "A Time of Mourning: The Politics of Commemorating the Tutsi Genocide in Rwanda," in *Public Memory, Public Media and the Politics of Justice*, eds. Philip Lee and Pradip N. Thomas (Hound Mills, UK: Palgrave Macmillan, 2014), 98; and Elisabeth King, "Memory

Controversies in Post-genocide Rwanda: Implications for Peacebuilding," *Genocide Studies and Prevention* 5, no. 3 (2010): 293–309.
4. See King, "Memory Controversies in Post-genocide Rwanda."
5. See Helen Hintjens, "Post-genocide Identity Politics in Rwanda," *Ethnicities* 8, no. 1 (2008): 5–41.
6. According to a Kinyarwanda announcement by the mayor of Kigali, Fidèle Ndayisaba, these individuals that I joined as they walked to the stadium were mainly from sectors nearest to the Amahoro Stadium. See Pascaline Umulisa, "Iwawa Ni Ho Hatangirijwe Icyumweru Cy'urukundo Nyakuri," *Kigali Today*, December 1, 2012, https://www.kigalitoday.com/ubuzima/urusobe-rw-ubuzima/Iwawa-ni-ho-hatangirijwe-Icyumweru-cy-Urukundo-Nyakuri.
7. See Roméo Dallaire, *Shake Hands with the Devil: The Failure of Humanity in Rwanda* (New York: Carroll & Graf, 2005).
8. Personal conversation with Pierre, Kigali, Rwanda, 2012.
9. Colin Cameron, "'The Second Betrayal?' Commemorating the 10th Anniversary of the Rwandan Genocide," in *Africa on a Global Stage*, eds. Tanya Lyons and Geralyn Pye (Trenton, NJ: Africa World Press, 2006), .
10. See: David Mwambari, "Music and the Politics of the Past: Kizito Mihigo and Music in the Commemoration of the Gerenocide Against the Tutsi in Rwanda." *Memory Studies* 13, no. 6 (2020): 1321–1336.
11. See Nyiramutuzo Nyirazana, "La problématique du silence comme défi à la mémoire des victimes du Génocide des Tutsi d'avril-juillet 1994: Cas du Secteur Gasaka, du District Nyamagabe" (MA, l'Université Nationale du Rwanda, 2007).
12. Ibreck, *A Time of Mourning*, 110.
13. See Ananda Breed, *Performing the Nation: Genocide, Justice, Reconciliation* (London: Seagull Books, 2013).
14. Ibreck, *A Time of Mourning*, 106–109.
15. Steve Terrill, "Rwanda Remembers Genocide 18 Years Later," *Voice of America*, April 7, 2012, http://www.voanews.com/content/rwanda-remembers-genocide-18-years-later-146586625/179994.html.
16. Fiona Gasana, "The Eighteenth Commemoration of the Tutsi Genocide," *IGIHE*, April 2, 2012, https://en.igihe.com/news/the-18th-commemoration-of-the-tutsi-genocide.html.
17. Colette Braeckman, "Rwanda: Deux Diplomates Belges Jugés Indésirables Par Kigali Ont Regagné Bruxelles," *Le Soir (Bruxelles)*, June 1, 2020, https://plus.lesoir.be/304340/article/2020-06-01/rwanda-deux-diplomates-belges-juges-indesirables-par-kigali-ont-regagne.
18. Though no law I could find emphasized dates for each individual commemoration, the CNLG president confirmed that April 13 is for politicians. "Murisanga," Radiyo Yacu VOA, Rwanda, 59:34, May 4, 2020, https://www.radiyoyacuvoa.com/a/5380993.html.
19. It is also not clear if April 8 is in written law, but it was confirmed in an explanation given by the government explaining why two Belgian diplomats were forced out of the country in 2020. See Braeckman, "Rwanda: Deux Diplomates."

20. See James Tasamba, "Rwanda: Nation Commemorates Genocide," *All Africa*, April 7, 2012, http://allafrica.com/stories/201204070008.html.
21. Rachel Ibreck, "The Politics of Mourning: Survivor Contributions to Memorials in Post-genocide Rwanda," *Memory Studies* 3, no. 4 (2010), 3.
22. Ibid. One of the discussions was on a selected group of Tutsi monarchs with an emphasis on their desire for greater unity among Rwandans.
23. On April 14, 2012, I spoke informally with a CNLG staff member named "Antoine" in Kigali, Rwanda, on the question of who selects participants. I wanted to know if there were any policies on who participated in community-level commemorations. He told me that he did not know of any but was aware that local leaders collaborate to appoint *inararibonye*, which means elder and wise people (who might include younger people) in the community.
24. This was from an informal conversation with Claire, a participant at a Kacyiru community event, April 10, 2012.
25. Ibid.
26. These were some of the events I attended: From April 7 to April 13, 2012, various afternoon community events in the districts of Kacyiru, and Kicukiro in Kigali City, including a candle vigil at Amahoro Stadium on April 7; then to Muhanga and Ruhango for events in the Ruhango sector on April 21, 2012, and a visit to a mass grave in Ruhango town; and similar commemorations events, at various times, in the southern (Huye), northern (Musanze), and eastern (Rwamagana town) regions and in Bugesera districts.
27. The rhetoric about the difference between good and bad governance was part of RPF government rhetoric since early commemorations. See Cameron, "Second Betrayal?," 9.
28. The music is composed by local choirs to suit the particular theme while referencing passages in the Bible. As we will see in Chapter 6, music plays a leading role in both formal and informal ceremonies.
29. On killings of Tutsi in this period, see Gérard Prunier, *The Rwanda Crisis: History of a Genocide* (London: Hurst, 1998, 60–62.
30. Interview, Ntamirambo, Muslim cleric, January 3, 2020.
31. *Frontline*, season 22, episode 6, "Ghosts of Rwanda," directed by Greg Barker, written by Greg Barker, aired April 1, 2004, http://www.pbs.org/wgbh/pages/frontline/shows/ghosts/video/.
32. There were many disagreements on facts about the genocide, especially at the United Nations. See David Mwambari, "Emergence of Post-genocide Collective Memory in Rwanda's International Relations," in *Beyond History: African Agency in Development, Diplomacy, and Conflict Resolution*, eds. Elijah Munyi, David Mwambari, and Alexi Ylönen (London: Rowman & Littlefield International, 2020).
33. This approach was also used in South Africa's Truth Reconciliation Commission, led by Archbishop Tutu, with significant challenges. For a discussion of this, see Richard Wilson, *The Politics of Truth and Reconciliation in South Africa: Legitimizing the Post-apartheid State* (Cambridge: Cambridge University Press, 2008).

34. It is also an occasion to call on private companies to support genocide survivors through their corporate social responsibility budgets. See, for example, "CNLG Calls for Companies to Support Survivors," *IGIHE*, January 21, 2012, http://en.IGIHE.com/news/cnlg-calls-for-companies-to-support-survivors.
35. He especially emphasized that Christian churches are not doing enough to organize commemorations and encourage church members to support this cause. See Dusabemungu Ange De La Victoire, "Religious Institution Urged to Be Part of Genocide Commemoration," IGIHE (Kigali), March 28, 2013, https://en.igihe.com/news/religious-institutions-urged-to-be-part-of.
36. Ibid.
37. See, for example, the following video, which shows a commemoration event held in Washington, D.C., during the eighteenth commemoration of the genocide in 2012: Fidelis Mironko, "18th Commemoration of the Genocide against the Tutsi in Washington DC, Part One," April 7, 2012, Georgetown University, YouTube video, 22:33, https://www.youtube.com/watch?v=sfKCwvUVQu0.
38. See "Outreach Program on the Rwanda Genocide and the United Nations," United Nations, 2012, http://www.un.org/en/preventgenocide/rwanda/.
39. Nyirazana, *La problématique du silence*, 13.
40. Interview with a university student, Huye, Rwanda, April 2011.
41. Jan Assmann, "Communicative and Cultural Memory," in *A Companion to Cultural Memory Studies*, eds. Astrid Erll and Ansgar Nunning (Berlin: De Gruyter, 2010), 37.
42. Espérance Mukasekuru, "*La réintégration sociale des femmes et filles victimes des violences sexuelles au cours du Génocide de 1994 au Rwanda*" (MA, Université Nationale du Rwanda, 2009), 56.
43. Ibid.
44. See Alexis Kagame, *Les organisations socio-familiales de l'ancien Rwanda* (Brussels: Académie Royale des Sciences Coloniales, 1954), 35.
45. Ibid.
46. Janet Jacobs, "Sacred Space and Collective Memory: Memorializing Genocide at Sites of Terror," *Sociology of Religion* 72, no. 2 (Summer 2011), 163.
47. Timothy Longman and Théoneste Rutagengwa, "Memory and Violence in Post-genocide Rwanda," in *States of Violence: Politics, Youth, and Memory in Contemporary Africa*, eds. Donald L. Donham and Edna G. Bay (Charlottesville: University of Virginia Press, 2007), 233.
48. Alyssa Juday, "Construction amidst Binaries," *Spaces of Memory–Lugares de memoria* 3-4 (2014): 74-79.
49. Institute of Research and Dialogue for Peace, *Reconstruire une paix durable au Rwanda: La parole au people* (Kigali, Rwanda: Institute for Research and Dialogue for Peace/WSP International, 2003), 77.
50. Kigero Muhire, "Analyse de la commémoration du Génocide des Tutsi dans le contexte socio-politique du Rwanda: 'Cas du District de Gasabo'" (BA, Université Nationale du Rwanda, 2011), 31.
51. Interview with Kayihura, 2011.

52. Jean Claude Mwambutse, "Jean Paul Samputu arabeshyuza ibyo Simburudare yavuze," *BBC Gahuzamiryango*, April 14, 2009, http://www.BBC.co.uk/greatlakes/news/story/2009/04/090415_rdaibukasamputu.shtml.
53. Jean-Paul Kimonyo, *Rwanda's Popular Genocide: A Perfect Storm* (Boulder, CO: Lynne Rienner, 2015,, 7.
54. Rodrigue Rwirahira, "Govt Vows to Push for Deportation of Fugitives," *East African (Nairobi)*, November 30, 2012, https://web.archive.org/web/20121201161554/http://www.theeastafrican.co.ke/Rwanda/News/Govt-vows-to-push-for-deportation-of-fugitives/-/1433218/1633766/-/1i8cbnz/-/index.html.
55. Terrill, "Rwanda Remembers Genocide."
56. Interview with Aline, April 2012.
57. "It is an affair of Tutsi where Hutu are confused"; see Institute of Research and Dialogue for Peace, *Reconstruire une paix durable*, 68.
58. Gishoma, "Crises traumatiques collectives d'Ihahamuka lors des commémorations du génocide des Tutsi," 158.
59. TIG is the French acronym for *Travail d'Intérêt Général*, or "work of general service," an assignment of work given to a prisoner who has confessed participation in the genocide. The legislation is quoted in "Rwanda (7) General Provisions," in the Natlex database, owned by the International Labor Organization, March 15, 2005; accessed January 5, 2013, http://www.ilo.org/dyn/natlex/natlex4.detail?p_lang=en&p_isn=71583&p_count=7&p_classification=01.
60. Kimonyo, *Rwanda's Popular Genocide*.
61. Ibid., 6–7.
62. Jessica Auchter, *The Politics of Haunting and Memory in International Relations* (New York: Routledge, 2014), 53.
63. Ibid.
64. Susan M. Thomson, *Whispering Truth to Power: Everyday Resistance to Reconciliation in Postgenocide Rwanda* (Madison: University of Wisconsin Press, 2013). See also: Susan Thomson, "Whispering Truth to Power: The Everyday Resistance of Rwandan Peasants to Post-genocide Reconciliation," *African Affairs* 110, no. 440 (2011): 439–456.
65. See Esther Marijnen, "Dealing with Dissent Across Borders: The 'Presence' of the Rwandan Government in the Rwandan Diaspora(s)," in *L'Afrique des Grands Lacs: Annuaire 2014–2015*, eds. Filip Reyntjens, Stef Vandeginste, and Marijke Verpoorten (Antwerp, Belgium: University Press of Antwerp, 2015), 287–305.
66. Prunier, *Africa's World War*, 3.
67. Edwin Musoni, "CNLG Releases Repot on Genocide Ideology in Schools," *New Times*, December 4, 2009, https://www.newtimes.co.rw/article/29935/National/cnlg-releases-report-on-genocide-ideology-in-schools.
68. Ibid.
69. Longman and Rutagengwa, "Memory and Violence in Postgenocide Rwanda," 246.
70. Ibid.
71. Ibid., 247.

72. On April 9, 2007, a man was arrested after dressing his dogs and informing his neighbors that he was remembering his dogs that died in 1994. See Godwin Agaba, "Dead Dogs Mourner to Appear in Court," *New Times*, April 11, 2007, archived at *All Africa*, https://allafrica.com/stories/200704110704.html.
73. Eugene Mutara, "Rwanda: 156 Genocide Survivors and Witnesses Killed," *New Times*, March 7, 2009, https://www.newtimes.co.rw/article/17565/National/156-genocide-survivors-and-witnesses-killed.
74. Longman and Rutagengwa, "Memory and Violence in Post-genocide Rwanda," 251.
75. Ibid.
76. It should be noted that Paris and Brussels police have refused to offer licenses to officiate these kinds of activities. For more on the genocide denial debate, see Michael Ngabo, "Rwanda: Deniers of the 1994 Genocide Against the Tutsi on Rampage," *All Africa*, April 23, 2011, https://allafrica.com/stories/201104250812.html.
77. Online opposition newspapers such as *Veritas Info News* and *Inyenyeri News* have carried many such stories in Kinyarwanda and have used those stories as platforms to gather support and call for individuals to protest and commemorate collectively on April 6. One of the first public protests was on April 6, 2011, in Brussels, Belgium, where there is a significant number of Hutu former elites.
78. Nyirazana, "La problématique du silence," 41.
79. On belonging and Rwandan youth who are of mixed heritage in postgenocide Rwanda, see Lyndsay McLean Hilker, "Rwanda's 'Hutsi': Intersections of Ethnicity and Violence in the Lives of Youth of 'Mixed' Heritage," *Identities* 19, no. 2 (2012): 229–247; and Anuradha Chakravarty, "Inter-ethnic Marriages, the Survival of Women, and the Logics of Genocide in Rwanda," *Genocide Studies and Prevention* 2, no. 3 (2007): 235–248.
80. Hutu resisters also want their dead remembered but do not always voice this concern. See René Lemarchand and Maurice Niwese, "Mass Murder, the Politics of Memory and Post-genocide Reconstruction: The Cases of Rwanda and Burundi," in *After Mass Crime: Rebuilding States and Communities*, eds. Simon Chesterman and Albrecht Schnabel (New York: United Nations University Press, 2007), 165–189; Helen Hintjens, "Conflict and Resources in Post-genocide Rwanda and the Great Lakes Region," *International Journal of Environmental Studies* 63, no. 5 (2006): 599–615; and Rachel Ibreck, "The Politics of Mourning: Survivor Contributions to Memorials in Post-genocide Rwanda," *Memory Studies* 3, no. 4 (2010): 330–343.
81. See Emma-Marie Umuherwa, "Kwibuka22: Ubuhamya bw'uko Depite Bazivamo yiciwe abana n'umugore .bwakoze benshi ku mutima," *IGIHE*, April 21, 2016, http://IGIHE.com/amakuru/u-rwanda/article/ubuhamya-bw-uko-depite-bazivamo-yiciwe-abana-n-umugore-bwakoze-benshi-ku-mutima?url_reload=21&debut_forum=20.
82. In 2019, a year outside the scope of this book, a debate on whether Hutu who killed should give testimonies and speak during commemoration raised tensions among Champions of memory primarily and Fatalists. See IGIHE, "Kuba Abakoze Jenoside Batanga Ubuhamya Mu Kwibuka Ntibivugwaho Rumwe," IGIHE (Kigali), 2019, https://IGIHE.com/amakuru/u-rwanda/article/kuba-abakoze-jenoside-batanga-ubuhamya-mu-kwibuka-ntibivugwaho-rumwe.

83. Richard P. Werbner, "Smoke from the Barrel of a Gun: Postwars of the Dead, Memory and Reinscription in Zimbabwe," in *Memory and the Postcolony: African Anthropology and the Critique of Power* (London: Zed Books, 1998), 71–102. Quoted in Ibreck, "Politics of Mourning," 4.
84. The United Nation's special representative to Rwanda, Rene Degni-Segui, reported in 1996 that an estimated 250,000–500,000 women were raped. This is a significant number of survivors. A study in 2000 showed that out of 1,000 women survivors tested, over 67% were HIV infected. See Nancy Sail, "Women under Siege: Rwanda."
85. See "Rwanda's Children of Rape," *Newsnight*, BBC, last updated June 30, 2010, http://news.BBC.co.uk/1/hi/programmes/newsnight/8768943.stm.
86. Shattered Lives: Sexual Violence during the Rwandan Genocide and Its Aftermath (New York: Human Rights Watch, September 24, 1996), 1, http://www.hrw.org/reports/1996/09/24/shattered-lives.
87. Sail, "Women under Siege: Rwanda."
88. Mukasekuru, *La réintégration sociale*, 72.
89. Interview with Aline, May 2012, Nyamagabe, South Province, Rwanda.
90. Ibreck, "Politics of Mourning," 2.
91. Interview with Soso, April 20, 2012, Rwamagana, Rwanda.
92. In April 2004, child-headed homes were estimated at 10,000, and most were supported by the Survivors Fund to care for their younger siblings. See the BBC program that carried an interview with one of the survivors caring for his siblings in a village near Kigali: "Rwanda: Child-Headed Households," *Woman's Hour*, BBC, April 7, 2004, http://www.BBC.co.uk/radio4/womanshour/2004_14_wed_04.shtml.
93. Burnet, *Genocide Lives in Us*.
94. See "Murisanga."

6
Expressing Memory after Genocide
The Art of Commemoration

Ababonangenda—Those who see me walking do not know the sorrow in my heart.
—Rwandan proverb

In July 2005, in the lobby of the United Nations headquarters in New York, an art exhibition was organized for the tenth commemoration of the Srebrenica genocide.[1] The exhibition included work from various artists, mostly from Bosnia and Herzegovina. One of the most powerful was the second version of Aida Šehovic's art installation of 1,705 coffee cups arranged in the geographic shape of Srebrenica.[2] The first version, "Što te Nema?" ("Why are you not here?"), presented a year earlier, was a display of 1,327 small porcelain coffee cups in front of a mosque in Sarajevo, the capital city of Bosnia and Herzegovina. The higher number of cups at the UN exhibition represented the victims of the Srebrenica genocide, whose bodies were found in that year and buried between the ninth and tenth anniversaries of this genocide. The exhibition as a whole, full of similarly creative and provocative work by other artists, attracted over 30,000 visitors in 2 weeks due to its unique and informal approach to commemorating a genocide that few people knew or remembered. Art and artists such as those who participated in this exhibition have played various roles in the memorialization of past atrocities, in both Rwanda and elsewhere. Although art provides mobility to memorialization and has always been a popular avenue to transmit ideas, memories, and stories in Rwanda's culture, little research exists that examines artworks and artists as they have responded to the master narrative as it emerged and evolved into a hegemonic memory of the genocide over the first 20 years.

In the previous chapters, we've seen how political memory itself evolved through changes in memorials, materials of memory such as the color of remembrance, or institutions and laws. I also discussed how Champions, Antagonists, and Fatalists have responded to the hegemonic master narrative as it emerged, evolved, and was enforced in various aspects of family and community life. This chapter focuses on individual responses and how individual positions within the analytical categories of Champion, Antagonist, and Fatalist evolved over time as the master narrative became solidified and turned into the hegemonic narrative. Thus, a closer look at individual narratives of artists and their supporters can help us examine why people emerge as Champions, Antagonists, or Fatalists and how their responses to the hegemonic master narrative also evolved and changed over time. The chapter finds one's position is not necessarily linked to one's ethnic or family belonging, but rather that social, political, personal attributes, economic factors, and history influence how one relates to the master narrative over time. I chose to analyze artists because while there exists extensive research in other contexts, analysis of the role of artists and art in emergence and evolution of memory in Rwanda is still relatively evolving.

This chapter analyzes artists' mnemonic messages transmitted through their various art forms to respond to the master narrative. While some works provoked conversations about reconciliation and nation-building, others aimed to activate individual reflection and the evolution of individual, social, communicative, and political memory all at once. Three artists' works and personal narratives inform analysis of this chapter. The first and the most discussed artist in this chapter is Kizito Mihigo, who was the most referenced by interviewees and most publicly associated in shaping the genocide political memory between 2008 and 2014.

Analysis of Mihigo's artwork and "iconic story" of surviving the genocide as a Tutsi[3] is then coupled with the next sections highlighting the work of two other artists, Edouard Bamporiki and Dorcy Rugamba. Each of these responded to the master narrative in their own ways, but their works discussed here had an impact on the master narrative and commemoration during the first 20 years in ways that diverge from Mihigo's. The chapter argues that through musical, poetic, and dramatic expressions of these artists' experiences, different memory forms evolved and interacted—especially through performance—as responses to the master narrative. But unlike memorials, laws, or institutions, artwork was also used by Champions, Fatalists, and Antagonists to channel their responses to the evolution of the master narrative and cultural memory in the first 20 years. This is a more difficult form of memorialization to evaluate than physical memorials because it is more evanescent and dynamic, being made up of performances, dispersed social connections, and attitudes rarely expressed in conventional media. It therefore demands close analysis of interviews and testimonials on the one hand and song lyrics, plays, film excerpts, and poems on the other hand as a way to get closer to understanding how Rwandans have responded to the official narrative and their diverse and dynamic experiences and expressions.

The Value of Expressing Memories of Mass Atrocities through Art

Going beyond music, many forms of art are used to commemorate the past. Art is an enabler of individual, social, communicative, and political memory forms. It provides a platform for healing and a way to face a brutal past that is difficult to capture in either spoken or written communication. Additionally, various forms of art provide means through which survivors and society at large can preserve the memory of victims while gaining insight into their individual and collective experiences. Art allows us to find "expressions that keep the memory of the victims, celebrate their dignity and remind [us] not to forget them."[4] It is one of the efficient carriers of memories. This is because it allows memories to circulate unsupervised beyond national borders, geographies, and generations.[5] Art can be disruptive, subversive, and does not need to heal. Art travels through music and films, as this chapter demonstrates, just like they do through other channels, including the media, as the next chapter argues, and through stories and objects and memorials as previous chapters have shown.

Beyond this, a filmmaker or musician who is a survivor or witness can confront his or her trauma through their art while creating a memory that is meaningful to his or her society.[6] In many societies that have experienced mass atrocities, Mödersheim argues: "Artists have felt the need to work through their memories and emotions by repeating the very incident that caused their trauma in images (or lyrics) that they create."[7] The artist re-establishes themselves through their creation "as a testifier, a survivor, a narrator that haunts their memory."[8] As Eric Fischl, the artist whose provocative sculpture *Tumbling Woman* memorializes the victims of September 11, asserted on the role of art: "This is what a culture looks to art for, to put image or voice or context to a way of rethinking, re-seeing, re-experiencing."[9] Thus art addresses "the gaps in healing and understanding that cannot be addressed through tribunals" or through formal laws and commemoration rituals like Rwanda's gacaca or the April 7 annual commemoration. Through its individuated and dynamic nature of memory,[10] art is more agile, more personal, and more immediate. The granules of commemorative art created by individuals are finer, whereas those of the artistic expressions of larger groups—and especially the state—are necessarily coarse.

Further, through representing violent past events, whether in very explicit or in implicit forms, art can be a potent weapon against denialism that such events ever took place. While commenting on art that emerged out of postconflict Sierra Leone, Mariama Ross has noted: "As our stomachs and hearts turn over at such sights, we get a small taste of what the artists felt."[11] By virtue of its immediacy and specificity and speaking to a particular experience, art is harder to refute than propositions or arguments. Paradoxically, the comparatively subtle yet powerful figure of the individual artist may well be more efficacious than official legislative measures that prohibit denialism speech, and the artist operates without risking democratic freedoms.

Art, Artists, and Postgenocide Commemorations

Context: Artists and the Pre- and Transgenocide Period

Following the Rwanda Patriotic Army's (RPA's) attack in October 1990, a small but influential group of Hutu elites intensified anti-Tutsi campaigns inside Rwanda. This group included politicians, business people, intellectuals, and artists. Prominent Hutu artist Simon Bikindi was among them. His art played an influential role in spreading hatred and eventually fueled the Genocide Against the Tutsi in 1994.[12] Bikindi was a celebrity, especially among pregenocide Rwandan politicians and ordinary people. Two of his compositions were especially associated with anti-Tutsi campaigns' key part of the pregenocide government master narrative on history: *Twasezereye ingoma ya cyami* ("We said goodbye to the monarchy"), a song about pre-1959 Tutsi monarchical rule, and *Njyewe nanga Abahutu* ("Me, I hate Hutu"), a song about his hatred for Hutu who were sympathizers of Tutsi. Both were often played at the privately owned popular Radio Télévision Libre des Mille Collines (known by its French acronym RTLM), notorious for its promotion of genocide.[13] After the genocide, Bikindi fled the country. However, in 2001 he was arrested in the Netherlands and transferred to the Tanzania-based

International Criminal Tribunal for Rwanda (ICTR).[14] While Bikindi was on trial, the prosecutor asserted that the artist's music "was an essential component in the genocide plan since it incited ethnic hatred against the Tutsis and urged people to attack the Tutsis and kill them because of their ethnic background."[15] Alison Des Forges observed that "when patrols went out to kill, they went off singing the songs heard on RTLM such as those of the popular Simon Bikindi."[16] There is no evidence that Bikindi himself instructed the radio to play his music or give it such interpretation, and his exact intentions are not known when he composed most of his songs before the genocide.[17] However, as the director of the Irindiro Ballet Company, the judges at the ICTR noted in their sentencing that Bikindi was a superstar, and therefore he used his influence to incite genocide through speech.[18] Bikindi was eventually convicted and imprisoned for 15 years.

Unlike Bikindi, artists who were Tutsi or perceived as Tutsi sympathizers were targeted and killed during the genocide. Rugamba Cyprien is one example among many. Cyprien, founder of a traditional dance company called *Amasimbi n'Amakombe*, was killed on April 7, the first day of the genocide.[19] Famous for lyrics that resonated with people at all levels of Rwandan society,[20] he was an icon and a critic of the pregenocide government and a committed Catholic in his later life.[21]

Music was central to the RPA's political and military campaign throughout the war. A study that examined the Rwanda Patriotic Front's (RPF's) songs between 1988 and 1995 found they were aimed at Rwandans within the movement, "diffusing an ideology within the movement itself for mobilization and education" and were not "a manipulative tool for an external audience."[22] Prior to attacking and arriving in Rwanda, songs circulated among the diaspora and in Rwanda.[23] Collective memory of *igihugu cy'amata n'ubuki* or "a country of honey and milk" featured in their lyrics helped some survive harsh conditions and rejections in refugee camps in Uganda, Kenya, Burundi, or then-Zaïre.[24] Like Burundian Hutu refugees in Tanzania, their displacement led them to create "nationness, history and identity."[25] Thus, collective remembering through song and poetry motivated them to undertake efforts to forget their terrible conditions as refugees[26] and propelled them to mobilize young refugees in the region to attack Rwanda in October 1990 in order to repatriate their communities. In this light, the RPA's attack was about more than returning home; it was also seeking to restore the glorious days of their beloved country that their ancestors once enjoyed. A former RPA soldier musician I spoke with remembered:

My role was to sing and create songs with a few other colleagues to warm up everyone. Especially during training for new recruits or even before going on battle, most of the mornings we were called with known songs or new songs to warm up everyone. It was a very important role to the point and so I was known by many senior military officers who also promoted me. I liked singing since I was very young given my mother always sang for us and told us stories of Rwanda [sic].[27]

Researchers who have written about music and the RPA's campaign have noted that RPA considered music was an important tool for not only its soldiers but also mobilization of support among the diaspora helped, by well-known musicians.[28] They broke into songs after winning or losing a battle in an evening around the fire they refer to as *ikitamaduni*.[29]

For Rémi Korman, one of the earlier researchers to discuss musicians in the RPF and music during commemoration, artists who were part of the RPA included men and women arriving with songs of victory. He lists songs such as *Turaje* ("We Are Arriving") composed by Rosalie Mukamutara; *Uraho Rwanda* ("Greetings to Our Rwanda") by Suzanne Nyiranyamibwa; and *Insinzi* ("Victory") by Maria Yohana Mukankuranga."[30] This last song on victory lasted the longest as an RPA song and was continuously played in RPF political meetings. Others included the songs of Jean-Paul Samputu, Cécile Kayirebwa, Maria Yohana Mukankuranga, and Masamba Intore, who "all performed songs in the late 1980s and early 1990s to raise money for the RPF's Liberation War and to inspire young people to join the RPA (the Rwanda Patriotic Army)."[31] Sometimes these songs were composed at a high risk. For example, Jean Paul Samputu was imprisoned as an *icyitso* or "spy" of the RPF in 1993, and his father was also killed in the genocide.[32] When played on airwaves, these songs represented a new Rwanda unlike, for instance, those of the famous Orchestre Impala. Orchestre Impala rarely ventured into political songs before or after the genocide. Their lyrics were mostly about relationships. It was part of the influencers of Rwandan society through music before the genocide, and it lost its members in 1994.[33] After the genocide, it was revived with caution because it brought memories of an old Rwanda that postgenocide political elites wanted forgotten for its bad governance and genocide mindset.[34] Many other artists who performed on weekly Tuesday drama that was aired on the radio were dead, in refugee camps, or traumatized. Some chose self-censorship with fears of reviving cultural production associated with *Abasope*, who would later revive concerts and meeting spots in Kigali that were reminiscent of the old Rwanda.[35]

Further, in the early periods after the genocide, some artists were afraid of engaging in a sensitive topic like memorializing the dead, especially after music and other forms of art were used to endorse and actively promote the genocide. They were wary of the potential dangers of cultural production and particularly hesitant about the prospect of entering the fraught political terrain of the genocide. Beyond this, the arts industry had been affected by the genocide: Artists had been targeted, and some killed. In addition, artists in general had meager means or support, given the austere material conditions that prevailed in the mid-1990s. Further, even for those artists who were composing, there were too many dead for different reasons; hence, the music that evolved did not commemorate only Tutsi or even Tutsi in particular. Finally, the current well-known artists associated with genocide commemoration are in their twenties and thirties, implying that they were young and dealing with their own loss and pain while trying to survive postgenocide hardships.[36] These artists' lives reflect the proverb "*Ababonangenda*," meaning "people who see me just walking cannot tell what pain, suffering or sorrow I am carrying or going through", meaning those who internalize pain and choose silence are reluctant to talk about it to anyone,[37] but have found in their respective arts an avenue for expression.

Young Artists in the Aftermath of the Genocide

After the genocide, members of ballets and media, magicians, and all kinds of artists were dead, outside the country, or inside the country with little means to participate in cultural production. Thus, the physical infrastructure on which such production depended was affected, as well as society in general. Few artists were known for their artwork on commemorating the recent past. The most well-known earlier composer of commemoration was Dieudonné Munyanshoza. He had been imprisoned in 1990 among accomplices or spies of the RPF. He joined the RPF after he was released from prison, and after returning to Rwanda, he was given permission to leave the army and returned to his home in Mibilizi in Cyangugu near the border with the Democratic Republic of Congo (DRC). Mibilizi, as he came to be known, was invited in different parts of Rwanda. His long songs based on his individual memory became an avenue for survivors to speak about their local experiences and those they lost by speaking their names and giving them back their humanity. During my research, Mibilizi was still one of the most prominent musicians associated with the master narrative and commemoration, with numerous well-known recordings. Two other important shifts followed Mibilizi's compositions.

The first was in 2003 with the composition of "Never Again" by Jean Paul Samputu; the second was in 2011 with the rise of Kizito Mihigo. With his rise to fame, Samputu's public engagement in matters of memory resulted in controversy and caused tensions among Champions. His music won him a prestigious KORA All Africa Music Award in 2004 as one of the most promising upcoming African artists, at a time around the tenth commemoration of the genocide. Africans were starting to recognize the seriousness of a genocide that took place on their continent. He toured many African festivals and around the world. He used his newly found fame to preach about reconciliation and forgiveness, a message that was applauded on international tours but not at home. In 2009, he disagreed sharply with survivor umbrella organization Ibuka on the issue of forgiveness and reconciliation, as covered in the previous chapter. Some Champions and Fatalists disagreed with what they perceived as Samputu's campaign to make forgiveness everyone's choice of coping and coming to terms with those who killed their victims. The suppression of this message in Rwanda was that it would evolve into a new public campaign around the master narrative that required survivors to forgive or else be ashamed of their individual experiences with traumatic memories of the past.

In April 2011 and 2012 when I was doing research, artworks of different forms were publicly incorporated into almost every aspect of commemoration, and some were made part of permanent memorial exhibitions in genocide museums around the country.[38] As the country continued to gain stability and economic prosperity in the decade that began in 2010, significant amounts of artwork were developed privately and in informal spaces as responses of individuals to personal experiences in the genocide. Art became an important channel through which Champions, Fatalists, and Antagonists began to respond to the evolving master narrative. Similarly, as formal memory became more organized and publicized, a new generation of remembrance artists emerged as well. Three of these young artists—Mihigo, Bamporiki, and Rugamba—rapidly gained popularity. Their art was the most referenced in my interviews and conversations with Rwandans of different generations. Thus, a close examination of their personal stories centered on their individual memories, and their best-known art is important for understanding the evolution of commemoration artists in the first 20 years after the genocide. Each in his own way broadly represents a particular channel for the evolution of social, communicative, and political memory, while simultaneously developing a personalized engagement with the genocide. Their works reside in a creative threshold, both public and private, individual and community, informed by their individual mnemonic experience of the genocide.

Evolution of Young Artists and Commemorations

Kizito Mihigo: A Tutsi Survivor's Tale

Profile
In April 2012, I attended Kizito Mihigo's concert at the Hotel Serena in Kigali. He was a Champion of the master narrative at that time. The concert was among many that Mihigo's organization, Kizito Mihigo for Peace (KMP). Mihigo was born in 1981 in the former Prefecture of Gikongoro into a family that lived near Kibeho. Mihigo's birth coincided with the appearance of the Virgin Mary, and therefore, he asserted, his parents raised him a strict Catholic.[39] In Kibeho, Mihigo started composing children's songs at the age of 9.

While addressing his audience at the concert, Mihigo reflected on a time shortly after the genocide when he met his father's killer, a former neighbor, Dr. Mutazihana. They were both in Burundi as refugees. "[He] had a daughter [Fifi]," Mihigo explained, "who was a close friend of mine during my primary school days at Kibeho primary school."[40] He remembered, "[Seeing him] naturally pushed me to try to avenge my father's death." Mihigo tried to join the RPA, but he was turned away for being too young. A few months later, however, when he returned to Rwanda, his career began to flourish, and then, too, he began to struggle with two of the emotional pillars of postgenocide memorialization, hatred and forgiveness.

In 1995, at the age of 14, Mihigo enrolled in the prestigious Petit Séminaire de Butare, a well-known Catholic secondary school, and joined the school's choir. Among choir members and schoolmates were boys whose parents had been leaders of Interahamwe in his town and had tried to exterminate

Mihigo's family. As he explained to the concert's audience, for a period he was terribly angry and wished he could bully them or somehow take revenge on them. Nevertheless, through interactions and meeting in choir practices, Mihigo saw the opportunity to reconcile with these boys.

It is also in this school that by the age of 19, young Mihigo had composed 200 liturgical songs popular in masses in Catholic churches nationally.[41] In addition, in 2000, he collaborated with other Rwandan musicians to compose the new Rwandan National Anthem. Following this national exposure, Mihigo was given a scholarship to study in France. During this period, as he related during a concert, he began to write lyrics that were crucial in his own journey, spoke to his memory, and called Rwandans to reconciliation and forgiveness.

In 2004, while visiting Rwanda, Mihigo found out that Dr. Mutazihana and his wife were imprisoned. Without access to them, he searched for his childhood friend Fifi. He told the audience at a concert his memories of the day they reunited:

> We shared a meal and I told her that I knew that her parents were involved in the death of my father and that is why they are serving time in prison. However, I told her not to be afraid, as I had moved on by forgiving her parents. Instead I asked her to recall the sweet memories we shared before the genocide.[42]

Their friendship was restored, and they continued to meet. After completing his studies in Paris in 2008, he taught music in Belgium, and his concerts of mainly Catholic songs became forums in which both radical and nonradical Hutu and Tutsi in France and Belgium could meet. Within this context, Mihigo evolved to focus on commemoration and found a platform in the Rwandan community, in both Rwanda and abroad. Although Mihigo had composed various commemoration songs that raised him to become a prominent Champion, his 2011 hit *Twanze Gutoberwa Amateka* meaning we resist those who want to change our history (hereafter *Amateka*), which he released in the seventeenth commemoration ceremony, is especially worthy of further examination, as it introduced him to larger Rwandan society, remained popular in the following three consecutive annual commemorations (i.e., through to 2014), and was the first song to provoke discussions in various audiences, including in prisons, which had mainly been isolated from commemoration activities.

Mihigo's Work

As he explained during a concert, Mihigo composed his songs while living in France or working in Belgium and reflecting on his earlier experiences. Two compositions that arose out of these reflections have shaped conversations among Rwandans during recent commemorations: the 2011 *Amateka* ("History") and the 2012 *Ijoro Ribara Uwariraye* (loosely, "The One Who Was Awake Narrates the Night Tales"; hereafter, *The One Who Was Awake*). As my interviews revealed, these songs gained fame in Rwanda during the commemoration period due to several factors, but two stood out. First, the songs frankly addressed key questions that had been at the center of debates on commemoration among Rwandans. Second, Mihigo used a unique style for his music and capitalized on his identity to engage with larger Rwandan society in ways that no other musician had done.

In conversations about commemoration, Rwandans debated who should be addressed and who should do the remembering in acts and events of commemoration, and these questions are dealt with in both songs. Mihigo explicitly calls on all Rwandans to take on this remembrance and conservation of memory as their responsibility. For example, in the second stanza of *Amateka*, he sings: "Dear Rwandan brothers and sisters, let us be united." He continues: "Our History, either the best or the worst, let us protect it from torturers with destroying thoughts, let the real love of our country induce us to defend it." *Amateka* includes all Rwandans, calling them to be part of the community that remembers.[43] In the second song, *The One Who Was Awake*, the question of who he is addressing is central in the opening lines of the song. Mihigo starts the song in the style he uses for most of his songs, playing soft keyboard sounds and singing: *Bana b'iwacu i Rwanda nimuze twibuke, twibuke Jenoside yakorewe Abatutsi* ("Children of our homeland Rwanda, come let us remember, remember the Genocide Against the Tutsi"). This is an even more direct and inclusive call to memory's Champions, Antagonists, and Fatalists to accept the duty of remembering. In the following lines, he explains this appeal: *"Rubanda banyimye amatwi, ngo akenshi njye mvuga ishavu, ntibazi ko muri iryo shavu ari ho hashibutse imbaraga z'u Rwanda"* ("The other people out there have denied me their attention, saying that often I talk about sorrow, yet they don't know that it's in that sorrow that Rwanda rediscovered its strength"). The song's release coincided with the announcement by the organizers of formal memory that commemoration would be taken to the village level for every Rwandan—and especially young Rwandans—to participate in. *The One Who Was Awake* was, in essence, a personal hymn to national unity and to a reconstructed, reconciled Rwandan nation.

Second, Mihigo capitalized on his identity as a Catholic, a youth, and a survivor and Champion to reach various audiences, organize campaigns, and transmit reconciliation messages. As an influential Catholic composer, he had a good reputation that was already well known to a large majority of Rwandans, given that even today the Catholic Church has the largest percentage of followers in Rwandan society (an estimated 56% of Rwandans were Catholic in 2006).[44] Thus, the Catholic Church remained influential despite some of its priests and nuns having been accused of participating in the genocide.[45] And as mentioned previously, the relationship between the Catholic Church and the postgenocide government was one of tensions throughout 1990s and 2000s. Mihigo's rhythm—though not necessarily his lyrics at this point—resonated with Antagonists, Champions, and Fatalists who were Catholics; as a reassuringly familiar musical cadence, it could be effectively paired with a deeply discomforting subject. Furthermore, his lyrical allusions to Christian rhetoric and concepts even attracted other Christians. Consider these lines of *Amateka*: "I am not trying to praise the Cross itself, I am rather commending the resurrection it has brought to me." He then ends the bridge with the following lines: "*Jenoside yakorewe Abatutsi, ni wo musaraba w'uru Rwanda*" ("Genocide Against the Tutsi is the cross for Rwanda"). Thus, in *Amateka*, Kizito uses the Christian image of the cross—an important symbol of the story of Jesus's crucifixion, which thereby points toward Easter and resurrection. His implicit conclusion is that the genocide was the cross for Rwanda; by implication, he compares the resurrection of Rwanda with the resurrection of Christ. Furthermore, in both songs he contrasts darkness to light, thus employing an opposition that is equally central to the Christian belief that Jesus died on the cross to bring light into the world.[46] These powerful allusions to the Bible were familiar terrain to not only Catholics but also other Christians.

Mihigo was among the first survivors to occupy a public stage in commemoration, with compositions that attracted a large audience with diverse views of the master narrative. His identity gave him the prerogative to directly urge survivors to use their testimonies as evidence that the genocide took place. The title *The One Who Was Awake* insists: "The one who was awake narrates the night's tale." In April 2012, I had an opportunity to discuss Mihigo's music with him during a community commemoration event where he had performed this song. He explained that he composed it not only to encourage survivors to speak up about their testimonies but also to empower the younger generation to build a positive future for themselves regardless of the history they hear from their parents, other adults, or teachers. His young audience was as important as those in prisons or survivors like those who were present at that community event.[47]

Although Mihigo's songs effectively united Champions, Antagonists, and Fatalists, part of *The One Who Was Awake* pointedly questions the last group, who do not want to remember because the history of Rwanda is terrible or too difficult; he further argued that even if the country's history is terrible or saddening, we must call events what they are and must narrate that painful past.[48] A video in which the song is played shows, in the background, photo images of victims and survivors at the Kigali Memorial Center's permanent exhibition as Mihigo sings about the importance of speaking out.[49]

The One Who Was Awake includes reconciliation rhetoric in other places besides those already mentioned: "Since we are the ones who were wronged, we will be the ones to sow the seeds of peace", and "Since we knew division, we will be the ones who will preach unity." Again here, Kizito not only used his identity to engage with survivor Fatalists but also regularly performed in prisons and led reconciliation conversations aimed at Antagonists. Programs organized under KMP in partnership with international and government agencies allowed him to create new spaces to engage memory through informal means.[50] He positioned himself as a survivor who gave forgiveness and who campaigned to persuade Antagonists to admit that the genocide happened. He also used his youthful status to reach out to secondary schools nationally and has engaged with thousands of young Rwandans who hold different perspectives on commemoration and the genocide. For his political songs in 2012, Kizito was criticized as having left his Christian songs for political ones. In his response through various concerts and in our conversations in 2021, he insisted that he sang about social issues and about history of his country but that that did not make him a politician. However, it was evident later that his songs were political.

Kizito Mihigo and Counternarrative Lyrics during the Twentieth Commemoration

However, as the twentieth commemoration ceremonies approached, Kizito Mihigo composed a new song, *Igisobanuro cy'Urupfu* ("The Meaning of Death"). In this song, he sang about the past as he had done in other songs analyzed in this chapter, but his lyrics, released in 2014 only through

YouTube, changed his message and challenged how the government viewed these commemorations, which he had previously supported in his songs.

His introductory lines were similar to his previous lyrics: "*Urupfu ni cyo kibi kiruta ibindi, ariko rutubera inzira, inzira igana icyiza kiruta ibindi*" ("Death is the worst thing that can happen, yet a path that leads to something better than anything else"). The next point he made in his lyrics was most relevant to commemoration controversies in postgenocide Rwanda: "*Nta rupfu rwiza rubaho, yaba Jenoside, cyangwa intambara, uwishwe n'abihorera, uwazize impanuka, cyangwa se uwazize indwara*" ("There is no good death, whether genocide, war, being killed in revenge attacks, in accident or dying from illness"); he concluded that all deaths are worthy of remembrance.

The Meaning of Death was equally revealing: "*Abo bavandimwe aho bicaye baradusabira*" ("Those relatives, wherever they are seated, they pray for us"). He continued: "Though the genocide orphaned me, let it not make me lose empathy for others. Their lives, too, were brutally taken but not qualified as genocide. Those brothers and sisters, they too are human beings. I pray for them. I comfort them. I remember them."[51]

Mihigo's words were interpreted by some as a declaration of his criticism against the government-endorsed program called *Ndi Umunyarwanda* ("I Am a Rwandan"). He continued in his song: "My dignity and love are not rooted in carnal life, nor in material possessions, but in humanity, humaneness. Let the words 'I am Rwandan' be preceded by 'I am HUMAN!'"[52] He referred to the concept of *Agaciro* in relation to the other's pain, something that the master narrative did not accept, especially when including discussions on Hutu victimhood during and or after the genocide.

Mihigo, who became viewed as an Antagonist to the master narrative because of this song, as in his other commemorative songs sang about death in contrast with light, with the Christian undertone of a promised better future with God. This was introductory, providing context for the rest of *The Meaning of Death*. However, it was the second stanza that caused controversy and questioned the master narrative. Mihigo, in his usual way of mastering Kinywarwanda, asserted that all deaths, including those not advantaged by the evolution of the master narrative and commemoration, were important and worthy of remembrance. He acknowledged that some died in revenge attacks. Although he did not clearly state which revenge attacks he was referring to, many Rwandans understood him to refer to Hutu killed by the RPA soldiers in the Kibeho camp massacre and in DRC refugee camps that Antagonists use in their comparative approach to the master narrative. In particular, the Antagonists in Rwanda and outside applauded Mihigo for finally acknowledging other versions of amateka, or history. The reference to those who died in accidents and in other circumstances was important to include in his declaration that all deaths were equally worthy of remembrance.

During online conversations and radio programs like *Ikondera* Info (an online news outlet critical of the government of Rwanda), Antagonists, some Fatalists, and others applauded Mihigo for acknowledging other Rwandans who died and for referring to them as relatives. In his song, he had comforted them as well, as he asserted that they are in a better place as well or advocated praying for them, just like lyrics about the genocide victims he had composed for many years. Furthermore, Antagonists approved *The Meaning of Death* for criticizing the Ndi Umunyarwanda program, which Edouard Bamporiki (covered further in this chapter), with the assistance of the first lady's foundation, introduced to all Rwandans. The program argued that everyone is Rwandan and minimized the importance of Hutu, Tutsi, and Twa identities, yet insisted that Hutu, even those who did not participate in the genocide, should apologize for the Interahamwe's actions in 1994.[53]

The Meaning of Death was a significant breaking point in which a prominent Champion became an Antagonist. But it also intensified debates around the master narrative and commemoration. More than any other artwork in the postgenocide period, it attracted a lot of attention and debate from different groups of Champions, Antagonists, and Fatalists, and since it was released just weeks before the twentieth commemoration ceremony, it caused many discussions about who is to be remembered. While it pushed the debate around the evolution of the master narrative and commemoration, it was also an opportunity for discourse around the master narrative to be policed and restricted and to create a new vocabulary that continued to evolve in the 5 years that followed, which are, nevertheless, outside the scope of this study.

After the song was released on YouTube on April 6, 2014, it was banned in Rwanda. Kizito Mihigo disappeared from public view, and his family reported he was missing. Online sources and social media forums speculated about what had happened, but it was not until a report by BBC Great Lakes news in Kinyarwanda on April 15, 2014, that the public learned that the police had arrested Mihigo.[54]

Even with an explanation in an interview with *IGIHE*,[55] a pro-government private famous online media, his arrest also provoked anger, especially from his fans. The police waited to confirm the news of his arrest after official commemoration ceremonies had ended and international dignitaries had left Rwanda. His absence from official functions and the absence of his songs from all media stations during the twentieth commemoration created suspicion that he had been killed or arrested. The police later explained that Mihigo had been arrested after investigations about him revealed he had been collaborating via online platforms with opposition parties banned in Rwanda and was a threat to national security.[56] Although BBC and the Associated Press captured the importance of his arrest, there was no international outcry about his importance or his music, even though such an outcry is usually provoked, for example, when an opposition politician is arrested in Rwanda.

However, when Mihigo finally appeared in court for his first hearing on April 21, many asked the police if his arrest was linked to his newly released song and its controversial lyrics. The police insisted that it was not due to his music, but that even Mihigo had acknowledged his wrongdoing and apologized for being part of a plan to destabilize the country. It is commonly believed among Rwandans that, given the previous support he received, the government, to protect itself against Mihigo's opposition, had to turn him into a terrorist, ban all his songs, lower his public profile, and, of course, disassociate itself from the message of *The Meaning of Death*. In the days that followed, Mihigo's art was banned in Rwanda, never to be played again on public radio or television as a channel for the master narrative. By September 2014, no further court hearings had been held in his case.

The government's treatment of Mihigo after the release of *The Meaning of Death* for the twentieth commemoration showed that the master narrative was to be protected regardless of who attempted to question it. His experience showed how debates and reflections are limited within the confines of the master narrative. In this case, laws to guard the master narrative were used to punish Mihigo; all memory institutions that he worked with distanced themselves from his work and removed him from their archives. He was restricted from accessing memorials and using materials of memory associated with the genocide; his art was banned from official commemorations and from being played countrywide; and the government's media disseminated the message of his disgrace. However, the new online media created more democratic spaces to discuss Mihigo's recent work and its importance in allowing a platform for multiple narratives of the genocide to exist. Yet, the Mihigo case showed also that even among Champions of the master narrative, there are some who privately hold

194   NAVIGATING CULTURAL MEMORY

similar views of multiple narratives of the genocide but keep it private, as they fear the consequences of expressing the same.

Edouard Bamporiki: Shouting from a Witness's Heart

Profile

In his semiautobiographical self-published work *Icyaha kuri bo, Ikimwaro kuri jye* ("Their Sin Is My Shame"), Edouard Bamporiki was a Fatalist initially then turned into a Champion of the master narrative. He wrote in his book and told stories in the public many times that on April 7, 1994, he was 11 years old and very ill in Kibogora Mission Hospital in Western Province near the border of Rwanda and Congo. As soon as the next day, Bamporiki remembers seeing patients arriving bleeding excessively and others coming to hide.[57] Bamporiki became fearful and repeatedly asked his mother, who was with him in the hospital, why those people were being hunted, but she gave him no response.[58] He writes in the book that a few days after that, a man called Pascal arrived in their ward with a baby, asking all patients for a hiding place. The hospital offered a bed, but he refused, claiming that killers would find him easily, and instead he chose to hide the child under Bamporiki's bed.[59] However, early the next morning killers arrived looking for Pascal, searched under each bed, and finally found him. They cut his head off and left the baby crying and Bamporiki screaming, fearing that he and his mother would also be killed. This, he writes, was when he insisted that his mother explain why these people were being killed. Seeing that his screaming and fear would attract the killers to return, his mother answered that he and she were safe because they were Hutu, and that only Tutsi were being hunted by Hutu.[60] This revelation would allow Bamporiki to move freely once they returned to their home, but, as the title of his book suggests, the same knowledge would burden his life after the genocide, especially during the commemoration period.

The RPA—who were referred to as *Inyenzi*, or cockroaches, to dehumanize them—had just arrived in the rural home of Bamporiki and his mother, and he, alongside other community members, ironically went to welcome them with applause even though they feared they would be targets of revenge killings.[61] Bamporiki's mother had refused to flee with her six children, given that his father had died and could not protect them during such a flight, and instead chose to wait for the Inyenzi to come and kill them. However, they were not killed; instead, normal life started to resume. His relatives and close family members gathered, and the older among them advised the family against joining Tutsi in their remembrance ceremonies.[62] Poems and songs of lament were being played on the radio, and as they gathered and listened, the adults kept on reminding young ones that with such anger in their music and poetry, the Tutsi would definitely use the commemoration period as a time for revenge.[63] In another instance, Bamporiki's aunt asked him why he thought the Tutsi would allow him to complete his studies even though the pregenocide Hutu government itself had a policy of streamlining the numbers of educated people, including Hutu.[64] With this discouragement and without enough money for tuition, he dropped out of secondary school and moved to Kigali to search for odd jobs and a better life. Thus, for Hutu like Bamporiki's family, early remembrance ceremonies were not their concern; instead, it was a period of fear and like Hakizimana's father discussed in the Introduction had alternative narratives about Rwanda's past.

Richard Benda, who interviewed and did an in-depth study of Bamporiki's narrative and the various ways he told it to Rwandans in over fifteen districts during Youth Connekt events, captures the moment Bamporiki's talent became recognized nationally. Benda quotes Bamporiki:

One day as I was cooking. . . . I remember I was frying chicken and my lady boss was screaming at me, "Edouard, do not burn my pot; it is worth more than you are!" Then I heard an advert on radio calling for poets and musicians to submit works on the importance of taxes! I composed a poem through the night and surprisingly I won the first prize for best poem![65]

The art gave him expert power that allowed him to recite the poem in a public event that was attended by the president of Rwanda, Paul Kagame, on the tenth anniversary of the genocide, which, according to Benda's interview with him, excited Bamporiki and gave him and his art national prominence.[66]

Bamporiki began to compose poetry about commemorations. The poem was titled *Iyo Badatsembwa* ("If They Had Not Been Massacred").[67] He often sold sugar cane to earn an income for his mother and sisters, and he remembers meeting survivors in the market and feeling a great deal of shame about being Hutu. This feeling would intensify during remembrances. He explained to Benda that the poem was well received by genocide survivors and other youth whose parents had been accused of the genocide. Benda writes:

> They [Tutsi genocide survivors] had never heard a Hutu so open about the pain, shame and humiliation brought upon them by what they had done. They could not believe that there were Hutu who could actually show empathy for the plight of Tutsi. But you know what amazed me? Many of them cried with me when they saw the turmoil of young Hutu racked by guilt of actions they had not committed. That night changed me![68]

It is that night according to this story that would turn Bamporiki from a Fatalist to a Champion of the master narrative. This would change him and, like Hakizimana discussed in the Introduction, lead him to go against his family's response to the master narrative. Bamporiki characterized his family as Antagonists of the master narrative like Hakizimana's father. This is especially when he spoke of his experiences of earlier commemorations, one being in 1995.

In 2004, as the various institutions encouraged Hutu and everyone else to participate in commemoration, Bamporiki attended one of the ceremonies, and he remembers asking to give a testimony as well. He could not be silent anymore and wanted to show that not all Hutu were killers. He narrated his story, explained his life burden, and was encouraged by survivors to consider himself a Rwandan more than anything else. This experience made him open to exhibiting his artwork publicly through various national competitions. In an interview with Maggie Ziegler of *Peace Magazine*, Bamporiki spoke of the silence he had maintained for a decade to obey his mother's request at the hospital:

> I started when I was in hospital because shouting shows that someone is not supporting. But I had to obey my parent, so I became quiet in public. But in my heart, I was not quiet. From 1994 to 2005, more than ten years, I was shouting in my heart, looking for a way to say something in public. It was not easy.[69]

However, after that first participation in commemoration, his artwork became widely accepted and shaped various conversations on commemoration. Yet as Richard Benda's research showed, Bamporiki recounted his story in a way it aligned with the master narrative, for instance equating[70] "Hutu killers, Hutu bystanders, Tutsi atrociously killed and child survivors" like him.

Bamporiki's Artwork and the Master Narrative

Bamporiki, who through his work shifted from a Fatalist to a Champion of the master narrative, has written or acted in various films that have won national and international awards in Rwanda, France, the United States, and Canada. His films, both shorts and features, and his poetry engaged with social issues related to memory. First, he used his work to encourage Hutu to use commemoration events as spaces to narrate what they did or what they witnessed in the genocide. Second, Bamporiki, like Mihigo, used his identity as a famous artist, and in his case as a prominent young Hutu, to engage with fellow Hutu Antagonists, compelling them to become Champions, especially on sensitive and controversial topics such as apologizing on a community's behalf. He has aimed his message especially at second-generation youth whose parents are suspected or convicted perpetrators.

During my fieldwork, I heard Bamporiki speaking at different forums while I was studying some of his work. He explained proudly that he felt freedom and could now participate in commemorative events with his survivor friends without feeling guilty. As he explained in a workshop in 2013, some of the people that disappointed him when he moved to Kigali were Hutu, and those who helped him heal were genocide Tutsi survivors.[71] His postgenocide and genocide life experiences have informed his work as an artist; however, he wants to create art that informs other Hutu that their participation in activities and events of commemoration is just as important as that of Tutsi. He said 5 years ago: "When we were commemorating, Tutsi, no Hutu, old or young, came to say what they had seen. Only Tutsi. And then I thought that's commemoration for whom? For Rwandans? [sic]"[72] However, he asserted that with time some Hutu are beginning to participate. He explained in the interview with *Peace Magazine*: "We are still having only survivor testimony. Not because they want to talk only themselves but because Hutu are still quiet [sic]."[73] This was the motivation behind his first feature film, *The Long Coat* (2009), which he wrote and acted as the main character. Its summary reads:

> *Long Coat* thematically focuses on the difficulty of leaving one's past behind. Following the story of a genocide survivor as well as son of a killer, the film revolves around the meaning of an old coat and its symbolic value for the young boy's dramatic past[74]

Bamporiki toured prisons—fifteen districts countrywide—and organized high-level events to publicize the notion of Hutu speaking up. In the film *Kinyarwanda* (2011), he acts as a Hutu insurgent who is forced to give an account of his violent actions during the genocide.[75] While reviewing the film, David DeWitt of the *New York Times* started with the words of Bamporiki's character: "From my heart, I ask for forgiveness"; this points to Bamporiki's other mission, to appeal to Antagonists to seek forgiveness.[76]

Bamporiki also used his identity as a Hutu to challenge Antagonists to sympathize with Tutsi during remembrance and apologize on behalf of the Hutu community. In a workshop attended by government-sponsored young artists from different parts of Rwanda, along with leaders that included President Kagame and First Lady Jeannette Kagame, under the umbrella of Youth Connekt Dialogue, Bamporiki made his message public. He argued that young men and women, especially those whose parents are Hutu, should apologize to Tutsi. Youth Connekt was a result of Bamporiki's transformation journey from a Fatalist to a Champion and had a profound impact on youth whose parents were accused of the genocide like Hakizimana. Benda, who followed these initiatives in over fifteen districts of Rwanda, confirms this in his paper on Youth Connekt. He followed how Bamporiki's testimony was used in these forums, which were both designed and organized by youth artists for peace but with the visible influence of government officials. Benda also shows how while many youth listened to Bamporiki, some openly expressed Antagonistic perspectives against the official history that was taught in all those forums.[77] In 2013, I attended two forums of Youth Connekt and found similar dynamic conversations going on. I recall being shocked that there were youth invited to conversations about their father's crimes and being allowed to ask questions, although they were never publicized.

In an interview with *New Times* after the event, he explained the criticism he received from various Hutu communities in Rwanda and especially in the diaspora. When the journalist asked him about the controversies, he said: "The main idea was about creating a platform for dialogue. If someone wants to apologize, it is fine, but no one was pushed or will be pushed to apologize in our subsequent dialogues." And he continued to assert a level of collective historical guilt: "One thing we can never erase from our history books is the fact that Genocide was committed by the Hutu against the Tutsi, so even those who didn't participate, it's a shame to us, which we need to first accept then chart a way forward."[78] President Paul Kagame, in a gathering of over 700 young people, affirmed Bamporiki's message. He endorsed that all Hutus should apologize, including those in the emerging generation who were teens during the genocide and the second generation born after the genocide. While his remarks attracted criticism from Rwandans and non-Rwandans, they benefited Bamporiki's personal life and transformed his political life. He emerged into a prominent Champion.[79] The events of Youth Connekt and those forums inspired the national policy on Ndi Umunyarwanda, discussed elsewhere in this book.

Bamporiki's and Mihigo's artwork of commemoration gained much publicity and support for two reasons. The works evolved from personal experiences, which other Rwandans, be they Antagonists, Fatalists, or Champions, can often identify with. They were personal experiences that could be readily deployed in national campaigns, and therefore the art can run along the main channels of memorialization. Additionally, the works were compatible with the master narrative and clearly relevant to the larger government agenda for postgenocide reconciliation. In some ways, they resemble Bikindi's art, which fitted into the larger pregenocide political agenda. They are popular like Bikindi's and are always played on radio and performed in public commemoration government events. Yet, they differ from Bikindi's in that, despite being popularized, they emerged out of personal experiences rather than being dictated by the custodians of formal memory. Furthermore, they have given visibility to or inspired the emergence of other artists.[80] These include Grace Mukankusi, who is a survivor and the only popular woman commemoration artist. She has composed two popular songs *Ikizere* ("Hope") and *Mfite Ibanga* ("I Have a Secret That My Parents Left Me"). Grace is unique since young women artists engaging with commemorations have emerged more slowly than men.[81]

Unlike Mihigo, however, Bamporiki gained popularity after he launched the Ndi Umunyarwanda program, which became a national project endorsed by the government, criticized by many for forcing Hutu youth to confess to crimes of their parents and as a political tool to reinvent Rwanda for its political interests.[82] He commented on the relevance of his acting and political career: "Being a poet and an actor has helped me learn how to transition from a politician to an actor. I have been acting for a long time until it is now part of me."[83] In 2013, Bamporiki declared his interest in politics and was elected as an RPF member of parliament. He is now one of the few artists, poet and politician, who is part of the ruling party and is famous in Rwanda and in the diaspora.[84] His work of supporting and championing the master narrative was continuously rewarded with positions of power.

Dorcy Rugamba: Activating Individual Memory

Profile
Dorcy Rugamba floats between being a Champion and Fatalist of memory and is one of the surviving children of the late pregenocide celebrity Rugamba Cyprien. Dorcy was away from his family home when his father and family members were killed in Kigali on April 7, 1994. Dorcy was in Butare visiting his relatives when he called his family home, and his father advised him not to return because it was dangerous. The family was killed shortly after that brief conversation. Dorcy fled with his relatives to Burundi as the genocide spread in different parts of the country, and later, through the assistance of family friends in France, he moved to Europe. However, Rugamba did not fully understand what he had experienced and did not start writing plays and engaging with his past for some time. Instead, he told Jon Henley of the *Guardian* in a 2007 interview: "For a long time, we were ignorant of the sheer scale of what had happened." He revealed: "[For years that followed,] I was in a kind of limbo; I had completely lost my bearings." He moved to Belgium to continue his studies, and even then, he did not know what he was doing or where he was. He asserted that he could not count the number of friends and family he had lost in circumstances he could not articulate or understand as a teen.[85]

While studying in Belgium, he began to express his pain and trauma through art. As official commemorations were popularized after the 10-year anniversary in 2004, Rugamba evolved as one of the few artists in the diaspora and in Rwanda whose artistic work provoked conversations among Rwandan and international audiences. However, Rugamba's style was unique in that it was about other genocides but at the same time addressed the Rwandan genocide. In his portrayal of Rugamba, Jon Henley wrote in 2007 that he was "a modest, soft-spoken, 24-year-old pharmacy student" and "part-time dancer in his father's troupe" who evolved "into an internationally acclaimed theatre director."[86] Rugamba has conducted various workshops for upcoming artists in Senegal, Rwanda, France, and Belgium while continuing to write various plays and has leading roles in various performances internationally.

Rugamba's Artwork
Although he does other performances and writes on various topics other than the memory of the genocide, Rugamba's work on genocide memory is particularly important because it engages with individual memory.[87] His approach

has been described as "humane and philosophical."[88] Among his well-known works is the documentary play *The Investigation*, which was based on the 1963–1965 Frankfurt Auschwitz trial.[89] While on tour in the United Kingdom, he commented on his work and personal story in an interview. He explained: "In many ways, it's exactly the right piece for us now, it's a play about two versions of history: the victims' and the executioners.'" Referring to the play and its relation to Rwanda's recovery context, he continued:

> It doesn't talk about our story, the Hutu-Tutsi story. It's a step removed from that whole context; it takes the real hard issues out of all the confused and confusing stuff that surrounds them. *The Investigation* takes a long hard look at another genocide and asks: what exactly was going on here?[90]

He asserted that: "watching as a Rwandan, it doesn't matter if you're the son of a killer or of a victim, because this play doesn't say: I accuse my neighbor's father. The values are more universal."[91] In this work, Rugamba found a unique way of connecting conversations about the memory of the Rwanda genocide to a topic that is well known in the Western world.

In 2004, Dorcy Rugamba returned to Rwanda and produced *The Investigation* in various community events, in both rural and urban areas. In an interview in the *Guardian* he described how he saw people experience his art.[92] He remembered that it was "an extraordinary thing." Although the performance attracted all kinds of people from the community, he particularly noticed the response from genocide survivors. He continued: "For genocide survivors, it was something far, far stronger than theatre." However, Rugamba related since his work is intense and provokes personal reflection: "Everywhere we performed, people—especially women, who had undergone unimaginable tortures—were howling, passing out where they sat."[93] Since the event organizers suspected this would happen, ambulances were ready to take people to hospitals, and organizers provided on-site counseling. He further reflected on that experience: "Rwandans have trouble expressing their emotions, you see. They don't like the raw and the crude, and this play was both. It was very real. It was like bursting a boil."[94]

In *The Investigation*, Rugamba effectively provoked reflection on the Rwandan genocide without even telling the story of that horror. In 2001 he coauthored *Rwanda 94*, a play that actually revisited the events of the genocide. In the 6-hour drama, which won various awards and has been staged at many venues in Europe, the Caribbean, and Canada, Rugamba played several different roles. In 2004, during the tenth anniversary of the genocide, *Rwanda 94* was presented in the city of Butare, Southern Province (where Dorcy lived during the genocide), and Bisesero, Western Province, an area where many Tutsi were killed. In 2005, Rugamba who, as his father had been, is a poet, published *Marembo*, a book of poems with photographs by Francis Busignies. *Marembo* is a poetic account of the last days of Rugamba's family in Rwanda.[95] While reviewing *Marembo*, Paul Kerstens wrote that it is "an act of defiance, of the refusal to allow the genocide to determine his memory and his identity."[96] Yet, as he recounts his last memories of his family, he shows that remembering the genocide and its victims is inevitable.

Rugamba and his artwork represented a minority of artists who have recently risen to prominence and are venturing into forms of art that are less popular with Rwandans, to engage with a subject that relates to a majority of Rwandans. Although he presented his work on the national stage, he remained generally distant from public discussions. His work was less about the politics of the day and dealt mostly with individual memories in a unique and abstract yet intense manner. It was less discussed in public domains such as on radio, televisions, or newspapers, but provoked many discussions and confronted its direct audiences in Rwanda and outside. Rugamba as an artist did not engage publicly in any political forums as Mihigo and Bamporiki did; rather, he maintained a low profile, and those who know him either associate his artistic ability with his father, Rugamba Senior, or have interacted with the younger Rugamba's work directly. Little was known or publicized about the artist himself, but more about his work and what inspires him.

Dorcy Rugamba continues to pursue his career in art internationally and lives in Belgium. His artwork was featured in the twentieth commemoration ceremony in Rwanda, and he authored two more works that were showcased in Brussels.[97]

The Significance of Artists in Commemoration Ceremonies

The works of Mihigo, Bamporiki, Rugamba, and other artists have shaped conversations and individual reflections on memory of the genocide among Rwandans. They have also influenced individuals to come to terms with their singular and collective pasts as well as shaped conversations around healing, reconciliation, and nation-building in many ways. First, the artists have explained in different interviews that creating art influenced their own healing process. Second, as my interviewees explained, Mihigo's and Bamporiki's art has shaped both their experiences of commemoration and those of the society at large.

In analyzing different interviews of these artists, it is evident that the artists' own works on memory have transformed them. During his concert at Serena that I attended in 2012, as his song *Amateka* gained popularity, Mihigo asserted that through composing some of his commemoration music in Belgium, he was inspired to search for and reconcile with Fifi. In reference to his reconciliation process with Fifi, he reflected that music helped him to slowly become a lovable person. For Bamporiki, on the other hand, who was inspired by what he witnessed at his hospital bed during the genocide, art has given him an avenue for self-actualization. He asserted in a *Peace Magazine* interview:

> When I got a chance to go to the public and express what was in me, I became a man. I became a real Edouard. Before I had this conflict within me; I had no unity and reconciliation in me. You could say I was like five Edouards, all fighting inside. But as I express what is in me, when I say what I saw, I get freedom.[98]

This statement demonstrates how he shifted from being a Fatalist to a Champion of the master narrative.

Similarly, Rugamba explained that after creating various artworks he was "pacified." He explained: "[This is] because I'm doing something. I may not be a judge or a politician or a soldier, but I am doing something in the aftermath of this. I'm battling with that whole period. I haven't abdicated. So, I'm not bitter about it. It hasn't sullied me. I do not hate life."[99] However, art has not only transformed individual artists but also generated various responses from the larger society. Fatalists have found a voice to express what cannot be spoken or commemorated in official functions. They find a voice to deal with a difficult, messy past that has resulted in traumas of all kinds.

When Mihigo first released *Amateka* in April 2011 as a Champion who shaped commemorations, it was widely played on radio, in public spaces like taxi parks countrywide, and in homes; as a result, the song became popular among Rwandans, as did the artist. That April, Mutoni, a university student and Champion I spoke with, was in the market and found herself singing the lyrics as the song played loudly. As she later told me in an interview, the song was especially captivating in its opening lines. She described them as powerful and attractive for an audience that was in a mourning mood. The song starts with a liturgical kind of rhythm and a calm sound, then Mihigo begins to sing softly, and one feels compelled to join in. She pointed to the song's opening lines: "Rwanda my mother, let me console you . . . that's why I was born and you brought me up." The song here calls every listener, like Mutoni in those public and private places, to remember the period they are in and to comfort the "mother," symbolizing the motherland. Rwanda is itself a unifying factor, and all—both Hutu and Tutsi listeners—are invited to belong and therefore participate and remember together. Mutoni, who before listening to Mihigo's music described herself in terms that could best be described as Fatalist, further explained:

> For me, listening to *Amateka* the first time, I felt like I had finally found a language to express the loss of my mother. I played it every time. My friends and I also listened to it together if one of us was having traumatic symptoms. We were encouraged because the song encouraged us not to ignore our history and was empowering in many ways because we could also reflect on a good future ahead of us.[100]

Yet, the song goes beyond what Mutoni and many other survivors referred to as comforting rhythm and lyrics; it engages difficult and sensitive questions publicly that are pertinent and have remained silenced in the formal memory. The song, for example, allows people to discuss why there had been a shift between calling the massacres of 1994 the Rwandan genocide and calling them the Genocide Against the Tutsi. *Amateka* provoked listeners with its bridge: "*Twibuke Jenoside yakorewe Abatutsi*" ("Let's remember the Genocide Against the Tutsi"). As discussed, the 2011 commemoration theme emphasized the question of who was being remembered. At the same time, the change in the official name of the genocide brought up a critical question among Rwandans, that of what happens to the memory of non-Tutsi who were killed in the genocide or civil wars that followed and what happens to the memory of others killed in the time following the genocide. However, as Mihigo explained at the concert in 2012, the term *genocide* itself was meant to emphasize and clarify who was targeted in the genocide even though he recognizes that non-Tutsis were also killed and are therefore remembered. The choice of language sought to distinguish the genocide memory from memories of civil wars and other killings of Rwandans in the 1990s. Through

Mihigo's art, Mutoni and many other youth could move from being a Fatalist to becoming Champions and gaining better understanding and endorsing of the master narrative.

Similarly, the line, *"Imyaka ibaye cumi n'irindwi twibuka"* ("It's been seventeen years remembering"), emphasized the "how long" question and affirmed that this had become a culture tradition for the past 17 years. However, as one of my interviewees explained, this opened debate between Antagonists and Champions, both of whom asked how long the remembering ritual would last. As if he had listened to his audience discussing these matters, Mihigo addressed this issue at the concert in 2012, reintroducing the song with the 17th-year emphasis removed and replacing that reference with "as remembrance and time passes." This was to emphasize and affirm that the genocide commemoration did not have a specific end time. By changing the words, he wanted to make the song accessible to all future generations that will engage in commemoration activities.

For Bamporiki, on the other hand, it was while going to prisons and showing his film to convicted genocide perpetrators who mostly were Antagonists that he saw how his work could bring about change in others or, simply said, to move them to become Champions of Memory: it gave them courage to confess. In Rilima Prison, for example, after a screening of *The Long Coat*, an inmate shouted: "I want to talk to Edouard." The man continued: "I want to tell you something, how you end the movie, the father killed a man and threw him in the latrine. That is what I did. I killed people and then I put them in the latrine. I'm here for another reason, and in four years I go out but I also did the genocide." The inmate was confessing to crimes that were unknown, for he had been jailed for looting and as a result had received a shorter sentence.[101]

Although in other cases the radical Hutu population has rejected Bamporiki, describing him as a Tutsi apologist,[102] this experience with prisoners shows the power of Bamporiki's art to shift even other Antagonists into becoming Champions. Yet he constantly speaks, engages, and represents a sensitive group of youth in Rwanda and the diaspora like Hakizmana discussed in the Introduction. This group is made of those whose parents committed the genocide crimes or are suspects and in some instances like his father continue to deny the genocide ever happened. After serving part of their time in prison, most of these parents are returning home because of illness or old age, and their interactions with the younger generation who grew up in a different Rwanda than they did will prove a challenge for policymakers. Although they have been rehabilitated, some organizations like Community-Based Social Therapy and many others are involved in their rehabilitation, but artists like Bamporiki occupy an important place to turn these youth into Champions in competition with their parents. One study found that the youth born of genocide survivors like Kayitesi or those like Hakizimana have anxiety, low self-esteem, stigma.[103] Majority of them are poor and have not accessed the promises of Vision 2020. They therefore make an easy target for any artist or politicians, Champions, Antagonists, or Fatalists. They were the audience that Kizito and Bamporiki and their sponsors compete for.

Bamporiki's art, though less accessible than some other forms, has given him fame and attracted many conversations in Antagonists communities given his focus on youth like Hakizimana. Diaspora former political elites and their offspring who continue to use online platforms to express their Antagonistic views on postgenocide Rwanda politics in general and the hegemonic master narrative critique his political activism as an RPF outspoken member. He is presented as the leading voice for a "promising generation."[104]

Artists' approaches, preferred art forms, and diverse messages to Rwandans reveal the plurality of expression of the genocide memory, but within the confines of the hegemonic master narrative and with risks. Furthermore, Mihigo's and Bamporiki's works have generated discussion and debate among communities of memory and, even when those works have engaged in reflection on the artists' own individual experiences as Champions and Antagonists, the works have provoked others to ask questions about their experiences and given others a language during the mourning period. The artists' choice to reveal their identities and therefore their position as either survivor or witness has allowed them to speak to specific communities and made them relevant to the formal memory's context. Mihigo and Bamporiki have often worked with other institutions of memory, like the National Commission for the Fight Against Genocide, National Unity and Reconciliation Commission, and different government ministries, as well as nongovernmental organizations (NGOs), to organize discussions, debates, and conversations geared toward reconciliation, confession, forgiveness, or education for younger generations. Mihigo and Bamporiki were often featured in national media engaging students in high schools, prisons, and other public forums. Consequently, their works have influenced and structured memory in different communities.

Both Mihigo and Bamporiki use a comparative memory approach in discussing the past even though the two artists remain distinct and independent. They have rarely put their works in public together or interacted with each other. Bamporiki's work stands as that of a Hutu who is remorseful and Mihigo's as that of a Tutsi survivor who diverges from the hegemonic narrative. Although research shows the youth still identify with ethnic[105] and other aspects of belonging associated with their families in postgenocide Rwanda, that is not the only determinant of their positions when it comes to their position vis-à-vis the Hegemonic master narrative. Rather, individual choices informed by political views and social economic issues matter as well. As we have seen at different times of Kizito and Bamporiki careers they made different choices that are based on their evolving political positions. And while their individual memory influences the kind of message they transmit using their art, their strategic choices define the outcomes of their artistic expressions and circulation among different groups of Rwandans. For instance, although Mihigo's Tutsi survivor identity, his close affiliation with a powerful institution such as the Catholic Church, and the fact that prior to his trial his music occupied a certain national prestige and benefited from extensive institutional support, these factors did not prevent him being punished when he turned into an Antagonist. Thus, it is not simply because one is a famous Tutsi survivor that they get to transmit whatever they want about the hegemonic master narrative rather if they agree to remain in support as a Champion. Other Champions, especially government officials, enforce demand and reward loyalty to the hegemonic master narrative.

In contrast to Mihigo's and Bamporiki's approaches, Rugamba's approach as a Fatalist of not capitalizing on his identity sets him and his art apart and generates a different reaction from his audience. Rugamba's style and less personalized approach often induce intense individual reflection. Unlike Mihigo's and Bamporiki's art, it does not seek to teach or to lead groups into organized debates. He is rarely discussed as an artist who engages in public debates or fits a particular message to a specific audience. His performances leave each individual in the audience to take away whatever messages they prefer.

However, as seductive as the notion may be, the mythology of a therapeutic art transcending political division and palliating the traumatized has certainly not been the universal experience in Rwanda—and Rugamba would not subscribe to such fantastical pretensions. The sort of authentic reflection and introspection on the part of the audience that he seeks to induce can clearly activate latent hatred as well as redemptive confession and conciliation.

Conclusion

Given the power of art, these artists have popularized commemoration of the Genocide Against the Tutsi, created new vocabulary, and influenced debates on personal and community levels that the laws and institutions could not generate. They are also powerful cultural tools that are attractive to youth, especially in the days of social media. Kizito knew that when he instituted programs through his KMP foundation and performed in secondary schools. And Bamporiki engaged equally with the youth as his main audience, but in official discourses that were permitted by the governing political elites and diaspora spaces through Rwanda Day around the world. As Mutoni asserted in reference to Mihigo's lyrics, she found an avenue to think about her mother and at the same time think about the future. Although their works are more accessible, and individuals can own them and therefore listen to or watch them year-round privately, the works come publicly alive in the April–June commemoration period. In this period, they set the tone and dictate the mood, both in live performances and in public places, whenever recordings of them are aired. They transform and ignite memorialization of the past.

In his own way, each artist is broadly representative of a particular channel for community memorialization, while simultaneously developing his own personalized engagement with the genocide. This chapter also has shown that it is possible to move from being a Champion to an Antagonist or vice versa, but one can also exist as a Fatalist or Champion without using their art for other purposes, as we have seen in the case of Dorcy Rugamba. Yet, it also means one's position can lead them to being punished or rewarded. The state enforces the message and demarcates lines to follow in support of the hegemonic master narrative through reward and punishment. In this case, Kizito was punished for undermining the narrative and turning into an Antagonist, while Bamporiki was rewarded for his constancy as a Champion and reinforcing the hegemonic master narrative, especially among the youth whose parents are imprisoned, like Hakizimana discussed in the Introduction. Thus, there is both the perceived power of art and the way political actors seek to manipulate artists through incentives and punishments to reproduce the hegemonic master narrative.

Art and artists are therefore crucial in our understanding of not only how memorialization of the master narrative emerged and evolved but also how these same tools can be used to respond to the official master narrative. While they play a crucial role in allowing master narrative mobility in Rwanda and around the world by Champions, especially in the age of social media, they can also be used to transmit dissent narratives by Antagonists as well as Fatalists. Examining artists over time and how they work emerges alongside the master narrative to show that actors' responses are not determined by one's personal history in the genocide. Rather, support and opposition for Fatalists to the master narrative are determined by many factors, including rural, urban, one's migration history, political ambitions, and many other factors.

Artists facilitate intergenerational dialogue and realization of "postmemory" phenomenon.[106] Postmemory refers to how the second-generation experience and construct memory about events they did not witness. They are transmitted to them to the point where they become powerful and to the point of the second generation claiming ownership of their own traumas and memories.[107] That is they allow new Champions, Antagonists, and Fatalists to emerge as guardians of various narratives official and vernacular. This chapter shows that music, dance, and many other artistic expressions are appealing to youth and can be a tool to promote healing and peaceful coexistence or resistance for hegemonic narrative.[108] This is important as artistic expressions are no longer restricted with social media tools such as TikTok, Instagram, Facebook, and many other digital avenues that permit memories to be transmitted by passing the state. As we will see in the next chapter and argues in other research, these platforms have become popular sites in Rwanda[109] and beyond that connect youth all around the world. In Rwanda in particular, they have facilitated an unsupervised conversation about narratives of Rwanda's pasts between youth in Rwanda who grew up with one narrative of the past and those in the diaspora who are divided among Champions, Antagonists, and Fatalists. The conversations, confrontations, or fake news created by the "born digital" generation[110] introduce all sets of questions that will need new theoretical thinking, including on their meaning in the Global South societies and the minorities expressing dissident narratives in the Global North.

The next chapter shows that journalists and media played a significant role in shaping the emergence of the official memory as well, but also media are used to respond and provide a popular accessible medium through which Champions, Antagonists, and Fatalists can contest the hegemonic memory as it emerges. It also shows how the hegemonic narrative is enforced in the media and across societies through a variety of Champion actors, mostly associates of the government.

Notes

1. The art exhibition was organized by the Academy of Bosnia and Herzegovina. See "Programs: Commemoration of the Srebrenica Massacre—Genocide and Aftermath Art Exhibit and Presentation at the United Nations," Academy of Bosnia and Herzegovina, accessed September 28, 2013, https://web.archive.org/web/20161013162553/http://www.academybh.org/abh_support/html/srebrenica.htm.
2. Martine Hawkes, "Transmitting Genocide: Genocide and Art," *Media and Culture Journal* 9, no. 1 (March 2006): 1, http://journal.media-culture.org.au/0603/09-hawkes.php.
3. Erin Jessee, "The Danger of a Single Story: Iconic Stories in the Aftermath of the 1994 Rwandan Genocide," *Memory Studies* 10, no. 2 (2017): 144–163.
4. Mödersheim, "Art and War," 5.
5. Astrid Erll, "Traveling Memory," *Parallax* 17, no. 4 (2011): 4–18.
6. See essays in this volume on the link between music and postatrocity contexts around the world: Helen Hintjens and Rafiki Ubaldo, "An Overview: Music for Healing, Peacebuilding and Resistance," in *Music and Peacebuilding: African and Latin American Experiences*, eds. Rafiki Ubaldo and Helen Hintjens (New York: Lexington Books, 2020), 1.
7. Ibid.
8. Ibid.
9. David Rakoff, "Post-9/11 Modernism: Questions for Eric Fischl," *New York Times Magazine*, October 27, 2002, 15.
10. Michael Rothberg, *Multidirectional Memory: Remembering the Holocaust in the Age of Decolonization* (Palo Alto, CA: Stanford University Press, 2009), 5.
11. Mariama Ross, "Representations of Violence: Bearing Witness," in *Representations of Violence: Art About the Sierra Leone Civil War*, eds. Patrick K. Muana, Chris Corcoran, and Russell D. Feingold (Madison, WI: Twenty-first Century African Youth Movement, 2005), 39.
12. Two forms of art were preferred in engaging with politics: music and cartoons. However, others who used art politically employed other art forms, which were mostly utilitarian and related to the decoration of everyday objects (e.g., mats, baskets, knife scabbards, and other tools used in the home). Those who make these are mainly

women. Men, on the other hand, are known to use the spoken word. For example, after battle or in modern gatherings men have used rhetoric to brag, drawing on a diverse Kinyarwanda vocabulary and exaggerated stories for entertainment purposes, such as at wedding ceremonies.

13. Jennifer A. Gowan, "Fanning the Flames: A Musician's Role in the Rwandan Genocide," *Nota Bene: Canadian Undergraduate Journal of Musicology* 4, no. 2 (2011): 49–66.
14. See Robert H. Snyder, "'Disillusioned Words like Bullets Bark': Incitement to Genocide, Music, and the Trial of Simon Bikindi," *Georgia Journal of International and Comparative Law* 35 (2006): 645–674.
15. Gowan, "Fanning the Flames," 51
16. Alison Liebhafsky Des Forges, *"Leave None to Tell the Story": Genocide in Rwanda* (New York: Human Rights Watch, 2014), 246.
17. Jason T. McCoy, "Mbwirabumva ('I Speak to Those Who Understand'): Three Songs by Simon Bikindi and the War and Genocide in Rwanda" (PhD, Florida State University, 2013), x.
18. Ibid., 11. Also Darryl Li, "Echoes of Violence: Considerations on Radio and Genocide in Rwanda," *Journal of Genocide Research* 6, no. 1 (2004): 9–27.
19. Jon Henley, "Scar Tissue," *Guardian,* October 31, 2007, http://www.theguardian.com/world/2007/oct/31/rwanda.theatre.
20. In the 1980s, for example, Cyprien's traditional music featured prominently in Radio Rwanda, even his critical songs. See Monique Alexis and Ines Mpambara, "The Rwanda Media Experience from the Genocide," International Media Support, 2003, 10, http://www.mediasupport.org/wp-content/uploads/2012/11/ims-assessment-rwanda-genocide-2003.pdf.
21. See, for example, his songs "Inda Nini" ("A Greedy Stomach") and "Akanigi" ("A Necklace"), in both of which he sings about the Tutsi refugees who had left their country in the 1950s and 1960s: Sipraiyani Rugamba and Amasimbi n'Amakombe, *Inda nini (+lyrics),* Murage Mwiza, May 11, 2018, YouTube, 4:32, https://www.youtube.com/watch?v=iIWdR6VxHkU&ab_channel=MurageMwiza; Sipriyani Rugamba and Amasimbi n'Amakombe, *Akanigi kanjye (+lyrics),* Murage Mwiza, January 12, 2018, YouTube, 6:26, https://www.youtube.com/watch?v=EVTgTtZDp4c&ab_channel=MurageMwiza
22. Benjamin Chemouni and Assumpta Mugiraneza, "Ideology and Interests in the Rwandan Patriotic Front: Singing the Struggle in Pre-genocide Rwanda," *African Affairs* 119, no. 474 (2020): 118.
23. Ibid.
24. See Gérard Prunier, *The Rwanda Crisis: History of a Genocide* (London: Hurst, 1998); Des Forges, *Leave None to Tell the Story,* 1999; and more recently Timothy Longman, *Memory and Justice in Post-genocide Rwanda* (Cambridge, UK: Cambridge University Press, 2017).
25. Liisa Helena Malkki, "Refugees and Exile: From 'Refugee Studies' to the National Order of Things," *Annual Review of Anthropology* 24 (1995): 1.
26. Ibid.

27. Interview with Kayiranga, a former RPF military officer, Kigali, Rwanda, December 2018.
28. Rémi Korman, "Indirimbo z'icyunamo. Chanter la mémoire du génocide," *Les Temps modernes* 4 (2014): 350–361.
29. Chemouni and Mugiraneza, "Ideology and Interests," 120.
30. Korman, "Indirimbo z'icyunamo," 352.
31. Andrea Mariko Grant, "The Making of a Superstar: The Politics of Playback and Live Performance in Post-Genocide Rwanda," *Africa* 87, no. 1 (2017): 160.
32. Marilyn Jones, "Difference Maker: Jean-Paul Samputu Practices Forgiveness—Even for His Father's Killer," *Christian Science Monitor*, July 19, 2013, http://www.csmonitor.com/World/Making-a-difference/2013/0719/Jean-Paul-Samputu-practices-forgiveness-even-for-his-father-s-killer.
33. See Rafiki Ubaldo and Helen Hintjens, "Rwandan Music-makers Negotiate Shared Cultural Identities after Genocide: The Case of Orchestre Impala's Revival," *Cultural Studies* 34, no. 6 (2020): 925–958.
34. Ibid.
35. Andrea Purdeková and David Mwambari, "Post-genocide Identity Politics and Colonial Durabilities in Rwanda," *Critical African Studies* 14, no. 1 (2021): 1–19.
36. For music and its complexity in Rwanda society during and after the war, see Chemouni and Mugiraneza, "Ideology and Interests"; Korman, "Indirimbo z'icyunamo"; McCoy, "Mbwirabumva"; and Grant, "The Making of a 'Superstar.'"
37. Jennie E. Burnet, *Genocide Lives in Us: Women, Memory, and Silence in Rwanda* (Madison: University of Wisconsin Press, 2012, 87.
38. Unlike in the pregenocide art scene, in Rwanda today many forms of art are becoming increasingly popular among Rwandans, and many of these forms engage with the genocide memory.
39. Yanditswe Kuya, "Minisitiri w'intebe ati 'Igitaramo cya Kizito Mihigo kiratanga amasomo ane," IGIHE (Kigali), April 17, 2012, https://igihe.com/imyidagaduro/muzika/abahanzi/kizito-mihigo/amakuru/minisitiri-w-intebe-ati-igitaramo-cya-kizito-mihigo-kiratanga-amasomo-ane.
40. Notes from a concert, *Ijoro ribara uwariraye*, that I attended at Serena Hotel on April 15, 2012.
41. See the home page of his official English website: Kizito Mihigo, "May Peace Be with You!" Fondation Kizito Mihigo pour la Paix (Kizito Mihigo Peace Foundation), accessed January 1, 2014, https://www.kizitomihigo.foundation/.
42. Concert, *Ijoro ribara uwariraye*.
43. For the song's lyrics, see Kizito Mihigo, "*Twanze Gutoberwa Amateka* Lyrics," *Afrika Lyrics*, accessed March 13, 2023 https://afrikalyrics.com/kizito-mihigo-twanze-gutoberwa-amateka-lyrics
44. See US Department of State, *International Religious Freedom Report 2007: Rwanda* (Washington, DC: Human Rights US State Department Bureau of Democracy and Labor, 2007), http://www.state.gov/j/drl/rls/irf/2007/90115.htm.
45. Although Christians and their role are discussed in various literature on the genocide, the most detailed is that given in Timothy Longman, *Christianity and Genocide in Rwanda* (Cambridge: Cambridge University Press, 2011).

46. The Bible often contrasts darkness and light. See, for example, John 1:3–5.
47. Notes from my fieldwork on April 22, 2012, Ruhango District, Southern Province, Rwanda, including conversations with Kizito Mihigo during a commemoration event.
48. See lyrics in Kinyarwanda in Kizito Mihigo, "Kizito Mihigo—Ijoro ribara uwariraye—Genocide Commemoration Song," YouTube.com, 5:57, 2012, http://www.youtube.com/watch?v=D1WiNvgNTgs.
49. Ibid.
50. For example, World Vision visited rural Rwanda with Mihigo, as documented in "Nyamagabe: Kizito Mihigo Foundation Entertains Youth in Peace Concert," *Rwanda Express*, September 22, 2013, http://rwandaexpress.blogspot.com/2013/09/nyamagabe-kizito-mihigo-foundation.html.
51. The translation comes from one of the few non-Rwandan online forums that captured the conversation: "*Artists in Politics: Kizito Mihigo's Fall in Rwanda*" (Jukwaa, Ghana: Kenyan Discussion Platform, May 3, 2014), http://jukwaa.proboards.com/thread/9017/artists-politics-kizito-mihigos-rwanda.
52. Ibid.
53. See discussion about the Ndi Umunyarwanda program in Robert Mbaraga, "States Pushes Campaign That Critics Say It Is Ethnically Divisive," *East African (Nairobi)*, November 16, 2013, http://www.theeastafrican.co.ke/Rwanda/News/Mixed-reactions-to--Ndi-Umunyarwanda-initiative-/-/1433218/2075366/-/6ktcmf/-/index.html.
54. The news was captured on Chris Kamo, BBC, Rwanda's Kizito Mihigo and Cassien Ntamuhanga arrested, 14th April 20214, https://www.bbc.com/news/world-africa-27028206.
55. "Kizito Mihigo yabonye umukobwa bazarushingana," IGIHE (Kigali), March 13, 2014, https://www.igihe.com/imyidagaduro/muzika/abahanzi/kizito-mihigo/amakuru/kizito-mihigo-yatangaje-uko-abona-umugore-w-agaciro.
56. See "Rwanda's Kizito Mihigo and Cassien Ntamuhanga Arrested," BBC News, BBC, aired April 14, 2014, http://www.BBC.com/news/world-africa-27028206
57. Edouard Bamporiki, *Icyaha kuri bo, ikimwaro kuri jye* (Kigali, Rwanda: E. Bamporiki Uwayo, 2010), 12.
58. Ibid.
59. Ibid., 13.
60. Ibid., 12.
61. The word *Inyenzi-Inkotanyi* was used to refer to RPF members and RPA soldiers; the expression can also be pronounced differently to mean "cockroaches," and this pronunciation had been used by the Interahamwe to dehumanize the Tutsi population during the genocide. The Interahamwe were saying the Tutsi were cockroaches and therefore had to be crushed. See Des Forges, *Leave None to Tell the Story*, 62.
62. Ibid., 24.
63. Ibid., 25.
64. Ibid.
65. Richard Benda, "Youth Connect Dialogue: Unwanted Legacies, Responsibility and Nation-building in Rwanda" (working paper 001, Nottingham, UK: Aegis Trust, September 2017), 10.
66. Ibid.

67. Ibid.
68. Ibid.
69. Maggie Ziegler, "Breaking the Silence on the Rwanda Genocide: An Interview with Edouard Bamporiki," *Peace Magazine*, July–September 2013, http://peacemagazine.org/archive/v29n3p16.htm.
70. Benda, "Youth Connect Dialogue," 10.
71. The survivors who helped Bamporiki included the well-known artist Mibilizi, who also sings commemoration songs but is less popular than Bamporiki and Mihigo. See workshop report documentary on Edouard Bamporiki: Ikaze Iwacu, "Ngira ipfunwe ryo kwitwa umuhutu Edouard Bampoyiki," Kigali, Rwanda, 13:33, 2013, http://www.youtube.com/watch?v=bykhj7mO2wI. (Note the different spelling of Bamporiki's name in the title.)
72. Ziegler, "Breaking the Silence on the Rwanda Genocide."
73. Ibid.
74. See Peter Bowen, "African Film Festival New York," *Focus Features, News & Views*, November 14, 2008, https://africanfilmny.org/films/long-coat/.
75. Alrick Brown, dir., *Kinyarwanda* (2011). Review blurbs and a list of awards the film won are shown at http://www.kinyarwandamovie.com/, accessed October 2, 2013.
76. See David Dewitt, "Linked Stories from the Months of the Rwanda Massacre," *New York Times*, December 1, 2011, http://www.nytimes.com/2011/12/02/movies/kinyarwanda-about-1994-genocide-of-tutsis-in-rwanda.html?_r=0.
77. Benda, "Youth Connect Dialogue," 12.
78. See "Rwanda: We Need to Step Out of Our Parents' Shadows—Poet Bamporiki," *AllAfrica*, July 23, 2013, https://allafrica.com/stories/201307230319.html.
79. Benda, "Youth Connect Dialogue," 12.
80. For example, Eric Senderi Mibirizi, known for his single "Twarabakundaga Turababura" ("We Loved You and We Lost You"), has also gained popularity. Equally, the 2001 film *100 Days*, produced by Eric Kabera, was one of the earliest works of a returnee artist to show Rwandans their stories on screen using Rwandan actors, including survivors. Then there are various groups of artists that gather during commemoration for a particular goal of composing a song or concert with a focus on commemoration. These include concerts by Maria Yohana Mukankuranga, Mani Martin, Patrick Nyamitari, Tonzi, Eric Rukundo, Sgt. Robert, Eric Senderi, Grace Kitoko, and Dieudonné Munyanshoza, as well as East African artists who performed the song "Never Again" in 2011, organized by cultural artist group Masamba.
81. Perhaps this slow emergence of women artists can be explained from the broader perspective that older Rwandan women have responded to the genocide memory with silence and have not been as vocal politically as men. See Burnet, Genocide Lives in Us.
82. On Ndi Umunyarwanda, see Andrea Purdeková, *Making ubumwe: Power, State and Camps in Rwanda's Unity-Building Project*, Vol. 34 (Oxford, NY: Berghahn Books, 2015); Susan Thomson, *Whispering Truth to Power: Everyday Resistance to Reconciliation in Postgenocide Rwanda* (Madison: University of Wisconsin Pres, 2013; and Caroline Williamson, "Genocide, Masculinity and Posttraumatic Growth in Rwanda: Reconstructing Male Identity through ndi umunyarwanda," *Journal of Genocide Research* 18, no. 1 (2016): 41–59.

83. See Andrew Israel Kazibwe, "Actor-cum-Politician Bamporiki Stars in *Umutoma—a Love Story*," *East African (Nairobi)*, June 27, 2014, http://www.theeastafrican.co.ke/Rwanda/Lifestyle/Actor-cum-politician-Bamporiki-stars-in-Umutoma-a-love-story-/-/1433242/2364116/-/m2n1et/-/index.html.
84. Ivan Ngaboka, "Rwanda's Youngest MP Is a Blend of Art and Politics," *New Times*, October 20, 2013, https://www.newtimes.co.rw/article/99187/rwandaas-youngest-mp-is-a-blend-of-art-and-politics#:~:text=DONNING%20A%20FITTING%20dark%20designer,of%20an%20ordinary%20young%20man.<<<
85. Henley, "Scar Tissue."
86. Ibid.
87. See a list of Rugamba's works, mostly written and performed in Europe, in Dorcy Rugamba, "Et si on interdisait les femmes dans l'espace public?" *La Revue des Ressources*, March 2, 2014, https://ressources.org/et-si-on-interdisait-les-femmes-dans-l-espace-public,2710.html.
88. Paul Kerstens, "Voice and Give Voice: Dialectics between Fiction and History in Narratives on the Rwandan Genocide," *International Journal of Francophone Studies* 9, no. 1 (2006): 102.
89. For more on the trials, see Devin O. Pendas, *The Frankfurt Auschwitz Trial, 1963–1965: Genocide, History, and the Limits of the Law* (Cambridge: Cambridge University Press, 2006).
90. Ibid.
91. See Henley, "Scar Tissue."
92. Ibid.
93. Ibid.
94. Ibid.
95. See Dorcy Ingeli Rugamba and Francis Busignies, *Marembo* (Saint-Maurice, Quebec, Canada: Da Ti M'beti, 2005).
96. Kerstens, "Voice and Give Voice."
97. Namely, Dorcy Rugamba, "Une société martiale et solidaire," interview by Colette Braekman, in *Rwanda: Mille collines, mille douleurs*, ed. Colette Braeckman (Brussels: Éditions Nevicata, 2014). And, he authored a reflective piece on the events of 1994: Dorcy Rugamba, "L'Angle mort de la bonne conscience française," *La Revue des Ressources*, December 30, 2013, https://ressources.org/l-angle-mort-de-la-bonne-conscience-francaise,2676.html.
98. See Ziegler, "Breaking the Silence on the Rwanda Genocide," 16.
99. See Henley, "Scar Tissue."
100. Interview with Mutoni, June 2011, Kigali, Rwanda.
101. Ziegler, "Breaking the Silence on the Rwanda Genocide."
102. On the BBC Gahuzamiryango program *Imvo n'imvano*, on July 13, 2013, a group of Hutu in the diaspora challenged Bamporiki's call for Hutu to confess to collective guilt. They accused him of wanting to shield and minimize memories of Hutu survivors of RPA killings. See Jastudio360, "Imvo n'imvano, gusaba imbabazi kw'abahutu," YouTube video, 57:12, 2013, http://www.youtube.com/watch?v=56QPn7LzQK0.

103. Emmanuel Biracyaza and Samuel Habimana, "Contribution of Community-Based Sociotherapy Interventions for the Psychological Well-being of Rwandan Youths Born to Genocide Perpetrators and Survivors: Analysis of the Stories Telling of a Sociotherapy Approach," *BMC Psychology* 8, no. 1 (2020): 1–15.

104. Richard M. Benda, "Promising Generations: From Intergenerational Guilt to Ndi Umunyarwanda," in *Rwanda Since 1994: Stories of Change*, Vol. 10, eds. Hannah Grayson and Nicki Hitchcott (Liverpool, UK: Liverpool University Press, 2019), 189.

105. See Lyndsay McLean Hilker, "Everyday Ethnicities: Identity and Reconciliation among Rwandan Youth," *Journal of Genocide Research* 11, no. 1 (2009): 81–100.

106. Marianne Hirsch, "The Generation of Postmemory," *Poetics Today* 29, no. 1 (2008): 104.

107. Ibid.

108. Aleida Assmann, Peter Novick, Gesine Schwan, and Janusz Reiter, "Bulletin Features," 2007; cited in Hintjens and Ubaldo, "Music for Healing, Peacebuilding and Resistance," 1.

109. Tugce Ataci, "Narratives of Rwandan Youth on Post-genocide Reconciliation: Contesting Discourses and Identities in the Making," *Journal of Youth Studies* 25, no. 10 (2021): 1–18.

110. Yvonne Liebermann, "Born Digital: The Black Lives Matter Movement and Memory after the Digital Turn," *Memory Studies* 14, no. 4 (2021): 713–732.

7

The Media, Commemoration, and the Enforcement of the Master Narrative

Umutemeli w'agahinda ni ijosi—The cover of sorrow is the neck.
—Rwandan proverb

On that unforgettable April morning in 1994 when the news broke on the radio that President Juvénal Habyarimana, Rwanda's leader since 1973, had been killed, many things changed in my life and the lives of all Rwandans. One of the changes was the introduction to strange-sounding classical music. I am yet to understand why the staff of Radio Rwanda found this music relevant. They announced that the president's plane had been shot down and then played this strange music as we waited for the next announcement. As I would learn later from those who were adults at the time, radio was a popular means of communicating news. It was used for announcing job opportunities, celebrating those who had passed national exams, or those few who got new appointments after graduating from the only university in Rwanda in our neighborhood in Butare. It was also used to announce the death of a loved one, including the president of the country and those on his plane this time around.

Another important avenue for communicating news was *Imvaho Nshya* (hereafter *Imvaho*), the main government newspaper published in Kinyarwanda. *Imvaho* served many purposes, including sharing weekly news, putting announcements and advertisements into print, and even helping people learn how to read and write. However, it was for the few as a majority of Rwandan adults did not have the means to buy it, and it was not distributed nationally to every house or address like newspapers in Western countries. It was limited to the towns and the literate working and middle classes.

Yet, radio's reach was larger and more accessible. As children we enjoyed listening to the radio in pregenocide Rwanda, especially on Tuesdays, when they aired an educational drama series "Igitaramo," which influenced Rwandans' thinking about culture, politics, family life, and the general development of the country. We listened to the radio in the morning while preparing to go to school and at lunch (which the working class took at home), and the workers in their fields always carried their radio, powered by batteries. From children to adults, people literate and illiterate alike had a relationship with a radio. Radio announcements were an integral part of everyday life, so it was a natural tool to announce the death of the president, play classical music, and then make an announcement that no one should leave their home. In addition to Radio Rwanda, there was one other private radio station that played a crucial role during the Genocide Against the Tutsi. Like music and other art forms, the radio and other media, such as print, new media, and television, became even more prominent and controversial in shaping everyday postgenocide life in the first two decades after the genocide. This chapter turns attention to how both local and international media responded to the evolution of the master narrative and commemoration in the first 20 years after the genocide. It looks at the media as an avenue whereby the master narrative is communicated and disputed and as a source of tensions for Champions, Antagonists, and Fatalists of the genocide memory.

As we've seen in previous chapters, laws, institutions, memorials, and artwork played key roles in both creating and responding to the emergence and evolution of the hegemonic master narrative of the Genocide Against the Tutsi. This chapter shows how the media played a dual role as well. It was another space where the hegemonic master narrative was constructed, disseminated, and enforced by Champions in the first two decades. Similarly, it was the most useful tool Antagonists and Fatalists used to respond to the hegemonic master narrative as it evolved. The evolution of new media emerged with the new millennium as the hegemonic master narrative was also evolving and transformed conversations on memorialization in postgenocide Rwanda. Just like the media played a crucial role in the execution of the genocide and Rwanda Patriotic Front (RPF) mobilizing their liberation war, both traditional and new media have played a principal role in shaping official memory and individual and collective responses to its emergence and evolution and provided a means for enforcing the hegemonic master narrative. In this chapter, I argue that through close analysis of the evolution of memory politics and the media in the first two decades that we can locate how the government and other Champions close to the government enforced the hegemonic narrative through rewarding and punishing public figures like artists. Furthermore, even though the government still controls the hegemonic master narrative and how it is discussed in local media, it faces competition and complications from online media outlets that defy geographic and national boundaries. The government, and in particular high-level politicians, dominates the social media space in Rwanda, but they are faced with an increasingly young population that is turning to social media to express their political views and positions on policies. Champions—especially the government—are also forced to engage with a wider global audience that questions the official genocide narrative that initially flourished online, propelled in some instances by other online movements that protest Western hegemonic narratives globally. More recently, this opposition has come from young Antagonists in the diaspora and some within Rwanda. New media accelerated their opposition to the hegemonic master narrative through social media influence on youth who grew up in the new Rwanda. Online spaces are increasingly becoming sites of narrative battles, competing for youth attention and energy.

Therefore, this chapter traces the evolution of various media in postgenocide Rwanda as platforms of engagement with the master narrative in its emergence. It finds that while international journalists and ORINFOR (Office Rwandais d'Information, which housed the radio we grew up listening to) shaped discussions about genocide memory in the early years after the genocide, economic development post-2000 has been characterized by the proliferation of private-sector media ownership. This proliferation allowed multiple sites of engagement but did not necessarily produce pluralism in debates over memory. As we will see, demographic change and increased access to technology tools, especially to urban youth, changed how Champions, Antagonists, and Fatalists related and responded to the master narrative and accelerated the representation of hegemonic master narrative, dissident narratives, and the genocide itself.

By analyzing secondary materials and the interviews I collected in 2012 and 2013 and in 2018-2019, I examine two periods that characterized the media memory evolution in postgenocide Rwanda. First, I discuss the dominance of ORINFOR and international journalists in shaping the period immediately following the Genocide Against the Tutsi and the preceding civil war. Then I move to the second period, from those first months until

2013, tracing the evolution of private media and their reporting during the annual mourning period. I also briefly discuss the slow emergence of social media, followed by a boom (especially among elites) in later years, as important platforms where multiple forms of the current master narrative and dissident narratives interact. This two-part analysis demonstrates how the government has carefully monitored and surveyed media programs during commemorations and continued to demarcate the legitimate boundaries of the genocide narrative, albeit with seemingly diminished efficacy over time. The chapter also examines recent developments in new media outlets and social media, though this analysis is brief and anecdotal rather than comprehensive, as it falls outside the scope of the study.[1] It seeks to contribute to emerging debates on the technology turn in memory studies explored in Chapter 1.

The First Period: Aftermath of the Genocide

In the past two decades, scholarship combining media research and memory studies has evolved. "Media memory" is a multilayer discipline of inquiry that examines how media agencies "operate as memory agents."[2] Media scholars Oren Myers, Motti Neiger, and Eyal Zandberg have argued that cultural memory depends on public expression, and that "memory studies focus on various forms of public expression such as rituals, ceremonial commemorations, and mass media texts." Thus, it follows that "collective memory is an inherently mediated phenomenon."[3] For Astrid Erll, media, television, and other such channels allow memory to travel over space and geographies, and "media disseminate versions of the past across time, space and mnemonic communities."[4] She asserts further:

> The current age of accelerated globalization has brought forth global media cultures, in which historical novels are quickly translated, movies dealing with the past are screened simultaneously in different corners of the globe, and worldwide TV-audiences can have mass-mediated experience in real time (as, for example, in the case of "9/11" or the inauguration of the American president Obama).[5]

Thus, the study of cultural memory necessarily involves the study of media. As this chapter demonstrates, Champions, Antagonists, and Fatalists understand the power of media and are transformed by it. The media and their role in generating political memory can be understood in a variety of ways. Jérôme Bourdon has claimed that a "life-story" approach creates an understanding of the media as giving "an elusive notion of the everyday."[6] He contends: "Certain narratives which have been told many times over, are stratified, and are less prone to change."[7] Media coverage of anniversaries of the September 11, 2001, terrorist attacks in the United States is a good example in support of his argument. Over the years, the reporting during the remembrance period has featured what Andrew Hoskins refers to as "flash frame" images.[8] The repetition of these images, such as the iconic picture of smoke coming out of the Twin Towers and a plane approaching in the sky featured in the *New York Times* on the tenth anniversary, has fixed a particular narrative of 9/11 events in a purportedly global, shared memory of 9/11.[9] The "born digital" generation[10] of champions has accelerated the use of online media to transmit, shape the emergence, and evolution of the master narrative and its hegemonic status in the offline and online worlds. Equally, it is the most preferred avenue for Antagonists. For instance, youth in Nigeria, Kenya, and other countries drew inspiration from the global Black Lives Matter protests around the world[11] and the RhodesMustFall movement to express their frustrations with hegemonic narratives in their own countries.[12] Likewise, Champions, Antagonists, and Fatalists have found a new avenue that accelerates the sharing of their narratives with the world without anyone's permission or with institutional gatekeepers. However, before we analyze new media and its relationship to memory politics, it is important to examine how various actors have used the media to respond to the emergence, evolution, and enforcement of the hegemonic master narrative.

In Rwanda, as in many other post–mass atrocity societies, journalistic witnesses pretended to a level of immediacy, spontaneity, and authenticity. However, the accounts of international and Rwandan journalists after the genocide also conveyed a strong, dynamic, market-driven imperative to achieve maximum affective or emotional impact on readers, viewers, and listeners.[13] Thus, the most appalling images were selected and shown.[14] A sharp, polar moral clarity was introduced for an audience encountering the images and story with limited context and limited attention—and the sharp polarity of victim and perpetrator flourished. As the most important actors in this space, journalists, editors, and media owners not only witnessed, but also selected with a preference for the most visible and most graphic horror, in some cases heavily influenced by their own traumas and individual memory.

In the case of Rwanda, there was much of this to witness after the fact, but its explanatory power was limited. Over time, journalists' accounts have come to be considered factual versions of what "really happened."[15] Thus, mostly international journalists and editors were positioned as the most legitimate storytellers and as authorities in establishing and guarding "the truth" about the violent past for Champions and contesting it for Antagonists.[16]

The journalistic construction of Rwanda's collective past was significantly augmented in 2004. On the tenth anniversary of the genocide in Rwanda, the BBC published an article, "In Pictures: Remembering the Genocide."[17] BBC's photojournalist Nick Danziger and a team reported on their encounters with survivors, imprisoned *génocidaire* suspects, and visitors to genocide memorials. In the introduction to a series of photos that included captions of stories, the report read: "These pictures and the individuals will haunt me forever. I cannot imagine what it must be like for the victims."[18] The dramatization and appropriation of these horrors could be read in a series of similar articles and learned about through radio and television programs produced by both large and small media houses. The sense of drama and emotion generated by such programs characterized the reporting of the genocide globally during the first two decades following 1994. The focus was on a narrative of victims, perpetrators, and heroes to use the language that was best understood by the Western public accused of forgetting or abandoning the Tutsi victims at their time of need.[19] Thus, primarily international journalists and a few Rwandan journalists working with BBC, Voice of America Great Lakes programs, and ORINFOR wrote the first draft of national memory.[20] As we will see in sections that follow, if the media got to tell the story however they pleased during the 1990s crisis in Rwanda and Democratic Republic of Congo (DRC), the RPF leadership designed a media strategy that would see them enforce their message at all costs as they rebuilt Rwanda. This was especially true for any news that questioned the script of the evolving hegemonic master narrative and events around it, particularly because of the media's legacy during the genocide and civil war.

The Media's Genocide Legacy

Survivors' recent history was the main concern for the new government, unlike with previous governments, which did not recognize or publicize earlier massacres. However, two factors complicated the engagement of Rwandan local media and individual journalists with genocide memory in the immediate period after the genocide. First, local media's involvement in the genocide and the consequent destruction of the media in 1994 affected their ability to engage.[21] Second, the impact of the RPF's informational management strategy, which insisted on constructing and disseminating its version of the "truth" of the recent past, was significant. In the first instance, media lost credibility during the genocide because of their role in the genocide. The Radio Télévision Libre des Mille Collines (RTLM) and selected radical newspapers left a negative perception of the media after their anti-Tutsi campaigns resulted in killings around the country.[22] Thus, ORINFOR—composed of Television Rwanda (TVR) and Radio Rwanda—was the only entity actively engaged in reporting and editorializing on such sensitive topics as genocide memory.[23] ORINFOR focused on survivors, victims, and the heroism of the RPF.

Every April, ORINFOR aired graphic images of genocide victims. It was a practice that arguably continued to traumatize the country, one that did not stop until 2011.[24] The airing of these images not only retraumatized Champions but also instilled fear in Antagonists and further paralyzed Fatalists, especially in urban areas. Until the ORINFOR-mediated messages were issued, many rural Rwandans might not have had any sense of the widespread nature of the genocide. Many knew only about what they had personally witnessed or survived. ORINFOR commemoration programs not only influenced these rural citizens' memories but also created a nationwide "event" for many communities living outside of urban areas that hosted some of the earliest commemorations. Their experiential memory, all too often horrific enough, was annually interlaced with nationally broadcast documentation of atrocity.

As Munyana, a community leader and mother of five explained to me in an interview, the commemoration period was a horrific time, and everyone dreaded it.

> The Rwandan national television [TVR] used to play all these images of dead people. I was young and sometimes my aunt would turn off the television. But we would still watch when she had gone to work during the day. The music was scary like that in [horror movies]. I remember an image of a woman lying down with a machete wound on her head and footage of children crying. Sometimes I used to have nightmares and it was hard to sleep.[25]

Munyana recounted how her relatives visited from rural Rwanda and would be shocked at what the urban folk were watching on their televisions. Television ownership in rural Rwanda remains a luxury, and large numbers of rural Rwandans followed radio programs that were focused on victims. As explained in the previous chapter, Edouard Bamporiki indicated that Hutu listened to the stories of angry survivors in different programs and wondered if there would be revenge against Hutu families. This Hutu fear was also expressed in an article, "Ubwoba bwumvikana" ("Understandable Fear"), that appeared in the April 24–30, 1995, issue of *Imvaho*. Author Mweusi Karake explained that Hutu might fear revenge from the RPF and other Tutsi after realizing that many Tutsi had been killed a year earlier. In an article that followed, the same author analyzed the experiences of many Hutu during April 1995:

> After the massacres and extermination in 1994, many Hutu had fled from their homes. This past month of April was a difficult month for them, as they feared that Tutsi and Inkotanyi or RPF would revenge and kill them. They also feared commemoration programs that had been planned for April 7, the day of remembering genocide victims.[26]

A closer look at scarce local accounts and viewpoints as published in *Imvaho* shows the diversity of concerns related to the commemoration periods. The April 3–9, 1995, issue of *Imvaho* contained a section called "Spécial Génocide: Umwaka urashize miliyoni y'abanyarwanda itikijwe" ("A Year Has Gone When One Million Rwandans Were Exterminated"), by Mweusi Karake. Karake began by explaining that during this week many people would be remembering, but he would not. He argued that remembering is for those in danger of forgetting what happened, and he would never forget those who were killed. In the same issue, Charles Gakumba analyzed the historical roots of the genocide in a piece, "Inkomoko y'irimbura-koko mu Rwanda" ("The Origin of Ethnic Cleansing in Rwanda").[27] Similarly, Béatrice Mutarabayire, of the survivor women's organization Avega Agahozo, expressed fear that former *Interahamwe* militia in the countryside and on Rwanda's borders continued to kill and wanted to kill all Tutsi.[28] In the same series of articles, others, like Frank Ndamage, questioned the progress of reconciliation. Equally, in the same newspaper's April 10–16, 1995, issue, two articles criticized the international community's lack of interest in aiding Rwandans.[29] In analyzing these articles in the only newspaper widely distributed and read throughout the country, I saw no indication whether these writers, at the time, were trained journalists or were simply individuals expressing their opinions on commemorations. Articles from this period helped frame the government's narrative of the recent past.[30]

The Postgenocide Government's Information Management Strategy

Additionally, the new RPF-led government developed a clear information management strategy based on what anthropologist Johan Pottier has called a "concept of morality, guilt and punishment."[31] To show their moral authority to speak on behalf of victims, the RPF's approach was to "capture the silent words of the victims giving them a meaning determined by current goals" and to "take over the private mourning of the survivors and transform it into a collective mourning."[32] The RPF political elites saw themselves as survivors—of not only the genocide but also earlier massacres and exile—and therefore they spoke not only for others but also for themselves. The stories generated by this approach were the stories that the international media and local media reported.

In many cases, the RPF authorized media houses to cover commemorations and ensured that the government's master narrative featured prominently. Thus, the RPF became the only moral authority to speak about the genocide and determine how the genocide is discussed. It is this moral authority and the attached perception of factual reliability that could not be challenged.[33] In many cases, international reporters cooperated, and this facilitated the subsequent international outpouring of "guilt" aid.[34]

Their strategy to convince the world with their narrative worked, and they ensured to follow through by showing confidence and determination, especially when interviewed by foreign media.[35] For example, then-Minister of Rehabilitation and Social Affairs Patrick Mazimpaka frankly asserted the RPF's uncontested claim to legitimacy 2 years later in the *Washington Post*: "We were (diplomatically) stronger because nobody could argue against us."[36] The then-vice president asserted that the Rwandan leadership used "communication and information warfare better than anyone" and had "found a new way of doing things."[37] Thus, the RPF convinced the world that they were the only ones with the credibility to reconstruct media institutions and oversee training of responsible journalists in the reconstruction of Rwanda in general.

Those in the media—whether individual journalists or human rights groups—who attempted to contradict the new government's framework were expelled from the country. Among the journalists were Christian Jennings of Reuters, expelled on February 9, 1997, and Stephen Smith of the French daily *Libération*, expelled on November 28 of the same year.[38] While some Rwandan journalists fled the country, others remained and opted for self-censoring strategies. It is this background and aggressive communication strategy that was also employed later that Champions used the radio as an avenue to promote the master narrative, and Antagonists used the media to contradict the master narrative. But, an understanding of the evolution of the postgenocide media industry is crucial to any analysis of the complex role of the media in the master narrative and commemoration.

The Second Period: Liberalization of Media Enforcement and Monitoring of Genocide Memory

Emergence of Private Media Companies

The second phase of media development after the genocide involved the liberalization of media ownership, but not necessarily the liberalization of the narrative.[39] This expansion of the media industry also included shifts in the very nature of media that paved the way for the later phase, which saw an increase in the use of new media. Liberalization grew out of the general economic, social, and political reconstruction that characterized Rwanda after the re-establishment of order and the securing of Rwanda's borders. In 2005, the now-well-established RPF government received public recognition internationally. In turn, international institutions and organizations and members of the diaspora from Western and African countries started to return and began investing in the "new" Rwanda. The RPF also grew stronger and further developed its media strategy to allow new radio stations and newspapers, but kept close control of those media's content, making sure they followed government directives on sensitive political issues, especially on the narrative of the recent past.

Through national forums that began under President Pasteur Bizimungu between May 1999 and March 2000, the new government outlined its development, economic, and peace agendas.[40] As a result of these consultations with the public, a new constitution was ratified by Parliament in 2003, and the "Vision 2020" document was popularized nationally. These events led to a boom in international aid in the post-2005 period, which grew local businesses, including new media houses. Given the popularity of radio stations in Rwandan society, this type of medium grew more rapidly than the less accessible television and newspapers. Contact FM and Radio 10 gained prominence, as did newspapers such as *The Weekly* and the government-controlled *New Times* and controversial newspapers such as *Umuvugizi* and *Umuseso*. Private radio stations introduced newer, more modern styles of broadcasting, such as the call-in shows Contact FM, Salus, and Radio 10, while online news sources such as *IGIHE*, *News of Rwanda*, and the *New Times* allowed readers to comment on each article. Inevitably, this led ORINFOR to adopt new styles as well, as it responded to the shift in the competitive environment, and in 2013 it changed its name to Rwanda Broadcasting Agency (RBA). In the earlier period, there was only one state radio station, but by 2005 there were over 20, though only one television broadcaster.[41]

Monitoring Media during Commemoration

With this evolution of new media, the government started a monitoring program that would establish rules for all media. This especially concerned coverage of sensitive political topics in radio, in print, and on television. In 2003, the Media High Council of the Press (hereafter MHC), a government watchdog body, began its work. The council claims that it produces independent reports such as the State of Media Freedom in Rwanda report, which had comprehensive views and a variety of views of media editors, owners, and journalists. It established a "Rwanda Media Monitoring Project," or RMMP. RMMP started to monitor all media outlets and their reports during the period of commemorations. The RMMP's aims were to "[enhance] professional standards of the Rwandan media, in providing key stakeholders with systematic data and a clear picture of deficiencies and performances in the sector," and to accomplish this "through periodic reports based on quantitative and qualitative analysis of media news items."[42] The RMMP monitored print, radio, and television media. The RMMP covered a range of topics, such as causes of the genocide; survivors' welfare; genocide prevention policies;

survivors' security; genocide memory (expressed in sites, testimonies, documents, plays on the genocide, apologies, etc.); the media's role in the genocide; and justice and reconciliation, among others.[43] The media mainly reported on official ceremonies with little coverage of private mourning.[44] An analysis of RMMP reports over the years from 2003 to 2012 showed that genocide memory was the most-discussed topic, while survivors' security received little attention.[45]

The monitors' findings reveal that a large percentage of contributions to the media's overall message came from the government, especially from high-ranking political RPF elites, not from ordinary survivors. The 2004 report asserted: "President Paul Kagame, Minister of Youth Robert Bayigamba and the President of IBUKA François Xavier Ngarambe appeared 64 times in different news items as sources of information," while the rest of the attention was devoted to foreigners such as Belgian Prime Minister Guy Verhofstadt and the former commander general of the United Nations Assistance Mission for Rwanda (UNAMIR), Roméo Dallaire, who "appeared respectively in 12 and 18 news items."[46] Thus, ordinary Rwandans' experiences and comments were afforded little presence in the media, despite the proliferation of new outlets. In its conclusion to the 2004 report on tenth commemoration ceremonies, the RMMP argued that only BBC, *Ingabo* magazine, Radio Rwanda, TVR, and *Ukuri* newspaper had reported accurately and given balance to discussions of their topics,[47] and half of the news items published or broadcast in the Gasabo, Inganzo, and Umurage districts were found to be biased.[48] The sources that were found to be biased were given warning, but no direct action against journalists or the papers was taken after the report. This lack of action on the part of the government showed small shifts in its approach to dealing with media that contradicted the master narrative.

Over time, levels of adherence to RMMP guidelines changed. In 2009, RMMP monitoring showed that the annual theme of commemoration was mentioned in 55% of media messages, down from 89% during the previous commemorations in 2008. This shows a diminished concordance between the officially mandated message and what was disseminated. It also provides at least a modest indicator that uncritical adherence to the government's line had faded somewhat over time.

Although the RMMP praised BBC Great Lakes radio programs for reporting balanced news, in 2009 BBC Great Lakes programs were suspended.[49] In particular, the government detested a 1-hour weekend program that was gaining popularity as a space for debate on Rwanda's recent past. The

BBC program, "Imvo n'Imvano" ("Analysis of a Problem from Its Source") was the first to be suspended, on April 25, 2009, during the commemoration period. The Rwandan government information minister had listened to a preview of the program and banned it because it included "most outrageous statements," as he later stated.[50] Similar accusations had been leveled against radio programs produced in Kirundi and Kinyarwanda by Voice of America in 2006 and 2008.[51]

In 2010, during the April mourning period, another two independent print media sources, *Umuvugizi* and *Umeseso*, were suspended for 6 months after being accused and threatened many times for their alleged controversial reports on the genocide and other RPF policies.[52] These two newly founded papers had published many articles with insightful language targeting mainly genocide survivors for mismanaging funds meant to pay for things like tuition for survivors. For instance, *Umuseso* published a series of articles between April 20 and April 23, 2009, "Ntibaduhagarariye bahagarariye ibifu byabo" ("They Do Not Represent Us But Their Own Stomachs"). The articles discussed the rampant mismanagement of survivors' organizations like Avega Agahozo and Ibuka. The author concluded that these organizations' leaders were comparable to the Interahamwe. When confronted by the government, *Umuseso* argued that it was quoting an angry survivor. In the same commemoration period of April 2009, another newspaper, *Rugari*, compared corrupt officials of the survivors' scholarship fund, Fonds national d'assistance aux rescapés du génocide et des massacres (FARG), to genocide perpetrators.[53] This emotive style of reporting and of opposing the RPF government narrative continued to increase in the new private media and articulated alternative opinions. Similarly, a daring article in *Rushyashya* in April 2009 even criticized how genocide survivors' human remains were used by Champions.[54] The article asserted:

> Every Interahamwe is searching for victims remains, while the RPF displays those same bones in windows for Westerners' attention! There are those survivors who were left with nothing, who live with terrible memories and will die with those memories as they do not have any "hope" of healing from this continued trauma.[55]

The RMMP noted that these claims had no substance and were not credible. The author compared the RPF government to Interahamwe and also criticized the theme of the fifteenth anniversary, which centered on hope for survivors.[56] Nevertheless, the presence of such open and provocative dissent indicated a transition from the timidity of the preceding decade.

Similarly, the BBC Great Lakes program was accused in 2012 of giving a voice to those who harbor a double genocide ideology or who compete for victimhood. Consider the following quotation from an RMMP annual report in 2012. The quotation refers to radio programs captured by the report. On April 6, 2012, at 20:30 (8:30 p.m.), BBC "Gahuzamiryango" aired the following message:

> It was said that some Rwandans have the right to bury their family members only if those members were killed in the genocide, but that there is another section of the population who has not been allowed to bury their family members that the RPF killed.[57]

While the BBC focused on sources from the diaspora, the other newspapers quoted above sourced their reports from Rwandans inside the country. RMMP reports took notice, and various parts of the government reacted, accusing the above newspapers of "negationism." In the same report, the RMMP authors concluded that the majority of programs were balanced, but they highlighted examples such as the ones discussed here that diverged from the government's narrative and therefore were, by definition, considered bad journalism.[58]

The RMMP legitimated the RPF information and communication strategy on memory and created a sense of rules to play by for those who invested in private media. The RMMP evolved into a strong institution mandated with controlling information on official memory and one that has the moral right to supervise the reporting of the memory narrative and punish those who do not follow government's ethics and laws. As a result of reports produced by the RMMP, the MHC forced antigovernment private media to close, and individual journalists or staff were exiled or killed in 2010, 2011, and 2012. Jean-Léonard Rugambage, the deputy editor-in-chief of *Umuvugizi*, was killed on June 24, 2010, and the editor-in-chief, Jean-Bosco Gasasira, was forced into exile and sentenced in absentia to two and a half years in prison in 2011.[59]

However, Gasasira and many others, both traditional journalists and individuals, took advantage of new media to launch a series of online newspapers, air their critical opinions on the RPF's memory narrative, and disseminate dissident narratives. This ushered in a new period, and post-2010 commemoration discussions moved to new social media spaces in a significant way. Sites such as Twitter and Facebook, mobile text messaging, YouTube, and various websites became part of the Rwandan vocabulary and opened new avenues for the sharing and generation of online genocide memory. The MHC, through the RMMP, took notice and started to monitor these new forums during the eighteenth anniversary period in 2012, and the council's observations have been documented in its reports since then. It monitored 196 news items and eight websites.[60] Thus, private media pushed to open space for debates on the genocide memory narrative in this second period while navigating a complex relationship with the government's MHC. A contest had begun—admittedly one in which the RPF remained largely ascendant. One researcher concluded: "Official policy not only controls the hygiene of bodies, but also the hygiene of the mind."[61]

A journalist and media owner interviewed for this study clarified that many journalists who continued to work in Rwanda and collaborate with the government chose a cultural of self-censoring, or *guceceka*, to keep silent on certain stories. Like another survivor who told me about how silence was used by some to avoid "trouble" during gacaca proceedings,[62] the journalists adopted strategies to keep quiet on some issues, especially the hegemonic master narrative and commemoration.[63] The proverb *Umutemeli w'agahinda ni ijosi*—meaning "the neck covers the sorrow" or "the cover of sorrow is the neck, when sorrow gets to the head, the head will act"—can be used to illustrate the media's self-censorship as a buffer between controversial narratives and the public. The journalist explained that this silence is even more evident when it comes to commenting on the master narrative or commemoration. He explained:

> Media has been silent as it fears to report about genocide related subject. It lives a dilemma of what and how to report a given event for fear to get into trouble since the law punishing crimes related to genocide is harsh. In addition to that law, silence also lies upon the post-genocide social situation, media outlets are forced to either interview genocide survivors or families of perpetrators. Yet people in both categories fear to report the kept secret realities of genocide. They want to avoid troubles of being accused by community members of having reported their community members. For instance, reporting a situation that can discover or reveal hidden facts about the genocide has become and continues to be taboo in media.[64]

His assertions clearly showed how individual journalists are influenced by their own traumas, individual memory, and fear of laws that evolved to protect the master narrative. They are aware that their first accounts are controlled and monitored.[65] In her dissertation on journalism in postgenocide Rwanda, Ruth Moon concurs. Moon studied postgenocide Rwanda through interviews, observations in newsrooms, and interactions with journalists and wrote that Rwandan journalists have some level of "autonomy to take powerful social position but instead they take a relatively weak social position in part because of shared social role as villains."[66] In an article she writes that some journalists reported that they do "puppet journalism."[67] Yet for Bert Ingelaere, communication in Rwanda is complex. Through his analysis of the concept of "ubwenge" in communication in Rwanda, he writes:

> This complex notion incorporates a range of elements, though in the broadest sense, it refers to a valorisation of the kind of intelligence that results in public self-control. *Ubwenge* is both an overall principle structuring behaviour and display, and also a specific way of communicating. In the traditional organization of Rwandan society, speech acts did not correspond to reality alone, and what one said did not necessarily correspond with what one thought. Subtle adjustments could be made according to the status differential between the interlocutors or other variables in the broader socio-political environment. Language was thus a means to an end, not an end in itself. From a Western perspective, the latter would be the truth and the former a lie. But in the Rwandan context, truth and lies existed, and still exist, in a dialectical relationship. The Rwandan system of communication was (and is) esoteric: statements reveal and conceal at the same time. Often, outsiders to Rwandan culture fail to take this into account.[68]

Thus, these journalists are not just self-censoring, but journalists, editors, and media owners responding through silence, actively criticizing the master narrative and either being rewarded for their position or punished for it.[69] In any case, the media continues to play a crucial role as a platform where individual, social, and political memory interact and travel to a younger generation and geographies.

Yet there are elements within the evolution of the master narrative, such as the naming of the Genocide Against the Tutsi, that send out contradictory messages that work against the promotion of Rwandanity. Policy analyst

Gretchen Baldwin, who conducted fieldwork in Rwanda on Kwibuka, put it this way:

> The contemporary Rwandan state's control of information continues the mythologizing work, but the same mythos does work for two different ideologies: the broader Rwandan nationalism which is encouraged year-round, and survivor nationalism which manifests publicly during Kwibuka commemoration.[70]

Therefore, Tutsi identity is revived around commemoration and whenever the atrocities are named, the audience inevitably thinks about Hutu, who were the majority of those who committed the genocidal crimes against the Tutsi. This naming temporarily replaces or suspends Rwandan identity and instead renders it vague or irrelevant in the politics of commemoration.

New Media and Memorialization

The evolution of the internet, mobile technology, and social media has revolutionized citizens' engagement and expression in the last two decades. These tools have become increasingly popular around the world and changed communication styles, content, and accessibility. They have also challenged traditional journalism because online information moves much faster and distributes the power of information control somewhat more widely. Thus, citizens can connect with and comment on politically sensitive issues in their own countries or in other countries through new platforms. In Rwanda and elsewhere, the use of advanced media technology has broken barriers and increased citizens' contributions to political discourse, including about the issues surrounding commemoration. This access has enabled a more symmetrical relationship between institutional media power and citizen memory.[71] As Amit Pinchevski points out, the online resources generate new forms of "personal memorabilia, perhaps more than any time before." She argues that the new spaces serve as "a basis for ephemeral society ties, as numerous users of Facebook, Myspace and YouTube experience every day."[72] The seemingly borderless online engagement with unfolding or past mass atrocities has accelerated the growth of "memorial mania" in twenty-first-century society and its use of communication media.[73] Social media and other new technologies have allowed representations of the past to "become mobilized, renewing, challenging and affecting memories" of the past.[74] Scholars of this recent and ever-changing phenomenon, such as Anna Reading, argue that new technologies are important because they fast-track "personal impressions into public memories,"[75] thus allowing the individual and collective memories to interact, a phenomenon Reading calls "mediality and representationality."[76]

Similarly, new communication tools have allowed citizens to respond to formal institutions' messages directly, thus democratizing debates on the past and lowering the levels of privilege required to engage in the construction of shared narratives.[77] As a result, dialogues have become increasingly rich. Although less articulate than trained or official contributors, ordinary citizens offer insights, and their views reflect larger community ideas about commemoration. These new forms tip into openly political dissent. Although this dissent is rarely conspicuous, its prevalence is not necessarily reassuring to the government—the very existence of more voices and more personal engagement occludes the polarized simplicity of the master narrative. The monotones of the annual theme now compete with the polyphonic, or even cacophonic, abundance of personalized contributions.

New Technology and Vision 2020 in Rwanda

In Rwanda, the rapid uptick in new social media tools resulted from pro-ICT (information and communication technology) government policies in the economic agenda outlined in Vision 2020.[78] Internet, mobile, and other technology projects have been given priority in the last decade.[79] Consequently, digital access has continued to penetrate more rapidly in urban towns than in rural Rwanda.[80] President Paul Kagame, government ministers, and some local rural leaders have popularized sites like Twitter, Facebook, YouTube, and websites with ordinary Rwandans.[81] In recent years, the government of Rwanda has begun to create new policies that have sought to control internet freedom; it has also passed new laws with the same purpose. Rwandan officials not only have become aggressively visible on these sites, engaging a wide range of issues with all kinds of people (not just Rwandans), but also have established laws that continue to give the government the right to prosecute anyone "misusing" these virtual spaces.[82]

Despite the general awareness and use of social media by Rwanda's government officials, penetration of rural Rwanda by the internet and social media is still slow, and significant obstacles remain. A 2013 report from Freedom House, an internet watchdog nongovernmental organization (NGO), mapped out the use of internet, social media, and online journalism in Rwanda. Since little research is available on the ever-growing number of ICT users in rural Rwanda, the report, despite its limits, gave much-needed analysis of the postgenocide media in Rwanda and their online activity. Although critical, the report acknowledges that the liberalization of media policy implemented in 2009 is apparent in the media law passed by Parliament in 2013.[83] The 2013 media law also allows for certain freedoms in online communication, though only in harmony with the Surveillance Act of 2012, which allows security agents to monitor online activity.[84] The report also pointed to poverty as a primary obstacle for most Rwandans to access the internet. It quoted statistics from the International Telecommunication Union (ITU) that recorded an 8% penetration rate in 2012.[85] The official Rwandan government's statistics put the penetration rate at 26%.[86] Another major obstruction to online usage is language, since 70%–90% of Rwandans speak Kinyarwanda rather than more global languages such as English or French.[87] However, mobile device penetration in 2012 ranked at 50% in both government and ITU statistics. So, with internet access remaining out of reach for most Rwandans, and despite mobile technology being much more accessible, Rwanda has a long way to go to meet the aspirations of Vision 2020, and the government is committed to further improving ICT accessibility.

In an effort to confront these obstacles, telecom companies working in Rwanda, in partnership with the government, have invented new products that have increased access to mobile technology and internet for rural citizens. For example, MTN, a leading telecommunications company that has 64% of mobile telephone subscribers nationally, created a solar portable charger called "Comeka Readyset" that individuals can use to recharge mobile phones in rural areas.[88] Furthermore, three telecom companies—MTN, TIGO, and AIRTEL—offer free limited internet, and they reduced prices significantly in 2011.[89] Additionally, in February 2013 MTN introduced "MTN Tweeter SMS," which gave access to more rural users. To counter the language factor, the government adopted English as the official language in Rwanda, and English language courses have been implemented nationally for young citizens as well as for the old.[90]

However, even as the use of mobile technology grows, a small number of elites with access to the internet often follow the master narrative of the genocide. A few programs on traditional media—especially radio—and on

236 NAVIGATING CULTURAL MEMORY

social media have attempted to create space for diverse political opinions, but not against the official genocide narrative. This is illustrated in programs like *Good Morning Rwanda* and *Good Evening Rwanda*, which are known to air text messages of citizens criticizing local authorities and policies. Most individuals who have attempted to criticize the genocide narrative or offer another version have done so via international media such as the BBC. For example, on April 1, 2014, Rene Mugenzi, an Antagonist of the master narrative, self-proclaimed Rwandan human rights activist, and blogger based in the United Kingdom, was interviewed on a BBC Great Lakes program. The BBC was concluding a series of programs on social media and the question of freedom. Mugenzi asserted that social media has allowed even those who are critical of the Rwandan government to engage with it on sensitive issues, including the question of memory. "I can tweet my opinions to the government and different leaders and they respond," Mugenzi revealed.[91] Mugenzi and other Rwandan activists in Belgium, France, and the United States understand that cyberspace is "an imaginatively constructed space" that can allow individuals in the diaspora to influence politics in their homeland.[92] However, due to his opinions, Mugenzi has been banned from entering Rwanda and is considered a genocide denier, an extreme version of an Antagonist of the master narrative.[93] What might have been possible in the "virtual" Rwanda met with a rather different reality when Mugenzi encountered its geographic counterpart, a telling illustration of the limits of these new media.[94]

New Technology and Champions, Antagonists, and Fatalists' Increasing Engagement with the Master Narrative

Although it is difficult to identify who first used social media to discuss genocide commemoration in Rwanda, and when, the first substantial online activity began on the tenth anniversary of the genocide in 2004 and was spearheaded by government institutions with little participation from ordinary Rwandans. Recognizing the potential of these media, by 2011 most memory institutions established their official presence online via websites and occasional YouTube videos and opened Facebook and Twitter accounts. For the seventeenth commemoration in 2011, official messages were transmitted globally using electronic technology, by not only the Rwandan government but also other institutions, such as the United Nations. For example, United Nations Secretary General Ban Ki-Moon appeared in a video on YouTube reading his annual statements in observance of the anniversary of the genocide, statements that normally would have been sent around as a letter to newspapers.[95] Similarly, official statements on, and notices concerning, the events of the seventeenth commemoration in Rwanda were widely circulated online through YouTube channels, on Facebook pages, and on Twitter.[96]

During the commemorations that followed, announcements of annual themes were first communicated online through various social media tools that the CNLG and government institutions had set up, and then circulated by the traditional media. The government used these platforms for different reasons, depending on their responsibility during the mourning period. While the CNLG, for example, tweeted the nineteenth commemoration theme first, and made other announcements through Twitter as well, the Rwanda National Police mostly used Twitter to send out security warnings and requests for the population to be vigilant. In many cases various users, including other agencies and ordinary citizens, redistributed police messages. For example, in preparation for the twentieth commemoration, the government set up #Kwibuka20, #RwandaRemembers, and other hashtags which became the center for discussions, but whose purpose was mostly to spread announcements of the flame-of-remembrance tour. Most importantly, they were the outlet for the official memory narrative.

What follows are examples of messages circulated through Twitter by CNLG (National Commission for the Fight against Genocide) and its officials to call on social media users to join commemoration activities. They demonstrate how Champions of the master narrative used Twitter during commemorations.

> **Mucyo Jean de Dieu** **@jdmucyo** MAR 21, "Share a message of remembrance, unity and renewal with the world. Be part of A Million Voices for #Kwibuka20 https://twitter.com/kwibukarwanda/status/481826703379939328 #**Rwanda**" or
> @Rwandaremembers "Genocide perpetrator Alphonse Hitiyaremwe giving a message of unity at Flame event in Bugesera District. #**Kwibuka20.**"
> There are also individuals who tweet their own messages, such as Mbabazi Lucy, who has been noticeably active in the past ten years during commemorations.
> **Mbabazi** **@LucyMbabazi April 10:** "rains our families braved" - #**Kwibuka10.**

Between the tenth and eighteenth commemoration ceremonies, the hashtag #Kwibuka was not popular, as few Rwandans were using Twitter, even for other topics.

For while Champions' social media has become spaces where the hegemonic master narrative is transmitted and enforced at all costs, for Antagonists it is a space where they can respond directly to Champions with counternarratives. Youth in Rwanda and the diaspora have started to own their own social media accounts and use them to gain views and influence in Rwanda and among the diaspora. YouTube channels have flourished online after the twentieth anniversary of the genocide as platforms where genocide denial takes place, counternarratives are produced and shared, and fake news confuses many youth. For those created in Rwanda, the most popular have programs on what happened during the genocide and civil war and how it is memorialized. For instance, in Rwanda, Real Talk Channel TV features journalists debating all kinds of issues, including debates among Champions, Antagonists, and Fatalists, including many critical perspectives that have not been heard in public in Rwanda for a long time. It features journalists' analysis and occasionally invited opposition leaders, like a well-known Antagonist who has been punished for it through imprisonment, Victoire Ingabire, to debates. Individuals who have used social media to express their disagreements with the hegemonic memory narratives and were punished were many, but three are prominent. These include Aimable Karasira, a genocide survivor and former lecturer at the University of Rwanda who used his YouTube channel to ask questions on how he can remember his family members killed by the RPF.[97] Another genocide survivor, Indamange Yvonne, equally critiqued approaches to the construction and transmission of the hegemonic master narrative. Innocent Bahati, who mostly critiqued the government through his famous poetry aired on his YouTube channel, went missing and has never been found.[98]

Platforms have also multiplied among an increasingly frustrated and traumatized diaspora. Their platforms include Ikondera (mostly pregenocide elite Antagonists), Radio Itahuka (former RPF members who turned into Antagonists), Jambo News (cofounded by grandchildren of the first postindependence interim president), Louise Uwacu's Facebook page (an independent critic who has a significant following and influence), Umutware TV, and many others that have aired constantly and gained influence and have started to shape conversations among Rwandans. Kizito Mihigo, discussed in a previous chapter, is an icon in this online world of

Antagonists. His music, which was banned on local media, has found a new audience and platforms where some of his songs have now been viewed over a million times, and programs dedicated to his memory multiplied.

These platforms and the actors who used them brought unprecedented changes to the hegemonic master narrative. Champions are increasingly forced to adapt with speed and creativity to try to stay ahead of the competition for the youth. It is no longer the Champions that set the agenda for the knowledge created about the hegemonic master narrative; they also do not have resources to dedicate or respond to each content creator. While it can be argued that only urban youth have access to the technologies and knowhow of using social media given the rural youth have not benefited from Vision 2020 as have those in urban areas,[99] these conversations happening online nevertheless travel through more accessible technologies like WhatsApp in rural areas and translate into physical popular disagreements offline, as seen the case of Miss Rwanda competition in 2019.[100] These online conversations circulate and also influence each other; as discussed in the concluding chapter, they have created new democratic spaces where the hegemonic master narrative can be transmitted by Champions but coexist with dissent narratives. These platforms have multiplied actors responding to the hegemonic memory narrative among Rwandans. Thus: "The agency has shifted, and it is now ordinary people who participate"[101] and whose response creates "more peer-to-peer" in memory creation and "perpetuation."[102] The interactions have created "multidirectional conversation [s]."[103] They serve as alternative[104] narratives for Rwandan youth to the hegemonic master narrative promoted by the state. However, if the technology turn has broken state-imposed barriers between Antagonists, Champions, and Fatalists, it has also provided a space for expressions of empathy and camaraderie during the commemoration period, as my respondents informed me. For instance, during my research I requested some of my interlocutors to share with me messages they received on their phones before WhatsApp, Instagram, and other social sites were popular. Below is an analysis of some of those messages.

Text Messages

In addition to Twitter, Facebook, and other online tools that became popular after the twentieth commemoration, mobile technology has also been a

240   NAVIGATING CULTURAL MEMORY

popular and growing space for transmitting messages during the mourning period. Unlike the messages on websites, YouTube, and other online public sites, text messages tend to be used for more personalized communication. The messages tend to be those of solidarity, encouragement, and comfort among different communities. Many Rwandans prefer this space because it offers a sense of intimacy and allows the sender and recipient to reciprocate sensitive messages. With the spread of mobile phones in rural areas, this is a growing phenomenon that has accelerated much more than other platforms. The following examples collected from my interviewees during my research in 2012 and 2013 reveal that individuals were able to shape and experience their text messages in an uncontrolled environment.

> Message 1: Josephine (not a survivor) to her survivor (Interviewee 1) classmate:
> This is the time for looking back, over what you have accomplished, and looking ahead with hope to bright new future. Be strong, we are together. You are not alone.[105]
>
> Message 2: Nonsurvivor to a survivor:
> Continue to be strong, we are uniting with you during this period. Remember they [victims] are on God's side. Be strong and courageous. This is what will make them proud. May God protect you.[106]
>
> Message 3: Solange to his survivor brother:
> Let's remember our genocide victims who left when we still needed them. We will always remember them. Let's work together, give each other advice, focus, study hard—it's when we want to make our parents proud. Strive to become a man and show those who killed us that we are standing in the gap [i.e., praying to God for mercy][107] for our departed families. We are together in this mourning period.[108]
>
> Message 4: A survivor to another:
> Let's unite and strive to live a good life. If we do it, we will have accomplished the greatness that characterized our victims. Continue to stand with dignity.[109]

Text messages thus provided a new platform giving the sender and receiver a sense of privacy while expressing sensitive messages to each other. As a new medium of communication, the text message provided a unique, potentially less visible, and less policed and political platform allowing individuals to mourn privately. It allowed individuals not to rely on public media to communicate with each other. It was, in a sense, a way to create personalized communal memories, existing below the state and beneath the open virtual space of institutionalized social media like Facebook and Twitter. The bonds here were local and personal, and the memory communities mapped onto preexisting relationships. While perhaps less fashionable, text messaging was arguably a more faithful and personalized vector for sharing a localized and intimate commemoration. Antagonists, Champions, and Fatalists alike used these spaces freely thinking they were open and democratic spaces that were not monitored like other avenues, even though we know government surveillance and technology can still be present.

Yet, these free spaces, as seen in other cases, can result in insults and provide a breeding ground for genocide denial, as we have seen in the case of Holocaust denial and promotion of terrorism online. They are also spaces that allow for bullying of survivors of atrocities and can therefore end up hurting and traumatizing people during commemorations.

Young genocide survivors I spoke to such as Solange, Kayitesi—whose story opened this book—and others who were born during the genocide did not have their own individual memories of the genocide. Instead, they acquired the memories of their departed parents or relatives from Champions whose individual memories travel to this generation through music, official events around commemorations, government messages, and youth camps such as Ingando. They experienced what Allison Landsberg calls "prosthetic memory." Landsberg's analysis of American society in the age of global media is relevant to Rwanda's mnemonic experience. She argues: "Modernity makes possible and necessary a new form of public cultural memory. This new form of memory, which I call prosthetic memory, emerges at the interface between a person and a historical narrative about the past."[110] In postgenocide Rwanda, prosthetic memory evolved between the youth and the master narrative and commemoration for both young Champions and the Fatalists and Antagonists, especially those who have emerged in the diaspora. For Landsberg:

> In this moment of contact, an experience occurs through which the person sutures himself or herself into a larger history.... In the process that I am describing, the person does not simply apprehend a historical narrative but

takes on a more personal, deeply felt memory of a past event through which he or she did not live. The resulting prosthetic memory has the ability to shape that person's subjectivity and politics.[111]

Rwandan youth were the key target of the master narrative during the period at the end of the first 20 years of remembrance. As commemoration moved closer to the twentieth commemoration, youth increasingly became central to commemoration and speeches, and were visibly involved in planning to commemorate a genocide some did not live through because their parents were in exile or were too young to remember. Many Champions, including Hakizimana, discussed in the Introduction, and those like Senga and Solange discussed in other chapters, were influenced by the mediated master narrative, and through art and media they find ways of responding to the evolution of commemoration. Gretchen Baldwin's research has concluded that:

> A blurring of "Tutsi" with "survivor" and the deliberate passing down of survivor identity to Tutsi youth have created, over time, conditions for a "survivor nationalism," exacerbating social tensions and risking sustainable peace in the long term.[112]

Conclusion

The radio shaped Rwandans' experiences of what unfolded during the genocide. As the chapter has shown, the influence of media has grown beyond the radio during the genocide to other media that have evolved in postgenocide Rwanda. Media has become a platform where individual, social, and political memory emerged but also where debate happens on the master narrative and commemoration. In the last two decades, the media in Rwanda have evolved from an almost nonexistent and fragile entity, virtually destroyed by civil war and genocide, into a state-controlled public space, then into a state-regulated sphere of private media, and more recently into a more dynamic new media landscape, albeit one with a substantial state presence. As this chapter has shown, even though the government still controls the master narrative and how it is discussed in local media, it faces competition from Antagonist actors who do not find their own narratives in the official narrative.

In addition, these new platforms increased the level of difficulty the MHC and other government watchdog institutions faced in monitoring and enforcing the hegemonic master narrative online and in mobile messages, compared to monitoring more traditional media. Vision 2020 has provided fast internet connectivity and access to mobile technology, at least among the urban wealthy and middle class. Memorialization was also affected by demographic change. Those born after the genocide became the majority of Rwanda's population. While youth are visible in policymaking positions and Rwanda has a pro-youth politics among its peers and globally, the majority are unemployed and rural. Some are unsettled and frustrated that they are not able to access the wealth created in the past two decades. These rural youth who are slowly connecting to the internet equally carry the weight of a history of their families, like Kayitesi and Hakizimana, a history that is full of unknowns. Unlike the older Champions, Antagonists, and Fatalists, who were more reserved and strategic in their approaches to responding to the hegemonic master narrative, today's, especially urban, youth are more expressive, especially online. Twitter in particular has become a tool to influence policymakers and keep their leaders under pressure. Therefore, new research is needed on what these factors mean in terms of how the hegemonic master narrative will be changed and be transformed as it "travels"[113] across generations, geographies, and communities of Champions, Antagonists, and Fatalists. As seen in other contexts, memories created online are vulnerable to factors like technology change, content being deleted[114] and therefore forgotten, or not only creating a temporary challenge to the hegemonic master narrative in the moment it becomes popular but also challenging it in fundamental and transformative ways. Regardless, the technology turn and postmemory turn in memory politics in Rwanda and elsewhere present both challenges and opportunities to the future of memory and knowledge production in memory studies explored in the concluding chapter. These opportunities for innovative and specific methodological and theoretical approaches, including those derived from Global South contexts such as Rwanda and in other contexts globally. This is the impetus for what I call the dignity turn in memory studies.

Notes

1. The use of social media data in research is developing, and new scholars have emerged to study this phenomenon. For example, new research has emerged that looks at social media and their relation to public opinion. See Amy Mitchell and Paul

Hitlin, "Twitter Reaction to Events Often at Odds with Overall Public Opinion," Pew Research Center, 2013, http://www.pewresearch.org/2013/03/04/twitter-reaction-to-events-often-at-odds-with-overall-public-opinion/. Social media have also fueled interest in sentimental analysis. I do not use this mode of analysis to analyze the text messages, blogs, tweets, or Facebook texts I have collected. The use of these methods by anonymous e-communities for expressing opinions and sentiments is still under investigation by a number of researchers.

For more on sentimental analysis, see Jamie Condliffe, "Flaming Drives Online Social Networks," *New Scientist*, 2010, http://www.newscientist.com/article/dn19821-flaming-drives-online-social-networks.html#.VQoPWmd0yUl; and Yasuhide Miura, Shigeyuki Sakaki, Keigo Hattori, and Tomoko Ohkuma, "Team X: A Sentiment Analyser with Enhanced Lexicon Mapping and Weighting Scheme for Unbalanced Data," Proceedings of the 8th International Workshop on Semantic Evaluation, Dublin, Ireland, Qatar Computing Research Institute, August 23–24, 2014.

2. In an analysis of American magazines and their influence on American national history, Kitch argues that media memory does not have to be an antithesis to cultural history. See Carolyn L. Kitch, *Pages from the Past: History and Memory in American Magazines* (Chapel Hill: University of North Carolina Press, 2005), 175–184.
3. Motti Neiger, Oren Meyers, and Eyal Zandberg, eds., *On Media Memory: Collective Memory in a New Media Age* (Basingstoke, UK: Palgrave Macmillan, 2011), 3.
4. Astrid Erll, "Travelling Memory," *Parallax* 17, no. 4 (2011): 9.
5. Ibid., 11.
6. Jérôme Bourdon, "Media Remembering: The Contributions of Life-Story Methodology to Memory/Media Research," in *On Media Memory: Collective Memory in a New Media Age*, eds. Motti Neiger, Oren Meyers, and Eyal Zandberg (New York: Palgrave Macmillan, 2011), 70.
7. Jérôme Bourdon, "Media Remembering: The Contributions of Life-Story Methodology to Memory/Media Research ., 64.
8. See Andrew Hoskins, *Televising War: From Vietnam to Iraq* (London: Continuum, 2004).
9. On the tenth anniversary of 9/11, the *New York Times*, in a series of articles, "911: The Reckoning," featured an image of the New York City skyline with smoke coming from the twin towers while they were under attack and with a plane approaching in the sky. The picture has become associated with societies' memories since it is one of the photos that feature prominently during the annual anniversary. See "Witness to Apocalypse," New York Times, September 8, 2011, http://www.nytimes.com/2011/09/08/us/sept-11-reckoning/escape.html.
10. Yvonne Liebermann, "Born digital: The Black Lives Matter Movement and Memory after the Digital Turn," *Memory Studies* 14, no. 4(2020), 1.
11. Yvonne Liebermann, "Born digital: The Black Lives Matter Movement and Memory after the Digital Turn.
12. See also Michael Rothberg, *Multidirectional Memory: Remembering the Holocaust in the Age of Decolonization* (Palo Alto, CA: Stanford University Press, 2009).
13. Kurt Lang and Gladys Engel Lang, "Collective Memory and the News," *Communication* 11 (1989): 123–129.

14. Sidney Eve Matrix, "Rewind, Remix, Rewrite: Digital and Virtual Memory in Cyberpunk Cinema," in *Save As . . . Digital Memories*, eds. Joanne Garde-Hansen, Andrew Hoskins, and Anna Reading (Basingstoke, UK: Palgrave Macmillan, 2009), 60–76.
15. Jill A. Edy, "Journalistic Uses of Collective Memory," *Journal of Communication* 49, no. 2 (1999): 73. See also Mary Harper, "Interview with Lindsey Hilsum about the 'Rwanda Genocide,'" *Witness*, radio broadcast, 09:00, BBC World Service, April 6, 2010, http://www.BBC.co.uk/programmes/p006xzww.
16. See Barbie Zelizer, *Covering the Body: The Kennedy Assassination, the Media, and the Shaping of Collective Memory* (Chicago: University of Chicago Press, 1992); and Michael Schudson, *Watergate in American Memory: How We Remember, Forget, and Reconstruct the Past* (New York: Basic Books, 1992).
17. BBC, "In Pictures: Remembering the Genocide," *One-Minute World News*, aired April 12, 2013, http://news.BBC.co.uk/2/shared/spl/hi/africa/04/photo_journal/rwanda/html/1.stm.
18. "In Pictures: Remembering the Genocide,"
19. See Linda Melvern, *A People Betrayed: The Role of the West in Rwanda's Genocide* (New York: Zed Books, 2019).
20. Office Rwandais d'Information (ORINFOR) is Rwanda's state-owned media agency. ORINFOR produces Radio Rwanda, Rwanda Television, and two national newspapers: the biweekly *Imvaho Nshya* in Kinyarwanda and the weekly *La Nouvelle Relève* in French. ORINFOR's offices are located in the capital city of Kigali. It has recently been renamed Rwanda Broadcast Agency, just as other government institutions have been renamed in English.
21. A number of books exist on this topic, to mention a few: Jean-Pierre Chrétien, Jean-François Duparquier, Marcel Kabanda, and Joseph Ngarambe, *Rwanda: Les médias du génocide* (Paris: Karthala, 1995); Allan Thompson, *Media and the Rwanda Genocide* (Ottawa, ON, Canada: IDRC, 2007).
22. On the role of RTLM, see Alison Liebhafsky Des Forges, *"Leave None to Tell the Story": Genocide in Rwanda* (New York: Human Rights Watch, 2014), 26 and 95. See also Chrétien, *Rwanda: Les médias du génocide*; and Allan Thompson, ed., *The Media and the Rwanda Genocide* (London: Pluto Press, 2007). This was given as the main reason for the slow evolution of media freedom in postgenocide Rwanda in the 2015 State of Media Freedom in Rwanda. See Bent Nørby Bonde, Jean-Pierre Uwimana, Francis Sowa, and Glenn O'Neil, "The State of Media Freedom in Rwanda," Rwanda Media Commission, May 2015, https://rsf.org/sites/default/files/6_5_2015_ib_-_final_report_on_state_of_the_media_freedom_in_rwanda_00.00.pdf, accessed July 6, 2015. . In the same report is a quotation that shows the government's vision to work with the media. For instance, it cites President Paul Kagame's speech at the Fifth East African Business Council Media summit in 2012: "The media will be an invaluable partner in communicating our agenda, advancing our interests, and being among the key narrators of our story." He insisted the government and the media did not have to "be adversaries as is sometimes the case." See Bonde et al., *The State of Media Freedom in Rwanda*, 11.

23. Rwanda Broadcasting Agency (RBA, as the former ORINFOR is now called) controls a television network broadcasting in English, French, and Kinyarwanda at different time slots. It remains the most watched television network, and Radio Rwanda also competes well with a dozen other new private radio stations.
24. See, for instance, the discussion in Frank Kanyesigye, "ORINFOR to Censure [i.e., censor] Shocking Genocide Images," *New Times*, March 22, 2011, https://www.newtimes.co.rw/article/52540/National/orinfor-to-censure-shocking-genocide-images.
25. Interview with Huye Munyana, 2013.
26. Mweusi Karake, "Spécial Génocide," *Imvaho Nshya* (Kigali), April 24–30, 1995.. The translation from the French of the news article is mine.
27. Mweusi Karake, "Spécial Génocide," *Imvaho Nshya* (Kigali).
28. Mweusi Karake, "Spécial Génocide," *Imvaho Nshya* (Kigali).
29. See Mweusi Karake, "Lack of International Aid to Survivors," *Imvaho Nshya* (Kigali), April 10–16, 1995. Karake contributed frequently to *Imvaho Nshya*. The translation is mine.
30. Other writers used the opportunity to interpret to the local audience what had been published in regional or international news concerning recent history. For example, a writer using the initials M. K. wrote that the East African newspaper had published a story of former president Habyarimana's family and had organized a service to remember him in Nairobi. See, for example, M. K., "Ikinani i Nairobi," Imvaho Nshya (Kigali), April 24–30, 1995.
31. Johan Pottier, *Re-imagining Rwanda: Conflict, Survival and Disinformation in the Late Twentieth Century* (Cambridge: Cambridge University Press, 2004), 203.
32. Claudine Vidal, "Les commémorations du génocide au Rwanda," *Les Temps Modernes* 613, no. 56 (2001): 44.
33. Pottier, *Re-imagining Rwanda*, 176.
34. In this period of 1994–2001, the genocide stories started to spread around the world. Individual countries and institutions started to support Rwanda's reconstruction, but mostly from a level of guilt, acutely mindful that they did not come to the rescue of Tutsi, who were now in power Jean-Paul Kimonyo, *Transforming Rwanda: Challenges on the Road to Reconstruction* (Boulder, CO: Lynne Rienner, 2019), 104.
35. *Le Monde*, October 26, 1996, as quoted in Filip Reyntjens, "Constructing the Truth, Dealing with Dissent, Domesticating the World: Governance in Postgenocide Rwanda," *African Affairs* 110, no. 438 (2011): 27.
36. *Washington Post*, July 14, 1998, quoted in Filip Reyntjens "Constructing the Truth, Dealing with Dissent," Domesticating the World.
37. Nik Gowing, "New Challenges and Problems for Information Management in Complex Emergencies: Ominous Lessons from the Great Lakes and Eastern Zaire in Late 1996 and Early 1997," paper presented at the Dispatches from Disaster Zones, Oxford, UK, May 28, 1998, 4. Quoted inFilip Reyntjens "Constructing the Truth, Dealing with Dissent, Domesticating the World, 26.
38. See Reyntjens, "Constructing the Truth," 4.
39. *Icyizere*, whose title means "hope," is the news magazine for CNLG, reporting what CNLG is doing in different parts of the country. In 2012, *Icyizere* published the following issue, now available from a third party publisher: CNLG, Icyizere, *Yumpu*,

February 21, 2013, https://www.yumpu.com/xx/document/read/10166717/icyizere-no20pdf-cnlg.
40. John Mutamba and Jeanne Izabiliza, "The Role of Women in Reconciliation and Peace Building in Rwanda Ten Years after Genocide: 1994–2004; Contributions, Challenges and Way Forward," *Journal of Culture and African Women Studies* 10 (2007): 11.
41. The radio was a better business to invest in than television, given that most Rwandans are in rural areas where distribution of TV signals is low, whereas radio has been part of urban and rural Rwandans' lives for decades.
42. The International Media Support (Denmark) and Norwegian People's Aid supported the setting up of the RMMP. See Rwanda Media High Council, *High Council of the Press Report* (Kigali: Republic of Rwanda, June 2004). See also Bonde et al., "The State of Media Freedom in Rwanda."
43. Rwanda Media High Council, *High Council of the Press Report*, 43–44.
44. Rwanda Media High Council, *High Council of the Press Report*, 77.
45. *Analysis of Media Coverage of the Eighteenth Commemoration of the Genocide against the Tutsi* (Kigali, Rwanda: Media High Council for the Press, 2012), 15.
46. *Analysis of Media Coverage of the Eighteenth Commemoration of the Genocide against the Tutsi.*, 99.
47. *Analysis of Media Coverage of the Eighteenth Commemoration of the Genocide against the Tutsi.*, 16.
48. *Analysis of Media Coverage of the Eighteenth Commemoration of the Genocide against the Tutsi.*
49. After the genocide, BBC created a new program that broadcasts from London with journalists stationed all over the Great Lakes Region. *BBC Gahuzamiryango* (meaning "the one that brings families together"), as it's popularly known, was established at first with a mission to help refugees and the displaced find each other after the genocide. Over the past two decades, it has covered general news and debates on Burundi, DRC, and Rwanda. The daily news reports are followed through FM radios in Burundi, DRC, Rwanda, and some regions of Uganda, as well as Tanzania. The programs are also aired online. The Saturday program, which was banned, has gained prominence among listeners because it tackles issues that local media in the region avoid. During commemoration periods, it gives platforms to not only survivors of the Genocide Against the Tutsi but also other Rwandans who have had different experiences and who often discredit the RPF version of 1994 events. This often displeases the Rwandan government, and therefore the program has been banned in Rwanda many times.
50. "La BBC et la VOA accusées par Kigali de 'Détruire l'unité des Rwandais,'" *Agence France-Presse*, August 19, 2008, http://www.lapresse.ca/international/200809/08/01-664254-la-BBC-et-la-voa-accusees-par-kigali-de-detruire-lunite-des-rwandais.php.
51. "Rwanda: Le chef de l'Etat inaugure une salve d'attaques verbales des autorités contre les journalistes," *Reporteurs sans Frontières*, January 31, 2006, https://rsf.org/fr/le-chef-de-letat-inaugure-une-salve-dattaques-verbales-des-autorit%C3%A9s-contre-les-journalistes.

52. See Lars Waldorf, "Censorship and Propaganda in Postgenocide Rwanda," In *Media and the Rwanda Genocide*, ed. Allan Thompson (London: Pluto Press, 2007), 404–416.
53. See Rwanda Media High Council, *Analysis of Media Coverage of the Fifteenth Commemoration of the Genocide against the Tutsi* (Kigali, Rwanda: Media High Council for the Press, December 2009).
54. "The Treatment of Genocide Victims Intolerable," *Rushyashya* (Kigali), April 7–15, 2009. The translation is mine.
55. "The Treatment of Genocide Victims Intolerable," *Rushyashya* (Kigali), April 7–15, 2009.
56. "The Treatment of Genocide Victims Intolerable," *Rushyashya* (Kigali), April 7–15, 2009.
57. *Analysis of Media Coverage of the Eighteenth Commemoration*, iii.
58. *Analysis of Media Coverage of the Eighteenth Commemoration*, iii.
59. *Analysis of Media Coverage of the Eighteenth Commemoration*, iii.
60. *Analysis of Media Coverage of the Eighteenth Commemoration*, iii.
61. Bert Ingelaere, "Do We Understand Life after Genocide? Center and Periphery in the Construction of Knowledge in Postgenocide Rwanda," *African Studies Review* 53, no. 1 (2010): 50, 53.
62. Interviewee 4, Kigali, Rwanda, 2019.
63. On how Rwandans used silence and especially in gacaca and generally postgenocide Rwanda, see also how various silences informed gacaca court proceedings: Max Rettig, Gacaca: truth, justice, and reconciliation in postconflict Rwanda?. *African Studies Review*, 51, no. 3 (2008): 25–50. See also Amnesty International, *Safer to Stay Silent: The Chilling Effect of Rwanda's Laws on "Genocide Ideology" and "Sectarianism"* (London: Amnesty International Report, 2010); and Anuradha Chakravarty, *Investing in Authoritarian Rule: Punishment and Patronage in Rwanda's Gacaca Courts for Genocide Crimes* (Cambridge: Cambridge University Press, 2016).
64. Interview with a media owner and editor, Kigali, Rwanda, 2018.
65. Ingelaere, "Do We Understand Life after Genocide?," 50.
66. Ruth Moon, "Constructing Journalism Practice between the Global and the Local: Lessons from the Rwandan Journalism Field" (PhD, Washington University, 2018).
67. Ruth Moon, "Beyond Puppet Journalism: The Bridging Work of Transnational Journalists in a Local Field," *Journalism Studies* 20, no. 12 (2019): 1725.
68. Ingelaere, "Do We Understand Life after Genocide?," 54.
69. There are accounts of foreign journalists who have discussed Rwanda's postgenocide and media politics. They have both been dismissed by the Kigali government as bias and full of malice. See Anjan Sundaram, *Bad News: Last Journalists in a Dictatorship* (New York: Bloomsbury, 2016) and recently Michela Wrong, *Do Not Disturb: The Story of a Political Murder and an African Regime Gone Bad* (London: 4th Estate, 2021), 488.
70. Gretchen Baldwin, "Constructing Identity through Commemoration: Kwibuka and the Rise of Survivor Nationalism in Post-conflict Rwanda," *Journal of Modern African Studies* 57, no. 3 (2019): 355–375.
71. Anna Reading explains that this is a phenomenon in what she calls a "globytal memory field," which she describes as a field that uses "dynamic methods of digital analysis

to understand the immersive and connective ecologies of social memory." See Anna Reading, "The Globytal: Towards an Understanding of Globalised Memories in the Digital Age," in *Digital Memories: Exploring Critical Issues*, eds. Anna Maj and Daniel Riha (Oxford, UK: Inter-Disciplinary Press, 2009), 31–40.

72. Amit Pinchevski, "Archive, Media, Trauma," in *On Media Memory: Collective Memory in a New Media Age*, eds. Mordechai Neiger, Oren Meyers, and Eyal Zandberg (New York: Palgrave Macmillan, 2013), 256.
73. On memorial mania, see Erika Lee Doss, *Memorial Mania: Public Feeling in America* (Chicago: University of Chicago Press, 2010).
74. Anna Reading, "Memobilia," in *Save As . . . Digital Memories*, eds. Joanne Garde-Hansen, Andrew Hoskins, and Anna Reading (New York: Palgrave Macmillan, 2009), 90.
75. Ibid.
76. Andrew Hoskins and Ben O'Loughlin, *War and Media: The Emergence of Diffused War* (Cambridge, UK: Polity Press, 2010).
77. Anna Reading has argued that this creates new online commemoration communities that are global. See also Anna Reading, "The London Bombings: Mobile Witnessing, Mortal Bodies and Globital Time," *Memory Studies* 4, no. 3 (2011): 298–311.
78. The Rwandan ICT for Development (ICT4D) process—or NICI (National Information and Communication Infrastructure) process—began in 1998 under the auspices of the African Information Society Initiative (AISI) of the United Nations Economic Commission for Africa (UNECA). Out of this, the government of Rwanda adopted a report: *An Integrated Framework for Socio-Economic and ICT Policy and Plan Development and Implementation for Rwanda* (Addis Ababa, Ethiopia: United Nations Economic Commission for Africa, 1999). See Marlene Holmner and Johannes J. Britz, "The Road Less Travelled: A Critical Reflection on Infrastructure Development in Africa from a Perspective of the New Economics of Information," *Mousaion* 29, no. 1 (2011): 1–16.
79. Increased use of ICT and the spread of its culture in Rwanda have taken place in three implementation phases. The first, from 2000 to 2005, focused on creating policies favorable to ICT initiatives. The second, from 2006 to 2010, concentrated on building the ICT backbone, including laying fiber-optic cables. The third phase, scheduled to run from 2011 to 2015, will speed up the introduction of services to exploit the new technology, and authorities are convinced that the new technology will push Rwanda ahead of regional rivals. During my research period of 2011 to 2014, Phases 1 and 2 had already been implemented, and Phase 3 was almost complete. The use of ICT was slowly changing the culture of how Rwandans learn and interact with each other. See Masimba Tafirenyika, "Information Technology Super-Charging Rwanda's Economy," *Africa Renewal*, April 2011, http://www.un.org/africarenewal/magazine/april-2011/information-technology-super-charging-rwandas-economy#sthash.UpvtXqVs.dpuf.
80. In 2010, one in four Rwandans had access to a mobile phone, the number was growing rapidly, and some of these mobile phones had access to the web. See Tafirenyika, "Information Technology."

81. President Paul Kagame emerged as one of the most popular presidents on Twitter in Africa in 2012, with 95,000 followers. See Allan Brian Ssenyonga, "Twitter 2012 Was a Very Interesting Year for "RwOT," New Times (Kigali), December 31, 2012.
82. For example, in August 2012, the Parliament of Rwanda passed a bill that gave security organs the power to tap people's phones, intercept private emails, and monitor social sites for security reasons. Article 3 also established an organ that would *monitor* those who *monitored* these media to ensure that the latter did not abuse their powers. However, critics of this law argued that, notwithstanding these safeguards, the law will give an advantage to government security agencies in their efforts to control freedom of expression and debates on sensitive political issues, like the genocide memory. Concerning adoption of the law, see "Rwanda," *Freedom on the Net 2013*, Freedom House, March 2, 2014, https://freedomhouse.org/sites/default/files/resources/FOTN%202013_Rwanda.pdf
83. *Freedom on the Net 2013*.
84. *Freedom on the Net 2013*.
85. See International Telecommunication Union, "Percentage of Individuals Using the Internet, 2000–2019" 2014, http://www.itu.int/en/ITU-D/Statistics/Pages/stat/default.aspx.
86. See Ministry of Youth and Culture, *Measuring ICT Sector Performance and Tracking ICT for Development (ICT4D)* (Kigali, Rwanda: Republic of Rwanda, 2013); Daniel Nkubito, "Issue Paper: Internet Connectivity and Affordability in Rwanda," 2012, cited in Freedom House Report, "Freedom on the Net 2013 – Rwanda" https://www.refworld.org/docid/52663adb14.html
87. Ann Garrison, "Rwanda Shuts Down Independent Press," *Rwandinfo*, April 14, 2010, https://rwandinfo.com/eng/rwanda-shuts-down-independent-press-ahead-of-presidential-elections/; and Beth Lewis Samuelson and Sarah Warshauer Freedman, "Language Policy, Multilingual Education, and Power in Rwanda," *Language Policy* 9, no. 3 (June 2010): 191–215.
88. Eric Bright, "MTN Launches Portable Renewable Energy System," *New Times* (Kigali), January 29, 2011, https://www.newtimes.co.rw/article/87360/News/mtn-launches-portable-renewable-energy-system.
89. Tafirenyika, "Information Technology."
90. The government changed the nation's official language from French to English for business and political reasons. Government officials argued in different forums that the change was necessary for Rwandans to connect to East African countries, that English was used more often in business, and that learning it at a young age would allow Rwandans to get more jobs regionally and internationally. However, others argued that it was also because Paris and Kigali postgenocide politicians have had a troubled relationship: The French Embassy has been closed, and both countries have expelled diplomats on numerous occasions. Throughout the past two decades the two governments have remained in disagreement on the origins and causes of the genocide, especially on the shooting of the plane that was carrying former President Habyarimana.
91. This was broadcast on *BBC Gahuzamiryango*, April 1, 2014, on the radio evening news that I listened to live and took notes.

92. See, for example, a study conducted on the use of cyberspace by Eritrean diaspora: Victoria Bernal, "Eritrea On-Line: Diaspora, Cyberspace, and the Public Sphere," *American Ethnologist* 32, no. 4 (2005): 660–675.
93. "Rwandan Exiles in London 'Threatened by Hitman,'" *BBC News*, May 21, 2011, https://www.BBC.com/news/world-africa-13475635.
94. Mugenzi was found guilty of theft in a church he worked for in the United Kingdom and sentenced to serve jail time. See "Cathedral Treasurer Stole £222,000 from Church to Feed Gambling Addiction," accessed January 20, 2020, https://www.votf.org/content/voice-faithful-focus-nov-6-2020.
95. For information on UN outreach programs and past Rwandan commemorations at the UN headquarters in New York City, see United Nations "Outreach Programme on the 1994 Genocide Against the Tutsi in Rwanda and the United Nations," https://www.un.org/en/preventgenocide/rwanda/commemorations-2021.shtml, accessed March 14, 2023.
96. See, for example, the president's speech: Paul Kagame, "17th Commemoration of the Genocide against the Tutsi," YouTube video, 4:54, 2011, http://www.youtube.com/watch?v=xUk6zBUUC0w
97. See Human Rights Watch, "Rwanda: Arrests, Prosecutions over YouTube Posts."
98. Ibid.
99. An Ansoms, "Striving for Growth, Bypassing the Poor? A Critical Review of Rwanda's Rural Sector Policies," *Journal of Modern African Studies* 46, no. 1 (2008): 1–32.
100. Andrea Purdeková and David Mwambari, "Postgenocide Identity Politics and Colonial Durabilities in Rwanda," *Critical African Studies* (2021): 1–19.
101. Liebermann, "Born Digital," 5.
102. Hoskins and Reading, "Save As: Digital Memories," 8.
103. Jason Gainous and K. M. Wagner, *Tweeting to Power: The Social Media Revolution in American Politics* (New York: Oxford University Press, 2017). Cited in Liebermann, "Born Digital," 5.
104. Ibid.
105. Message given by Interviewee 1, Kigali, Rwanda, 2013.
106. Message given by Interviewee 2, Kigali, Rwanda, 2013.
107. The writer of the message is alluding to the Jewish prophet Ezekiel (Ezekiel 22:30).
108. Message given by Solange during an interview, Kigali, Rwanda, 2013.
109. Text given by Interviewee 4, Kigali, Rwanda, 2013.
110. Alison Landsberg, *Prosthetic Memory: The Transformation of American Remembrance in the Age of Mass Culture* (New York: Columbia University Press, 2004), 2.
111. Ibid., 2.
112. Baldwin, "Constructing Identity through Commemoration."
113. Erll, "Travelling Memory," 9.
114. Liebermann, "Born Digital," 15.

Conclusion

The Malleability of Memory and Reflections on the Future of Knowledge Production on Rwanda, Dignity, and in Memory Studies

One evening when I was studying in the United States with some friends from Rwanda and other African countries, we heard there was an East African party not far from where we were celebrating a friend's birthday. We drove to the party divided among a couple vehicles. When we arrived, one of our friends went ahead to check if there was a cover charge or any other rules to enter the venue. He returned, angry, having had an argument with the doorman. It turned out this was a party organized by Hutu youth who had just ended a symposium on Rwandan politics. Such meetings were popular among Hutu elites in the diaspora as avenues to denounce the Rwandan government and in some cases lament their relatives who lost power in 1994.[1] The doorman followed him to the parking lot where we were waiting. Within minutes, the situation turned into a verbal altercation between the two. Another young man who had come out of the party said this was not a party for Tutsi or any sympathizers of the Kigali government. As soon as we heard that, we knew something was wrong. More people joined, and the mood became intense. The Hutu youth threatened to call the police on our group. We rushed to our cars. Our group included Tutsi survivors, Hutus, and those of us who do not care about ethnic affiliation or were from mixed Hutu and Tutsi backgrounds. We had genocide survivors among us and knew immediately that our encounter with such angry Hutu youth might turn into a heated debate. After phoning some friends who knew the organizers, we learned that they had just concluded a conference discussing Rwanda's past and, among other topics, the Hutu who had been killed by the Rwanda Patriotic Front (RPF) during the war in Rwanda and in then-Zaire after fleeing the Rwandan Patriotic Army (RPA). The organizers of the party, who I have called Antagonists in this book, disagreed with the master narrative, which was circulating around the United States at that time. Ultimately, I have come to realize that the events of that evening and the verbal altercation that took place are the direct result of the politics around the hegemonic master narrative of the 1994 Genocide Against the Tutsi. The salience of this narrative prohibited the existence of a conversable space between my own heterogeneous group and that of the party organizers—we all assumed that the members of the other were homogeneous in their antagonism toward this master narrative. This not only prevented all of us from acknowledging the possibility of nuance among the "other" but also prohibited the possibility of compassion between members of my own group and those of the party organizers.

I reflected on this moment for many years after that evening. How divided are we as young Rwandans, I wondered? How long will we fight over the past and our different versions of it? What did our parents, guardians, or older uncles and aunts, and books mostly authored by foreigners, tell us about the 1994 genocide and larger violence of the 1990s that we cannot tolerate each other at a party in a foreign country?

The party and the evening that I have just recounted took place in 2010, and these questions about memory became heavier as I talked to many elderly Rwandans in the diaspora and in Rwanda on my frequent visits back. I had friends in the RPA with varied access to RPF strategic meetings who told me their version of events in great detail. I also knew some descendants of former pregenocide elites, who hated the fact that I frequently talked about the struggles and pain that Tutsi refugees had endured when their parents were in power and the agony that Tutsis who remained in Rwanda lived through for decades. From my involvement in Nairobi with the diaspora, to my research in villages in Rwanda, Melbourne, and across many cities in the United States, where we organized commemorations during my graduate studies, and to travels around Europe, questions about Rwanda's multiple pasts followed me. The fact that I had the ambition to study and travel to learn about the world and was fortunate enough to do so meant that I carried the history of our country to different audiences with varied knowledge of Rwanda.

In my first and second master's degrees, I explored the questions of the politics of identity in Rwanda's pasts. Researching Rwanda's memory politics was an easy choice to make as I embarked on my doctoral studies in Australia. Yet, as I finished my PhD in 2015, it felt like I had only begun to learn how to engage with the question of the complexities of examining contexts in which histories of violence interact in the public arena, the actors who shape these conversations, relationships among these actors, and the dynamic factors that swirl around them. It is this feeling of the unfinished manuscript about this debate that led me to seek new ways to think about Rwanda's past, present, and future and especially the question of how debates on future memory will evolve. Yet even as I write this, it is difficult to imagine a tidy ending to such a complex question of what happened that night at the party or the many other responses to the master narrative I have encountered while working on this project.

In this book, I have tried to argue that over the 20 years following 1994, the master narrative of the Genocide Against the Tutsi emerged and evolved out of plural collective practices, was turned into an inward and outward hegemonic master narrative, and was enforced by various actors from both Rwanda and outside. I have shown that strategic decisions were taken to inspire its creation in line with the hegemonic and global Holocaust "paradigm," which was already in circulation, combined with Rwandan perspectives. Through this process two forms of hegemonic narratives emerged: one that seeks to establish a "model" or commemorating (Western hegemony) and another on how the master narrative in Rwanda's context has evolved to silence other versions of the past.

In both forms, language, art, laws, memorials, and other materials of memory were all used to create an official master narrative of one event—"the genocide"—among other competing, interlinked memories of violence that unfolded before and after 1994 in Rwanda and in the Great Lakes Region. Through consolidation of power, the postgenocide government enforced the implementation of this hegemonic master narrative through various strategies (including rewarding those who support the hegemonic master narrative and punishing those Antagonists who challenged it). Through this book I have also tried to counter the dominant perception in the postgenocide memory politics literature that overemphasizes the centrality of the government and makes invisible other actors, who equally influenced the emergence and evolution of the hegemonic master narrative.

With empirical evidence of the lived experiences of many Rwandans I interviewed and the anecdotal evidence of my own life, I have shown that many other actors (international donors, postconflict experts, and survivors) were involved in creating the script of a Genocide Against the Tutsi that empowered the master narrative to transform into a hegemonic one. The recognition of the "Rwandan genocide" in international forums—before it evolved into the Genocide Against the Tutsi—was one of the biggest gains for postgenocide government political elites in the years since 1994. But, this transition into a global and hegemonic master narrative was not without criticism. It attracted various responses from Rwandans and foreigners alike. In later years, closer to the twentieth anniversary of the genocide, older Rwandans, as well as youth born after the genocide, falling into the Champion, Fatalists, or Antagonist category, took advantage of evolving online platforms to proliferate conversations that sometimes turned into heated debates on Rwanda's past, present, and future.[2]

In examining the evolution of the official memory of the genocide in the two decades since 1994, Rwandans and other interested parties took contradictory approaches to coming to terms with the past and building the present and the future. While commemorations were both inward and outward looking, the Gacaca courts were mostly inward. Rwandans responded to both inward- and outward-facing approaches by gravitating toward the analytically fluid and dynamic political categories of Champions, Antagonists, and Fatalists. While some Rwandans, including respondents in this study, like Hakizimana, Soso, and Nsenga, became Champions of the master narrative; others, such as Mugenzi and Kayitesi, emerged as Antagonists and rejected the master narrative and commemorations or certain aspects thereof. Kayitesi and Kizito became indifferent to the ceremonies—Fatalists to the master narrative who both later shifted positions to become Antagonists. These categories and positions were not static or even binary, but rather malleable, depending on factors including individuals' circumstances, the prevailing political environment, and the ever-changing context shaped by internal RPF politics, regional dynamics, and international actors. The tensions were fierce, even in the diaspora.

Perhaps unsurprisingly, it is difficult to write a conclusion on such a sensitive and complex topic that is continuously evolving. Rather, I propose a set of reflections and key questions that I hope can lead to research and reflections on memory in the future. I then end with some theoretical proposals about studying Rwanda and knowledge production in memory studies and especially those struggling with the fallout of colonial pasts.

Reflections on Empirical Insights on Rwanda's Past, Present, and Future

Rwanda's postgenocide mnemonic experience, with the evolution of its master narrative and commemorative practices, as well as the varied responses to these, is important for a broader understanding of mnemonic experiences after mass violence. Creating a master narrative and accompanying forms of commemoration after mass violence is an inherently complex political, social, and economic process carried out by local, national, and international actors. When a competitive memory approach is chosen, it has the potential to breed tensions and create new or different conflicting narratives left out of official histories. While some individual memories can be mobilized for social or political memory, others resist a single master narrative and simple commemorations of a complex past, putting into sharp relief what author Chimamanda Ngozi Adichie calls "the danger of a single story."[3] The danger of selecting and writing a single story that ignores other interrelated stories inevitably raises tensions between individual and political memory. This is especially true when these individuals include youth who are creative, frustrated, idle, and able to access online tools that can be used to respond to, and contradict, the master narrative. It is even more dangerous for those of us who live with traumas of the violence we witnessed during the genocide or other violent histories that happened before and after the genocide.

Political elites in RPF mobilized the hegemonic narrative of the Holocaust. International perspectives on reconciliation and other homegrown ideas were leveraged to construct a narrative that has resulted in controversies. This selective remembering and forgetting of certain victims is not specific to Rwanda. Western right-wing politicians have constructed and mobilized old (and new) hegemonic master narratives that promote white-centric history. For instance, Vlaams Belang, a right-wing political party in Flanders in Belgium, continuously promotes their own narrative of Belgium's past[4] in Germany, it's the Alternative for Germany party (AFD); in France, it's the National Rally; and in the United States we saw the rise of right-wing parties during Republican President Donald Trump's tenure.

Ordinary citizens, liberals or conservatives, in Europe and North America, have also responded. Some choose to champion their hegemonic master narratives that promote former powerful oppressors and deny the significance, or even existence, of past colonial crimes. Champions of these hegemonic narratives resist evolving curricula, political changes, or institutional reforms and insist on the erasure of minority and dissident narratives even within democracies (France, United Kingdom, United States, Canada, Germany, etc.).[5]

Likewise, in the same democracies we find Antagonists who, for various reasons, are also engaging in protesting these hegemonic master narratives that, for example, commemorate only heroic accounts of the world wars or tales of resilience in the Holocaust. However, the same Antagonists are less active in commemorating victims of slavery and colonialism perpetrated by their societies and reject narratives that reckon with these in any substantive way.[6] Some, in fact, turn into Fatalists and remain indifferent to surging public debates about these countries' pasts. Regardless of the context, diaspora Antagonists of hegemonic narratives in Western contexts equally compete for recognition of their pasts in Western curricula, official narratives, and public debates. Thus, Antagonists' protests in these different contexts have put questions of coloniality embedded within these hegemonic master narratives, and contestations around them, right at the center of politics, not only in national contexts, but also as part of a global struggle for political and epistemic decolonization both off- and online.[7] As I point out further in this chapter, while contexts are different, there are threads that connect these undemocratic and democratic contexts that dominant literature tends to analyze into different categories of how memory is created.

Claiming and Naming Memory

The most complex and urgent question in debates around the master narrative and its current hegemonic status surrounds the use of rewards and punishment to safeguard the economic and reconciliation achievements of the Rwandan government and postgenocide society in general of the two decades since 1994 and creating a peaceful future for the country's youthful population. Like the adults who take part in commemorations, Rwandan youth have evolved to navigate and strategically present themselves as Champions, Fatalists, and Antagonists of the master narrative in recent decades. The youth are involved in a delicate game that is sometimes a matter of life and death: to ask or not ask questions or to act as vessels through which narratives of a past they did not witness travel. As Alison Landsberg put it: "The resulting prosthetic memory has the ability to shape that person's subjectivity and politics."[8] Rwandan youth who have chosen to articulate their positions as Champions or Antagonists deploy Rwanda's competing histories as a platform to deploy these histories at home, in the diaspora, and online. Thus, the evolution and representation of Rwanda's mediated memory among youth has started to stimulate unhealthy, and sometimes dangerous, debates within Rwanda and, more visibly, abroad in the diaspora, as evidenced in the opening of this chapter and in the online forums discussed in previous chapters.

This dilemma of prosthetic memory has ramifications in and outside Rwanda. The dynamics of power surrounding the emergence and evolution of the master narrative of the genocide have been influenced by powerful insiders and outside actors from the beginning. Colonial ideology is based on the notion that the colonizer can appropriate whatever he wants from the colonized. This not only applies to land, resources, and labor, but also extends to knowledge, life experiences, and trauma. Colonizer logics render the trauma of the colonized as simply another task for the colonizer. Rwanda's example is key: In the midst of grappling with the scope of the horror that took place in 1994, the new government, while simultaneously trying to manage basic public services and safety, had to continuously consider how to manage the emotions and attention of the West. This is demonstrated plainly in the case of former US President Bill Clinton being more warmly welcomed than former UN Secretary General Kofi Annan, a Ghanian who received a lukewarm reception, despite the fact that both held powerful offices and bore responsibility for abandoning Rwandan Tutsi in the middle of a genocide and a civil war. Equally, the new government also had to manage the emotions of its own traumatized citizens, which included both survivors and perpetrators of violence. For the new government, positioning the genocide as a cause célèbre was crucial in securing its own legitimacy as well as obtaining the resources necessary to rebuild Rwanda and keep the postgenocide mess under control. While all these factors are understandable and should always be in view of analysis, one cannot ignore the challenges that these considerations and tactics introduced into the process evolving from an emergency situation to the stability Rwanda enjoys today. The challenge this book has sought to document and articulate are what Roland Junod and Paul Rutayisire have identified as the resultant "memory politics" in their studies on commemoration in Rwanda.[9] These memory politics discussed next are the ones that shape present and future debates on Rwanda, and that were potentially going to turn messy that night in the United States with my friends.

Old Fears, New Challenges

On the ground, current debates reanimate an old dilemma for Rwandan society because, as detailed previously, past master narratives have been used to egregious and violent ends. The old PARMEHUTU (Party of the Hutu Emancipation Movement) ideology, based on grievances generated by both individual memory and colonial narratives of the monarchy, was used to inspire earlier massacres and genocidal killings by Rwandan youth. Other Rwandan youth who took up arms in the RPA, meanwhile, were inspired by stories that their parents told them about the monarchical past and the politics that led them into exile; in some ways, this dissident narrative, once espoused by exiles, helps inform the evolving master narrative in Rwanda today. The monarchical period itself produced master narratives that drove dissident narratives underground, creating its own Champions and Antagonists. The dilemma now is how a country with such a complex and fiercely debated history can ensure that various interpretations of the past can be rigorously discussed while sustaining peace for not only the aging generation who lived this disputed history firsthand, but also current and future generations, without risking future cycles of violence. The need for a space where competing memories can coexist is therefore urgent. There are a number of possibilities within unfolding conversations and the transformation of memory politics in Rwanda that Champions, Fatalists, and Antagonists can utilize to move forward, where differing historical interpretations do not need to lead to war and insecurity.

This reflection begs the question: Can discourses on Rwanda's past move away from a competitive memory approach that encourages a "zero-sum game"[10] and instead identify how varying memories of Rwanda's pasts can interact, relate to each other, and even coexist in public discourses on memorialization? For Rwanda, and other contexts where actors are navigating sensitive and violent pasts, this approach would help move away from seeking a moral equivalence of violence and victims.[11] While the effort to categorize the Genocide Against the Tutsi as a genocide (a grave crime) was historically accurate and is legally binding both locally and internationally, other types of mass violence that unfolded before, during, and after the genocide are similarly worthy of attention and debate.[12] The dilemma is equally how to overcome limitations in this Western approach that creates political pressure to call certain types of violence "genocide" in order to make them worthy of action and redress. There is an assumption that southern actors massacre each other all the time, so violence must be labeled as a "genocide"[13] in order to be worthy of global attention. The war in the Tigray region in Ethiopia is a recent example where old political elites have claimed there was a genocide, and the Western political elites and media responded with attention. Yet, the recent security challenges in this context are as a result of interconnected histories of conflicts that have taken different shapes in the past decades. Obviously, what happened to the Tutsi in Rwanda was a genocide: The Interahamwe actors planned to exterminate the Tutsi and put this plan into practice. Yet, the perceived advantages and resources gained by the postgenocide government because of Western "guilt" over ignoring the Genocide Against the Tutsi, in contrast to the continued neglect of interconnected violence against Hutus, present a stark lesson and a problem for international politics. It is likely a part of what fuels Antagonists, who develop their narratives to mourn their loved ones, and among political elites (old and new), including old ones, who want similar resources and attention paid to their relatives killed when the RPF attacked the north, and in the DRC (Democratic Republic of the Congo) violence. None of these meet the legal definition of genocide, and should it not matter as it causes ongoing trauma, pain, and anger among the Antagonists. This need to justify all violence as genocide for it to matter is equally rampant in Burundi, the DRC, Darfur, and China and in many other contexts. "Rwanda 1994" has unfortunately become a cliché mobilized to gain attention in international diplomacy.[14] While it is important to point out where extreme violence has turned into genocide, urgent care should be taken that other violent crimes that do not meet the threshold of such infamous atrocity are not ignored or considered unimportant if human dignity is to be protected.

There is a need to dismantle the development of hegemonic narratives and instead cultivate a space for the variable stakeholders debating these issues and those facilitating the discussion, such as journalists, scholars, or online commentators, to negotiate and develop a sensitive, specific, and shared vocabulary and "conversable spaces"[15] that are peaceful. This is because memories or silences that are mobilized do not belong to one group. Michael Rothberg writes:

> Memories are not owned by groups—nor are groups "owned" by memories. Rather, the borders of memory and identity are jagged; what looks at first like my own property often turns out to be a borrowing or adaptation from a history that initially might seem foreign or distant.[16]

CONCLUSION 261

Thus, in Rwanda's case, to what extent can a single group, be it Hutu, Tutsi, or Twa, claim memories as their personal purview? In employing lenses of multidirectional memory, one finds that some who identify their families as Hutu can be Champions of the master narrative—as in the cases of Edouard Bamporiki or Hakizimana. Survivor Kizito Mihigo, who was a Tutsi and whose controversial song expressed empathy for the Hutu and those killed in other instances of violence that surrounded the genocide, is considered to have evolved from being an influential Champion to becoming an Antagonist.[17] In this sense, the master narrative of the genocide does not belong to only one group, despite the vocabulary used. It is shared by different Hutu, Tutsi, and Twa who, for various reasons, take part in commemorations.

And yet, where should we draw the line on who can claim authority and ownership over an experience? Indeed, many Champions who are visible, and who continuously engage in the debate on what happened in the genocide, were not present in Rwanda during the events in question and did not undergo the trauma of those who were. Genocide survivors such as Kizito Mihigo have turned into Antagonists. Even high-profile genocide survivor Protais Mitari, the Minister who banned Mihigo's music and who helped create the master narrative, later also fled Rwanda. Similarly, former leaders of Ibuka in Rwanda and the diaspora have disputes on the master narrative, especially when Mihigo died mysteriously. It is telling that other genocide survivors who influenced early debates have slowly vanished from public political discussion on the past in Rwanda. The most visible Antagonists in the diaspora are equally not always those who themselves survived the Kibeho massacre, RPF killings in the North prior to 1994, or those that took place in DRC after 1994. The most visible are mostly political elites or their descendants who were absent when the violence happened or had protection against the violence. The master narrative has evolved into a political tool for both Champions and Antagonists competing for political power. However, the evolution has also pushed many into becoming Fatalists.

Few survivors of any instance of interrelated mass violence are called by either side to give evidence and testimony during official commemorations or in online forums and unofficial commemorative events that I have previously mentioned. This debate unfolds largely between political elites with or against foreign journalists, scholars, and politicians engaged in conversations about events none of them actually experienced. Many survivors of the genocide and civil war crimes are Fatalists, who choose varied strategic silences and withdraw from public debates over the history they lived through, which still shapes their everyday lives in Rwanda and in the diaspora.[18] Many politicians and policymakers rely on the hegemonic master narrative to warn their populations or gain international attention to "not to repeat what happened in Rwanda." Those survivors who are involved in public debates do so in an individual capacity. Regardless of the analytical category in which they fit, they have to strike a delicate balance and align their story with the version advanced by either Champions or Antagonists. For Champions, Antagonists, and Fatalists, a Western audience or resources like aid funding are the ultimate target, for various reasons, but mostly because of the assumption that the Global North is where stories of suffering are legitimized and granted global significance.

Since I opened this book with a reflection on my positionality, it is only fitting to point out that I am also using Western resources, which fund my research, to influence global debates. Where does international support become an unequal distribution of narrative power to the Global North? Where does legitimacy based on the hegemonic master narrative become neocolonialism? How does a society transition to having inclusive conversations about a past in a sincere and peaceful way?

Problems and Promises of Technology and Memory

Beyond these debates over colonization and memory, we need to recognize that Rwanda's youth have been handed not only the most important tool of advancement in a fast-paced, globalized world, but also the most dangerous for transformation of these conversations. Online spaces are fast becoming agents of memory in which the master narrative and dissenting narratives travel across generations and geographies at a higher speed than ever before.[19] It is these platforms that unite those permitted to take part in the memory politics conversations in Rwanda, those who are alienated therein and those acting in an individual capacity. This conversable space is a physical or online platform that matters to communities, scholars, practitioners, and all other actors. The internet is increasingly becoming accessible in rural communities, and with this comes disinformation promoted via online channels to a youthful population who were not allowed to study history subjects comprehensively, and that is striking, given that some see the mismatch between their relatives' narratives and those dictated by the hegemonic master narrative. While there are youth like Hakizimana who actively support the government, there are also many like Kayitesi who have and will continue to shift their positions and are curious about what the online world has to provide to express their grief.

While the master narrative has been used in online and offline channels to travel around Rwanda, Africa, and the world with the support of the current government, the Antagonists' dissident narratives are increasingly creating and finding their own paths into formerly restricted national spaces and debates to influence interested urban and rural youth with alternative versions of the past. This raises an important question as to how these evolving factors will shape offline conversations on politics, or peace and security in Rwanda, leading to further reflections on the possibilities of transformation of conflicts and inter-group relationships.

There are, of course, offline spaces that have been used to foster debates about other aspects of rebuilding Rwanda in the first two decades that are worth examining as conversable spaces to resolve memory politics in Rwanda. These include demobilization camps, where former rebels who returned from the DRC were resocialized and engaged in debates about Rwanda's pasts with the goal to win them over from their dissident narrative towards co-opting them within the hegemonic one. Other public spaces for discourse include *Umushyicyirano wi Gihugu* (Rwanda's national annual dialogue); Rwanda Day (a convention that travels around the world with the president meeting Rwandans in the diaspora); *Umuganda* (monthly community services that bring together Rwandans); and many others that are designed to foster conversations over Rwanda's past, present, and future. These offline spaces are embedded within Rwandan political and cultural practices and are familiar to Rwanda's youth. They are important conversable spaces where Rwandans can debate and settle their disagreements on various versions of the past without violence.

Online and offline conversations are by turns honest, confrontational, and threatening for those on any side. The question of how conversations happening offline and online shape each other must be explored further. These conversations often target youth, who were not yet born in 1994 and yet, prompted by different events and circumstances close to them, are now engaged in this debate at various levels. For instance, a program aired on the Voice of America (VOA) Kinyarwanda/Kirundi service on May 4, 2020, featured those who I have called Champions, Antagonists, and Fatalists engaged in conversation about contentious issues surrounding the genocide and its twenty-sixth commemoration.[20] Speculation around the death of

Kizito Mihigo in February 2020 further exemplifies the intersection of online and offline debates. Contention over the cause of his death unfolded online and offline among Antagonists, Champions, and Fatalists, including non-Rwandans.[21] Youth were engaged because Kizito was a celebrity of their own time.

Future research will need to examine to what extent online platforms allow actors to express and change their positions in relation to the master narrative. It will be important to study what powers these platforms give to government elites and which ones they take away and distribute to ordinary people, whether in democratic contexts or not. Rwanda researchers will need to unpack the influence of demographic changes and technology on shaping memorialization that is perhaps more inward focused on Rwandan youth. This is because Champion, Antagonist, and, to a lesser extent, Fatalist narratives have the potential to find alliances in regional and international master narratives or dissident narratives that render them powerful, visible, and therefore able to mobilize support for either side to maintain a presence and shape Rwanda's future memory politics. Further, research on future memory politics in Rwanda will have to grapple with these shifts and interactions, which are unfolding quickly, and will need to assess what these conversations will mean for knowledge production on Rwanda's past, present, and future. The malleability of memory is unavoidable but should be determined by peaceful transfer of power.

Theoretical, Methodological, and Epistemological Implications

From a theoretical perspective, this book shows how the master narrative became hegemonic, as it emerged and developed, and responses to it became increasingly subject to institutional policing. By showing how the master narrative of memory discourse in Rwanda has evolved, this book demonstrates the contingent nature of political discourses. But this contingency is always linked to limitations of agency, that is, to the capacity of political actors to adapt their discourses to new situations beyond their control. Doing so in a coherent way, in relation to various social, political, and cultural situations, requires politicians to continuously adapt their strategies of enforcing the master narrative or sometimes losing control without necessarily admitting it.

From an epistemological point of view, the book shows the difficulty of studying a master narrative and its trajectory over time. The problem is that in researching this discourse, either one forgets or minimizes the way in which other discourses develop and influence the master narrative or one begins to define other perspectives using the characteristics and rationalities of the hegemonic discourse as one's baseline. And this last remark is very important because hegemonic and nonhegemonic discourses often have different characteristics because they obey different rationalities and interests and serve constituencies whose relationships to institutional power vary significantly.

In considering alternative perspectives to the master narrative discourse, we forget to distinguish between their social and political objectives. Sometimes, alternative discourses are created in response to objectives that the hegemonic discourse does not or cannot pursue. Thus, if we look at discourses on the basis of their political or social objectives and their targets, then perhaps we can redefine the very ideas of hegemony and master narrative. Hegemonic memory silences alternative narratives and gives privilege to the most powerful actors. Actors mobilize the hegemonic master narrative to ensure it always serves their specific and defined interests. From this point of view, the master narrative of memory that becomes hegemonic memory is concerned with power that creates realities and produces consequences in terms of what can be seen, thought, and felt. These discourses define who is right and who is wrong. They produce a particular form of truth that enables the activation and legitimization of symbolic or state violence. Such discourses are thus one of the many ways in which not only the powerful and governing control people, but through which societies and institutions police the boundaries of acceptable behavior and discourse.

Theoretical and Methodological Implications beyond Rwanda

By studying, from a Rwandan perspective, an issue that has been highly examined in the West, this book illustrates the debates on the dichotomous relationship between universalism and particularism that are very strongly criticized in decolonial or postcolonial studies.[22] Decolonial literature insists on the need for social sciences today to interrogate, from not only the fields of the Global South but also different positionalities, the knowledge produced in humanities and social sciences.[23]

In postcolonial and postconflict societies in the Global South, coloniality logics continue to influence the most intimate parts of people's lives. Those political elites who benefit from coloniality, whether in the Global North or Global South, continuously conspire to dominate knowledge production, ideas of organizing the past, and dictate particular methods of how history, including those of their crimes, should be written and understood.[24] But, how we do repair the ruptures that have been exacerbated by colonial power? For Mudimbe, it is important to challenge and confront ideas that have been produced in the past in what he called "the colonial."[25] This involves finding perspectives of life and death that respondent communities mobilize in contesting hegemonic knowledge on how the past should be remembered. I therefore end the book with a proposition of *Agaciro* or dignity that was put forward by a respondent in another study on Rwanda's vernacular memory.

Agaciro (dignity, self-worth) in Rwanda reframes remembrance to focus on the value and dignity afforded to every human being. Its power is derived from how, as a philosophy, it connects today's youth with their ancestors, their families, and their dead. It provides an inherently relational and social approach to preserving the dignity of the people in their communities. It also provides an avenue through which to find connections between Antagonists, Champions, and Fatalists and their distinct approaches to addressing memory politics. While Agaciro is specifically Rwandan in its modalities, Norman Ajali's work, and many others that study dignity, shows that many cultures have some kind of cosmological framework about respecting the dignity of human life.[26] It is Agaciro—dignity of their loved ones and themselves—that Champions, Antagonists, and Fatalists are fighting for at different levels. Champions fight for the dignity of their dead relatives on local and international levels where actors have increasingly endorsed the master narrative. Equally, Antagonists are fighting for the same recognition against the hegemonic master narrative in local official history and internationally. However, as I have highlighted previously, it should not be the case that their claims need to be termed as genocide for their fight for dignity to be taken seriously.

Dignity is a universal principle that manifests itself in different languages and forums but nevertheless centers the importance of human beings in life and beyond. Its definition is dynamic and context specific.[27] But, it is different from the discourse on human rights that emphasizes the individual and not the collective. As argued elsewhere, the Agaciro approach is one that is "derived from 'actors' interpretations rather than from the artifacts of memory."[28] It is complex and layered as it allows for a researcher to locate the connections between different actors' claims to memory. The Agaciro approach to dignity provides the researcher with a common analytical anchor through which to explore and understand the shifting memory politics and humanity of respondents—namely, the understanding that the pursuit of dignity is inherently relational and not merely individual. This approach to dignity facilitates the broader cultivation of compassion. It warrants clarifying that this Agaciro approach to dignity remains aligned with the broader understanding of dignity as intrinsic; it does, however, expand understandings of dignity to acknowledge and centralize the social and interrelational dimensions of the pursuit of dignity among people. It is dignity-centered thinking that both of our groups lacked when we encountered each other in the United States in the story that I discussed in the opening of this conclusion.

This is not to romanticize vernacular memory; on the contrary, narratives themselves can prove antagonistic, and as discussed in chapter 2, the process of supplanting one hegemonic narrative with another can be violent. Yet allowing a meaningful democratic space for a plurality of narratives opens up the possibility of recognizing the dignity of many, and brings into focus the power struggles over what is remembered, what is forgotten, and what is silenced.

In many ways, Champions, Antagonists, and Fatalists alike are fighting for their dignity and the dignity of their loved ones killed in these violent histories. It through respecting each other's dignity that their relationships can be restored and developed. Restoring dignity through remembrance can help alleviate conflicts over the past, and in many contexts simultaneously serves an important decolonial function. It restores the dignity denied to the enslaved or massacred; it also charts a path forward to consider how remembering the past is constructed and how to produce knowledge about the ever-changing nature of memory. More research is needed to explore how different communities understand the multiple meanings of dignity and how the concept can be deployed in studies about the past or peacebuilding and in those communities that are interested in fostering a peaceful present and future.

Notes

1. On memory narratives of Hutu diaspora, see Claudine Kuradusenge, "Denied Victimhood and Contested Narratives: The Case of Hutu Diaspora," *Genocide Studies and Prevention: An International Journal* 10, no. 2 (2016): 7; and Claudine Kuradusenge-McLeod, "Belgian Hutu Diaspora Narratives of Victimhood and Trauma," *International Journal of Transitional Justice* 12, no. 3 (2018): 427–443.
2. On youth perspectives on memory politics in Rwanda, see Tugce Ataci, "Narratives of Rwandan Youth on Post-genocide Reconciliation: Contesting Discourses and Identities in the Making," *Journal of Youth Studies* (2021): 1–18; and see Andrea Mariko Grant, "Bringing the *Daily Mail* to Africa: Entertainment Websites and the Creation of a Digital Youth Public in Post-genocide Rwanda," *Journal of Eastern African Studies* 13, no. 1 (2019): 106–123.
3. Chimamanda Ngozi Adichie, "The Danger of a Single Story," July 23, 2009, Oxford, UK, TED Talk, 18:33, https://www.ted.com/talks/chimamanda_ngozi_adichie_the_danger_of_a_single_story/transcript?language=en. See also Erin Jessee, "The Danger of a Single Story: Iconic Stories in the Aftermath of the 1994 Rwandan Genocide," *Memory Studies* 10, no. 2 (2017): 144–163.
4. Curiously fewer of these right-wing parties flourish in the Francophone Belgium region for different historical processes; see Léonie de Jonge, "The Curious Case of Belgium: Why Is There No Right-Wing Populism in Wallonia?" *Government and Opposition* 56, no. 4 (2021): 598–614.
5. See; Ann Laura Stoler, "Colonial Aphasia: Race and Disabled Histories in France," *Public Culture* 23, no. 1 (2011): 121–156; and/or Christina Sharpe, *In the Wake: On Blackness and Being* (Durham, NC: Duke University Press, 2016).
6. Michael Rothberg's book *Multidirectional Memory: Remembering the Holocaust in the Age of Decolonization* (Palo Alto, CA: Stanford University Press, 2009) is one of those examples that have tried to provide clarity on these questions of colonial and slavery pasts that are continuously mobilized among many others authored by Western-based scholars, including the diaspora.
7. David Mwambari, "Can Online Platforms Be e-Pana-Africana Liberation Zones for Pan-African and Decolonization Debates?," *CODESRIA Bulletin Online* 5 (February 2021): 5, https://web.archive.org/web/20210215185323/http://www.codesria.org/IMG/pdf/5-_mwambari_codbul_online_21.pdf.
8. David Mwambari, "Can Online Platforms Be e-Pana-Africana Liberation Zones for Pan-African and Decolonization Debates.
9. See Roland Junod and Paul Rutayisire, "Citoyenneté et réconciliation au Rwanda," *Collection du centre de recherche sociale*, OAPEN, https://library.oapen.org/handle/20.500.12657/33028, 80.
10. Michael Rothberg, "From Gaza to Warsaw: Mapping Multidirectional Memory," *Criticism* 53, no. 4 (2011): 523–548.
11. See Philip Verwimp, "Testing the Double-Genocide Thesis for Central and Southern Rwanda," *Journal of Conflict Resolution* 47, no. 4 (2003): 423–442; or also see Lars

Waldorf, "Revisiting Hotel Rwanda: Genocide Ideology, Reconciliation, and Rescuers," *Journal of Genocide Research* 11, no. 1 (2009): 101–125.

12. As I was concluding this book, Champions, Antagonists, and Fatalists' conversations took a new turn. Through online platforms, such as the Real Talk Channel hosted by Etienne Gatanizi, topics that were previously deemed taboo started. One conversation included Champions like the CNLG (Commission National de Lutte contre le Génocide) director Dr. Jean Damascene Bizimana engaging in conversations with the host, who might be seen to be an Antagonist. See "Bizimana, Ubwami si bwo bwateje Inzangano mu Banyarwanda. Kuba harategekaga Abatutsi byari umuco" ["Kingdoms are not the source of hatred amongst Rwanda. It was cultural to have a Tutsi Kingdom"], *Real Talk Channel*, YouTube video, 49:19, September 17, 2020, https://www.youtube.com/watch?v=jDzSpV01Gi8; or this one on the question of ethnicity: "Amoko 'Hutu Tutsi' Mu Mator Y'abameya. Byaturutse He Ko Amoko 'yaciwe' Mu Betegetsi Bw'URwanda," YouTube video, Real Talk Channel, 1:04:35, January 23, 2021, https://www.youtube.com/watch?v=Dyzl1JhkeWg.

13. See Mahmood Mamdani, "The Politics of Naming: Genocide, Civil War, Insurgency," *London Review of Books* 29, no. 5 (March 8, 2007), https://www.lrb.co.uk/the-paper/v29/n05/mahmood-mamdani/the-politics-of-naming-genocide-civil-war-insurgency

14. Wouter Reggers, David Mwambari, and Valérie Rosoux, "In Memory of Peacekeepers: Belgian Blue Helmets and Belgian Politics," *Journal of International Peacekeeping* 29, no. 2 (January 2022): 258-281.

15. Funmi Olonisakin, Alagaw Ababu Kifle, and Alfred Muteru. "Shifting Ideas of Sustainable Peace Towards Conversation in State-Building," *Conflict, Security & Development* 21, no. 4 (2021): 1–22.

16. Rothberg, Multidirectional Memory, 5.

17. See, for instance, the interview that aired on *Real Talk* referenced above footnote 12, "Bizimana." In this discussion, Champions, including CNLG leaders, agree that the Genocide Against the Tutsi is appropriately named and focused. Then annually, on April 13, Rwandans are called to also remember Hutu politicians who died while protecting Tutsi. However, a distinction is made. These Hutu politicians are not genocide victims like Tutsi victims; they were killed due to their heroic acts, not because they were Tutsi.

18. See, for instance, activists and writers based in the United States or France, such as the most prominent in past two decades: On the genocide in Rwanda, see Immaculée Ilibagiza and Steve Erwin, *Left to Tell: Discovering God Amidst the Rwandan Holocaust* (New York: Hay House, 2006); Consolee Nishimwe, *Tested to the Limit: A Genocide Survivor's Story of Pain, Resilience, and Hope* (Bloomington, IN: Balboa Press, 2012); or Yolande Mukagasana and Patrick May, *La mort ne veut pas de moi: document* (Paris: Éditions Fixot, 1997). About DRC and refugees around Africa, see Clemantine Wamariya and Elizabeth Weil, *The Girl Who Smiled Beads: A Story of War and What Comes After* (Crown, 2018). These books, especially the ones featuring women's trauma, have been subjects of other books. See, for instance, Catherine Gilbert, *From Surviving to Living: Voice, Trauma and Witness in Rwanda Women's*

Writing (Toulouse, France: Presses universitaires de la Méditerranée, 2018). However, few books, theses, and documents that were written in Kinyarwanda or written in Rwanda, such as those referenced throughout this book, gained such international prominence, confirming coloniality plays a role when it comes to mobility of ideas produced from Global South.

19. Astrid Erll, "Travelling Memory," *Parallax* 17, no. 4 (2011): 4–18.
20. See "Murisanga," 59:34, Radiyo Yacu VOA, May 4, 2020, https://www.radiyoyacuvoa.com/a/5380993.html, radio broadcast.
21. As I was concluding this book, Mihigo's life story took a dramatic and tragic turn. On September 14, 2018, he was released by presidential pardon after spending 4 years in prison. A few days earlier, it was reported he had abandoned his appeal claim. The presidential mercy was also given to other over two thousand prisoners, including the controversial politician Victoire Ingabire.

    Then on February 13, 2020, the Rwandan police announced they had arrested Mihigo as he tried to flee the country through the border between Rwanda and Burundi. On February 14, 2020, a few weeks before the Twenty-Sixth Commemoration period, the Rwanda Investigative Bureau (RIB) announced Kizito Mihigo had been found dead in his jail cell. They informed the public that they suspected it was suicide. After human rights groups and media complained of declaring suicide before investigation, the RBI announced investigations were underway, but suicide was evident. On February 26, 2020, the National Public Prosecution Authority confirmed he died after hanging himself.

    After his death, Rwandans mourned Mihigo at a funeral with his family. Champions wrote numerous op-eds analyzing where he had gone wrong. Radicals among them accused him of being a genocide denier. For Antagonists, Kizito's death became that of a martyr. His music, especially the controversial song "Igisobanuro cy'urupfu" (The Meaning of Death), was continuously played and shared over the internet. Antagonists organized masses and eulogized him, and others became activists in memory politics. His death was as controversial as his life since 2014 when he released that song. His story was reported by local news organizations like IGIHE and the *New Times* and globally, including in major news outlets such as Al Jazeera and the BBC. The stories told about his life intensified debates and conversations privately and publicly about Rwanda's past and allowed the master narrative and contestations around it to travel both online and geographically to a new generation of youth globally.

    For more on Mihigo's death, see "Kizito Mihigo: Singer Found Dead in Rwandan Police Cell," BBC News, February 17, 2020, https://www.bbc.com/news/world-africa-51528526; "Popular Rwandan Singer Found Dead in Police Cell: Police," Al-Jazeera, February 17, 2020, https://www.aljazeera.com/news/2020/02/popular-rwandan-singer-dead-police-cell-police-200217150952317.html; "Rwanda: Ensure Justice over Kizito Mihigo Death; Popular Singer Died in Police Custody," updated February 20, 2020, https://www.hrw.org/news/2020/02/20/rwanda-ensure-justice-over-kizito-mihigo-death; and Glory Iribagiza, "Autopsy Confirms Kizito Died by Suicide," *New Times* (Kigali), February 26, 2020, https://www.newtimes.co.rw/news/autopsy-confirms-kizito-died-suicide.

22. Naoki Sakai, "Modernity and Its Critique: The Problem of Universalism and Particularlism," in *Postmodernism and Japan*, eds. Masao Miyoshi and Harry Harootunian (Durham, NC: Duke University Press, 1989), 93–122; or/and Dipesh Chakrabarty, "Provincializing Europe: Postcoloniality and the Critique of History," *Cultural Studies* 6, no. 3 (1992): 337–357.
23. See, for instance, Sabelo J. Ndlovu-Gatsheni, *Epistemic Freedom in Africa: Deprovincialization and Decolonization* (New York: Routledge, 2018); and André Keet, "Epistemic 'Othering'and the Decolonisation of Knowledge," *Africa Insight* 44, no. 1 (2014): 23–37.
24. Aymar N. Bisoka, David Mwambari, and Ndlovu Gisheni, "From Summity to Counter-summit: Imperialism, Françafrique and Decololonization," *Review of African Political Economy*. December 13, 2021, https://roape.net/2021/12/13/from-summit-to-counter-summit-imperialism-francafrique-and-decolonisation/
25. V. Y. Mudimbe, *The Invention of Africa: Gnosis, Philosophy, and the Order of Knowledge* (Bloomington: Indiana University Press, 1988).
26. See, for instance, Eleni Coundouriotis, "The Dignity of the 'Unfittest': Victims' Stories in South Africa," *Human Rights Quarterly* 28, no. 4 (2006): 842–867; Norman Ajari, *La Dignité ou la mort: Éthique et politique de la race* (Paris: Éditions La Découverte, coll. Les Empêcheurs de penser en rond, 2019); and Drucilla Cornell, *Law and Revolution in South Africa* (New York: Fordham University Press). Also see Zaynab El Bernoussi, *Dignity in the Egyptian Revolution: Protest and Demand During the Arab Uprisings* (Cambridge: Cambridge University Press, 2021); Ana Luisa Guerrero, *Deconstrucción y genealogía del concepto de dignidad de los pueblos originarios en el pensamiento latinoamericano* (Mexico City: Bonilla Artigas Editores, 2015); Sandra M. Rios Oyola, "Dignification of Victims through Exhumations in Colombia," *Human Rights Review* 22 (2021): 483–499. As well, see Sandra M. Rios Oyola, "Restoring the Human Dignity of Absent Bodies in Colombia," in *Post-conflict Memorialization: Missing Memorials, Absent Bodies*, eds. Luisa Gandolfo, Olivette Otele, and Yoav Galai (London: Palgrave Macmillan, 2021). doi:10.1007/978-3-030-54887-2_10.
27. Catherine Dupré, *The Age of Dignity: Human Rights and Constitutionalism in Europe* (London: Bloomsbury, 2016), 16.
28. Gregor Feindt, Félix Krawatzek, Daniela Mehler, Friedemann Pestel, and Rieke Trimçev, "'Entangled Memory: Toward a Third Wave in Memory Studies," *History and Theory* 53, no. 1 (2014): 27. Cited in David Mwambari, *Agaciro*, Vernacular Memory, and the Politics of Memory in Post-genocíde Rwanda," *African Affairs* 120, no. 481 (October 2021): 628.

Bibliography

Adekunle, Julius O. *Culture and Customs of Rwanda*. Westport, CT: Greenwood Press, 2007.
Aegis Trust. "What We Do." https://www.aegistrust.org/what-we-do/.
African Rights. *Rwanda: Death, Despair, and Defiance*. London: African Rights, 1995.
Agaba, Godwin. "Dead Dogs Mourner to Appear in Court." *New Times* (Kigali), April 11, 2007. http://allafrica.com/stories/200704110704.html.
Alexis, Monique, and Ines Mpambara. *The Rwanda Media Experience from the Genocide*. Copenhagen: International Media Support, 2003. http://www.mediasupport.org/wp-content/uploads/2012/11/ims-assessment-rwanda-genocide-2003.pdf.
Allen, Brenda. "Feminist Standpoint Theory: A Black Woman's (Re)View of Organizational Socialization." *Communication Studies* 47, no. 4 (1996): 257–271.
"Amagambo Y'ngenzi (a Glossary of Important Words and Phrases)." *prévenirgénocideinternational*, accessed September 9, 2021. http://www.preventgenocide.org/rw/amagambo2.htm.
Amnesty, International. *Rwanda—Gacaca: A Question of Justice*. London: Amnesty International, International Secretariat, 2002.
"Amoko (Hutu Tutsi) Mu Mator Y'abameya. Byaturutse He Ko Amoko "Yaciwe" Mu Butegetsi Bw'urwanda?" YouTube video, Real Talk Channel, 1:04:35, January 23, 2021. https://www.youtube.com/watch?v=Dyzl1JhkeWg.
Andrews, Molly. *Narrative Imagination and Everyday Life*. Oxford, UK: Oxford University Press, 2019.
Anita Kwizera. "Nyamasheke: Local Leadership to Look for Missing Bodies." *News of Rwanda* (Kigali), June 29, 2012. https://web.archive.org/web/20210127110924/http://www.newsofrwanda.com/ibikorwa/7737/nyamasheke-missing-genocide-bodies-traced/.
Anna, Reading. "The London Bombings: Mobile Witnessing, Mortal Bodies and Globital Time." *Memory Studies* 4, no. 3 (2011): 298–311.
Annan, Kofi A., and Nader Mousavizadeh. *Interventions: A Life in War and Peace*. New York: Penguin, 2013.
Ansoms, An. "Striving for Growth, Bypassing the Poor? A Critical Review of Rwanda's Rural Sector Policies." *Journal of Modern African Studies* 46, no. 1 (2008): 1–32.
Ansoms, An, Esther Marijnen, Giuseppe Cioffo, and Jude Murison. "Statistics versus Livelihoods: Questioning Rwandas Pathway Out of Poverty." *Review of African Political Economy* 44, no. 151 (2017): 47–65.
Asiimwe, Arthur. "Rwanda's Ex-President Freed from Prison." *Reuters* (Kigali), April 6, 2007. https://www.reuters.com/article/us-rwanda-president/rwandas-ex-president-freed-from-prison-idUSL0650070720070406.
Assmann, Aleida. "Memory, Individual and Collective." In *The Oxford Handbook of Contextual Political Analysis*, edited by R. E. Goodin and C. Tilly, 210–224. Oxford, UK: Oxford University Press, 2006.

Assmann, Jan. "Communicative and Cultural Memory." In *A Companion to Cultural Memory Studies*, edited by Astrid Erll and Ansgar Nunning, 109–118. Berlin: De Gruyter, 2010.

Assmann, Jan. *Cultural Memory and Early Civilization: Writing, Remembrance, and Political Imagination*. Cambridge: Cambridge University Press, 2011.

Assmann, Jan. *Das Kulturelle Gedächtnis: Schrift, Erinnerung und Politische Identität in Frühen Hochkulturen*. Munich: Beck, 1977.

Associated Press. "More Graves Found at New Site, Canadian Indigenous Group Says." *NPR*, July 1, 2021. https://www.npr.org/2021/07/01/1012100926/graves-found-at-new-site-canadian-indigenous-group-says?t=1625388369719

Ataci, Tugce. "Narratives of Rwandan Youth on Post-genocide Reconciliation: Contesting Discourses and Identities in the Making." *Journal of Youth Studies* 25, no. 10 (2021): 1–18.

Augé, Marc. *Oblivion*. Minneapolis: University of Minnesota Press, 2004.

Australian War Memorial. "Rwanda (UNAMIR), 1993–1996." Accessed March 15, 2023. https://www.awm.gov.au/collection/U60680/.

Ba, Mehdi. "Comment une reine a sauvé la vie de Paul Kagame." *Jeune Afrique*, June 21, 2017. http://www.jeuneafrique.com/mag/446543/politique/reine-a-sauve-vie-de-paul-kagame/.

Baldwin, Gretchen. "Constructing Identity through Commemoration: Kwibuka and the Rise of Survivor Nationalism in Post-conflict Rwanda." *Journal of Modern African Studies* 57, no. 3 (2019): 355–375.

Bamporiki, Edouard. *Icyaha Kuri Bo, Ikimwaro Kuri Jye*. Kigali, Rwanda: E. Bamporiki Uwayo, 2010.

Barahona de Brito, Alexandra, Carmen González-Enríquez, and Paloma Aguilar, eds. *The Politics of Memory Transitional Justice in Democratizing Societies*. Oxford, UK: Oxford University Press, 2004.

Barker, Greg, dir. *Frontline*. Season 4, episode 6, "Ghosts of Rwanda." Aired April 1, 2004 on PBS. https://www.pbs.org/wgbh/pages/frontline/shows/ghosts/.

Barsalou, Judith Marie, and Victoria Baxter. *The Urge to Remember: The Role of Memorials in Social Reconstruction and Transitional Justice*. Washington, DC: United States Institute of Peace, 2007.

Batsinduka, Richard. "The Rwanda Conflict." In *Regional and Ethnic Conflicts: Perspectives from the Front Lines*, edited by Judy Carter, George Emile Irani, and Vamik D. Volkan, 130–158. Hoboken, NJ: Taylor and Francis, 2015.

"La BBC et la VOA accusées par Kigali de 'détruire l'unité des Rwandais.'" *Agence France-Presse*, August 19, 2008. http://www.lapresse.ca/international/200809/08/01-664254-la-BBC-et-la-VOA-accusees-par-kigali-de-detruire-lunite-des-rwandais.php.

Behuria, Pritish. "Centralising Rents and Dispersing Power While Pursuing Development? Exploring the Strategic Uses of Military Firms in Rwanda." *Review of African Political Economy* 43, no. 150 (2016): 630–647.

Bell, Duncan, ed. *Memory, Trauma and World Politics: Reflections on the Relationship between Past and Present*. Basingstoke, UK: Palgrave Macmillan, 2006.

Bell, Duncan S. A. *Memory, Trauma and World Politics: Reflections on the Relationship between Past and Present*. Basingstoke, UK: Palgrave Macmillan, 2010.

Ben-Amos, Avner, Ilana Bet-El, and Moshe Tlamim. "Holocaust Day and Memorial Day in Israeli Schools: Ceremonies, Education and History." *Israel Studies* 4, no. 1 (1999): 258–284.

Beoku-Betts, Josephine. "When Black Is Not Enough: Doing Field Research among Gullah Women." *NWSA Journal* 6, no. 3 (1994): 413–433.

Bergson, Henri. *Matter and Memory*. Hong Kong: Casimo Classics, 2007. First published New York: G. Allen; Macmillan, 1912.

Berlins, Marcel. "Victims of the Holocaust Get a Memorial Day. Victims of Other Atrocities Do Not. Isn't It Time We Dropped the Whole Idea?" *Guardian*, September 14, 2005. https://www.theguardian.com/theguardian/2005/sep/14/features2.g2.

Bernal, V. "Eritrea on-Line: Diaspora, Cyberspace, and the Public Sphere." *American Ethnologist* 32, no. 4 (2005): 660–675.

Berry, Marie E. "From Violence to Mobilization: Women, War, and Threat in Rwanda." *Mobilization* 20, no. 2 (2015): 135–156.

Berry, Marie E. *War, Women, and Power from Violence to Mobilization in Rwanda and Bosnia-Herzegovina*. Cambridge: Cambridge University Press, 2018.

Berry, Marie E. "When Bright Futures Fade: Paradoxes of Women's Empowerment in Rwanda." *Signs: Journal of Women in Culture and Society* 41, no. 1 (2015): 1–27.

Berthold, Molden. "Resistant Pasts versus Mnemonic Hegemony: On the Power Relations of Collective Memory." *Memory Studies* 9, no. 2 (2016): 125–142.

Bickford, Louis, Patricia Karam, Hassan Mneimneh, and Patrick Pierce. *Documenting Truth*. New York: International Center for Transitional Justice, 2009. https://www.ictj.org/sites/default/files/ICTJ-DAG-Global-Documenting-Truth-2009-English.pdf.

"Bizimana: Ubwami si bwo bwateje Inzangano mu Banyarwanda. Kuba harategekaga Abatutsi byari umuco." YouTube video, 49:19. Real Talk Channel, 2020. https://www.youtube.com/watch?v=jDzSpV01Gi8.

Bizimana, Jean Demascène. *L'Eglise et le genocide au Rwanda: les peres blancs et le negationnisme*. Paris: Editions L'Harmattan, 2001.

Bizimungu, Pasteur. "Report on the Reflection Meetings Held in the Office of the President of the Republic from May 1998 to March 1999." Kigali: Republic of Rwanda, Office of the President of the Republic (1999).

Bloomfield, Sean, and Immaculee Ilibagiza, dir. *If Only We Had Listened*. 2011; Kigali: Stella Mar Films, 2011. DVD.

Bobbio, Norberto. "Gramsci and the Concept of Civil Society." In *Civil Society and the State: New European Perspectives*, edited by John Keane, 73–99. London: Verso, 1988.

Bolin, Annalisa. "Imagining Genocide Heritage: Material Modes of Development and Preservation in Rwanda." *Journal of Material Culture* 25, no. 2 (2019): 196–219.

Bolin, Annalisa. "On the Side of Light: Performing Morality at Rwanda's Genocide Memorials." *Journal of Conflict Archaeology* 7, no. 3 (2012): 199–207.

Boothman, Derek. "The Sources for Gramsci's Concept of Hegemony." *Rethinking Marxism* 20, no. 2 (2008): 201–215.

Bouka, Yolande. "Nacibazo, 'No Problem': Moving Behind the Official Discourse of Post-genocide Justice in Rwanda." In *Emotional and Ethical Challenges for Field Research in Africa: The Story Behind the Findings*, edited by Susan Thomson, An Ansoms, and Jude Murison, 107–122. New York: Palgrave Macmillan, 2013.

Bourdon, Jérôme. "Media Remembering: The Contributions of Life-Story Methodology to Memory/Media Research." In *On Media Memory: Collective Memory in a New Media Age*, edited by Motti Neiger, Oren Meyers, and Eyal Zandberg, 62–76. New York: Palgrave Macmillan, 2011.

Braeckman, Colette. "Rwanda: Deux diplomates Belges jugés indésirables par Kigali ont regagné Bruxelles." *Le Soir* (Bruxelles), June 1, 2020. https://plus.lesoir.be/304340/arti

cle/2020-06-01/rwanda-deux-diplomates-belges-juges-indesirables-par-kigali-ont-regagne.

Brandstetter, Anna-Maria. *Contested Pasts: The Politics of Remembrance in Post-genocide Rwanda*. Wassenaar, Netherlands: NIAS, 2010.

Brauman, Rony, Stephen Smith, and Claudine Vidal. "Politique de terreur et privilège d'impunité au Rwanda." *Esprit* 8, no. 9 (2000): 147–161.

Breed, Ananda. *Performing the Nation: Genocide, Justice, Reconciliation*. London: Seagull Books, 2013.

Brett, Sebastian, Louis Bickford, Liz Ševčenko, and Marcela Rios. "Memorialization and Democracy: State Policy and Civic Action." From the international conference Memorialization and Democracy, International Center for Transitional Justice, Santiago, Chile, June 20–22, 2007.

Bright, Eric. "MTN Launches Portable Renewable Energy System." *New Times* (Kigali), January 29, 2013. http://allafrica.com/stories/201301300035.html.

Brockmeier, Jens. *Beyond the Archive: Memory, Narrative, and the Autobiographical Process*. Oxford, UK: Oxford University Press, 2018.

Brockmeier, Jens. "Remembering and Forgetting: Narrative as Cultural Memory." *Culture & Psychology* 8, no. 1 (2002): 15–43.

Brockmeier, Jens. "Texts and Other Symbolic Spaces." *Mind, Culture, and Activity* 8 (2001): 215–230.

Brown, Alrick, dir. *Kinyarwanda*. 2011; Alrick Brown, Tommy Oliver, and Darren Dean, prod. 1:40:00. Film/.

Brown, Sara E. "Female Perpetrators of the Rwandan Genocide." *International Feminist Journal of Politics* 16, no. 3 (2014): 448–469.

Brubaker, Rogers, and Margit Feischmidt. "1848 in 1998: The Politics of Commemoration in Hungary, Romania, and Slovakia." *Comparative Studies in Society and History* 44, no. 4 (2002): 700–744.

Buckley-Zistel, Susanne. "Development Assistance and Conflict Assessment Methodology." *Journal for Conflict, Security and Development* 1 (2005): 119–127.

Buckley-Zistel, Susanne. "Remembering to Forget: Chosen Amnesia as a Strategy for Local Coexistence in Post-genocide Rwanda." *Africa: Journal of the International African Institute* 76, no. 2 (2006): 131–150.

Bucyensenge, Jean Pierre. "How Tending to a Memorial Site Helps Unite Genocide Survivors, Perpetrators." *New Times* (Kigali), January 30, 2014.

Burke, Peter. "History as Social Memory." In *Memory: History, Culture and the Mind*, edited by Thomas Butler, 97–113. Oxford, UK: Basil Blackwell, 1989.

Burnet, Jennie E. "Gender Balance and the Meanings of Women in Governance in Post-genocide Rwanda." *African Affairs* 107, no. 428 (2008): 361–386.

Burnet, Jennie E. *Genocide Lives in Us: Women, Memory, and Silence in Rwanda*. Madison: University of Wisconsin Press, 2012.

Burnet, Jennie E. "The Injustice of Local Justice: Truth, Reconciliation, and Revenge in Rwanda." *Genocide Studies and Prevention* 3, no. 2 (2008): 173–193.

Cameron, Colin. "'The Second Betrayal?' Commemorating the 10th Anniversary of the Rwandan Genocide." Paper presented at the 26th Annual Conference, African Studies Association of Australasia and the Pacific, 'Africa on a Global Stage,' Flinders University, October 1–3, 2003.

Carter, Nancy, Denise Bryant-Lukosius, Alba DiCenso, Jennifer Blythe, and Alan J. Neville. "The Use of Triangulation in Qualitative Research." *Oncology Nursing Forum* 41, no. 5 (2014): 545–547.
Casey, Edward S. *Remembering: A Phenomenological Study*. Bloomington: Indiana University Press, 1987.
Césaire, Aimé. *Discourse on Colonialism*. Paris: Présence Africaine, 1955.
Chakravarty, Anuradha. "Inter-Ethnic Marriages, the Survival of Women, and the Logics of Genocide in Rwanda." *Genocide Studies and Prevention* 2, no. 3 (2007): 235–248.
Chakravarty, Anuradha. *Investing in Authoritarian Rule: Punishment and Patronage in Rwanda's Gacaca Courts for Genocide Crimes*. Cambridge: Cambridge University Press, 2016.
Chakravarty, Anuradha. "Navigating the Middle Ground: The Political Values of Ordinary Hutu in Post-genocide Rwanda." *African Affairs* 113, no. 451 (2014): 232–253.
Chan, Kimberly. "Landscaping for Hope: Further Development of the Kigali Memorial Center." Undergraduate thesis, University of California Davis, 2007.
Chemouni, Benjamin, and Assumpta Mugiraneza. "Ideology and Interests in the Rwandan Patriotic Front: Singing the Struggle in Pre-genocide Rwanda." *African Affairs* 119, no. 474 (2019): 115–140.
Chilisa, Bagele. *Indigenous Research Methodologies*. Thousand Oaks, CA: Sage, 2019.
Chilisa, Bagele, Thenjiwe Emily Major, and Kelne Khudu-Petersen. "Community Engagement with a Postcolonial, African-Based Relational Paradigm." *Qualitative Research* 17, no. 3 (2017): 326–339.
Chrétien, Jean-Pierre. *Rwanda: Les médias du génocide*. Paris: Editions Karthala, 2002.
Chrétien, Jean-Pierre, Jean-François Duparquier, Marcel Kabanda, and Joseph Ngarambe. *Rwanda: Les médias du génocide*. Paris: Editions Karthala, 1995.
Clark, Philip. "Bringing the Peasants Back in, Again: State Power and Local Agency in Rwanda's Gacaca Courts." *Journal of Eastern African Studies* 8, no. 2 (2014): 193–213.
Clark, Philip. *The Gacaca Courts, Post-genocide Justice and Reconciliation in Rwanda: Justice without Lawyers*. Cambridge: Cambridge University Press, 2011.
Clark, Philip. "The Legacy of Rwanda's Gacaca Courts." *Think Africa Press*, March 23, 2012. https://web.archive.org/web/20120326005430/http://thinkafricapress.com/rwanda/legacy-Gacaca-courts-genocide.
Clark, Philip, and Zachary D. Kaufman, eds. *After Genocide: Transitional Justice, Post-conflict Reconstruction and Reconciliation in Rwanda and Beyond*. Oxford, UK: Oxford University Press, 2013.
CNLG (La Commission Nationale de Lutte contre le Genocide [National Commission for the Fight against Genocide]). Icyizere. *Yumpu*, February 21, 2013, https://www.yumpu.com/xx/document/read/10166717/icyizere-no20pdf-cnlg.
"CNLG Calls for Companies to Support Survivors." *IGIHE*, January 21, 2012. http://en.igihe.com/news/cnlg-calls-for-companies-to-support-survivors.
Cobb, Sara B. *Speaking of Violence: The Politics and Poetics of Narrative Dynamics in Conflict Resolution*. Oxford, UK: Oxford University Press, 2013.
Cohen, Stanley. *States of Denial: Knowing about Atrocities and Suffering*. Cambridge, UK: Polity Press, 2001.
Condliffe, Jamie. "Flaming Drives Online Social Networks." *New Scientist*, 2010. http://www.newscientist.com/article/dn19821-flaming-drives-online-social-networks.html#.VQoPWmd0yUl.

Connerton, Paul. "Seven Types of Forgetting." *Memory Studies Memory Studies* 1, no. 1 (2008): 59–71.
"Corruption in Farg." *Rugari* 2, no. 44 (April 2009).
Crane, Susan A. *Museums and Memory*. Palo Alto, CA: Stanford University Press, 2000.
Crownshaw, Rick, ed. *Transcultural Memory*. New York: Routledge, 2016.
Crumley, Carole L. "Exploring Venues of Social Memory." In *Social Memory and History: Anthropological Perspectives*, edited by Jacob J. Climo and Maria G. Cattell, 39–52. Lantham, MD: AltaMira Press, 2002.
Curtis, Devon E. A. "What Is Our Research For? Responsibility, Humility and the Production of Knowledge About Burundi." *Africa Spectrum Africa Spectrum* 54, no. 1 (2019): 4–21.
Dallaire, Roméo, and Brent Beardsley. *Shake Hands with the Devil: The Failure of Humanity in Rwanda*. New York: Carroll & Graf, 2005.
Daniel, Levy, and Sznaider Natan. "Memory Unbound: The Holocaust and the Formation of Cosmopolitan Memory." *European Journal of Social Theory* 5, no. 1 (2002): 87–106.
De La Victoire, Dusabemungu Ange. "Religious Institution Urged to Be Part of Genocide Commemoration." *IGIHE* (Kigali), March 28, 2013. http://en.igihe.com/news/religious-institutions-urged-to-be-part-of.html.
De Saint-Exupéry, Patrick. *L'Inavouable: La France au Rwanda*. Paris: Editions Les arènes, 2004.
Des Forges, Alison Liebhafsky. *Defeat Is the Only Bad News: Rwanda under Musinga, 1897–1931*. Madison: University of Wisconsin Press, 2014.
Des Forges, Alison Liebhafsky. *"Leave None to Tell the Story": Genocide in Rwanda*. New York: Human Rights Watch, 2014.
Dewitt, David. "Linked Stories from the Months of the Rwanda Massacre." *New York Times*, December 1, 2011. http://www.nytimes.com/2011/12/02/movies/kinyarwanda-about-1994-genocide-of-tutsis-in-rwanda.html?_r=0.
Donà, Giorgia. "'Situated Bystandership' During and after the Rwandan Genocide." *Journal of Genocide Research* 20, no. 1 (2018): 1–19.
Doss, Erika. *Memorial Mania: Public Feeling in America*. Chicago: University of Chicago Press, 2012.
Dumas, Helen, and Rémi Korman. "Espaces de la mémoire du génocide des Tutsi au Rwanda." *Mémoriaux et lieux de mémoire, Afrique contemporaine* 238, no. 2 (2011): 11–27.
Dusabemungu, Ange de la Victoire. "It's Grey Not Purple for Genocide Commemoration." *IGIHE*, August 2, 2013. http://en.igihe.com/news/it-s-grey-not-purple-for-genocide-commemoration.html.
Eastmond, Marita, and Johanna Mannergren Selimovic. "Silence as Possibility in Postwar Everyday Life." *International Journal of Transitional Justice* 6, no. 3 (2012): 502–524.
Edwards, Jason A. "The Mission of Healing: Kofi Annan's Failed Apology." *Atlantic Journal of Communication* 16, no. 2 (2008): 88–104.
Edy, Jill A. "Journalistic Uses of Collective Memory." *Journal of Communication* 49, no. 2 (1999): 71–85.
Eltringham, Nigel. "The Past Is Elsewhere." In *Remaking Rwanda: State Building and Human Rights after Mass Violence*, edited by Scott Straus and Lars Waldorf, 269–282. Madison: University of Wisconsin Press, 2011.
Erll, Astrid. "Travelling Memory." *Parallax* 17, no. 4 (2011): 4–18.

Eyre, Anne. "Remembering: Community Commemoration after Disaster." In *Handbook of Disaster Research*, edited by Havidán Rodríguez, Enrico L. Quarantelli, and Russell Dynes. Handbooks of Sociology and Social Research, 441–455. New York: Springer, 2007.

Fanon, Frantz. *Black Skin White Masks*. New York: Grove Press, 1952.

Fassin, Didier, and Richard Rechtman. *The Empire of Trauma: An Inquiry into the Condition of Victimhood*. Princeton, NJ: Princeton University Press, 2009.

Fisher, Jonathan. "Writing about Rwanda since the Genocide: Knowledge, Power and 'Truth.'" *Journal of Intervention and Statebuilding* 9, no. 1 (2015): 134–145.

"Forgiveness; a Choice Not a Command." *New Times* (Kigali), May 10, 2009. https://www.newtimes.co.rw/section/read/86651.

Forty, Adrian, and Susanne Küchler, eds. *The Art of Forgetting*. Oxford, UK: Berg, 2001.

Fox, Nicole. *After Genocide: Memory and Reconciliation in Rwanda*. Madison: University of Wisconsin Press, 2021.

Frankema, Ewout, and Frans Buelens. *Colonial Exploitation and Economic Development: The Belgian Congo and the Netherlands Indies Compared*. London: Routledge, 2015.

Freeman, Mark. "Discerning the History Inscribed Within." In *Handbook of Culture and Memory*, edited by Brady Wagoner, 65–84. New York: Oxford University Press, 2017.

Freeman, Mark. *Hindsight: The Promise and Peril of Looking Backward*. New York: Oxford University Press, 2010.

Freeman, Mark. "Open Wounds: Discerning, Owning, and Narrating Deep History." In *Race, Rage, and Resistance*, edited by Mark Freeman, 14–33. New York: Routledge, 2019.

Friedman, Rebekka. *Competing Memories: Truth and Reconciliation in Sierra Leone and Peru*. Cambridge: Cambridge University Press, 2017.

Fujii, Lee Ann. *Killing Neighbors: Webs of Violence in Rwanda*. Ithaca, NY: Cornell University Press, 2011.

Fujii, Lee Ann. "Shades of Truth and Lies: Interpreting Testimonies of War and Violence." *Journal of Peace Research* 47, no. 2 (2010): 231–241.

Gahongayire, Liberata. "The Contribution of Memory in Healing and Preventing Genocide in Rwanda." *International Journal of Innovation and Applied Studies* 10, no. 1 (2015): 109–118.

Gakwenzire, Philibert. "Contribution à la gestion de la mémoire du génocide des du Rwanda en 1994" (MA, Université Senghor, 2005).

Gallen, James. "Jesus Wept: The Roman Catholic Church, Child Sexual Abuse and Transitional Justice." *International Journal of Transitional Justice* 10, no. 2 (2016): 332–349.

Gansemans, Jos. *Les Instruments de musique du Rwanda: Etude ethnomusicologique*. Tervuren, Belgium: Musée royal de l'Afrique centrale, 1988.

Garrison, Ann. "Rwanda Shuts Down Independent Press." *Rwandinfo*, April 14, 2010. https://rwandinfo.com/eng/rwanda-shuts-down-independent-press-ahead-of-presidential-elections/.

Gasana, Fiona. "The 18th Commemoration of the Tutsi Genocide." *IGIHE*, April 2, 2012. http://en.igihe.com/news/the-18th-commemoration-of-the-tutsi-genocide.

Gatwa, Tharcisse. *The Churches and Ethnic Ideology in the Rwandan Crises, 1900–1994*. Oxford, UK: Oxford Center for Mission Studies, 2005.

Gearoid, Millar. "Performative Memory and Re-Victimization: Truth-Telling and Provocation in Sierra Leone." *Memory Studies* 8, no. 2 (2015): 242–254.

Gedi, Noa, and Yigal Elam. "Collective Memory: What Is It?" *History and Memory* 8, no. 1 (1996): 30–50.
Geismar, Haidy. "Building Sites of Memory: The Ground Zero Sonic Memorial Sound Walk." *Fabrications* 15, no. 2 (2005): 1–13.
Giblin, John. "The Performance of International Diplomacy at Kigali Memorial Centre, Rwanda." *Journal of African Cultural Heritage Studies* 1, no. 1 (2017): 49–67.
Gilbert, Catherine. *From Surviving to Living: Voice, Trauma and Witness in Rwanda Women's Writing.* Montpellier, France: Presses universitaires de la Méditerranée, 2018.
Gillies, J., R. A. Neimeyer, and E. Milman. "The Meaning of Loss Codebook: Construction of a System for Analyzing Meanings Made in Bereavement." *Death Studies* 38, no. 4 (2014): 207–216.
Gilroy, Paul. *Postcolonial Melancholia.* New York: Columbia University Press, 2005.
Gishoma, Darius. "Crises traumatiques collectives d'ihahamuka lors des commémorations du génocide des Tutsi: Aspects cliniques et perspectives thérapeutiques" (PhD, University of Louvain, 2014). http://hdl.handle.net/2078.1/143580.
Gishoma, Darius, and Jean-Luc Brackelaire. "Quand le corps abrite l'inconcevable: Comment dire le bouleversement dont témoignent les corps au Rwanda?" *Cahiers de psychologie clinique* 30, no. 1 (2008): 159–183.
Gishoma, D., J. L. Brackelaire, N. Munyandamutsa, J. Mujawayezu, A. A. Mohand, and Y. Kayiteshonga. "Supportive-expressive group therapy for people experiencing collective traumatic crisis during the genocide commemoration period in Rwanda: Impact and implications." *Journal of Social and Political Psychology* 2, no. 1 (2014): 469–488.
"Gisozi Memorial Site: Voices of the Past Immortalized." *IGIHE* (Kigali), December 11, 2012. http://en.igihe.com/arts-culture/gisozi-memorial-site-voices-of-the-past.html.
Gourevitch, Philip. "The Life After: Fifteen Years after the Genocide in Rwanda, the Reconciliation Defies Expectations." *New Yorker*, May 4, 2009. http://www.newyorker.com/magazine/2009/05/04/the-life-after.
Gourevitch, Philip. *We Wish to Inform You That Tomorrow We Will Be Killed with Our Families: Stories from Rwanda.* London: Picador, 1998.
Gov.UK, Department of International Development and the Rt. Hon. Lynne Featherstone. "UK International Development Minister Lynne Featherstone Visits Ntarama Genocide Memorial Site." June 2, 2014. https://www.gov.uk/government/news/uk-international-development-minister-lynne-featherstone-visits-ntarama-genocide-memorial-site
Government of Rwanda. *An Integrated ICT-led Socio-Economic Development Policy and Plan for Rwanda, 2001–2005.* Kigali: Republic of Rwanda, 2001. https://www.minict.gov.rw/index.php?eID=dumpFile&t=f&f=1107&token=19a0fd85a4bcc12c0543ac8c0dc3d969a358b1d8
Gowan, Jennifer A. "Fanning the Flames: A Musicians Role in the Rwandan Genocide." *Nota Bene: Canadian Undergraduate Journal of Musicology* 4, no. 2 (2012). Accessed March 15, 2023. https://ojs.lib.uwo.ca/index.php/notabene/article/view/6576
Gowing, Nik. "New Challenges and Problems for Information Management in Complex Emergencies: Ominous Lessons from the Great Lakes and Eastern Zaire in Late 1996 and Early 1997" (paper presented at the Dispatches from Disaster Zones, Oxford, UK, May 28, 1998).
Grant, Andrea Mariko. "Bringing the Daily Mail to Africa: Entertainment Websites and the Creation of a Digital Youth Public in Post-genocide Rwanda." *Journal of Eastern African Studies* 13, no. 1 (2019): 106–123.

Grant, Andrea Mariko. "Ecumenism in Question: Rwanda's Contentious Post-genocide Religious Landscape." *Journal of Southern African Studies* 44, no. 2 (2018): 221–238.

Grant, Andrea Mariko. "The Making of a Superstar: The Politics of Playback and Live Performance in Post-genocide Rwanda." *Africa* 87, no. 1 (2017): 155–179.

Guichaoua, André, and René Dégni-Ségui. *Rwanda, De La Guerre Au Génocide Les Politiques Criminelles Au Rwanda (1990–1994)*. Paris: La Découverte, 2010.

Guyer, Sara. "Rwanda's Bones." *Boundary 2* 36, no. 2 (2009): 155–175.

Halbwachs, Maurice. *On Collective Memory*. Translated by Lewis A. Coser. Chicago: University of Chicago Press, 2008.

Halsey, Katie, and Jane Slinn. *The Concept and Practice of Conversation in the Long Eighteenth Century, 1688–1848*. Newcastle, UK: Cambridge Scholars, 2008.

Hammack, Phillip L. "Narrative and the Politics of Meaning." *Narrative Inquiry* 21, no. 2 (2011): 311–318.

Hawkes, Martine. "Transmitting Genocide: Genocide and Art." *Media and Culture Journal* 9, no. 1 (2006). http://journal.media-culture.org.au/0603/09-hawkes.php.

Henley, Jon. "Scar Tissue." *Guardian*, October 31, 2007. http://www.theguardian.com/world/2007/oct/31/rwanda.theatre.

Hertefelt, Marcel D., and André Coupez. *La royauté sacrée de l'ancien Rwanda: Texte, traduction et commentaire de son rituel*. Tervuren, Belgium: Koninklijk Museum voor Midden-Afrika, 1997.

Hilker, Lyndsay McLean. "Rwanda's 'Hutsi': Intersections of Ethnicity and Violence in the Lives of Youth of 'Mixed' Heritage." *Identities: Global Studies in Culture and Power* 19, no. 2 (2012): 229–247.

Hilsum, Lindsey. "Rwanda Genocide." *Witness History*, 9:00. BBC World Service. April 6, 2010. http://www.BBC.co.uk/programmes/p006xzww.

Hintjens, Helen. "Post-genocide Identity Politics in Rwanda." *Ethnicities* 8, no. 1 (2008): 5–41.

Hirsch, Marianne. *Family Frames: Photography, Narrative, and Postmemory*. London: Harvard University Press, 2014.

Hoelscher, Steven, and Derek H. Alderman. "Memory and Place: Geographies of a Critical Relationship." *Social & Cultural Geography* 5, no. 3 (2004): 347–355.

Hoffman, Eva. *After Such Knowledge: A Meditation on the Aftermath of the Holocaust*. London: Vintage, 2005.

Holmes, Georgina. "Rwanda and the Commonwealth: The Evolution of the BBC's Institutional Narrative on the 1994 Rwandan Genocide." *Round Table* 100, no. 416 (2011): 519–530.

Holmner, Marlene, and Johannes J. Britz. "The Road Less Travelled: A Critical Reflection on Infrastructure Development in Africa from a Perspective of the New Economics of Information." *Mousaion* 29, no. 1 (2011): 1–16.

Hoskins, Andrew. *Televising War: From Vietnam to Iraq*. London: Continuum, 2010.

Hoskins, Andrew, and Ben O'Loughlin. *War and Media: The Emergence of Diffused War*. Cambridge, UK: Polity Press, 2012.

Human Rights Watch. "Shattered Lives: Sexual Violence during the Rwandan Genocide and Its Aftermath." September 24, 1996. http://www.hrw.org/reports/1996/09/24/shattered-lives.

Huyssen, Andreas. "Trauma and Memory: A New Imaginary of Temporality." In *World Memory: Personal Trajectories in Global Time*, edited by Jill Bennett and Rosanne Kennedy, 16–29. Basingstoke, UK: Palgrave Macmillan, 2003.

Huyssen, Andreas. *Twilight Memories: Marking Time in a Culture of Amnesia*. New York: Routledge, 1995.

Ibreck, Rachel. "International Constructions of National Memories: The Aims and Effects of Foreign Donors' Support for Genocide Remembrance in Rwanda." *Journal of Intervention and Statebuilding* 7, no. 2 (2013): 149–169.

Ibreck, Rachel. "The Politics of Mourning: Survivor Contributions to Memorials in Postgenocide Rwanda." *Memory Studies* 3, no. 4 (2010): 330–343.

Ibreck, Rachel. "A Time of Mourning: The Politics of Commemorating the Tutsi Genocide in Rwanda." In *Public Memory, Public Media and the Politics of Justice*, edited by Philip Lee and Pradip N. Thomas, 98–120. Hound Mills, UK: Palgrave Macmillan, 2014.

"Ibuka Strategic Plan, 2011–2015." 2011. http://survivors-fund.org.uk/wp-content/uploads/2011/11/IBUKA-Strategic-Plan-2011-2015.pdf.

Ikaze Iwacu. *Ngira Ipfunwe Ryo Kwitwa Umuhutu Eduard Bampoyiki*, August 10, 2013, YouTube, 13:32, http://www.youtube.com/watch?v=bykhj7mO2wI.

Ilibagiza, Immaculée, and Steve Erwin. *Left to Tell: Discovering God Amidst the Rwandan Holocaust*. Carlsbad, CA: Hay House, 2006.

Ilibagiza, Immaculée, and Steve Erwin. *Our Lady of Kibeho: Mary Speaks to the World from the Heart of Africa*. Carlsbad, CA: Hay House, 2012.

Imam, Ayesha M., Amina Mama, and Fatima Sow, eds. *Engendering African Social Sciences*. Dakar, Senegal: CODESRIA Book Series, 1999.

Imbs, Françoise, and Florent Piton. *Emmanuel Ntezimana (1947–1995): Être historien et citoyen engagé au Rwanda*. Toulouse, France: Presses universitaires du Midi, 2021.

Ingabire, Chantal Marie Ingabire, Grace Kagoyire, Diogene Karangwa, Noella Ingabire, Nicolas Habarugira, Angela Jansen, and Annemiek Richters. "Trauma Informed Restorative Justice through Community Based Sociotherapy in Rwanda." *Intervention* 15, no. 3 (2017): 241–253.

Ingelaere, Bert. "Do We Understand Life after Genocide? Center and Periphery in the Construction of Knowledge in Postgenocide Rwanda." *African Studies Review* 53, no. 1 (2010): 41–59.

Ingelaere, Bert. *Inside Rwanda's Gacaca Courts: Seeking Justice after Genocide*. Madison: University of Wisconsin Press, 2018.

"Institute of National Museums of Rwanda." http://www.museum.gov.rw/index.php?id=2.

International Labour Organization. "Rwanda (7) General Provisions." Natlex Database. http://www.ilo.org/dyn/natlex/natlex4.detail?p_lang=en&p_isn=71583&p_count=7&p_classification=01.

International Telecommunication Union. "Individuals Using the Internet, 2000–2012." 2014. http://www.itu.int/en/ITU-D/Statistics/Pages/stat/default.aspx.

Iribagiza, Glory. "Autopsy Confirms Kizito Died by Suicide." *New Times* (Kigali), February 26, 2020. https://www.newtimes.co.rw/news/autopsy-confirms-kizito-died-suicide.

Jacobs, Janet. "2010 Paul Hanly Furfey Lecture: Sacred Space and Collective Memory: Memorializing Genocide at Sites of Terror." *Sociology of Religion* 72, no. 2 (2011): 154–165.

Jakaswanga. "Artists in Politics: Kizito Mihigo's Fall in Rwanda." Jukwaa: Kenyan Discussion Platform. May 3, 2014. http://jukwaa.proboards.com/thread/9017/artists-politics-kizito-mihigos-rwanda.

James, E. K. Parker. *Acoustic Jurisprudence: Listening to the Trial of Simon Bikindi*. Oxford, UK: Oxford University Press, 2015.

Jarvis, Jill. *Decolonizing Memory: Algeria and the Politics of Testimony.* Durham, NC: Duke University Press, 2021.

Jastrow, Morris, Jr., Crawford Howell Toy, Marcus Jastrow, Louis Ginzburg, and Kaufman Kohler. "Ashes." *The Jewish Encyclopedia.* Accessed March 15, 2023. http://www.jewishencyclopedia.com/articles/1944-ashes.

Jastudio360°. "Invo N'imvano Gusaba Imbabazi Kw'abahutu." YouTube, 57:12. 2013. http://www.youtube.com/watch?v=56QPn7LzQK0.

Jelin, Elizabeth. *Silences, Visibility and Agency: Ethnicity, Class and Gender in Public Memorialization.* ICTJ Research Brief. New York: International Center for Transnational Justice, 2009.

Jessee, Erin. "The Danger of a Single Story: Iconic Stories in the Aftermath of the 1994 Rwandan Genocide." *Memory Studies* 10, no. 2 (2017): 144–163.

Jessee, Erin. *Negotiating Genocide in Rwanda: The Politics of History.* New York: Palgrave Macmillan, 2019.

Jessee, Erin. "Promoting Reconciliation through Exhuming and Identifying Victims of the 1994 Rwandan Genocide." Africa Initiative Discussion Paper Series 4. Waterloo, ON, Canada: Center for International Governance Innovation, 2012.

Jessee, Erin. "Rwandan Women No More: Female Génocidaires in the Aftermath of the 1994 Rwandan Genocide." *Conflict and Society* 1, no. 1 (2015): 60–80.

Jessee, Erin, and Sarah E. Watkins. "Good Kings, Bloody Tyrants, and Everything in Between: Representations of the Monarchy in Post-genocide Rwanda." *History in Africa* 41 (2014): 35–62.

Jinks, Rebecca. *Representing Genocide: The Holocaust as Paradigm?* London: Bloomsbury, 2016.

Jones, Adam. "Gender and Genocide in Rwanda." *Journal of Genocide Research* 4, no. 1 (2002): 65–94.

Jones, Marilyn. "Difference Maker: Jean-Paul Samputu Practices Forgiveness—Even for His Father's Killer." *Christian Science Monitor*, July 19, 2013. http://www.csmonitor.com/World/Making-a-difference/2013/0719/Jean-Paul-Samputu-practices-forgiveness-even-for-his-father-s-killer.

Jordan, Paul William. *The Easy Day Was Yesterday: The Extreme Life of an S.A.S Soldier.* Newport, NSW, Australia: Big Sky, 2012.

Juday, Alyssa. "Construction amidst Binaries—The Remaking of a Remembered Rwanda." *Trialog* 118/119, no. 3–4 (2014): 74–79.

Kabanda, Marcel. "Droit des archives et droits de l'homme." *La Gazette des archives* 206, no. 2 (2007): 97–105.

Kagame, Alexis. *Un Abrégé de l'histoire du Rwanda.* Butare, Rwanda: Editions universitaires du Rwanda, 1972.

Kagame, Alexis. *Les Milices Du Rwanda Précolonial.* Brussels, Belgium: Académie royale des sciences coloniales, Classe des sciences morales et politiques, 1963.

Kagame, Alexis. *Les organisations socio-familiales de l'ancien Rwanda.* Brussels, Belgium: Académie Royale des Sciences Coloniales, 1954.

Kagame, Paul. *Paul Kagame's Speech at the 7th Anniversary of the Genocide in Rwanda at the Nyakibanda Memorial Site.* Rukumberi, Rwanda: Government of Rwanda, 2001.

Kagame, Paul. "17th Commemoration of the Genocide Against the Tutsi." YouTube video, 4:54. 2011. http://www.youtube.com/watch?v=xUk6zBUUC0w.

Kagame, Paul. "Speech by His Excellency Paul Kagame." Paul Kagame, July 4, 2009. https://www.paulkagame.com/liberation-day-kigali-4-july-2009/

Kamanzi, M. S. "Rwanda: Quelle Reconciliation?" *Etudes* 400, no. 5 (2004): 581–586.
Kamo, Chris. "BBC: Abanyarwanda Bamaze Kuvumbura Ikinyoma Cya Kagame Mugushaka Gucecekesha." YouTube. 2014. https://www.youtube.com/watch?v=5QMA04FB0lo.
Kamukama, Dixon. *Rwanda Conflict: Its Roots and Regional Implications*. Kampala, Uganda: Fountain, 1998.
Kanimba, Célestin. "Préservation de la mémoire du genocide: Roles, actions et strategies." *Etudes Rwandaises* (September 2015): 128–147.
Kantengwa, Sharon. "Remembering Is a Healing Remedy for Genocide Survivors." *New Times* (Kigali), April 7, 2016. https://www.newtimes.co.rw/section/read/198752.
Kanyesigye, Frank. "Rwanda: Orinfor to Censure [i.e., Censor] Shocking Genocide Images." *All Africa*, March 22, 2011. http://allafrica.com/stories/201103220859.html.
Karake, Mweusi. "Lack of International Aid to Survivors." *Imvaho Nshya* (Kigali), Apri 10–16, 1995.
Karake, Mweusi. "Spécial génocide." *Imvaho Nshya* (Kigali), April 24–30, 1995.
Karkowska, M. "On the Usefulness of Aleida and Jan Assmann's Concept of Cultural Memory for Studying Local Communities in Contemporary Poland: The Case of Olsztyn." *Polish Sociological Review* 2013, no. 3 (2013): 369–388.
Karuhanga, James. "Government Suspends BBC Programmes." *New Times* (Kigali), April 26, 2009. http://allafrica.com/stories/200904260007.html.
Kazibwe, Andrew Israel. "Actor-Cum-Politician Bamporiki Stars in Umutoma—A Love Story." *East African* (Nairobi), June 27, 2014. http://www.theeastafrican.co.ke/Rwanda/Lifestyle/Actor-cum-politician-Bamporiki-stars-in-Umutoma-a-love-story-/-/1433242/2364116/-/m2n1et/-/index.html.
Kerstens, Paul. "'Voice and Give Voice': Dialectics between Fiction and History in Narratives on the Rwandan Genocide." *International Journal of Francophone Studies* 9, no. 1 (2006): 93–110.
Kimani, Martin. "For Rwandans, the Pope's Apology Must Be Unbearable." *Guardian*, May 29, 2010. http://www.guardian.co.uk/commentisfree/belief/2010/mar/29/pope-catholics-rwanda-genocide-church.
Kimonyo, Jean-Paul. *Rwanda's Popular Genocide: A Perfect Storm*. Boulder, CO: Lynne Rienner, 2015.
Kimonyo, Jean-Paul. *Transforming Rwanda: Challenges on the Road to Reconstruction*. Boulder, CO: Lynne Rienner, 2019.
King, Elisabeth. "From Data Problems to Data Points: Challenges and Opportunities of Research in Postgenocide Rwanda." *African Studies Review* 52, no. 3 (2009): 127–148.
King, Elisabeth. "Memory Controversies in Post-genocide Rwanda: Implications for Peacebuilding." *Genocide Studies and Prevention* 5, no. 3 (2010): 293–309.
King, Régine Uwibereyeho, and Izumi Sakamoto. "Disengaging from Genocide Harm-Doing and Healing Together between Perpetrators, Bystanders, and Victims in Rwanda." *Peace and Conflict: Journal of Peace Psychology* 21, no. 3 (2015): 378–394.
Kinzer, Stephen. *A Thousand Hills: Rwanda's Rebirth and the Man Who Dreamed It*. Hoboken, NJ: John Wiley & Sons, 2008.
Kitch, Carolyn L. *Pages from the Past: History and Memory in American Magazines*. Chapel Hill, NC: University of North Carolina Press, 2005.
"Kizito Mihigo: Singer Found Dead in Rwandan Police Cell." *BBC News*. 2020. https://www.BBC.com/news/world-africa-51528526.

"Kizito Mihigo Yabonye Umukobwa Bazarushingana." *IGIHE* (Kigali), March 13, 2014. http://igihe.com/imyidagaduro/muzika/abahanzi/kizito-mihigo/amakuru/article/kizito-mihigo-yatangaje-ko-yabonye.

Knittel, Susanne C., and Sofia Forchieri. "Navigating Implication: An Interview with Michael Rothberg." *Journal of Perpetrator Research* 3, no. 1 (2020): 6–19.

Korman, Rémi. "Bury or Display? The Politics of Exhumation in Post-genocide Rwanda." In *Human Remains and Identification: Mass Violence, Genocide, and the 'Forensic Turn,'* edited by Élisabeth Gessat-Anstett and Jean-Marc Dreyfus, 203–220. Manchester, UK: Manchester University Press, 2017.

Korman, Rémi. "Commémorer Sur Les Ruines: L'État Rwandais face à la mort de masse dans l'après-coup du génocide (1994–2003)" (PhD, EHESS, 2020). http://www.theses.fr/2020EHES0135.

Korman, Rémi. "Indirimbo Z'icyunamo. Chanter La Mémoire Du Génocide." *Les Temps Modernes*, 4--5, no. 680–681 (2014): 350–361.

Korman, Rémi. "Le Rwanda face à ses morts ou les cimetières du génocide." In *Génocides et politiques mémorielles*, edited by F. Blum, 1–4. Paris: Centres d'histoires sociales du XXe siècle, 2011.

Korman, Rémi. "L'État Rwandais et la mémoire du génocide commémorer sur les ruines (1994–1996)." *Vingtième Siècle. Revue d'histoire* 122, no. 2 (2014): 87–93.

Korman, Rémi. "Mobilising the Dead? The Place of Bones and Corpses in the Commemoration of the Tutsi Genocide in Rwanda." *Human Remains and Violence: An Interdisciplinary Journal* 1, no. 2 (2015): 56–70.

"Kuba Abakoze Jenoside Batanga Ubuhamya Mu Kwibuka Ntibivugwaho Rumwe." *IGIHE* (Kigali), 2019. https://igihe.com/amakuru/u-rwanda/article/kuba-abakoze-jenoside-batanga-ubuhamya-mu-kwibuka-ntibivugwaho-rumwe.

Kuradusenge, Claudine. "Denied Victimhood and Contested Narratives: The Case of Hutu Diaspora." *Genocide Studies and Prevention* 10, no. 2 (2016): 59–75.

Kuya, Yanditswe. "Minisitiri W'intebe Ati 'Igitaramo Cya Kizito Mihigo Kiratanga Amasomo Ane." *IGIHE* (Kigali), April 17, 2012. http://igihe.com/imyidagaduro/muzika/abahanzi/kizito-mihigo/amakuru-137/minisitiri-w-intebe-ati-igitaramo-cya-kizito-mihigo-kiratanga-amasomo-ane.html.

Kwibuka, Eugene. "What Does 'Ndi Unuyarwanda' Mean to You?" *New Times* (Kigali), December 3, 2013. http://www.newtimes.co.rw/section/article/2013-12-03/71264/.

Lacey, Marc. "10 Years Later in Rwanda, the Dead Are Ever Present." *New York Times*, February 26, 2004. http://www.nytimes.com/2004/02/26/world/10-years-later-in-rwanda-the-dead-are-ever-present.html.

Laclau, Ernesto, and Chantal Mouffe. *Hegemony and Socialist Strategy: Towards a Radical Democratic Politics*. New York: Verso, 2014.

Landsberg, Alison. *Prosthetic Memory: The Transformation of American Remembrance in the Age of Mass Culture*. New York: Columbia University Press, 2006.

Lang, Kurt, and Gladys Engel Lang. "Collective Memory and the News." *Communication* 11 (1989): 123–129.

Lemarchand, René. *The Dynamics of Violence in Central Africa*. Philadelphia: University of Pennsylvania Press, 2009.

Lemarchand, René. "Genocide, Memory and Ethnic Reconciliation in Rwanda." *L'Afrique des Grands Lacs: Annuaire, 2006–2007* (2007): 21–30.

Lemarchand, René. "A History of Genocide in Rwanda." *Journal of African History* 43, no. 2 (2002): 307–311.

Lemarchand, René. *Rwanda and Burundi*. London: Pall Mall, 1970.
Lemarchand, René. "Rwanda: The Rationality of Genocide." *Issue: A Journal of Opinion* 23, no. 2 (1995): 8–11.
Lemarchand, René, and Maurice Niwese. "Mass Murder, the Politics of Memory and Post-genocide Reconstruction: The Cases of Rwanda and Burundi." In *After Mass Crime: Rebuilding States and Communities*, edited by Béatrice Pouligny, Simon Chesterman, and Albrecht Schnabel, 165–189. New York: United Nations University, 2007.
Lewis, Paul. "Rebels in Rwanda Said to Slay 3 Bishops and 10 Other Clerics." *New York Times*, June 10, 1994. http://www.nytimes.com/1994/06/10/world/rebels-in-rwanda-said-to-slay-3-bishops-and-10-other-clerics.html.
Li, Darryl. "Echoes of Violence: Considerations on Radio and Genocide in Rwanda." *Journal of Genocide Research* 6, no. 1 (2004): 9–27.
Liebermann, Yvonne. "Born Digital: The Black Lives Matter Movement and Memory after the Digital Turn." *Memory Studies* 14, no. 4 (2021): 713–732.
Linden, Ian, and Jane Linden. *Church and Revolution in Rwanda*. Manchester, UK: Manchester University Press, 1977.
Lischer, Sarah Kenyon. "Narrating Atrocity: Genocide Memorials, Dark Tourism, and the Politics of Memory." *Review of International Studies* 45, no. 5 (2019): 805–827.
Longman, Timothy. *Christianity and Genocide in Rwanda*. Cambridge: Cambridge University Press, 2011.
Longman, Timothy. *Memory and Justice in Post-genocide Rwanda*. Cambridge: Cambridge University Press, 2017.
Longman, Timothy, and Théoneste Rutagengwa. "Memory and Violence in Postgenocide Rwanda." In *States of Violence: Politics, Youth, and Memory in Contemporary Africa*, edited by Donald L. Donham and Edna G. Bay, 236–260. Charlottesville: University of Virginia Press, 2007.
K., M. "Ikinani I Nairobi." *Imvaho Nshya* (Kigali), April 24–30, 1995.
MacCoy, Jason. "Making Violence Ordinary: Radio, Music and the Rwandan Genocide." *African Music: Journal of the African Music Society* 8, no. 3 (2009): 85–96.
Mackintosh, Anne. "The International Response to Conflict and Genocide: Lessons from the Rwanda Experience Edited by David Millwood." *Journal of Refugee Studies* 9, no. 3 (1996): 334–342.
Malkki, Liisa Helena. *Purity and Exile: Violence, Memory, and National Cosmology among Hutu Refugees in Tanzania*. Chicago: University of Chicago Press, 2006.
Malkki, Liisa Helena. "Refugees and Exile: From 'Refugee Studies' to the National Order of Things." *Annual Review of Anthropology* 24 (1995): 495–523.
Mamdani, Mahmood. *Neither Settler nor Native: The Making and Unmaking of Permanent Minorities*. Cambridge, MA: Belknap Press of Harvard University Press, 2020.
Mamdani, Mahmood. "The Politics of Naming: Genocide, Civil War, Insurgency." *London Review of Books*, March 8, 2007. https://www.lrb.co.uk/the-paper/v29/n05/mahmood-mamdani/the-politics-of-naming-genocide-civil-war-insurgency.
Mamdani, Mahmood. *Saviors and Survivors: Darfur, Politics, and the War on Terror*. New York: Pantheon, 2009.
Mamdani, Mahmood. *When Victims Become Killers: Colonialism, Nativism, and the Genocide in Rwanda*. Princeton, NJ: Princeton University Press, 2002.
Mathys, Gillian. "Bringing History Back In: Past, Present, and Conflict in Rwanda and the Eastern Democratic Republic of Congo." *Journal of African History* 58, no. 3 (2017): 465–487.

Matrix, S. E. "Rewind, Remix, Rewrite: Digital and Virtual Memory in Cyberpunk Cinema." In *Save As . . . Digital Memories*, edited by Joanne Garde-Hansen, Andrew Hoskins, and Anna Reading, 60–76. Basingstoke, UK: Palgrave Macmillan, 2009.

Mbaraga, Robert. "States Pushes Campaign That Critics Say It Is Ethnically Divisive." *East African* (Nairobi), November 16, 2013. http://www.theeastafrican.co.ke/Rwanda/News/Mixed-reactions-to--Ndi-Umunyarwanda-initiative-/-/1433218/2075366/-/6kt cmf/-/index.html.

Mbashimishe, Cecili. "D.O.T. Rwanda Commemorates the 1994 Genocide against Tutsi." *Digital Opportunity Trust*, July 7, 2014. http://rwanda.dotrust.org/blogs/publicnews/dot-rwanda-commemorates-the-1994-genocide-against-.

Mbonyinshuti, J. Tabaro, and Irene Nayebare. "Genocide Survivor Reunites with Family after 19 Years." *New Times* (Kigali, Rwanda), June 1, 2013. https://www.newtimes.co.rw/article/93295/National/genocide-survivor-reunites-with-family-after-19-years.

McCoy, J. T. "Mbwirabumva ('I Speak to Those Who Understand'): Three Songs by Simon Bikindi and the War and Genocide in Rwanda" (PhD, Florida State University, 2013).

McDoom, Omar. *Rwanda's Ordinary Killers: Interpreting Popular Participation in the Rwandan Genocide*. London: Development Research Center, Crisis States Program, 2005.

McDowell, Sara. "Commemorating Dead 'Men': Gendering the Past and Present in Post-conflict Northern Ireland." *Gender, Place & Culture* 15, no. 4 (2008): 335–354.

McKinley, James C., Jr. "Tide of Rwanda Refugees Flows Back to Tanzania Camps." *New York Times*, December 14, 1996. http://www.nytimes.com/1996/12/14/world/tide-of-rwanda-refugees-flows-back-to-tanzania-camps.html?pagewanted=all&src=pm.

Media High Council. *Analysis of Media Coverage of the Eighteenth Commemoration of the Genocide Against the Tutsi*. Kigali, Rwanda: Media High Council for the Press, 2012.

Media High Council. *Analysis of Media Coverage of the Fifteenth Commemoration of the Genocide Against the Tutsi*. Kigali, Rwanda: Media High Council for the Press, December 2009.

Meierhenrich, Jens. "Topographies of Remembering and Forgetting." In *Remaking Rwanda: State Building and Human Rights after Mass Violence*, edited by Scott Straus and Lars Waldorf, 283–296. Madison: University of Wisconsin Press, 2011.

Meierhenrich, Jens. "The Transformation of Lieux De Mémoire: The Nyabarongo River in Rwanda, 1992–2009." *Anthropology Today* 25, no. 5 (2009): 13–19.

Meierhenrich, Jens, and Martha Lagace. "Through a Glass Darkly: Genocide Memorials in Rwanda 1994–Present." 2020. http://maps.cga.harvard.edu/rwanda/home.html.

Melvern, Linda. *Conspiracy to Murder: The Rwandan Genocide*. London: Verso, 2006.

Melvern, Linda. *A People Betrayed: The Role of the West in Rwanda's Genocide*. Cape Town, South Africa: New Africa Education, 2001.

Mignolo, Walter D. *The Darker Side of Western Modernity: Global Futures, Decolonial Options*. Durham, NC: Duke University Press, 2011.

Mihelj, Sabina. "Between Official and Vernacular Memory." In *Research Methods for Memory Studies*, edited by Emily Keightley and Michael Pickering, 60–75. Edinburgh: Edinburgh University Press, 2013.

Mihigo, Kizito. "Kizito Mihigo—Ijoro Ribara Uwariraye—Genocide Commemoration Song." YouTube video, 5:57. 2012. http://www.youtube.com/watch?v=D1WiNvgNTgs.

Minow, Martha. *Between Vengeance and Forgiveness: Facing History after Genocide and Mass Violence*. Boston: Beacon Press, 1998.

Mironko, Charles. "Igitero: Means and Motive in the Rwandan Genocide." *Journal of Genocide Research* 6, no. 1 (2004): 47–60.

Mironko, Fidelis. "18th Commemoration of the Genocide Against the Tutsi in Washington, DC, Part One." 2012. YouTube video, 22:33. https://www.youtube.com/watch?v=sfKCwvUVQu0.

Misztal, Barbara A. *Theories of Social Remembering*. Buckingham, UK: Open University Press, 2003.

Mitchell, Amy, and Paul Hitlin. "Twitter Reaction to Events Often at Odds with Overall Public Opinion." Pew Research Center, 2013. http://www.pewresearch.org/2013/03/04/twitter-reaction-to-events-often-at-odds-with-overall-public-opinion/.

Miura, Yasuhide, Shigeyuki Sakaki, Keigo Hattori, and Tomoko Ohkuma. "Team X: A Sentiment Analyzer with Enhanced Lexicon Mapping and Weighting Scheme for Unbalanced Data." Proceedings of the 8th International Workshop on Semantic Evaluation, Dublin, Ireland, Qatar Computing Research Institute, August 23–24, 2014.

Mödersheim, Sabine. "Art and War." In *Representations of Violence: Art about the Sierra Leone Civil War*, edited by Patrick K. Muana, Chris Corcoran, and Russell D. Feingold, 15–20. Madison, WI: 21st Century African Youth Movement, 2005.

Moon, Ruth. "Beyond Puppet Journalism: The Bridging Work of Transnational Journalists in a Local Field." *Journalism Studies* 20, no. 12 (2019): 1714–1731.

Moon, Ruth. "Constructing Journalism Practice between the Global and the Local: Lessons from the Rwandan Journalism Field" (PhD, Washington University, 2018).

Moore, Lisa M. "Recovering the Past, Remembering Trauma: The Politics of Commemoration at Sites of Atrocity." *Journal of Public & International Affairs* 20, Spring (2009): 213–244.

Mudimbe, V. Y. *The Invention of Africa: Gnosis, Philosophy, and the Order of Knowledge*. Bloomington: Indiana University Press, 1988.

Mugabe, Aggée M. Shyaka. "Community Conflicts in Rwanda: Major Causes and Ways to Solutions." NURC, 2007. http://www.nurc.gov.rw/fileadmin/templates/nurc/css/Community_conflict_in_Rwanda.pdf.

Mugesera, Antoine. *Les conditions de vie des Tutsi au Rwanda de 1959 à 1990: Persécutions et massacres antérieurs au génocide de 1990 à 1994: Essai*. Paris: Ibuka, 2014.

Mugesera, Antoine. *Imibereho Y'abatutsi Mu Rwanda 1959-1990: Itotezwa N'iyicwa Bihoraho*. Kigali, Rwanda: Les Editions Rwandaises, 2015.

Mugiraneza, Assumpta. "Les écueils dans l'appréhension de l'histoire du génocide des Tutsi." *Revue d'histoire de la Shoah*, 190 (2009): 153–172.

Muhire, Kigero. "Analyse de la commémoration de genocide des Tutsi dans le context socio-politique de Rwanda: 'Cas Du District De Gasabo'" (BA, Université National du Rwanda, 2011).

Mukagasana, Yolande, and Patrick May. *La mort ne veut pas de moi: Document*. Paris: Fixot, 1997.

Mukagasana, Yolande, Patrick May, Anna Cinzia Sciancalepore, and Lisa Foa. *La morte non mi ha voluta*. Molfetta, Italy: La meridiana, 2008.

Mukamana, Donatilla, and Petra Brysiewicz. "The lived experience of genocide rape survivors in Rwanda." *Journal of Nursing Scholarship* 40, no. 4 (2008): 379–384.

Mukasekuru, Espérance. "La reintegration sociale des femmes et filles victimes des violences sexuelles au cours du génocide de 1994 au Rwanda" (MA, l'Université National du Rwanda, 2009).

Munene, Macharia. "Mayi and Interahamwe Militias: Threats to Peace and Security in the Great Lakes Region." In *Civil Militia: Africa's Intractable Security Menace?*, edited by David J. Francis, 251–280. Burlington, VT: Ashgate, 2005.

Munyandamutsa, N., P. Mahoro Nkubamugisha, M. Gex-Fabry, and A. Eytan. "Mental and Physical Health in Rwanda 14 Years after the Genocide." *Social Psychiatry and Psychiatric Epidemiology* 47, no. 11 (2012): 1753–1761.

"Murisanga," audio recording, 59:34. Radiyo Yacu VOA, May 4, 2020. https://www.radiyoyacuVOA.com/a/5380993.html.

Musilikare, Jérémie. *La vie des pygmées Batwa au Rwanda*. Paris: L'Harmattan, 2015.

Musoni, Edwin. "CNLG Releases Report on Genocide Ideology in Schools." *All Africa*, December 4, 2009. http://allafrica.com/stories/200912040034.html.

Musoni, Edwin. "Maintenance of Memorial Sites a Collective Responsibility—CNLG." *New Times* (Kigali), April 17, 2012. http://allafrica.com/stories/201204170166.html.

Mutamba, John, and Jeanne Izabiliza. "The Role of Women in Reconciliation and Peace Building in Rwanda: Ten Years after Genocide, 1994–2004: Contributions, Challenges and Way Forward." The National United and Reconciliation Commission (NURC), May 2005. https://repositories.lib.utexas.edu/bitstream/handle/2152/4786/3871.pdf%3Bsequence=1

Mutara, Eugene. "Rwanda: 156 Genocide Survivors and Witnesses Killed." *All Africa*, March 7, 2009. http://allafrica.com/stories/200903090569.html.

Mwambari, David. "*Agaciro*, Vernacular Memory and the Politics of Memory in Post-genocide Rwanda." *African Affairs* 120, no. 481 (2021): 611–628.

Mwambari, David. "Can Online Platforms Be E-Pana-Africana Liberation Zones for Pan-African Decolonization Debates?" *CODESRIA Bulletin Online*, 2021. https://kclpure.kcl.ac.uk/portal/en/publications/can-online-platforms-be-epanaafricana-liberation-zones-for-panafrican-and-decolonization-debates(9b329fbc-cd9b-4fd0-b8db-b703014e7032).html

Mwambari, David. "Emergence of Post-genocide Collective Memory in Rwanda's International Relations ". In *Beyond History: African Agency in Development, Diplomacy, and Conflict Resolution*, edited by Eijah Munyi, David Mwambari, and Aleksi Ylönen, 119–134. London: Rowman & Littlefield International, 2020.

Mwambari, David. "Inventing Ethnicity: The Malleability of Identity in Rwanda" (MA, Syracuse University, 2010).

Mwambari, David. "Leadership Emergence in Post-genocide Rwanda." *Leadership & Developing Societies* 2, no. 1 (2017): 88–104.

Mwambari, David. "Local Positionality in the Production of Knowledge in Northern Uganda." *International Journal of Qualitative Methods* 18 (2019): 160940691986484.

Mwambari, David. "Music and the Politics of the Past: Kizito Mihigo and Music in the Commemoration of the Genocide Against the Tutsi in Rwanda." *Memory Studies* 13, no. 6 (2019): 1321–1336.

Mwambari, David. "Women-Led Non-Governmental Organizations and Peacebuilding in Rwanda." *African Conflict and Peacebuilding Review* 7, no. 1 (2017): 66–79.

Mwambari, David, Alfred Muteru, Barney Walsh, Irenee Bugingo, Thomas Munyneza, and Funmi Olonisakin. "Reframing Narratives of Statebuilding and Peacebuilding in Africa," African Leadership Center, Nairobi, Kenya, 2016.

Mwambari, David, Barney Walsh, and Funmi Olonisakin. "Women's overlooked contribution to Rwanda's state-building conversations." *Conflict, Security & Development* 21, no. 4 (2021): 475–499.

Mwambari, David, and Sarah Schaeffer. "Post-conflict Education: The Case of History Curriculum in Post-genocide Rwanda." In *Contemporary Issues in African Studies: A Reader*, edited by Ernest E. Uwazie and Chaunce Ridley, 167–186. Dubuque, IA: Kendall Hunt, 2011.

Mwambutse, Jean Claude. "Jean Paul Samputu Arabeshyuza Ibyo Simburudare Yavuze." *BBC Gahuzamiryango*, April 14, 2009. http://www.BBC.co.uk/greatlakes/news/story/2009/04/090415_rdaibukasamputu.shtml.

Naidu, Ereshnee, and Cyril Adonis. *History on Their Own Terms: The Relevance of the Past for a New Generation*. Braamfontein, South Africa: Center for the Study of Violence and Reconciliation, 2007.

National Institute of Statistics of Rwanda. "Districts Baseline Survey." National Institute of Statistics, Kigali, Rwanda, May 2012. http://www.statistics.gov.rw/survey/districts-baseline-survey.

National Unitey and Reconcilation Commission. *Rwanda Reconciliation Barometer*. Kigali: Republic of Rwanda, 2010.

Ndahiro, Tom. "Genocide-Laundering: Historical Revisionism, Genocide Denial and the Role of the Rassemblement Républicain Pour La Démocratie Au Rwanda." In *After Genocide: Transitional Justice, Post-conflict Reconstruction and Reconciliation in Rwanda and Beyond*, edited by Philip Clark and Zachary D. Kaufman, 311–320. Oxford, UK: Oxford University Press, 2013.

Ndlovu-Gatsheni, Sabelo. "Coloniality of Power in Development Studies and the Impact of Global Imperial Designs on Africa." Inaugural lecture. University of South Africa, Department of Development Studies, Pretoria, October 16, 2012.

Ndlovu-Gatsheni, Sabelo. *Epistemic Freedom in Africa: Deprovincialization and Decolonization*. New York: Routledge, 2018.

Neiger, Motti, Oren Meyers, and Eyal Zandberg, eds. *On Media Memory: Collective Memory in a New Media Age*. New York: Palgrave Macmillan, 2011.

Newbury, Catharine. *The Cohesion of Oppression: Clientship and Ethnicity in Rwanda, 1860–1960*. New York: Columbia University Press, 1994.

Newbury, Catharine, and David S. Newbury. "A Catholic Mass in Kigali: Contested Views of the Genocide and Ethnicity in Rwanda." *Canadian Journal of African Studies* 33, no. 2/3 (1999): 292–328.

Newbury, David, and Catharine Newbury. "Bringing the Peasants Back In: Agrarian Themes in the Construction and Corrosion of Statist Historiography in Rwanda." *American Historical Review* 105, no. 3 (2000): 832–877.

Newbury, David S. "The Clans of Rwanda: An Historical Hypothesis." *Africa* 50, no. 4 (1980): 389–403.

Newbury, David S. *Kings and Clans: Ijwi Island and the Lake Kivu Rift, 1780–1840*. Madison: University of Wisconsin Press, 2010.

Newbury, David S. "Les campagnes de Rwabugiri: chronologie et bibliographie." *Cahiers d'études africaines* 14, no. 53 (1974): 181–191.

Ngabo, Michael. "Rwanda: Deniers of the 1994 Genocide Against the Tutsi on Rampage." *All Africa*, April 23, 2011. http://allafrica.com/stories/201104250812.html.

Ngaboka, Ivan. "Rwanda's Youngest MP Is a Blend of Art and Politics." *New Times*, October 20, 2013. https://www.newtimes.co.rw/article/99187/rwandaas-youngest-mp-is-a-blend-of-art-and-politics#:~:text=DONNING%20A%20FITTING%20dark%20designer,of%20an%20ordinary%20young%20man.

Ngoga, Martin. "The Institutionalization of Impunity: A Judicial Perspective of the Rwandan Genocide." In *After Genocide: Transitional Justice, Post-conflict Reconstruction and Reconciliation in Rwanda and Beyond*, edited by Philip Clark and Zachary D. Kaufman, 321–322. Oxford, UK: Oxford University Press, 2013.

Ngoga, Martin. "Why Rwanda Needs the Law Repressing Genocide Denial and Ideology." *Umuvugizi* (Kigali), June 4, 2011. https://umuvugizi.wordpress.com/2011/06/04/why-rwanda-needs-the-law-repressing-genocide-denial-and-ideology/.

Nhema, Alfred G., and Paul Tiyambe Zeleza, eds. *The Roots of African Conflicts: The Causes & Costs*. Oxford, UK: James Currey, 2008.

Nichols, Terence L. *Death and Afterlife: A Theological Introduction*. Grand Rapids, MI: Brazos Press, 2010.

Nishimwe, Consolee. *Tested to the Limit: A Genocide Survivor's Story of Pain, Resilience, and Hope*. Bloomington, IN: Balboa Press, 2012.

Nkubito, Daniel. "Issue Paper: Internet Connectivity and Affordability in Rwanda." 2012. http://ppd.rw/wp-content/uploads/2012/12/internet-connectivity-and-affordability-in-Rwanda-issue-paper-Final.pdf.

Nkusi, David. "The Historical Significance of Mulindi Museum." *New Times* (Kigali), September 20, 2014, https://www.newtimes.co.rw/article/111546/Opinions/the-historical-significance-of-mulindi-museum.

Nora, Pierre. "Between Memory and History: Les Lieux De Mémoire." *Representations*, no. 26 (1989): 7–24.

Nora, Pierre. *Realms of Memory. Rethinking the French Past*. Vol. 2. Translated by Lawrence D. Kritzman. New York: Columbia University Press, 1996.

"Nyamagabe: Kizito Mihigo Foundation Entertains Youth in Peace Concert." *Pleader*, 2015. http://rwandaexpress.blogspot.com/2013/09/nyamagabe-kizito-mihigo-foundation.html.

Nyirazana, Nyiramutuzo. *Building Lasting Peace in Rwanda: Voices of the People*. Kigali, Rwanda: Institute of Research and Dialogue for Peace, 2004.

Nyirazana, Nyiramutuzo. "La problematique de silence comme défi a la mémoire des victimes du génocide des Tutsi D'avril-Juillet 1994: cas du Secteur Gasaka, du District Nyamagabe" (MA, l'Université National du Rwanda, 2007).

Okech, Awino. "Gender and State-Building Conversations: The Discursive Production of Gender Identity in Kenya and Rwanda." *Conflict, Security, & Development* 21, no. 4 (2019): 1–15.

Okpewho, Isidore. *African Oral Literature: Backgrounds, Character, and Continuity*. Bloomington: Indiana University Press, 2013.

Olesen, Virginia L. "Feminist Qualitative Research and Grounded Theory: Complexities, Criticisms, and Opportunities." In *The Sage Handbook of Grounded Theory*, edited by Antony Bryant and Kathy Charmaz, 417–435. Thousand Oaks, CA: SAGE, 2010.

Olick, Jeffrey K. *The Politics of Regret: On Collective Memory and Historical Responsibility*. New York: Routledge, 2007.

Olick, Jeffrey K., and Joyce Robbins. "Social Memory Studies: From 'Collective Memory' to the Historical Sociology of Mnemonic Practices." *Annual Review of Sociology* 24, no. 1 (1998): 105–140.

Olick, Jeffrey K., Vered Vinitzky-Seroussi, and Daniel Levy, eds. *The Collective Memory Reader*. Oxford, UK: Oxford University Press, 2011.

Olonisakin, Funmi, Alagaw Ababu Kifle, and Alfred Muteru. "Shifting ideas of sustainable peace towards conversation in state-building." *Conflict, Security & Development* 21, no. 4 (2021): 409–430.
Olonisakin, Funmi. *Peacekeeping in Sierra Leone: The Story of Unamsil*. Boulder, CO: Lynne Rienner, 2008.
Olonisakin, Funmi, Alagaw Ababu Kifle, and Alfred Muteru. "Shifting Ideas of Sustainable Peace Towards Conversation in State-Building." *Conflict, Security, & Development* 21, no. 4 (2021): 409–430.
Omeje, Kenneth C., and Tricia M. Redeker Hepner. *Conflict and Peacebuilding in the African Great Lakes Region*. Bloomington: Indiana University Press, 2013.
Oomen, Barbara. "Donor-Driven Justice and Its Discontents: The Case of Rwanda." *Development and Change* 36, no. 5 (2005): 887–910.
Orth, Richard. "Rwanda's Hutu Extremist Genocidal Insurgency: An Eyewitness Perspective." *Small Wars & Insurgencies* 12, no. 1 (2001): 76–109.
Otake, Yuko. "Suffering of Silenced People in Northern Rwanda." *Social Science & Medicine* 222 (2019): 171–179.
Oyebade, Adebayo, and Abiodun Alao. *Africa after the Cold War: The Changing Perspectives on Security*. Trenton, NJ: Africa World Press, 1998.
Pendas, Devin Owen. *The Frankfurt Auschwitz Trial, 1963–1965: Genocide, History and the Limits of the Law*. Cambridge: Cambridge University Press, 2011.
Peters-Little, Frances, Ann Curthoys, and John Docker. *Passionate Histories: Myth, Memory and Indigenous Australia*. Canberra, Australia: ANU Press, 2010.
"In Pictures: Remembering the Genocide." *One-Minute World News*, April 12, 2013, on BBC. http://news.BBC.co.uk/2/shared/spl/hi/africa/04/photo_journal/rwanda/html/1.stm.
"Pictures of the Day: 9 April 2019." *Telegraph*, April 9, 2019. https://www.telegraph.co.uk/news/2019/04/09/pictures-day-9-april-2019/, Accessed March 10, 2023.
Pinchevski, Amit. "Archive, Media, Trauma." In *On Media Memory: Collective Memory in a New Media Age*, edited by Mordechai Neiger, Oren Meyers, and Eyal Zandberg, 253–264. New York: Palgrave Macmillan, 2013.
Piton, Florent. "Ii/le Rwanda indépendant (1959–1990)." In *Le génocide des Tutsi du Rwanda*, edited by Florent Piton, 33–66. Paris: La Découverte, 2018.
"Pope Says Church Is Not to Blame in Rwanda." *New York Times*, March 21, 1996. https://www.nytimes.com/1996/03/21/world/pope-says-church-is-not-to-blame-in-rwanda.html.
"Popular Rwandan Singer Found Dead in Police Cell: Police." *Al-Jazeera*, 2020. https://www.aljazeera.com/news/2020/02/popular-rwandan-singer-dead-police-cell-police-200217150952317.html.
Pottier, Johan. *Re-imagining Rwanda: Conflict, Survival and Disinformation in the Late Twentieth Century*. Cambridge: Cambridge University Press, 2004.
Press, Robert M. "In Rwanda's 'Slave Ship' Prison, Life Is Grim for Suspected Killers." *Christian Science Monitor* November 18, 1994. https://www.csmonitor.com/1994/1118/18011.html.
"Programs: Commemoration of the Srebrenica Massacre—Genocide and Aftermath Art Exhibit and Presentation at the United Nations." Academy of Bosnia and Herzegovina, 2013. http://www.peacebuildinginitiative.org/index2d35.html?pageId=1895
Prunier, Gerard. *Africa's World War: Congo, the Rwandan Genocide, and the Making of a Continental Catastrophe*. Oxford, UK: Oxford University Press, 2009.

Prunier, Gerard. *The Rwanda Crisis: History of a Genocide*. London: Hurst, 1998.
Purdeková, Andrea. *Making Ubumwe: Power, State and Camps in Rwanda's Unity-Building Project*. New York: Berghahn Books, 2015.
Purdeková, Andrea, and David Mwambari. "Post-genocide Identity Politics and Colonial Durabilities in Rwanda." *Critical African Studies* 14, no. 1 (2021): 1–19.
Radstone, Susannah, ed. *Memory and Methodology*. Oxford, UK: Berg, 2000.
Raeymaekers, Timothy, and Koen Vlassenroot. *Conflict and Social Transformation in Eastern DR Congo*. Ghent, Belgium: Academia, 2004.
Rakoff, David. "The Way We Live Now: 10-27-02: Post-9/11 Modernism: Questions for Eric Fischl." *New York Times Magazine*, October 27, 2002, Section 6, 15, https://www.nytimes.com/2002/10/27/magazine/the-way-we-live-now-10-27-02-questions-for-eric-fischl-post-9-11-modernism.html
Rankine, Claudia. "The Condition of Black Life Is One of Mourning." In *The Fire This Time: A New Generation Speaks About Race*, edited by Jesmyn Ward, 145–155. New York: Scribner, 2019.
Reading, Anna. "The Globytal: Towards an Understanding of Globalised Memories in the Digital Age." In *Digital Memories: Exploring Critical Issues*, edited by Anna Maj and Daniel Riha, 31–40. Oxford, UK: Inter-Disciplinary Press, 2009.
Reading, Anna. "Memobilia." In *Save As . . . Digital Memories*, edited by Joanne Garde-Hansen, Andrew Hoskins, and Anna Reading, 81–95. New York: Palgrave Macmillan, 2009.
Reconstruire une paix durable au Rwanda: La parole au peuple. Kigali, Rwanda: Institute for Research and Dialogue for Peace/WSP International, 2003.
Renan, Ernest. "What Is a Nation?" In *Nation and Narration*, edited by Homi K. Bhabha, 8–22. New York: Routledge, 2008.
Rennie, J. K. *The Banyoro Invasions and Interlacustrine Chronology*. Los Angeles: University of California, Los Angeles, 1973.
Rennie, J. K. "The Precolonial Kingdom of Rwanda: A Reinterpretation." *Transafrican Journal of History* 2, no. 2 (1972): 11–54.
Republic of Rwanda. "Law No. 02/98 of 22 January 1998 Establishing a National Assistance Fund for Needy Victims of Genocide and Massacres Committed in Rwanda between 1 October 1990 and 31 December 1994." http://www.refworld.org/cgi-bin/texis/vtx/rwmain/opendocpdf.pdf?reldoc=y&docid=52df99854.
Republic of Rwanda. "The 19th Commemoration of the 1994 Genocide Against Tutsi Will Be Marked in Each Umudugudu Village under the Theme 'Let Us Commemorate the Tutsi Genocide as We Strive for Self Reliance.'" 2013. https://web.archive.org/web/20130218063625/http://www.gov.rw/The-19th-Commemoration-of-the-1994-Genocide-against-Tutsi-will-be-marked-in-each-Umudugudu-village-under-the-theme-Let-us-commemorate-the-Tutsi-Genocide-as-we-strive-for-self-reliance.
Republika Y'u Rwanda. *Ingingo Z'ingenzi Mu Mateka Y'u Rwanda*. Kigali, Rwanda: Office of the President, 1972.
Reyntjens, Filip. "Constructing the Truth, Dealing with Dissent, Domesticating the World: Governance in Post-genocide Rwanda." *African Affairs* 110, no. 438 (2011): 1–34.
Reyntjens, Filip. *The Great African War: Congo and Regional Geopolitics, 1996–2006*. New York: Cambridge University Press, 2009.
Reyntjens, Filip. "Rwanda: Genocide and Beyond." *Journal of Refugee Studies* 9, no. 3 (1996): 240–251.

Reyntjens, Filip. "Rwanda, Ten Years On: From Genocide to Dictatorship." *African Affairs* 103, no. 411 (2004): 177–210.
Riot, Thomas, Herrade Boistelle, and Nicolas Bancel. "Les politiques d'itorero au Rwanda un dispositif éducatif et guerrier à l'épreuve de la reconstruction nationale." *Revue tiers-monde* 228 (2016): 101–120.
Roediger, Henry L., and James V. Wertsch. "Creating a New Discipline of Memory Studies." *Memory Studies* 1, no. 1 (2008): 9–22.
Rosoux, Valérie. "La gestion du passé au Rwanda: Ambivalence et poids du silence." *Genèses* 61, no. 4 (2005): 28–46.
Rosoux, Valérie. "Rwanda, La Mémoire Du Génocide." *Etudes* 390, no. 6 (1999): 731–742.
Ross, Mariama. "Representations of Violence: Bearing Witness." In *Representations of Violence: Art about the Sierra Leone Civil War*, edited by Patrick K. Muana, Chris Corcoran, and Russell D. Feingold, 35–40. Madison, WI: 21st Century African Youth Movement, 2005.
Rothberg, M. "From Gaza to Warsaw: Mapping Multidirectional Memory." *Criticism* 53, no. 4 (2011): 523–548.
Rothberg, Michael. *The Implicated Subject*. Palo Alto, CA: Stanford University Press, 2020.
Rothberg, Michael. *Multidirectional Memory: Remembering the Holocaust in the Age of Decolonization*. Palo Alto, CA: Stanford University Press, 2009.
Ruburika, Sam. "M.H.C. Lauds Media for 2008 Genocide Commemoration Coverage." *AllAfrica*, April 10, 2009. https://allafrica.com/stories/200904130135.html.
Rugamba, Dorcy. "Et si interdisait les femmes dans l'espace public?" March 2, 2014. http://dorcyrugamba.wordpress.com/.
Rugamba, Dorcy. "L'Angle Mort De La Bonne Conscience Francaise," December 30, 2013, http://dorcyrugamba.wordpress.com/2013/12/30/langle-mort-de-la-bonne-conscience-francaise/.
Rugamba, Dorcy. "Une société martiale et solidaire." In *Rwanda: Mille collines, mille douleurs: L'Âme des Peuples*. Edited by Colette Braekman. Paris: Nevicata, 2014.
Rugamba, Dorcy Ingeli, and Francis Busignies. *Marembo*. Saint-Maurice, QC, Canada: Da Ti M'beti, 2005.
Rugamba, Sipriyani. *Akanigi kanjye (+lyrics)*. Amasimbi n'Amakombe. Murage Mwiza. January 12, 2018. YouTube, 6:26. 2011. https://www.youtube.com/watch?v=EVTgTtZDp4c&ab_channel=MurageMwiza.
Rugamba, Sipriyani. *Inda Nini (+lyrics)*. Amasimbi n'Amakombe. Murage Mwiza. May 11, 2018. YouTube, 4:32. https://www.youtube.com/watch?v=iIWdR6VxHkU&ab_channel=MurageMwiza.
Rutayisire, Emmanuel. "RDF Defends War Memorial Monuments at Parliament."*East African* (Nairobi), July 18, 2014. https://www.theeastafrican.co.ke/rwanda/News/RDF-defends-war-memorial-monuments-at-parliament/1433218-2389352-12463aw/index.html.
Rutayisire, Paul. "Approche locale du génocide la région de Nyarubuye." *Vingtième Siècle. Revue d'histoire* 122, no. 2 (2014): 37–49.
Rutayisire, Paul. "L'Évangélisation du Rwanda (1922–1945) (PhD, Université de Fribourg, 1984).
Rutayisire, Paul. *La christianisation du Rwanda (1900–1945): Méthode missionnaire et politique selon Mgr. Léon Classe*. Fribourg, Switzerland: Éditions Universitaires Fribourg, 1987.

Rutazibwa, Olivia Umurerwa. "Studying Agaciro: Moving Beyond Wilsonian Interventionist Knowledge Production on Rwanda." *Journal of Intervention and Statebuilding* 8, no. 4 (2014): 291–301.

"Rwanda." *Freedom on the Net 2013*. Freedom House. March 2, 2014. https://freedomhouse.org/sites/default/files/resources/FOTN%202013_Rwanda.pdf.

Rwanda Development Board. "Rwanda Tourism: Things to Do and Cultural Experience." http://www.rwandatourism.com/.

"Rwanda: Child-Headed Households." April 7, 2004, *Woman's Hour*, BBC. http://www.BBC.co.uk/radio4/womanshour/2004_14_wed_04.shtml.

"Rwanda: Ensure Justice over Kizito Mihigo Death; Popular Singer Died in Police Custody." Updated February 20, 2020, https://www.hrw.org/news/2020/02/20/rwanda-ensure-justice-over-kizito-mihigo-death.

"Rwanda: Le chef de l'état inaugure une salve d'attaques verbales des autorités contre les journalistes." *Reporters sans Frontières*, January 31, 2006. https://rsf.org/fr/le-chef-de-letat-inaugure-une-salve-dattaques-verbales-des-autorit%C3%A9s-contre-les-journalistes.

"Rwanda Marks Genocide Anniversary." *One-Minute World News*, BBC, April 6, 2004. http://news.BBC.co.uk/1/hi/world/africa/3602859.stm.

"Rwanda: We Need to Step Out of Our Parents' Shadows—Poet Bamporiki." *All Africa*, July 23, 2013. http://allafrica.com/stories/201307230319.html.

"Rwandan Exiles in London 'Threatened by Hitman.'" *BBC News*, May 21, 2011. https://www.BBC.com/news/world-africa-13475635.

"Rwandan Soldiers Arrive in Sudan." *One-Minute World News*, BBC, August 15, 2004. http://news.BBC.co.uk/2/hi/africa/3562096.stm.

"Rwanda's Children of Rape." June 30, 2010, *Newsnight*, BBC. http://news.BBC.co.uk/1/hi/programmes/newsnight/8768943.stm.

"Rwanda's Kizito Mihigo and Cassien Ntamuhanga Arrested." *BBC News*, April 14, 2014. http://www.BBC.com/news/world-africa-27028206.

Rwanda 2020. "Bill Clinton Visits Rwanda—March 26, 1998." YouTube, 18:58. 2012. https://www.youtube.com/watch?v=avJr2qRbPcQ.

Rwanda Media High Council. *High Council of the Press Report*. Kigali: Republic of Rwanda, June 2004.

RwandaTV. "Inama Y'igihugu Y'umushyikirano | Day 2–14 Ukuboza 2018." YouTube, 3:08:18. December 23, 2018. https://www.youtube.com/watch?v=aWglCJJKNno.

Rwirahira, Rodrigue. "Govt Vows to Push for Deportation of Fugitives." *East African* (Nairobi), November 30, 2012. https://web.archive.org/web/20121201161554/http://www.theeastafrican.co.ke/Rwanda/News/Govt-vows-to-push-for-deportation-of-fugitives/-/1433218/1633766/-/1i8cbnz/-/index.html.

Said, Edward W. "Invention, Memory, and Place." *Critical Inquiry Critical Inquiry* 26, no. 2 (2000): 175–192.

Sai, Nancy. "Conflict Profile: Rwanda." Women's Media Center, February 8, 2012. https://womensmediacenter.com/women-under-siege/conflicts/rwanda.

Saint-Exupéry, Patrick de. *Complices de l'inavouable: La France au Rwanda*. Paris: Arènes, 2009.

Samuelson, Beth Lewis, and Sarah Warshauer Freedman. "Language Policy, Multilingual Education, and Power in Rwanda." *Language Policy* 9, no. 3 (2010): 191–215.

Sanders, Edith R. "The Hamitic Hypothesis: Its Origin and Functions in Time Perspective." *Journal of African History* 10, no. 4 (1969): 521–532.

Santayana, George. *Reason in Common Sense: Volume One of the Life of Reason.* New York: Dover, 1980.

Schudson, Michael. "The Present in the Past versus the Past in the Present." *Communication* 11 (1989): 105–113.

Schudson, Michael. *Watergate in American Memory: How We Remember, Forget, and Reconstruct the Past.* New York: Basic Books, 1993.

Scully, Shannon. "The Politics of Memory and the Display of Human Remains: Murambi Genocide Memorial, Rwanda." Paper presented at Conflict, Memory, and Reconciliation: Bridging Past, Present and Future, Kigali, Rwanda, January 1, 2012.

Sebarenzi, Joseph, and Laura Mullane. *God Sleeps in Rwanda: A Journey of Transformation.* Oxford, UK: Oneworld, 2009.

Ševčenko, Liz, and Maggie Russell-Ciardi. "Sites of Conscience: Opening Historic Sites for Civic Dialogue, Forward." *Public Historian* 30, no. 1 (2008): 9–15.

Sharpley, Richard, and Mona Friedrich. "Genocide Tourism in Rwanda: Contesting the Concept of the 'Dark Tourist.'" In *Dark Tourism: Practice and Interpretation*, edited by Glenn Hooper and J. John Lennon, 146–158. New York: Routledge, 2016.

Sherwod, Harriet. "Pope Francis Asks for Forgiveness for Church's Role in Rwanda Genocide." *Guardian*, March 20, 2017. https://www.theguardian.com/world/2017/mar/20/pope-francis-asks-for-forgiveness-for-churchs-role-in-rwanda-genocide.

Sibomana, Eric, and Brooker Chambers. "Remembering from a Distance: Genocide Commemoration in Rwanda and Covid-19." *Society Pages*, April 6, 2021. https://thesocietypages.org/Holocaust-genocide/remembering-from-a-distance-genocide-commemoration-in-rwanda-and-covid-19/.

Sinalo, Caroline. *Rwanda after Genocide: Gender, Identity and Post-traumatic Growth.* Cambridge: Cambridge University Press, 2018.

Smith, James M. *A Time to Remember: Rwanda: Ten Years after Genocide.* Retford, Nottinghamshire, UK: Aegis Institute, 2004.

Snyder, Robert H. "'Disillusioned Words Like Bullets Bark": Incitement to Genocide, Music, and the Trial of Simon Bikindi." *Georgia Journal of International and Comparative Law* 35, no. 3 (2007): 645–674.

Sodaro, Amy. *Exhibiting Atrocity: Memorial Museums and the Politics of Past Violence.* New Brunswick, NJ: Rutgers University Press, 2018.

Sodaro, Amy. "Politics of the Past: Remembering the Rwandan Genocide at the Kigali Memorial Centre." In *Curating Difficult Knowledge: Violent Pasts in Public Places*, edited by Erica Lehrer, Cynthia E. Milton, and Monica Eileen Patterson, 72–88. Basingstoke, UK: Palgrave Macmillan, 2011.

Sontag, Susan. "Regarding the Pain of Others." *Diogène* 201, no. 1 (2003): 127–139.

Sperling, C. "Mother of Atrocities: Pauline Nyiramasuhuko's Role in the Rwandan Genocide." *Fordham Urban Law Journal* 33, no. 2 (2006): 637–664.

Ssenyonga, Allan Brian. "Twitter 2012 Was a Very Interesting Year for 'RwOT.'" *New Times* (Kigali), December 31, 2012, https://www.newtimes.co.rw/article/85803/twitter-2012-was-a-very-interesting-year-for-arwota.

Stover, Eric, and Harvey M. Weinstein, eds. *My Neighbor, My Enemy: Justice and Community in the Aftermath of Mass Atrocity.* Cambridge, UK: Cambridge University Press, 2004.

Straus, Scott. *The Order of Genocide: Race, Power, and War in Rwanda.* Ithaca, NY: Cornell University Press, 2006.

Straus, Scott, and Lars Waldorf, eds. *Remaking Rwanda: State Building and Human Rights after Mass Violence*. Madison: University of Wisconsin Press, 2011.

Sturken, Marita. *Tangled Memories: The Vietnam War, the AIDS Epidemic, and the Politics of Remembering*. Berkeley: University of California Press, 1997.

Swedlund, Haley J. *The Development Dance: How Donors and Recipients Negotiate the Delivery of Foreign Aid*. Ithaca, NY: Cornell University Press, 2018.

Tabaro, Jean de la Croix. "Genocide Commemoration Week Taken to Village Level." *New Times* (Kigali), February 8, 2013. https://www.newtimes.co.rw/article/87822/National/genocide-commemoration-week-taken-to-village-level.

Tabaro, Jean de la Croix. "Know Your History: Rukara, an Icon of Resistance to Colonialists." *New Times* (Kigali), October 22, 2014. https://www.newtimes.co.rw/section/read/182210.

Tadjo, Véronique. "Genocide: The Changing Landscape of Memory in Kigali." *African Identities* 8, no. 4 (2010): 379–388.

Tafirenyika, Masimba. "Information Technology Super-Charging Rwanda's Economy." *Africa Renewal*, April 2011. http://www.un.org/africarenewal/magazine/april-2011/information-technology-super-charging-rwandas-economy#sthash.UpvtXqVs.dpuf.

Tamale, Sylvia. *Decolonization and Afro-Feminism*. Ottawa, Canada: Daraja Press, 2020.

Tasamba, James. "Rwanda: Nation Commemorates Genocide." *All Africa*, April 7, 2012. http://allafrica.com/stories/201204070008.html.

Tashoa, Athan. "Genocide Memorial Sites in Sorry State, Says Report." *New Times* (Kigali), April 29, 2014. http://www.newtimes.co.rw/section/article/2014-04-29/74929/.

Tashobya, Athan. "Genocide Memorials Inch Closer to Becoming UNESCO Heritage Sites." *New Times* (Kigali), April 6, 2018. https://www.newtimes.co.rw/news/genocide-memorials-inch-closer-becoming-unesco-heritage-sites.

Taylor, Christopher C. "Kings and Chaos in Rwanda: On the Order of Disorder." *Anthropos* 98, no. 1 (2003): 41–58.

Taylor, Christopher C. *Sacrifice as Terror: The Rwandan Genocide of 1994*. New York: Routledge, 2020.

Terrill, Steve. "Rwanda Remembers Genocide 18 Years Later." *Voice of America*, April 7, 2012. http://www.VOAnews.com/content/rwanda-remembers-genocide-18-years-later-146586625/179994.html.

Tertsakian, Carina. "'All Rwandans Are Afraid of Being Arrested One Day': Prisoners Past, Present, and Future." In *Remaking Rwanda: State Building and Human Rights after Mass Violence*, edited by Scott Straus and Lars Waldorf, 210–220. Madison: University of Wisconsin Press, 2011.

Thomas, Grace Elizabeth. "Re-imagining Framework for Leadership Analysis." *Leadership and Developing Societies* 5, no. 1 (2020): 69–73.

Thompson, Allan, ed. *The Media and the Rwanda Genocide*. London: Pluto Press, 2007.

Thomson, Susan. "Academic Integrity and Ethical Responsibilities in Post-genocide Rwanda: Working with Research Ethics Boards to Prepare for Fieldwork with Human Subjects." In *Emotional and Ethical Challenges for Field Research in Africa: The Story Behind the Findings*, edited by Susan Thomson, An Ansoms, and Jude Murison, 139–154. New York: Palgrave Macmillan, 2013.

Thomson, Susan. *Rwanda: From Genocide to Precarious Peace*. New Haven, CT: Yale University Press, 2018.

Thomson, Susan. *Whispering Truth to Power: Everyday Resistance to Reconciliation in Postgenocide Rwanda*. Madison: University of Wisconsin Press, 2013.

Thomson, Susan, An Ansoms, and Judith Murison. *Emotional and Ethical Challenges for Field Research in Africa: The Story behind the Findings*. New York: Palgrave Macmillan, 2013.

Totten, Samuel, and Rafiki Ubaldo. *We Cannot Forget: Interviews with Survivors of the 1994 Genocide in Rwanda*. New Brunswick, NJ: Rutgers University Press, 2011.

"The Treatment of Genocide Victims Intolerable." *Rushyashya* (Kigali), April 7–15, 2009.

Turner, Thomas. *The Congo Wars: Conflict, Myth, and Reality*. New York: Zed Books, 2007.

Umuherwa, Emma-Marie. "Kwibuka22: Ubuhamya Bw'uko Depite Bazivamo Yiciwe Abana N'umugore Bwakoze Benshi Ku Mutima." *IGIHE* (Kigali), April 21, 2016. http://igihe.com/amakuru/u-rwanda/article/ubuhamya-bw-uko-depite-bazivamo-yiciwe-abana-n-umugore-bwakoze-benshi-ku-mutima?url_reload=21&debut_forum=20.

Umulisa, Pascaline. "Iwawa Ni Ho Hatangirijwe Icyumweru Cy'urukundo Nyakuri." *Kigali Today*, December 1, 2012. https://www.kigalitoday.com/ubuzima/urusobe-rw-ubuzima/Iwawa-ni-ho-hatangirijwe-Icyumweru-cy-Urukundo-Nyakuri.

United Nations. *Convention on the Prevention and Punishment of the Crime of Genocide*. New York: United Nations, 1960.

United Nations. Outreach Program on the Rwanda Genocide and the United Nations. 2012. http://www.un.org/en/preventgenocide/rwanda/.

United Nations. "Outreach Programme on the 1994 Genocide Against the Tutsi in Rwanda and the United Nations." United Nations. Accessed March 14, 2023. https://www.un.org/en/preventgenocide/rwanda/commemorations-2021.shtml.

United Nations Children's Fund (UNICEF). *UNICEF Annual Report 2013–Rwanda*. New York: UNICEF, 2013.

United Nations Visiting Mission to Trust Territories in East Africa. *Report on Ruanda-Urundi*. New York: United Nations, 1960.

US Department of State. *International Religious Freedom Report 2007: Rwanda*. Washington, DC: Bureau of Democracy, Human Rights, and Labor, 2007. http://www.state.gov/j/drl/rls/irf/2007/90115.htm.

Uvin, Peter. *Aiding Violence: The Development Enterprise in Rwanda*. West Hartford, CT: Kumarian Press, 1998.

Uwineza, Peace, Elizabeth Pearson, and Elizabeth Powley. *Sustaining Women's Gains in Rwanda: The Influence of Indigenous Culture and Post-genocide Politics*. Washington, DC: Institute for Inclusive Security, 2009. https://www.inclusivesecurity.org/wp-content/uploads/2012/08/1923_sustaining_womens_gains_nocover.pdf.

Vansina, Jan. *Antecedents to Modern Rwanda: The Nyiginya Kingdom*. Oxford, UK: James Currey, 2005.

Vansina, Jan. *Oral Tradition as History*. Madison: University of Wisconsin Press, 1985.

Verwimp, Philip. "Testing the Double-Genocide Thesis for Central and Southern Rwanda." *Journal of Conflict Resolution* 47, no. 4 (2003): 423–442.

Vesperini, Helen. "Rwanda Warms to UN Chief." *BBC News*, September 4, 2001. http://news.BBC.co.uk/2/hi/africa/1524704.stm.

Vidal, Claudine. "La commémoration du génocide au Rwanda: Violence symbolique, mémorisation forcée et histoire officielle." *Cahiers d'Études Africaines* 44, no. 175 (2004): 575–592.

Vollhardt, Johanna Ray, and Michal Bilewicz. "After the Genocide: Psychological Perspectives on Victim, Bystander, and Perpetrator Groups." *Journal of Social Issues* 69, no. 1 (2013): 1–15.

Waldorf, Lars. "Censorship and Propaganda in Post-genocide Rwanda." In *Media and the Rwanda Genocide*, edited by Allan Thompson, 404–416. London: Pluto Press, 2007.

Waldorf, Lars. "Revisiting Hotel Rwanda: Genocide Ideology, Reconciliation, and Rescuers." *Journal of Genocide Research* 11, no. 1 (2009): 101–125.

Waldorf, Lars. "Rwanda's Failing Experiment in Restorative Justice." In *Handbook of Restorative Justice: A Global Perspective*, edited by Dennis Sullivan and Larry Tifft, 422–434. London: Routledge, 2006.

Wamariya, Clementine, and Elizabeth Weil. *The Girl Who Smiled Beads: A Story of War and What Comes After*. New York: Crown, 2018.

Watkins, Sarah E. "Tomorrow She Will Reign: Intimate Power and the Making of a Queen Mother in Rwanda, C.1800–1863." *Gender & History* 29, no. 1 (2017): 124–140.

Watkins, Sarah E., and Erin Jessee. "Legacies of Kanjogera: Women Political Elites and the Transgression of Gender Norms in Rwanda." *Journal of Eastern African Studies* 14, no. 1 (2020): 84–102.

Watkins, Sarah Elizabeth. "Iron Mothers and Warrior Lovers: Intimacy, Power, and the State in the Nyiginya Kingdom, 1796–1913" (PhD, University of California, Santa Barbara, 2014). https://alexandria.ucsb.edu/downloads/7d278t181.

Waugh, Colin M. *Paul Kagame and Rwanda: Power, Genocide and the Rwandan Patriotic Front*. Jefferson, NC: McFarland, 2004.

Weah, Aaron. "Declining Ethnic Relations in Post-war Liberia: The Transmission of Violent Memories." *International Review of the Red Cross* 101, no. 910 (2019): 151–171.

Weaver, Tom. "Art, Memory and Genocide: UVM staffer, alumna and artist's Sarajevo installation honors the victims of the 1995 Srebrenica massacre." *Vermont Quarterly Magazine*, September 28, 2004, www.uvm.edu/theview/pdfs/092904.pdf.

Weinstein, Warren. "Military Continuities in the Rwanda State." *Journal of Asian and African Studies* 12, no. 1–4 (1977): 48–66.

Werbner, Richard P. "Smoke from the Barrel of a Gun: Postwars of the Dead, Memory and Reinscription in Zimbabwe." In *Memory and the Postcolony: African Anthropology and the Critique of Power*, edited by Richard Werbner, 71–102. London: Zed Books, 1998.

Westover, Jeff. "National Forgetting and Remembering in the Poetry of Robert Frost." *Texas Studies in Literature and Language* 46, no. 2 (2004): 213–244.

Whitaker, Beth. "Refugees and the Spread of Conflict: Contrasting Cases in Central Africa." *Journal of Asian and African Studies* 38, no. 2–3 (2003): 2–3.

Whitaker, Beth Elise, and John F. Clark, eds. *Africa's International Relations: Balancing Domestic & Global Interests*. Boulder, CO: Lynne Rienner, 2018.

Wielenga, Cori. "Healing and Reconciliation after Violent Conflict: The Role of Memory in South Africa and Rwanda." *Acta Academica* 45, no. 1 (2013): 209–231.

Wilde, Alexander. "Chile's Memory and Santiago's General Cemetery" (Paper presented at the Latin American Studies Association Congress, Montreal, Canada, September 5–8, 2007).

Willems, Eva. "Open Secrets and Hidden Heroes: Violence, Citizenship and Transitional Justice in (Post-)Conflict Peru" (PhD, Ghent University, 2019). https://biblio.ugent.be/publication/8641074.

Williams, Paul Harvey. *Memorial Museums: The Global Rush to Commemorate Atrocities*. Oxford, UK: Berg, 2007.

Wilson, Richard. *The Politics of Truth and Reconciliation in South Africa: Legitimizing the Post-apartheid State*. Cambridge: Cambridge Univ. Press, 2008.

Winter, Jay. *Remembering War: The Great War between Memory and History in the Twentieth Century.* New Haven, CT: Yale University Press, 2006.

Winter, Jay. *Sites of Memory, Sites of Mourning the Great War in European Cultural History.* Cambridge: Cambridge University Press, 2014.

Winter, Jay, and Emmanuel Sivan. *War and Remembrance in the Twentieth Century.* New York: Cambridge University Press, 2005.

"Witness to Apocalypse." *New York Times*, September 8, 2011. http://www.nytimes.com/2011/09/08/us/sept-11-reckoning/escape.html.

Wood, Julia T. "Critical Feminist Theories." In *Engaging Theories in Interpersonal Communication: Multiple Perspectives*, edited by Leslie A. Baxter and Dawn O. Braithwaite, 323–334. Thousand Oaks, CA: Sage, 2008.

Wosińska, Małgorzata. "Murambi Is Not Auschwitz: The Holocaust in Representations of the Rwandan Genocide." In *Replicating Atonement*, edited by Mischa Gabowitsch, 187–208. New York: Palgrave Macmillan, 2017.

Wouk, Herman. *War and Remembrance.* Boston: Little, Brown, 1978.

Young, James E. *Writing and Rewriting the Holocaust: Narrative and the Consequences of Interpretation.* Bloomington: Indiana University Press, 1998.

Yusin, Jennifer. "The Itinerary of Commemoration in the Kigali Memorial Centre: On Trauma, Time and Difference." *Culture, Theory and Critique* 57, no. 3 (2016): 338–356.

Zeleza, Paul Tiyambe. "Manufacturing and Consuming Knowledge." *Development in Practice* 6, no. 4 (1996): 293–303.

Zeleza, Paul Tiyambe. "Reckoning with the Pasts and Reimagining the Futures of African Studies for the 21st Century." Keynote address, African Peacebuilding Network APN Lecture Series 4: 2019. https://www.semanticscholar.org/paper/Reckoning-with-the-pasts-and-reimagining-the-of-for-Zeleza/f60a31b198a1cd865a221b0a4e0940f8578e1e11.

Zelizer, Barbie. *Covering the Body: The Kennedy Assassination, the Media, and the Shaping of Collective Memory.* Chicago: University of Chicago Press, 2005.

Ziegler, Maggie. "Breaking the Silence on the Rwanda Genocide: An Interview with Edouard Bamporiki." *Peace Magazine*, July–September 2013. http://peacemagazine.org/archive/v29n3p16.htm.

Index

For the benefit of digital users, indexed terms that span two pages (e.g., 52–53) may, on occasion, appear on only one of those pages.

Adichie, C. N., 256
Aegis Trust, 100, 119
AERG (Association des Étudiants et Éleves Rescapés du Genocide), 99–100
Agaciro-centered approach
    general discussion, 266–67
    identifying and examining principles of, 37–38
    overview, 7–8
Ajali, N., 37–38
Amagaju, 132
Amahoro Stadium, Kigali, 96–97, 147
Amateka ("History") (Mihigo), 187–89, 203
Andrews, M., 5
Annan, K., 83–84, 105n.35, 126–27
Antagonists of master narrative
    dignity approach and, 266–67
    general discussion, 10–11
    Kizito Mihigo as, 190–94
    in other cultures, 257
    prosthetic memory, 257–58
    responses to commemoration activities, 163–68
    social media use, 235–39, 262–64
    view of KGM exhibits, 128–29
antidenial laws, 98
anxiety around commemoration activities, 163–65
art
    in aftermath of genocide, 184–86
    of Dorcy Rugamba, 200–2, 207–8
    of Edouard Bamporiki, 194–99, 205
    expressing memories of mass atrocities through, 180–81
    of Grace Mukankusi, 199
    of Kizito Mihigo, 186–94, 203

    overview, 178–80
    in pre- and transgenocide period, 181–84
    significance in commemoration ceremonies, 202–8
    of Simon Bikindi, 48–49, 181–82, 199
aspirations, shared, xii–xiii
Assmann, A., 28–29
Assmann, J., 28
Association des Étudiants et Éleves Rescapés du Genocide (AERG), 99–100
AVEGA Agahozo, 99–100

Bahati, I., 238
Baldwin, G., 232–33, 242
Bamporiki, E.
    artwork and master narrative, 197–99
    impact of work, 205–7
    profile, 194–96
banners, 120
Bayigamba, R., 228
Bazivamo, C., 168
BBC
    Great Lakes radio programs, 228–29, 230, 235–36, 247n.49
    "In Pictures: Remembering the Genocide," 222
Belgian colonial rule, 50–51, 55
Benda, R., 10–11, 95, 195, 196, 198
Bikindi, S., 48–49, 181–82, 199
Bisesero Memorial, 145–46
Bizimungu, P., 86, 87, 96, 97–98, 105n.30, 106n.41
Black Lives Matter, 32–33, 35–36, 220–21
Bolin, A., 120, 130
Bonde, B. N., 245n.22

Boniface, R., 10, 22n.19
Bourdon, J., 220–21
Brandstetter, A.-M., 85–86
Buckley-Zistel, S., 117
burial of dead
　debates about, 77–78
　informal commemorations, 58–60
　mass graves and memorials, 131–33
　reburials, 134–35, 136–37
Butare, Rwanda, 112–13

case selection, 15–16
Catholic Church, 141–42n.44, 142n.55
　commemoration innovations reducing influence of, 121–25
　informal commemorations, 58–59
　Kizito Mihigo's identification with, 189
Central Court, 47, 48–49, 50, 51–52
Champions of master narrative
　co-creation of master narrative, 75
　dignity approach and, 266–67
　Dorcy Rugamba as, 200–2
　Edouard Bamporiki as, 196–99, 205–6
　emergence of, 60–61
　general discussion, 9–10
　Kizito Mihigo as, 186–87, 203
　memorials, 119
　in other cultures, 256–57
　prosthetic memory, 257–58
　responses to commemoration activities, 160–62
　social media use, 236–39
　view of KGM exhibits, 128–29
child-headed homes, 177n.92
Children's Memorial at Kigali Genocide Memorial, 128–29
Chilisa, B., 15
Christianity, 50–51, 153, 154–55, 158
churches as memorials, 121–22
civic education, 150–56
Clark, P., 106n.37
class divisions, 50–51
Clinton, B., 83–84, 105n.35
CNLG. See Commission Nationale de Lutte contre le Genocide
"cockroaches," use of term, 194–95, 213n.61

coerced obedience, 163–68
collective guilt, 8, 198–99, 215n.102
collective memory, 27–29, 182, 220
colonialism, 34, 50–52, 266
color of remembering, change in, 96–97, 123–24
commemorations. See also memorials
　Antagonist view of, 10–11
　Champion view of, 9
　community-level activities and civic education, 150–56
　Fatalist view of, 11
　graphic images aired by media during, 223–24
　international endorsement of master narrative, 83–84
　internationalization of, 88–91
　media monitoring during, 227–33
　national, 147–50
　official period for, 57–58, 71n.62
　political tensions immediately following genocide, 57–62
　private and family events, 157–60
　regional dynamics, 94–95
　reluctance to participate in, 1–2
　social media discussions about, 236–39
　themes for events, 79, 81–82, 85, 86, 87, 88, 90, 91–92, 93, 94
Commission Nationale de Lutte contre le Genocide (CNLG)
　building of memorials, 118–19
　lesson plans from, 151
　planning of commemoration events, 94
　protection of commemorations, 97–100
　social media use, 236–38
communicative memory, 28, 157
community-level commemoration activities, 150–56
comparative memory approach, 165–68, 207
competitive memory approach, 31, 41n.45, 165, 167, 256, 259–60
Congo wars, 80–81
constitution, adoption of new, 87–88
cosmopolitan memory, 30
countermemory activities, 165–68
cross symbol, replacement of, 124–25

cultural memory, 28–29, 220–21
Cyprien, R., 182

Dallaire, R., 228
Danziger, N., 222
Darfur, genocide in, 90
dark tourism, 35
dates for commemorating other victims, 150
decentralization of commemoration, 95–97
decolonial turn, 34–37
decolonization, 14–15, 52–55, 72–73n.87
Decolonization and Afro-Feminism (Tamale), 34
denial of genocide
    addressed in commemoration themes, 91–92
    antidenial law, 98
    national framework for reconstruction viewed as, 86–87
    by perpetrators, 2–3
    by radical Antagonists, 165–67
Department for International Development (DFID), British, 119
Des Forges, A., 88–89, 121–22, 181–82
DeWitt, D., 198
diaspora
    Antagonists in, 166–67, 219, 252–53, 261
    civic education among, 155–56
    music and mobilization in, 182–83
    online media platforms, 238–39
dignity approach
    general discussion, 266–67
    identifying and examining principles of, 37–38
    overview, 7–8
Diop, B. B., 133
double genocide ideology, 122, 165–66, 167, 230
Dusingizemungu, J. P., 61, 77–78, 123, 136–37

empirical insights, 256–57
English, adoption as official language, 235, 250n.90

epistemological implications, 265
Erlinder, P., 110n.94
Erll, A., 31, 220
ethnic hierarchy, establishment of, 50–52
evening commemoration sessions, 152–55
expansion wars, precolonial, 47–48, 49

family commemoration events, 157–60
Fatalists of master narrative
    dignity approach and, 266–67
    Dorcy Rugamba as, 200–2
    Edouard Bamporiki as, 194–96
    general discussion, 11–12
    in other cultures, 257
    prosthetic memory, 257–58
    responses to commemoration activities, 168–70
    social media use, 236–39
    view of KGM exhibits, 128–29
fear
    among repatriated refugees, 81
    during commemoration periods, 224–25
    self-censoring by journalists, 231–33
films
    by Edouard Bamporiki, 197–99
    Hotel Rwanda, 89–90, 107n.54
Fischl, E., 180–81
flames of remembrance, 124–25
foreign aid, 100–1
foreigners, role in creation of narrative, 116–17
forgiveness, 162, 185, 198–99
Freedom House, 234–35

gacaca courts, 2–3, 84–85, 91–92, 105–6n.36
Gakumba, C., 224–25
Gakwenzire, P., 117–18
Gasasira, J.-B., 230–31
Gatsinzi, M., 34–35
gendered analyses, 16, 30
generational anxiety, xi–xii, 2–3
genocide, adoption of term, 81–83, 108n.59, 259–60

Genocide Against the Tutsi. *See also* commemorations; memorials
  accounts of, 69–70n.58
  adoption of term "genocide," 81–83, 108n.59, 259–60
  in *Amateka* song, 204–5
  beginning of, 76–77
  burial of dead after, 58–60, 77–78
  community-level activities and civic education, 150–56
  domestic political realities and actors, 84–88
  emergence of narrative, 60–61, 254–55
  evolution of narrative, 56–57
  as hegemonic master narrative, 4
  international endorsement of, 83–84, 116–17
  internationalization of commemoration and global outreach, 88–91
  Kigali Genocide Memorial and, 127–31
  local discussion of reconstruction, 91–93
  mapping master narrative of, 8–12
  media monitoring during commemoration, 227–33
  national commemorations, 147–50
  national policies, institutions, and laws protecting, 97–101
  New Rwanda, 101–2
  overview, 1
  political tensions immediately following, 57–62
  private and family events, 157–60
  regional dynamics, 94–97
  role of church in, 124
  RPF information management strategy, 225–26
  setting tone for domestic commemoration, 76–83
  shifting responses to, 2–3
genocide memorials. *See* memorials
Genocide Survivors Students Association, 99–100
German East Africa, 50–51
Gishoma, D., 82, 92–93, 98, 117–18, 164
Gitera, J. H., 52
globytal memory field, 248–49n.71
God Sleeps in Rwanda: A Journey of Transformation (Sebarenzi), 84

Gourevitch, P., 88–89
grassroots courts, 84–85
gray, as color of mourning, 96–97, 123–24
Great Lakes radio programs, BBC, 228–29, 230, 235–36, 247n.49
group memory, 28–29
guceceka, 231–33
guilt, collective, 8, 198–99, 215n.102

Habyarimana, J., 54, 55, 76–77, 166–67, 217
Hammack, P., 5
hatred
  of Hutu, 161–62
  of Tutsi, 181–82
hegemonic master narrative. *See also* Genocide Against the Tutsi
  artists and, 206–7
  dismantling development of, 259–61
  emergence of, 254–55
  master narrative versus, 5–8
  overview, 4
Henley, J., 200
Hirsch, M., 32
historical master narratives
  colonial, 50–52
  current dilemmas due to, 259
  evolution of Genocide against the Tutsi narrative, 56–57
  of liberation and oppression, 52–55
  overview, 45–46
  political tensions immediately following genocide, 57–62
  precolonial oral tradition, 46–50
Hoffman, E., 32
holidays, changes in, 101
Holocaust memory, 30–31, 34–35, 59–60
Hotel Rwanda (film), 89–90, 107n.54
humanitarian assistance, 103n.3, 104n.8
Hutu. *See also* Genocide Against the Tutsi
  Antagonist desire for commemoration of, 167–68
  anxiety around commemoration activities, 163–65
  collective guilt, 198–99, 215n.102
  colonial narratives, 50–52
  family commemorative events, 159–60
  fear during commemoration periods, 224–25

hatred of, 161–62
massacres of 1959, 52–55, 72–73n.87
narratives of liberation and oppression, 52–55
precolonial narratives, 48–49

ibipinga (Antagonists). *See* Antagonists of master narrative
Ibuka, 99–100, 160
ICT (information and communication technology) policies, 234–35, 249n.78, 249n.79
ICT for Development (ICT4D) process, 249n.78
Icyaha kuri bo, Ikimwaro kuri jye ("Their Sin Is My Shame") (Bamporiki), 194–95
identity cards, 51
"If They Had Not Been Massacred" (Bamporiki), 195–96
Igisobanuro cy'Urupfu ("The Meaning of Death") (Mihigo), 190–94
ihahamuka (traumatism/being traumatized), 92–93
Ijoro Ribara Uwariraye ("The One Who Was Awake") (Mihigo), 188–90
ikiriyo, 152–55
Imvaho Nshya (newspaper), 217, 224–25
"In Pictures: Remembering the Genocide" (BBC), 222
inanga, 46–50
individual memory, 27–29, 200–2
informal commemorations, 58–59
information and communication technology (ICT) policies, 234–35, 249n.78, 249n.79
information management strategy, 225–26
Ingabire, V., 99, 129
Ingelaere, B., 88–89, 94–95, 232
Ingoma Kalinga (royal drum Kalinga), 52
insider/outsider positionality, x–xiv
Insinzi ("Victory") (Mukankuranga), 183–84
Institute of Research and Dialogue for Peace (IRDP), 160–61
institutionalized memories, 28
institutions protecting commemorations, 96–97
international aid, 100–1

International Criminal Tribunal for Rwanda (ICTR), 105n.32, 181–82
international endorsement of master narrative, 83–84
international journalism, 221–22, 225–26
Internet. *See* online media
interviews, 12–13
intore (Champions). *See* Champions of master narrative
Investigation, The (documentary play), 200–1
Inyenzi-Inkotanyi, 194–95, 213n.61
itorero camps, 9
Iyo Badatsembwa ("If They Had Not Been Massacred") (Bamporiki), 195–96

Jacobs, J., 157
Jennings, C., 226
Jenoside (genocide), 81–83
journalists
emergence of private media companies, 226–27
in first period, 220–26
genocide legacy, 222–25
media monitoring during commemoration, 227–33
overview, 217–20
postgenocide government's information management strategy, 225–26
in second period, 226
self-censoring by, 231–33
social media, 233–39
Junod, R., 258

Kabatende, A.-M., 59
Kagame, P., 86, 97–98, 142n.55, 163, 198–99, 228, 245n.22, 250n.81
Kanimba, C., 117–18
Kanjogera (queen mother), 48–49, 50, 51–52
Karake, M., 224–25
Karasira, A., 238
Karengera, I., 112
Karuhimbi, S., 153–54
Kayibanda, G., 54
Kerstens, P., 201–2
Kibeho massacres, 121–22, 167
Kigali conference, 34–35

Kigali Genocide Memorial (KGM)
  flame of remembrance, 120, 124–25
  master narrative sustained at, 127–31
  overview, 125–27
Kimonyo, J. P., 51–52, 87–88, 92, 121, 163, 164
Ki-Moon, B., 236–37
Kinyarwanda (film), 198
Kizito Mihigo for Peace (KMP), 186
Korman, R., 59, 78, 116–17, 183–84
kwibuka, 77

Landsberg, A., 32, 241–42, 257–58
language
  adoption of term "genocide," 81–83, 108n.59
  related to commemorations, 77
  related to survivors, 85–86
  related to trauma, 92
  used by Antagonists, 165–66
laws protecting genocide memory, 96–97
Leave None to Tell the Story (Des Forges), 88–89
Lemarchand, R., 88–89
lesson plans from CNLG, 151
Levi, P., 161
liberalization of media ownership, 226–27
liberation and oppression, narratives of, 52–55
Liberation Day, 101
Liebermann, Y., 32–33
local commemoration ceremonies, 95–97
local memorials, 135–37
localizing master narrative
  by Antagonists, 163–68
  by Champions, 160–62
  community-level activities and civic education, 150–56
  by Fatalists, 168–70
  national commemorations, 147–50
  overview, 145–46
  private and family events, 157–60
Long Coat, The (film), 197, 205
Longman, T., 102, 166–67

Mamdani, M., 37, 53–54
Mansudae project, 72n.85
Marembo (Rugamba), 201–2
mass graves, 131–33
mass violence
  memorials in commemoration of, 114–15
  mnemonic experiences after, 256–57
master narrative. *See also* localizing master narrative; memorials
  domestic political realities and actors, 84–88
  hegemonic master narrative versus, 5–8
  international endorsement of, 83–84
  internationalization of commemoration and global outreach, 88–91
  Kigali Genocide Memorial and, 127–31
  local discussion of reconstruction, 91–93
  mapping, 8–12
  national policies, institutions, and laws protecting, 97–101
  New Rwanda, 101–2
  overview, 74–76
  regional dynamics, 94–97
  role of church in, 124
  role of foreigners in creation of, 116–17
  setting tone for domestic commemoration, 76–83
  shifting responses to, 2–3
materials of memory. *See* memorials
Mazimpaka, P., 225–26
Mbaye, D., 154
Mbiti, J., 37–38
McDowell, S., 30
Meaning of Death, The (Mihigo), 190–94
media
  emergence of private media companies, 226–27
  first period, 220–26
  genocide legacy, 222–25
  monitoring during commemoration, 227–33
  overview, 217–20
  postgenocide government's information management strategy, 225–26
  second period, 226
  self-censoring by journalists, 231–33
  social media, 233–39
  text messages, 239–42

Media High Council of the Press (MHC), 227–28, 230–31
media memory, 220
Meierhenrich, J., 132, 133, 134
memorials
   in commemoration of mass atrocities, 114–15
   debates on function of, 116–18
   discourse on other sites, 134–37
   innovations reducing influence of Catholic Church, 121–25
   Kigali Genocide Memorial, 125–31
   local, 135–37
   overview, 112–14
   permanence and mobility of, 131–34
   reburial in, 134–35, 136–37
   as tools of memory, 120–25
   for various purposes and needs, 118–20
memory, forms of, 28–29
memory politics, 258–59, 264
memory studies
   Agaciro-centered approach, 37–38
   decolonial turn, 34–37
   key concepts in literature, 27–29
   online platforms, 32–33
   overview, 4, 26–27, 29–31
   transcultural turn, 31–32
mental crises, 92–93
methodological implications, 265–66
methodology, 12–15
MHC (Media High Council of the Press), 227–28, 230–31
Mibilizi, 184–85
Mibirizi, E. S., 214n.80
Mignolo, W., 34
Mihigo, K., 11, 238–39, 261
   Amateka, 187–89, 203–5
   counternarrative lyrics by, 190–94
   death of, 263–64, 270n.21
   profile, 186–87
   work of, 188–90, 206–7
Mitari, P., 261
mobile technology. *See* online media
Mödersheim, S., 180–81
Molden, B., 5–6
monarchy, precolonial, 47–50
monitoring of media, 227–33, 250n.82
monuments. *See* memorials

Moon, R., 232
mourning rituals, Rwandan, 157
MTN, 235
Mucyo, J. de D., 123, 136–37, 149–50, 155
Mugenzi, R., 235–36, 251n.94
Mugo, M., 37–38
Mugonero Memorial, 131–32
Mukankuranga, M. Y., 183–84
Mukankusi, G., 199
Multidirectional Memory: Remembering the Holocaust in the Age of Decolonization (Rothberg), 31
Munyanshoza, D., 184–85
Murambi Memorial, 132–33
Murangira, E., 132–33
museums. *See* memorials
music
   in aftermath of genocide, 184–86
   of Kizito Mihigo, 186–94, 203
   in pre- and transgenocide period, 181–84
   significance in commemoration ceremonies, 202–8
   of Simon Bikindi, 48–49, 181–82, 199
Musinga, 51–52
Muslims, 153–54, 158
Mutarabayire, B., 224–25
Mutsindashyaka, T., 126
Mwizerwa, J. L., 137

national commemorations, 147–50, 223–24
National Commission for the Fight against Genocide. *See* Commission Nationale de Lutte contre le Genocide
national framework for reconstruction, 86–87
national policies protecting genocide memory, 96–97
National Reconciliation Barometer, 117–18
national symbols and holidays, 101
National Unity and Reconciliation Commission (NURC), 88, 97–100, 117–18
Ndamage, F., 224–25
Ndi Umunyarwanda ("I am a Rwandan") program, 93, 191, 192, 199

Ndlovu-Gatsehni, S., 34
Ndori, 48
"Never Again" (Samputu), 185
new Rwanda, 101–2
newspapers
  concerns related to commemoration periods, 224–25
  emergence of private media companies, 226–27
  monitoring during commemoration, 227–33
  overview, 217
Ngarambe, F. X., 228
Ngoga, M., 98
NGOs, 99–100
9/11 commemorations, 220–21, 244n.9
Nkubito, A.-M., 58, 71n.72
Nora, P., 28
northern Rwanda, commemoration in, 94–95
Nsengimana, A., 57
Ntarama memorial, Rwanda, 121
ntibindeba (Fatalists). *See* Fatalists of master narrative
NURC (National Unity and Reconciliation Commission), 88, 97–100, 117–18
Nyamasheke Memorial, 135–36
Nyamata Memorial, 121
Nyiginya dynasty, 48
Nyundo Memorial, 121

Office Rwandais d'Information (ORINFOR), 222, 245n.20

physical space. *See* memorials
Pinchevski, A., 233–34
playwrites, 200–2
poetry, 194–96
political memory, 28–29, 220–21
political messages at commemorations, 150–51
political tensions immediately following genocide, 57–62
positionality, insider/outsider, x–xiv
postmemory, 32, 209
Pottier, J., 225
precolonial narratives, 46–50
Press, R. M., 70n.59

prisons, 70n.59
private commemorations, 58–59, 157–60
private media, 226–27, 230
private organizations, commemoration by, 155–56
prosthetic memory, 32–33, 241–42, 257–58
Protais, M., 96–97
public experience of master narrative
  community-level activities and civic education, 150–56
  national commemorations, 147–50
  private and family events, 157–60
  public organizations, commemoration by, 155–56
purple as color of remembering, 123–24

queen mothers, 48–49

race science, 51
radio
  announcement of Habyarimana's death on, 217
  emergence of private media companies, 226–27
  monitoring during commemoration, 227–33
  pregenocide, 218
Radio Télévision Libre des Mille Collines (RTLM), 181–82, 222–23
RBA (Rwanda Broadcasting Agency), 226–27, 245n.20, 246n.23
RDF (Rwanda Defense Force), 80–81
Reading, A., 233–34, 248–49n.71
Real Talk Channel, 238, 269n.12, 269n.17
Rebero (Rwanda), 1995 commemoration in, 78
reburials, 134–35, 136–37
reconciliation
  Fatalist view of, 169
  forgiveness and, 162, 185
  in music, 190
  role of commemorations and memorials, 117–18, 156
reconstruction
  liberalization of media ownership, 226
  local discussion of, 91–93
  national framework for, 86–87
refugee repatriation, 79–81

regional dynamics in commemoration, 94–97
"Remember all" events, 167
Renan, E., 29
repatriation of refugees, 79–81
responses to master narrative
   by Antagonists, 163–68
   by Champions, 160–62
   community-level activities and civic education, 150–56
   by Fatalists, 168–70
   national commemorations, 147–50
   overview, 145–46
   private and family events, 157–60
retraumatization, 147–49, 223
revenge killings, 80–81
Rhodes Must Fall, 32–33, 35–36, 220–21
RMMP (Rwanda Media Monitoring Project), 227–31
Rosoux, V., 116–17
Ross, M., 181
Rothberg, M., 31, 260
royal drum Kalinga (*Ingoma Kalinga*), 52
RPA (Rwanda Patriotic Army), 182–84
RPF (Rwanda Patriotic Front), 56–57
RTLM (Radio Télévision Libre des Mille Collines), 181–82, 222–23
Rubanda nyamwishi, 52–55
Rudahigwa, 51–52
Rugamba, C., 182, 211n.20, 211n.21
Rugamba, D., 203
   artwork, 200–2
   impact of work, 207–8
   profile, 200
Rugambage, J.-L., 230
Rugari (newspaper), 229
Rukara, 47
Rukara rwa Bishingwe inanga, 47
Rusesabagina, P., 89–90, 107n.54
Rushyashya (newspaper), 229–30
Rutagengwa, T., 166–67
Rutayisire, P., 258
Rutazibwa, O., 14
Rwabugiri, 48–49
Rwabugiri, Kigeli IV, 47
Rwanda 94 (play), 201–2
Rwanda Broadcasting Agency (RBA), 226–27, 245n.20, 246n.23

Rwanda Defense Force (RDF), 80–81
Rwanda Media Monitoring Project (RMMP), 227–31
Rwanda Patriotic Army (RPA)
   civil war, 54, 56–57
   first Congo war, 80
   Kibeho camp massacre, 121–22, 167
   role of music, 182–84
Rwanda Patriotic Front (RPF). *See also* master narrative
   civil war, 56–57
   creation of master narrative, 86–87
   domestic political realities and actors, 84–88
   information management strategy, 225–26
   liberalization of media ownership, 226–27
   media monitoring during commemoration, 227–33
   monitoring of media, 227–33, 250n.82
   national policies, institutions, and laws protecting commemorations, 97–101
   national victory celebration in 1994, 58
   new Rwanda, 101–2
   overview, 1
Rwandan Genocide, 83, 254–55
Rwanda's Popular Genocide (Kimonyo), 121
Rwanyonga and Rwabugiri inanga, 47

Said, E., 29–30
Samputu, J. P., 162, 183–84, 185
Santayana, G., 57–58
scholarship on Rwanda, 63–66n.2, 89–90
Schreiber, J.-P., 116–17
Sebarenzi, J., 84, 86–87, 106n.42
self-censoring by journalists, 231–33
semantic innovation
   adoption of term "genocide," 81–83, 108n.59
   related to commemorations, 77
   related to survivors, 85–86
   related to trauma, 92
Sendashonga, S., 87
September 11 commemorations, 220–21, 244n.9
shared aspirations, xii–xiii

Shoah, 116–17
Simburudari, T., 162
Smith, S., 226
social amnesia, 29
social media
    in commemoration processes, 32–33
    increasing engagement with master narrative, 236–39
    monitoring of, 230–31
    overview, 220–21, 233–34
    research on, 243–44n.1
    text messages, 239–42
    Vision 2020 and, 234–36
social revolution, 52–55, 72–73n.87
Srebrenica genocide commemorative art exhibit, 178
storytelling, during commemorations, 152–55
survivor nationalism, 242
survivors
    Champion view of, 9, 160–62
    Fatalist response to commemoration, 168–70
    killings of, 166–67
    terms related to, 85–86
    tour guides in KGM, 129–30

Tamale, S., 34
Tanzania, refugees in, 79–80
technology, impact on cultural memory, 32–33. *See also* social media
Tertsakian, C., 70n.59
testimonials during commemorations, 152–55
text messages, 239–42
Their Sin Is My Shame (Bamporiki), 194–95
theoretical implications, 264, 265–66
"Through a Glass Darkly: Genocide Memorials in Rwanda" project, 132, 133, 134
transcultural turn, 31–32

trauma
    during commemoration, 92–93, 147–49
    Fatalist response to commemoration, 168–70
    retraumatization, 147–49, 223
Tutsi. *See also* Genocide Against the Tutsi
    Champion view of survivors, 9, 160–62
    colonial narratives, 50–52
    hatred of, 181–82
    massacres of 1959, 52–55, 61, 72–73n.87
    narratives of liberation and oppression, 52–55
    precolonial narratives, 48–49
    terms related to survivors, 85–86
Twa, 48–49, 50–52
Twanze Gutoberwa Amateka (Mihigo), 187–89
Twitter, 236–38, 250n.81

ubwenge, in communication, 232
"Ubwoba bwumvikana" ("Understandable Fear") (Karake), 224
Umeseso (newspaper), 229
umubiri, 77
Umuvugizi (newspaper), 229, 230
United Nations, 83–84, 156, 178, 236–37
Urwanda Rushya, 100–1
urwibutso (monument), 118
utu, concept of, 37–38
Uwilingiyimana, A., 78

Verhofstadt, G., 228
vernacular memory, 16, 36–37, 38
Vidal, C., 116–17
Vision 2020, 226–27, 234–36
vocabulary
    adoption of term "genocide," 81–83, 108n.59
    related to commemorations, 77
    related to survivors, 85–86
    related to trauma, 92